Dancing in Utopia

Dancing in Utopia

Dartington Hall and its Dancers

Larraine Nicholas

DANCE BOOKS

First published in 2007 by Dance Books Ltd
The Old Bakery
4 Lenten Street
Alton
Hampshire GU34 1HG

ISBN: 978 1 85273 1212

A CIP catalogue record for this book is available from the British Library

Printed and bound in Great Britain by Latimer Trend and Company Ltd,
Plymouth, Devon

Cover Photographs
Front: The Courtyard, Dartington Hall. © Larraine Nicholas.
Inset: Children taught by Jenny Gertz dancing in the gardens at Dartington
Hall, early 1940s. © Lisa Ullmann Archive, National Resource Centre for
Dance, LU/F/1/55
Back: Dartington College of Arts students performing in the open-air
theatre, a project directed by Deborah Levy, 1993. © Graham Green

Contents

For all of Dartington's dancers, especially the many whose names and dances do not appear in these pages. Each of their steps has informed the narrative that follows.

Acknowledgements

The research and writing of this book has been a long journey that I could not have undertaken without the help of numerous others. It began in earnest on my first visit to the Dartington Hall Trust Archive in Spring 2001. During many periods of research since then, I have deeply appreciated the friendliness, knowledge and professionalism of its staff, especially Yvonne Widger, Angie St John Palmer, John Sanford (also of the Dartington College of Arts library) and Heather McIntyre. Other archivists have supported me in my quest, putting at my disposal their funds of specialist knowledge that simply cannot be encompassed by a cataloguing system. I want to mention especially Chris Jones at the National Resource Centre for Dance at Surrey University (and also its manager, Helen Roberts); Jane Fowler at the Laban Archive; Nicolas Bell of the Music Collections at the British Library; and Mike Brewis of the South West Film and Television Archive. There have been many other contacts with staff at various archives, all of whom have contributed to the sum of knowledge and understanding that has informed my work. I thank the National Co-operative Archive, The Place Videoworks Library, the Victoria and Albert Museum's Archive of Art and Design and Theatre Museum Collection, and the New York Public Library for the Performing Arts, Jerome Robbins Dance Division. My special gratitude goes to Pauline Manley, who undertook research work for me with great thoroughness in the State Library of New South Wales, Sydney (Margaret Barr Collection).

Many individuals gave me their time, encouragement and invaluable information, from the perspective of their specialist knowledge or from their own intensive experience of living the history of *Dancing in Utopia*. Their names follow in alphabetical order:

Jenna Agate, Ric Allsopp, Angus Balbernie, Jill Beddard, Joy Bolton-Carter (Skinner), Laurie Booth, Emilyn Claid, Nic Cottis, Peter Cox, Peter Curtis, Ann David, Iain Davison, Katie Duck, Janet Eager, William Elmhirst, Kevin Finnan, Anne-Marie Gaston (Anjali), Janet Goodridge, Graham Green, Pauline de Groot, Ann Hutchinson Guest, David Henshaw, Peter Hulton, Cathy Kiddle and Peter Kiddle, Colette King, Gary Lester, Claire MacDonald, Fionna McPhee, Julia Morel, Karen Morgan, Geraldine Morris, Charlie Morrissey, Mary O'Donnell (Fulkerson), Steve Paxton, Valerie Preston-Dunlop, Prarthana Purkayastha, Alan Read, Eloise Sharman, Frances

Shepherd, Nahid Siddiqui, Kirstie Simson, David Slater, Janet Smith, Yolande Snaith, Geraldine Stephenson, Diana Theodores, Sam Thornton, Mara de Wit.

Every one of these contacts has informed the narrative of Dartington that follows. I acknowledge my debt to them. Needless to say, I have had to find my own path through the narrative, and any inaccuracies or shortcomings in the text are entirely my own.

A number of colleagues have taken time out from their own busy research and teaching schedules to read drafts and give me helpful comments to feed into revisions. They are Henrietta Bannerman, Renate Brauninger, Alexandra Carter, Mollie Davies, Stephanie Jordan, Angela Kane, Ann Nugent and Stacey Prickett. I am acutely aware of how much I owe to their scholarly perceptions. Stephanie Jordan deserves special thanks for her mentoring of my career over many years and through all stages of this project. I feel deeply the warmth and friendship of the network of dance scholars, those based at Roehampton University and in other UK institutions. We have a close and supportive community—a dance utopia indeed.

Finally, I must thank David Leonard of Dance Books and my editor Rod Cuff for guiding me as I attempted to negotiate the shoals of major publication for the first time.

Photographic images are included with thanks to repositories, individual photographers and copyright holders: Chris Crickmay; *The Dancing Times* (thanks to Jonathan Gray); Dartington Hall Trust Archive; Deutsches Tanzarchiv Köln; Getty Images; Hugo Glendinning; Graham Green; Nancy Grimes; Fritz Henle Archive; Cathy and Peter Kiddle; Margaret Barr Collection, Mitchell Library, State Library of New South Wales; National Resource Centre for Dance, Rudolf Laban and Lisa Ullman Archives; V&A Images/ Victora and Albert Museum, London. I have researched copyright with due diligence and acknowledged it when known. Thanks go to Clare Freestone and Bernard Horrocks of the National Portrait Gallery for their expert advice.

Research and writing of this book was funded by the Arts and Humanities Research Council (Small Grant in the Creative and Performing Arts and The Research Leave Scheme) and by Roehampton University.

Introduction: Making Dance History

> I knew that one day I should visit Dartington Hall.... I had heard so much
> about it from friends and acquaintances that I seemed to know it person-
> ally. But I suspected that 'my' Dartington was very different from the real
> thing; and my suspicions were fully justified.
>
> The first shock was the length of the journey from London and the re-
> moteness of Totnes, up the River Dart on the edge of Dartmoor. Even more
> intimidating was the long drive to the Hall through the estate, and the
> grey, feudal magnificence of the Hall itself: it was hard to associate the
> ample, placid beauty of the gardens and buildings with the sweat and
> excitement of artistic pioneering.
>
> Fernau Hall, 1950[1]

So wrote a London-based dance and theatre critic, arriving at Dartington
Hall for a weekend conference in 1950. At the time of his visit, Dartington
already had a twenty-five-year history of development in education, arts and
industry from the moment the estate and medieval hall had been bought by
Dorothy and Leonard Elmhirst in 1925. By 1950, those estate industries
were built around its core agricultural businesses of farming, forestry and
horticulture. There was a carpentry business making use of Dartington's
own wood; woollen textiles were being made at Dartington's own mill. Although these trades were steeped in the tradition of the English countryside,
Dartington always set itself on the path of research and progress. Amongst
other things, it had pioneered the artificial insemination of cattle and the
commercial production of apple juice in Britain. Advancement was not only
to be seen in agriculture: Dartington Hall School was a well-known seat of
progressive child education. But it was the 'artistic pioneering' in dance and
theatre that interested Fernau Hall, and it is my fascination with that subject
that is the foundation for this book. In particular, this narrative will be concerned with Dartington's pioneering in the field of dance, although it will
become clear that often dance and other forms of performance have gone
hand in hand, sometimes difficult to disentangle and define separately.

In order to write about Dartington, we have to arrive there. The notion
that it is a location at the end of a journey is commonplace in accounts of
its life and work, as if its pastoral setting and aura of being far from
London condense its unique essence. (My own first journey to Dartington
begins Chapter 1.) Fernau Hall identified some of the physical features of
Dartington that visitors have typically noticed down the years, and still do.
The beauty of nature in its rolling countryside environment is matched by
the decidedly unnatural beauty of its huge gardens with their planted walks,

steps and statuary. The hierarchical connotations of the medieval Courtyard range of buildings seem to be in tension with Dartington's ethos of democracy and experiment.

Perhaps Hall's description deliberately exaggerated the distance and difficulty of the journey, as if he wanted to be congratulated for venturing 200 miles from the bright lights of London. By most standards it is not a long drive from Totnes through the estate to the medieval Courtyard buildings, although remoteness has certainly been an issue from time to time. Artists at Dartington have needed to be able to work productively 'out of the loop' of metropolitan circles. Now, of course, the visitor encounters a Dartington different from Fernau Hall's. The Elmhirst founders have deceased, the Trust they set up in the 1930s has largely withdrawn from agricultural and rural business, and their progressive school closed down in 1987. On the other hand, the Trust has moved on to businesses more in line with twenty-first-century financial priorities such as tourism and conference facilities, while supporting research in ecology, social studies, education and the arts, which are all implicit in the original foundation. Dartington College of Arts, originally an offshoot of the Trust and of the Elmhirsts' plans, still flourishes as a semi-independent body on the estate, developing all the artistic ideas that are implicit in the foundation.

Defining the beauty and uniqueness of Dartington, its apparently natural landscape and architectural attractions, has long been one thread in establishing its credentials as a 'utopia'. The other is the belief system that was ingrained after the Elmhirsts bought the estate in 1925. In Chapter 1, I discuss the founders and their ideas in more detail. For the moment it is sufficient to outline that their vision was about creating a community on this estate where industry and agriculture would be carried out according to the most recent and enlightened scientific practice; where the arts should be available to all workers; and where education of children should be governed by their own developing interests rather than a repressive, book-bound regime. It is these two threads, the recourse to nature and the vision of a less oppressive society, that place Dartington within the tradition of utopia.

In normal usage, we often invest the words 'utopia' and 'utopian' with heavy sarcasm. Those who begin such projects are generally assumed to be unrealistic dreamers who are bound to be disappointed by the failure of human nature and the environment to deliver their vision of a perfect life. But the word itself, invented by Sir Thomas More for his book *Utopia* in 1516, embodies a play upon the ideas of the desirable and the impossible. From ancient Greek roots, 'utopia' combines *eutopia* (a good place) and *outopia* (no place). William Morris must have had *outopia* in mind when he titled his socialist utopian fantasy *News from Nowhere* (1891). In the genre of literary utopias invented by More (and their polar opposites, the dystopias such as

Aldous Huxley's *Brave New World* of 1932) fantasy is a necessary part, but not the whole of the story. Utopias are essentially radical acts of imagination that critique contemporary society by holding up a reversing mirror. This is what life *could* be like! Society is not perfect but *is* perfectible, not necessarily doomed to perpetuate the same mistakes.[2]

As a primary example, William Morris conceived of an imagined English egalitarian society of the twenty-first century that has rolled back the nineteenth-century 'progress' in industrialisation and urbanisation. The urban poor have returned to the land to take up the old pre-industrial handcrafts. No longer being wage slaves or machine slaves, they take pride and pleasure in their work and decorate even the most utilitarian objects. The distinction between craft and high art collapses because rich art consumers no longer exist. Sadly, we are not allowed to see these people dance. The narrator's waking dream begins to fade as he enters the Harvest Festival; all are seated for a feast, but it seems only natural that the evening would progress to dancing and that these inhabitants of utopia would dance in the 'folk' mode that reflects Morris's anti-modernity.[3] While there is a thread of Morris's utopia detectable at Dartington in the confluence between crafts and high arts and in its references back to a medieval past (for example, tournaments with 'jousting' between neighbouring hamlets were held during the 1950s), Dartington's ethos was not just about retrogressive nostalgia, because from the beginning it embraced notions of modernity and of twentieth-century progress, including in the contemporary arts.

More and Morris exemplify the literary utopias that have nourished practical attempts to create the earthly utopias that are in Dartington's lineage. For centuries, social and economic inequality and religious sectarianism have been the wellsprings of such experiments. Persecuted religious minorities such as the Shakers (see Chapter 1) sought salvation in communal living. The nineteenth century provided other catalysts in the shape of social and educational theorists such as Henri Saint-Simon, Charles Fourier, Leo Tolstoy and Johann Pestalozzi. Political movements, including Chartism, communism and anarchism, posited their own versions of the better life. Philanthropists tried to improve the abject conditions of industrial workers by building model communities. (In Chapter 1 I discuss one of these, Robert Owen's New Lanark.) There were attempts to give the dispossessed and have-nots a stake in the land and in the product of their own labour by means of cooperative societies, agricultural communes and novel ways of self-government. It has to be said that most of what was attempted failed within a short time, but the significance of these experiments is their place in the groundswell towards what are, even in the twenty-first century, the incomplete projects of democracy and social inclusion. Utopias, whether conceptual or practical, arise from passionate beliefs and imagination; for without the desire for change and the ability to imagine change, how can change happen?

As varied as they are, there are strong similarities in the ideas that set utopian plans in motion. They often draw power from the notion that there was once a Golden Age in human relationships to which society can return: a romantic state of communion with nature, for example. So utopian communities often seek out somewhere to set down roots where nature appears to be at its most lovely. For William Morris, the pre-industrial medieval society, where the craftsman had ownership of his own labour, seemed to provide a model of the just society. In times and places when poverty has been the norm, utopias have held out a vision of plenty. If there were justice and equality, if no one took more than they were entitled to, then surely there would be no need for poverty and hunger? But utopian communities cannot survive just on their hopes and beliefs. Utopia needed to be constructed within a built environment especially designed for its needs, with buildings often coming to symbolise the relations within the community, between people and between the different communal activities. To a remarkably consistent degree, utopias have put education at the centre of their beliefs, even when universal education was not the norm.

The Elmhirsts' Dartington, especially in its early years, had a strong family resemblance to other utopian schemes – pastoral charms, promotion of educational reform, more equitable social relationships and a programme of informed building construction for all its cultural, commercial and residential needs. [4] As with other utopias, we can challenge the rightness or success of Dartington's own vision, but this does not devalue the utopian quest. After all, *outopia* is by its nature unattainable. The utopian act is to strive for *eutopia*, the 'good place', in the face of all the contradictions and paradoxes. Without making any inflated claims to a utopian dream, Dartington's founders set off upon the quest for the good place. So one half of the title of this book is explained: Dartington as 'utopia in the making'.

But why dance? This is a question I will begin to answer here and go into more fully in Chapter 1. The Elmhirsts saw the value of the arts to society, including the art of dance. Dancing has more than once been a feature of utopian projects, as I will outline in Chapter 1. However, Dartington seems to have produced an environment that encouraged the participation of dancers as artists at times when their status in Britain was not assured in comparison to the other arts.

Making dance history: Dartington's role

The central narrative of this book is that Dartington played a special role in the making of British dance history in the twentieth century, being at the forefront of several waves of dance innovation: Dartington 'made dance history'. 'Making history' – that phrase resounds with all the exaggerated claims that pepper the popular media when some feat is hailed as the first of its kind, but here I disassociate it from this loose meaning. In the sense I mean it here, 'history' stands for the past, and obviously everyone had a part in its making. The most disregarded dance studio in the land made history just as much as Dartington did. While acknowledging this truism, the dance history that Dartington made lends itself to an extended narrative from the 1920s up to the present. It is not only that it is so full of interest, exceptional personalities and cross-fertilisations, but also I will be arguing that its history crystallises important issues in twentieth-century British dance more generally.

In common with some other utopias, Dartington made a place for dance from the beginning. Is this surprising? It is surely not a surprise that social dancing should be part of the fabric of the place. If we look only at the 1920s and 1930s, for example, we see a time when there were limited opportunities for entertainment, when dancing was one of the normal ways for young men and women to interact freely, and when ballroom dancing was part of the necessary social competence of the middle class. In 1927 Dorothy Elmhirst wrote in a letter about a dancing class in the Private House at Dartington Hall, when Dartington Hall School had recently been installed there.

> On Tuesdays we have a Dancing Class, composed of Seniors [*adults including the Elmhirsts and School staff*], the older Juniors [*schoolchildren*], the gardener's children, the maids of our household, and our second man [*footman*]. It is a most wonderful and unique affair, about thirty of us in all. We are learning the charleston, the tango, and all the tricks of the trade, and even Whitney [*her eldest son*] has decided that we are thoroughly up to date.[*Explanatory notes added*] [5]

This scene also brings to the surface some aspects of Dartington's version of utopian democracy: employers, employed staff and children could participate in dancing together (and in fact were on first-name terms), but the typical upper-class domestic hierarchy of the time was still in place.

Ballroom dancing and also traditional (folk) dancing had their place at Dartington, where anything that encouraged sociability was prized. The unusual matter is that the art of dance was also brought there. I define the art of dance as distinct from social dancing by its perceived main intention. The art of dance has an expressive intention. Its genres (ballet, modern dance, contemporary dance, South Asian dance, for example) are normally associated with performance to an audience. They use techniques founded in training an eloquent body for that purpose. Creativity, the making and performing of new dance works, is of prime importance. Social dances, on the other hand, are intended for general social interaction, bringing people to-gether and allowing them to enjoy movement, rhythm and a sense of community. Obviously these definitions are hugely generalised and break down under many circumstances. Social dances clearly have expressive qualities: we can, for example, easily distinguish the difference between an Argentinian tango and an English longways set country dance in the ways they express character, rhythm and social relationships. Therefore, the art of dance sometimes purloins social dance techniques for its own expressive pur-poses. The art of dance can also become social, as for example at Dartington, when it was a participatory activity for adult amateurs and schoolchildren, not necessarily leading to performance.

In a commonsense way, we can distinguish the techniques of social dance from the techniques of the art of dance, at least in relation to our own cul-tures although the conventions are often blurred. While the notion of performance is embedded in what we expect from the art of dance, including the framing of a performance on stage with an audience present, these ex-pectations can be subverted when the artist wants to challenge them. Playing to the theatricality of everyday life, for example, can bring into play all manner of indoor and outdoor spaces, different opportunities for siting performance and different opportunities for audience interaction, sometimes with people who had no prior intention to be an audience. (We can see this happening at Dartington in Chapters 5 and 6.) Into this complex mix come ceremonial dances such as Morris dancing, an area of traditional dance where the expressiveness of the form and display to an audience are certainly the intentions behind the dance in current practice, although formations and stepping are similar to the social forms of traditional dance. Because they originally had a close relationship with Dartington Hall itself, I will include a little on the foundation of the Dartington Morris Men at an appro-priate point in Chapter 4.

The focus of this book is on the art of dance at Dartington (the sense in which I will generally use the term 'dance') and on the succession of dance artists who worked there over the seventy-five years of its history in the twentieth century. This is not to deprecate social and traditional dance forms. I recognise that they have their own history at Dartington, albeit with fewer archival sources to draw upon. This is of itself an interesting historical issue, suggesting that the ubiquity of social dancing in some ways made it invisible because its nature was taken for granted. The fascination with the art of dance, on the other hand, gave rise early on to a great deal of documenta-tion, reflecting a seriousness of purpose in the eyes of the founders. Although Dartington has changed in many ways from the 1920s to the present, the beliefs of the founders have been a touchstone for its frequent metamorphoses, so that it is possible to trace a concern with the art of dance even at times when it was absent from the place or subsumed into other concepts of performance.

I credit the Elmhirsts with a policy towards dance that was unusual or even unique for its time in early twentieth-century Britain. While making available for their community the facilities for music making, arts and crafts and drama, they also wished to introduce dance, thus acknowledging its place alongside the other art forms recognised as 'high arts'. This contrasts with the prevailing lower esteem and visibility of dance in relation to the other arts.

This marginalisation of dance has turned out to be a prominent issue in dance scholarship as it has developed in the latter part of the twentieth century, in part instigated by the very fact that serious dance scholarship was so late to develop, in Britain only from the 1970s. Over-generalisation can be misleading however, and the issue needs teasing out on a number of levels if it is to be of help in contextualising Dartington's dance policy. I want first of all to give a very specific historical context for dance in 1920s Britain before going on to more deep-seated issues affecting the status of dance generally in the West.

Before the twentieth century, the theatre-dance form of ballet had become widespread in Europe.[6] Having developed from the dance of the French baroque with royal patronage, it expanded further, in major part promoted by royal, imperial and ducal flamboyance. Grand opera houses with permanent ballet companies and established schools became features of many capitals and large cities – Paris, Copenhagen, Stockholm, Milan and St Petersburg, to take some examples. But Britain lacked royal patrons with sufficient interest and had not established major dance institutions. Nevertheless, there were times when London saw a great vogue for dance, and particular London theatres were noted for it. From the 1830s to the 1850s, with the contemporary appeal of romanticism on stage, much-acclaimed foreign ballet stars and choreographers visited the city.[7] By this time, ballet had taken on feminine connotations. Women were the stars, but their status (and consequently the status of the art) was low, even though ballet was largely managed and choreographed by men.

From the late nineteenth century into the first decade of the twentieth century, ballet's greatest visibility in London was in the major music halls: the Alhambra and the Empire. These productions, as part of a variety bill, were spectacular and popular in the sense of appealing across the class divide, often showing off accomplished foreign ballerinas. The music hall ballet was framed as popular entertainment and was an integral part of the lively, socially inclusive world of Victorian theatre. But social processes were at work that would solidify the class boundaries of culture. The Theatre Licensing Act of 1843 had tried to draw the line between the legitimate theatre (plays) and other kinds of entertainment, while the late century saw West End theatre managers discouraging, the lower classes from their audiences, emphasising the West End as the domain of 'serious' theatrical art.[8] The effect was to separate the entertainment of the masses from the high arts, with the latter as markers of a 'cultured' middle class. But ballet in Britain failed to make that transition, remaining culturally on 'the other side', along with variety and pantomime.

A snapshot of ballet's position at the turn of the century can be gleaned from a book published in 1895, *Dancing* by Mrs Lilly Grove.[9] Her antipathy to the stage dancing of her day and to ballet in particular, with its 'painful tip-toe tripping' is made quite clear.

> Efforts are being made to-day towards a revival of the ballet, which forms such a large *element* in the entertainment at music halls.... These ballets, however, are pageants, and have very little in them of the dance in its more artistic form.[10]

If we now move forward in time to the 1920s, the decade in which the Elmhirsts' Dartington Hall was founded, we can observe a change in the social context of dance. Serge Diaghilev brought his Ballets Russes to London first in 1911 and for many subsequent seasons. Here was the basis for a change of perception about theatre dance as an art form alongside the others, not least because the music and design were by artists who could be respected in their own right and not just as theatrical hacks. Nevertheless, it remained 'the Russian ballet'; its dancers, such as Vaslav Nijinsky and Tamara Karsavina, and even Anna Pavlova, who made London her base for touring with her own company, were foreign exotics. London did have a number of good-quality private ballet studios, some, including those of Serafina Astafieva and Francesca Zanfretta, teaching authentic Russian and Italian technique. Consequently there were a few British and Irish dancers able to dance in and even star in the companies of Diaghilev and Pavlova, most changing their names to sound foreign: Anton Dolin, Alicia Markova, Lydia Sokolova and Ninette de Valois being the most prominent. Diaghilev died in 1929 and the company collapsed. Pavlova died in 1931. Already in the late 1920s there were efforts to found Britain's own ballet companies in schools and performing groups under Ninette de Valois and Marie Rambert, sowing the seeds of what would become the Royal Ballet and Ballet Rambert. These formidable women, both with experience under Diaghilev, were pressing for the place of the art of ballet to be on a level with the other high arts. The price of this was to be the repudiation of Britain's own recent ballet history in the music halls in favour of drawing a more acceptable lineage from Diaghilev.

At the same time, another genre of the art of dance was making an appearance. Isadora Duncan, dancing in a simple tunic and bare or sandaled feet, arrived in London in 1899, becoming a sought-after dancer in upper-class salons before moving to mainland Europe the following year, where she would be fêted. Duncan is a legend of dance, mythologised by controversy and tragedy, so it makes for a nice narrative point that she came quite close to Dartington. Her lover, the sewing-machine heir Paris Singer, inherited Oldway Mansion, a palatial residence about ten miles away at Paignton. She was here only briefly in 1910:[11] it gave sea air, true, but not exactly the environment for a woman whose intellectual and artistic circles encompassed the more stimulating surroundings of London, Paris and Berlin. We cannot pretend that she would have been interested in looking at the run-down farm that was Dartington Hall then.[12] For her and for others, Greek statuary set the standards for graceful, curving body lines – the antithesis to ballet, which seemed incapable of making the transfer to a twentieth-century dance. Even before Duncan arrived in London, Lilly Grove had endorsed the 'graceful movements' of dancers photographed in Graeco-Roman classical robes. Duncan also inspired other creative artists who made quite individual contributions to dance. For instance, the Canadian Maud Allan made a sensation with her dances, particularly *The Vision of Salomé*, which she performed for more than a year in London from 1908.[13]

Three British women stand out: Madge Atkinson, Ruby Ginner and Margaret Morris. Because they took inspiration from ancient Greek statuary and friezes, they are often labelling 'Hellenic' dancers, although they varied in the degree to which they looked to the Greek model. None of them saw their dance as just a reconstruction of movements from friezes and statues. They were taking something from those Greek female figures, dancing with ease in their loose tunics, that spoke to the desire of the twentieth-century woman to be free of restrictions in movement, dress and patriarchy. In music they often looked to the subjective emotion of the nineteenth-century romantic composers such as Schubert, Chopin and Mendelssohn. They were striving for simple, expressive movement that appeared to arise organically from the body and was directly counter to the technique and impression of ballet. They were 'barefoot dancers', the antithesis of the ballerinas in their sharp, tight shoes.

The resurgence of ballet and the development of dance that looked to Hellenic models were characteristic of 1920s Britain, the decade when Dartington was founded, but this does not indicate that dance had stepped out of the margins of cultural life. If the measure is the number of dance performances in comparison with musical concerts and plays, or if the measure is the number of publications devoted specifically to dance, then dance remained in the margins. If the measure is the stable existence of national

institutions, some with state patronage, set up to establish artistic merit and
transfer of knowledge, such as the National Gallery, the Royal Academy of
Music or the Royal Academy of Dramatic Art, then dance was still struggling
for recognition. (For example, the Society of Operatic Dancing, set up in
1920 to improve the teaching of ballet, received its royal charter as the Royal
Academy of Dancing only in 1935.) Nevertheless, the Elmhirsts decided
upon a place for dance at Dartington alongside the other arts. In Chapter 1, I
argue that they brought their ideas about the value of dance from their previous experiences, Dorothy's in her native New York and Leonard's in
imperial India.

I have outlined some historically specific conditions affecting the status of
dance in early twentieth-century Britain. I now intend to explore some more
deep-seated notions about the nature of dance in order to show that, despite
its strong position in some Western societies at particular historical moments, there remains an essential burden that dance must bear, always
making it difficult to establish its comparable worth in relation to the other
arts in prevailing Western thought.

By its very nature, dance exists only in the fleeting moment and is mostly
unrecorded, in spite of twentieth-century developments in dance notation,
film and video. Therefore dance does not lend itself to connoisseurship as the
visual arts do: it cannot be possessed, hung on the wall or exhibited in a
gallery. It is not held permanently within the pages of a book and sold on
every high street like literature. Consequently, its economy, measured as public consumption and funding for professional performance, is much smaller.
Its non-verbal nature makes it slippery to define and to write about, and also
puts it outside one of the dominant themes in the history of culture, that of
language – orality, literacy and reasoning. Ephemerality is a condition
shared by the other performing arts, but works of drama and music can be
represented by non-performance versions that form a basis and some would
say a prescription for the performance, although this is debatable. Drama,
equally as ephemeral as dance, can be captured in the pages of a script;
indeed, the aspiration for a more literary form of drama, plays written for
publication, was part of the bourgeoisification of late Victorian theatre.[14]
Performed music also has its material forms in musical scores, with the additional long history of recorded music from piano rolls to compact discs in the
present. Music consumption in the nineteenth century shifted towards the
kind of knowledgeable connoisseurship practised in the visual arts, the concert hall becoming the equivalent of the gallery where the canon of great
master works of the past was to be relished.[15] There is a long history of
drama and music being 'sold on every high street'. Their permanence and
availability give them a status that dance lacks. Although the twentieth century has seen some viable dance notation systems (mainly Benesh Notation

and Labanotation), choreographers and performers are predominantly not notation-literate. Few can go to the expense of hiring a notator, and as a result few dance works are recorded. Even if we assume that many choreographers now will have recorded their work for personal use, film and videotape have proved to be extremely sensitive to the destructive effects of time. The ephemerality of dance may have been one of the factors influencing its failure to become institutionalised as a high art in Britain during the nineteenth century, and this has continued.

On the other hand, ephemerality has been positively embraced by some twentieth-century artists in dance, visual arts and theatre. Sometimes this has been in a political challenge to the situation where arts are perceived as marketable commodities. So self-destructive art, 'happenings', Dada and Fluxus have been pitted against the notion that the arts must leave value-laden traces for the connoisseur. If the nature of dance is to be ephemeral, then, as some of Dartington's dancers would themselves perceive, improvised performance, never twice the same, explores and celebrates the true temporal nature of dance, existing only in its moment.

Another fundamental issue regarding the nature of dance, and one which has implications for the value attached to it by society, is its material manifestation in the body of the dancer. How do western societies view the body? The Christian tradition has been at best ambivalent towards the body, seen as the baser part of human existence, with its sexual appetites, excretions and ultimate decomposition, whereas the soul can rise to a higher plane, freed from its bodily prison. Thus dance has been generally excluded from Christian ritual, and under Puritanism suppressed even in its social function. There is also a long history of philosophical enquiry around 'the mind–body problem' (the attempt to understand the way they interact) that has treated these two as separate entities, hierarchically linked. The seventeenth-century Frenchman René Descartes famously wrote, 'Cogito ergo sum' (I am thinking, therefore I exist). Cartesian dualism conceptualised the mind and body as distinctly different things, but there was no doubt which was better. The mind, located in the brain but essentially non-physical and also identified with the soul, could exist without the body. The mind-soul's essential occupation was abstract thought, while the body was machine-like and ultimately fallible. Passions, sense-perceptions and imagination in which the mind needed to attend to the body were described as belonging to the body rather than to the mind.[16] These features of human emotional life are of course essential to the arts and to dance. Although dualism did not originate with Descartes (Plato had also subscribed to a form of it) and his ideas were controversial, various notions of dualism have persisted. We only have to think about the seemingly 'natural' distinction between manual labour (the body) and the professions (mind), or between the 'blue collar' (body, dirty) and the 'white colour' (mind, clean) worker.

But as we examine the dance at Dartington throughout the twentieth century, we will notice how the art form challenged its status. A number of Dartington's dancers, both male and female, were on a quest for a wholeness of self that defied dualism. In the 1970s and 1980s there were practices explicitly developing mind–body unity through the notion of 'the thinking body'; but even right from the beginning of dance at Dartington there were beliefs, rather vaguely articulated at first, about the place of dance or another kind of expressive movement in educational and societal wholeness. The separation of the art of dance from everyday life was questioned. Other challenges disputed the fixed identity of dance in the public mind. The feminist critique of the notions of female identity implicated in dance came later in the century; but before this, Dartington's female dancers had shown themselves to be independently minded and adventurous, not at all content to be directed by men. Frequently dance at Dartington redefined itself towards performance practices using spoken text or mundane gesture, challenging its boundary with drama. I am not suggesting that these trends were specific to Dartington, but that Dartington is a lens through which to watch them at work in the country at large.

I earlier sketched out the artistic context of theatre dance in 1920s Britain, focusing on the genres of classical ballet and Hellenic 'barefoot' dancing. It is clear from the beginning that Dartington's founders, Dorothy and Leonard Elmhirst, had no intention of introducing classical ballet as their dance genre. Why was that? Perhaps they perceived that ballet's overwhelming concern with perfection was not appropriate for the educational and social role they had in mind, but also, as I argue in the next chapter, their experience of dance in other continents was very specific and different from that of the London ballet world. A Hellenic dancer became the first dance teacher at Dartington. That may have been a pragmatic situation that arose by chance. Yet in the 1920s Hellenic dance represented a solution to the freeing of the body to meet the challenges of the twentieth century. This must have appealed to the Elmhirsts' pursuit of modernity and progress in all aspects of Dartington – scientific, agricultural, educational and artistic. Even after their direct input into Dartington matters had waned, the influence of those founding values persisted through the institutions they set up – the still existing Dartington Hall Trust, Dartington Hall School (closed in 1987) and the Arts Department that became first the Arts Centre and then the present-day Dartington College of Arts.

So Dartington has continued to provide a nurturing environment for the new and the experimental. For the most part, the genres of dance that have positioned themselves in opposition to classical ballet, those that tend to be categorised as modern or postmodern, have been the ones practised at Dartington. Even when there was a sustained effort to give practical support to a ballet company, it was because it seemed to confront contemporary themes. This book will not be concerned with marking out an aesthetic history justifying broad concepts such as modern dance and postmodern dance, although Dartington as an extended case-study says much about the development of these genres in Britain and abroad in the twentieth century. I take an alternative route through Dartington's history. While the focus is on specific dancers and choreographers and their interaction with the place, I will weave around these a topic that characterises Dartington throughout the century: an emerging exploration and questioning of the function of dance in society.

Perhaps this was no more than the concomitant of a socially informed view of the arts in general, but its rather striking presence at Dartington draws attention to issues that have been more widely important in British dance in the twentieth century. It is demonstrable that there has been a question haunting the stage, as it were: What can the art of dance do in people's lives? It is at least reasonable to wonder whether this serious question has been conditioned by the marginalised position of dance in the West. Perhaps dance has to validate its worth through advancing notions that it is both educationally and socially beneficial. Now at the beginning of the twenty-first century, when dance is thriving as a degree subject in universities (although we can still question how well it is doing in schools); when the community dance movement is bringing dance to people who might never experience it; when non-Western dance forms are being taught in an ethnically diverse population; and when professional dance companies make 'outreach' a priority, it is important to remember that eighty years ago none of this was part of the dance culture of the country. Reflected in Dartington's history we can see the growth of the ideology and practice that made this possible. But I am not implying a narrative of linear progress towards a version of dance that looks desirable from today's perspective. Like utopia, the vision of dance in society is an incomplete and fluctuating project that is continually remade in the light of political and artistic contexts.

If I say that these debates were embedded in Dartington's culture, I mean culture in the broadest sense, to include all the living-out of everyday life. In this history, ideologies will be seen gradually formulating from various levels of experience, not necessarily clearly articulated at first. Often beliefs will have to be inferred from the practice of dance creation, performance and pedagogy or from institutional decisions. I will argue that it is possible to observe dance in the process of being defined in relation to its function – as performance and audience reception; an education for children and adult amateurs; an academic subject; a vocational training; a philosophy of life; a tool of community engagement; and a vehicle for conveying political ideas. These functions entwine, emerge, decline and re-emerge. They form a varied pattern underlying the creative work of Dartington's dancers.

Making dance history: The historian's role

History is a complex word with multiple meanings: the past, a representation of the past, an academic discipline, to name a few. The notion of 'making history' is likewise complex. While I have insisted that Dartington (by which I mean every person concerned with it) 'made history' (that is, its past), and that this history is a particularly interesting one, I must now insist that this history (this past) is logically not accessible unless someone can invent time travel. So I now turn to another use of the word, meaning the way the past is represented. In this meaning I, as the historian, am making history (attempting to represent the past), which takes material shape in this book. Dartington's people made its history in the past. I make my history in the present. How can these two perspectives ever meet?

The time when the historian's work was received as an objective revelation of the truth of the past has long gone. In that scientific (positivist or certaintist) understanding of the historical undertaking, most associated with the nineteenth-century German historian Leopold von Ranke, rigour in searching out and interpreting documents and relics was the method that appeared to guarantee a correct version of the past. But, quite apart from raising any concerns about how truth can be retrieved from such documents, those methods were developed from a time when history meant the study of rulers and nations – huge power structures with a large investment in documentary evidence. I will later deal with doubts about how documents of the past are assumed to speak to the present, but now I want to point out that traces of the past are patchy when we are investigating marginalised people or art forms. Crucially for dance history, those ephemeral dancing bodies are absent, as are their dances. However, dance historians should not become obsessed about this: all historical events are ephemeral, be they dances or battles. Everything about the past has passed away.

In recent decades, the pendulum has swung from that scientific view of the historian's craft to a postmodern, relativist scepticism about the possibility of knowing in the present the truth about the past. The strongest arguments relate to the critique of language as an accurate representation of the world, coming from structural and post-structural linguistics and from such thinkers as Roland Barthes, Jacques Derrida and Michel Foucault. If we start to see language as inherently arbitrary in the way it represents reality, this strikes at the heart of our claims both to be able to read the past from the written source material and to pass on an accurate representation of the past in written histories. There is, for example, nothing in the word 'dance' that looks or sounds like a dance, and I have already pointed out some of the problems around defining what I will mean when I use that word. Nevertheless, there remains a strong attachment in the practice of historians to the notion that they can discover and convey a truth about the past which, although it may not be the only truth, is at least one of a range of valid ones.

In Alun Munslow's categorisation, historians range themselves along a continuum from conservative 'reconstructionists', who believe in the accuracy of their picture of the past, to 'deconstructionists', who have taken their scepticism about historical truth to an extreme. Branching off from reconstructionism are the 'constructionists', who place their historical interpretations within pre-existing laws of social theory such as Marxism or feminist theory. But Munslow states that, in current practice, 'most historians range themselves around the methodological point at which constructionism branches from reconstructionism'.[17] This is where I place myself. I find this to be a good position from which to listen to the arguments of all parties and to be informed by the multiplicity of critical standpoints that characterise the work of history today.

The swing of the pendulum back and forth between extreme and intermediate positions in this debate has been documented profusely.[18] Its presence in dance-history scholarship today is attested, for example, by Alexandra Carter's collection *Rethinking Dance History* (2004). The debate encompasses such philosophical issues as the nature of knowledge and the possibility of historical truth, which I will not enter into here. I will rather focus on three issues that arise from it, because they impinge directly on the research and writing of this book about Dartington. They concern the nature of narrative history, the role of the historian, and the use and interpretation of sources.

The notion of history as a chronological narrative took rather a battering in the 1970s and 1980s. Deconstructionists such as Hayden White drew attention to the way in which the forms and devices of fiction are utilised to impose a plot upon the past.[19] The historian selects, emplots and writes an account that the reader will relish without too many frustrating loose ends and culs-de-sac – in other words, something that does not in the least resemble real life. Deconstructionists such as White view narrative as something imposed upon the past. The historian is implicated in an invention, an act of imagination; but more importantly, the narrative form itself is an unacknowledged but powerful mode of explanation in its own right, telling a story that can be epic, tragic or comedic, or that has the dynamics of unassailed progress, ascent and decline or cyclical recurrence. Do these devices render narrative history academically suspect as real knowledge about the past? Too often, narrative history can seem to incorporate the authority of the only plot that is available for this set of circumstances. This is especially so when the historian adopts an all-knowing authorial voice, as if telling the story from a position of ultimate and perfect knowledge.

However, there are also some reasoned arguments that narrative history deserves to remain one of the most prominent historical forms. First of all, we can observe that the historian's role is always essentially an imaginative one. The distinction between the past and history means that any communication attempting to bring the past to life must be an imaginative engagement with unknown people, always with attention to the historical sources. Sometimes, in order to give a voice to the vast majority who have left no personal evidence of themselves, historians have positively embraced the imaginative. In such a way, our only access to the absent voice of a nineteenth-century 'ballet girl' (Cara Tranders of the Empire Music Hall) is in her fictional reverie by Alexandra Carter.[20] I would suggest that there is a continuum from fiction to narrative history along which we must place ourselves according to the story we have to tell.

We can also enquire into the beguiling nature of narrative itself. Is there something about the human experience that is 'story-shaped'? We do seem to be creatures of narrative, making and repeating our own histories of short events or whole lifetimes, not just socially but also when telling our own stories to ourselves. Is it relevant that several European languages have the same name for history and story (in French, *histoire*, in Italian, *istoria*, in German *Geschichte*)?[21] I believe there are things in the nature of Dartington's past that suit it to the form of narrative history. My argument is based upon David Carr's defence of narrative history, coming from the philosophical direction of phenomenology.[22] He disagrees that narrative is an alien form imposed upon the past, arguing that it is consistent with our everyday experience of time. We perceive actions and events in a present moment that is conditioned by a past moment and looks towards an intention or expectation for a future moment. Individual moments of time are thus laid out in a story-like way in which we grasp that each moment is part of a longer whole. He argues that we really do experience the narrative forms of beginnings, middles and ends in our daily actions and experience. Our temporal sequences are varied and multiple, ranging from single events to whole lifetimes. To those who would argue that the experience of real life is of a continuous succession of events without the meaningful selection given in a narrative, he would counter that, when we try to grasp one of our life's more complex past–present–future temporal sequences to reflect upon, we are in effect becoming the narrator of it to ourselves or to others.[23]

So Carr's argument is that the bedrock of the human experience of time is something very like literary narrative. These narrative structures, large and small, include what he calls 'relay-form' or historicity[24] – our sense of being placed in relation to others in a lineage of past, present and future, at its most basic form in the generations of family life.[25] Historicity is a very palpable expression at Dartington, where the 'relay-form' from the founders to the present day and the perceived obligation to convey that into the future has a constituting effect on policy. Historicity can also be embodied in dance history in the way in which dancers perceive their own position in relation to predecessors (perhaps teachers), peer groups experiencing the current aesthetic and cultural environment, and a future of the next step in developing their art. I am not implying here the simplistic notion of 'family trees' based upon entrenched and highly selective versions of the canon of 'greats' that has been an element of dance-historical writing.[26] I am suggesting a much more diverse sense of connectedness through physical practice, one which acknowledges the presence of past movement experience in the body now, and which shares or contends the current field with many overlapping others and is always pressing on towards the next dance. So predecessors are acknowledged even as a dancer goes beyond them, forming new contemporary groupings and passing on embodied knowledge. Dancers' lives seem to be essentially 'story-shaped'.[27]

One of the outcomes of the deconstructionist critique of reconstructionist history has been to foreground the role of the historian in formulating history as the representation of the past. It is no longer tenable to assume a mantle of objectivity. Most historians now, myself included, will reflect on their own position in relation to the historical material. To what extent do my own biases and predilections structure the way I think about the past? Those questions have to be part of the historian's self-reflexivity. But it is not enough to keep this to myself, because the reader needs to understand my position too. As Peter Burke states:

> Historical narrators need to find a way of making themselves visible in their narrative, not out of self-indulgence but as a warning to the reader that they are not omniscient or impartial and that other interpretations beside theirs are possible.[28]

I have attempted to be a presence in the text through my occasional appearances in my own voice. Meanwhile, I introduce myself as someone passionate about dance and history and particularly gleeful in the presence of hitherto untold stories. As a teacher trained at the Laban Art of Movement Studio (the debt of this organisation to the Elmhirsts becomes clear in Chapter 4) and a latecomer to university education and academia, I believe in the educational and social functions of dance and their transformational possibilities. My own history in dance, as amateur participant, teacher and audience member, has run parallel to most of the last fifty years of Dartington's history, so in a way I have a personal investment in it, although

I remain an outsider at Dartington itself. Like all historical researchers, I sit somewhere between my enthusiasms and hypotheses and my conviction that I must use all care in making a valid interpretation of the sources. I am aware that, like all histories, this narrative is just one of the ways of joining up the dots of the past.

The methods of empirical research, discovering and interpreting historical sources, remain the bedrock of most historical research, even though the reconstructionist–deconstructionist debate reminds us to think carefully about what we do. We must now recognise that, without the intervention and interpretation of the historian, the sources in themselves say nothing about the past; far from being pristine and objective, they have already been loaded with implicit meaning that goes beyond the surface story they tell.

This is of course true for the already existing published accounts that include dance at Dartington. I survey the most important book-length sources here, starting with those coming from an institutional perspective.

Victor Bonham-Carter, Dartington's first archivist, wrote *Dartington Hall: The History of an Experiment* (1958) as a condensed version for publication of a much longer history prepared for the use of the Trustees, looking to the future as 'a permanent and authoritative record for posterity'.[29]   Michael Young's *The Elmhirsts of Dartington* was first published in 1982. Both mention dance at Dartington before World War II but superficially, with some factual errors and without appropriate artistic contextualisation. In Young's case his viewpoint is necessarily coloured by his experience as a schoolboy there in the 1930s. He was also a close family friend and later Trustee, so his knowledge is privileged in particular ways: he is able to give a portrait of the Elmhirsts as personalities 'from close up'. At the point where memoir merges with history, we can expect that there will be factual inaccuracies where memories are not checked. This is so for some of his memories of dance at Dartington.[30]

Another text giving a broad overview and that includes dance in its remit is Peter Cox's memoir of over forty years of involvement, *The Arts at Dartington 1940–1983: A Personal Account* (2005), an edited version of his previous unpublished document.[31]   As Administrator of the Arts Department, Warden of the Arts Centre and Principal of Dartington College of Arts until 1983, Cox, more than any other personality, has joined together the world the Elmhirsts dominated and the world of Dartington in recent decades. Of necessity his perspective on dance is both personal and institutional, constituted within his overall policy for the institutions he was nurturing. His account reminds us of the institutional constraints within which dancers and other artists must negotiate their practice.

From the dance-historical perspective, a number of biographies document dance careers partially spent at Dartington: Erik Näslund on Birgit Cullberg

(1978), Caryll von Sturmer on Margaret Barr (1993), Valerie Preston-Dunlop on Rudolf Laban (1998), Patricia Stöckemann on Kurt Jooss and Grete Müller on Sigurd Leeder (both 2001). With the exception of Stöckemann, all these authors were writing about a person known to them and, with the exception of Cullberg, deceased. They vary in the range of sources used, including the choreographer's own memories, the writer's own recollections and archival sources. The comments I made previously about the reflexive positioning of the historian apply equally to biographers. We need to be able to recognise whose voice is speaking, the relationship of author to subject and the source material used.

All of the above speak of a first intensive period of dance at Dartington that had mainly passed away by the 1940s, although, as I show in Chapter 4, there remained important connections with the dance world over the next two decades. It was not until the 1960s that Dartington once more had a consistent dance presence. The interest for dance scholars in this later period has been in analysing the successional influences and cross-fertilisations of dance technique and aesthetic between Britain and the USA. For example, Stephanie Jordan's *Striding Out* (1992) brings dance-analytic as well as historical frameworks to the context of 'British new dance' in the 1970s and 1980s, when the Dance at Dartington festivals became so influential (1978–87) and Dartington's dancers formed a hub for the dissemination of ideas.

Recently, the new phenomenon of publishing on CD-ROM and DVD has enabled many more various visual and aural sources to be brought to published dance history. So, looking to the period directly previous to the one that Jordan describes, Valerie Preston-Dunlop and Luis Espana brought together archive moving and still images and on-camera interviews for their DVD *The American Invasion 1962–72* (2005). This charts a decade in which American modern dance first came into an academic setting, with Dartington College of Arts playing a central role. New technologies may well be significant in future for the transmission of historical research. They offer new, bright ways of bringing to life the dance of the past. They also offer challenges in how to keep the balance between presenting imaginatively and making evident a firm bedrock of well-researched data.

This book differs from all the publications listed above in attempting a connected narrative of dance at Dartington through a large part of the twentieth century. The major part of my research has been in archives of various sorts, including documentary, video and photographic collections along with collections of specialist journals held in libraries. The Dartington Hall Trust Archive is the one I have used most consistently. In addition I have accessed the National Resource Centre for Dance archives at Guildford, Surrey, where there are major collections relating to Rudolf Laban and Lisa Ullmann as well as a small collection from Leslie Burrowes and a large but, at present, mainly unsorted one from the critic Fernau Hall. Through my research assistant, Pauline Manley, I was able to obtain documents from the State Library of New South Wales, Sydney (Margaret Barr Collection). As well as proving a source of rarer books, the British Library houses special collections, including the papers of the composer Alan Bush, providing a background to Barr's activities in London in the late 1930s. The National Co-operative Archive, based in Manchester, enabled me to see the film of the *Towards Tomorrow* pageant of 1938, which included Barr and others dancers of that period. The Victoria and Albert Museum's Archive of Art and Design and Theatre Museum Collection gave me access to a variety of sources related to individual choreographers and their works, as well as the huge documentary repository of the Arts Council of Great Britain. The New York Public Library for the Performing Arts, Jerome Robbins Dance Division, provided a range of print and audio-visual sources unobtainable elsewhere. Other audio-visual archive material came from the archive at Laban, in London, where a considerable collection relating to twentieth-century dance is being created. I also accessed audio-visual material at The Place Videoworks in London. The South West Film and Television Archive in Plymouth preserves the film and television record of that region, including Dartington's own early filmed records as well as television programmes made there.

Even these primary sources come with deep layers of implicit meaning. We must ask not only why these sources were created and what codes and conventions governed their form, but also why they have survived and what values are reflected in their preservation.[32]

The Dartington Hall Trust Archive is a case in point. Its origin as an archive (originally Records Office) is in the 1950s as part of the project for Bonham-Carter's history of Dartington. He decided on four broad categories: commercial records (archived in boxes prefixed C); the work of the Trust, which included the arts (prefixed T); and correspondence and documents in Dorothy's domain (DWE) and in Leonard's (LKE). These prefixes will become very familiar in notes to the chapters, although the archive has now grown beyond these categories. The archive is rich with the mundane documentation of the Estate offices as well as the private records of the Elmhirsts. What factors have enabled these to be preserved for the present? we should ask. Is it that the Elmhirsts had personal secretarial help; that there was ample room for storage of documents; that there were no 'efficiency consultants' making them trash their elderly records? There is also, I think, a sensitivity to Dartington's history that is absolutely fundamental, because being positioned within a long past and future is implicit in the Elmhirsts' acquisition of Dartington Hall. The earliest decades of records also reflect a manner of working when ideas, rebukes, commands and concerns were put into writing rather than speaking them face to face or on the phone, even between people who were often working a short walk from each other. The fact is that the phone was new here in the 1920s and 1930s and not all offices had even an extension, let alone a direct line. Even later on there seems to have been a persistence of thought that the correct way to do business was in writing. This written richness peters out towards the present day. A further complication for this research is that, for other reasons, the records of Dartington Arts Society and Dartington College of Arts as represented in the archive are much thinner. Each organisation had a life that was semi-independent, the College eventually becoming separated from the Trust in the late 1980s. This falling-off in volume of sources is compounded by the standard restrictions on access to documents from the preceding thirty years. There are a number of factors here in relation to preservation and archiving practices that structure the records.

Sequences of dated paper records such as letters, minutes and reports sometimes make it possible to pin down the gradual formation of ideas or the conceptual roots of events (or at least their public articulation).They help us put these into chronological sequence. Yet their voices are sometimes obscure: sometimes they fail to identify the originator and date; sometimes they give information contradicted elsewhere; often they are hedged about with the writing conventions and idiosyncrasies of their period. They must be interpreted and compared with other sources.

Status and money gave to the Elmhirsts a mighty ability to draw attention to the artistic work that was happening at Dartington, a fact that of itself affects the richness of the written record, not only in archived sources but in newspapers and journals. From 1929 to 1934 members of the family were personally involved in dance performances, and those performances were well-covered by local press, with the reviews carefully preserved in the archive. Throughout the 1930s, the family's keen interest in Dartington's dance and their network of influential friends were constructive in getting wider recognition in print, for example in the British journal *The Dancing Times* and in the American *Theatre Arts Monthly* (which was also being supported by Dorothy's New York-based charity). After this, the personal artistic involvement of the Elmhirsts tended towards drama and music. When dance was once more permanently situated in Dartington from 1965, the intense physical participation of family members no longer applied. Dorothy Elmhirst died in 1968 and Leonard in 1974. I believe that at least part of the cause of the falling-off in written records of dance at Dartington is related to the changing interests of the Elmhirsts.

In a more general way, Dartington has always been aware of the need for good internal and external communications, so its own news publications are now useful primary sources for its artistic life. The little news-sheet called *News of the Day* was first produced by Leonard Elmhirst in November 1927.

It is now amongst the most useful tools for tracing Dartington's early every-day existence. It gives an invaluable chronicle of a little community in all its aspects – lost fountain pens and problems with water supply, 'what's on' at the cinemas in Paignton and Totnes, comings and goings at the Hall (reading a little like the Court Circular at times), classes, rehearsals and performances. In 1967 this was superseded by a much more professional illustrated news-paper, *Dartington Hall News*, which later became *Dartington Hall News and South Devon Scene*. It remained in existence until 1984, promoting in particu-lar the arts in Dartington and the South West. Another periodical, *Dartington Voice* (1976–89), published longer articles literally voicing the various and often conflicting perspectives, including artistic, within the complex organi-sation.

Oral history interviews form a contrast with paper-based sources: how can we evaluate them, collected many years after the events themselves? Current research on the neuroscience of memory suggests that memories are not, as it were, recorded whole and stored in one part of the brain, but that memory recall is a constructive process in which the individual brings together different aspects of the same memory stored separately.[33] This proc-ess is not infallible in terms of accuracy. Dates and names may be distorted and similar events may be conflated. Present needs also shape the memory. We all consciously rehearse our memories to construct our autobiographies in a more easily retrievable version. Oral history is subject to the same evalu-ations as other historical sources, but there is absolutely nothing that can replace the physical contact with an actual participant in historical events. Crucially, such contacts advise the historian of her own uncomfortable role between moulding all the various sources into a valid interpretation and her obligation to a story that belongs to others.

To be true to the subject, the challenge for the dance historian is to make a historical narrative that creates a space for dance to come alive. How, then, can this be done in the absence of the dances themselves? The traces they leave behind seem all too often to be pathetically inadequate reminders of the real thing – photographs of a few moments, reviews by critics (sometimes partisan or with an axe to grind), too rarely a decent filmed or video record. The films or videos made for the artist's own record often have a sad afterlife, deteriorating in quality unless they are properly archived.[34] We must also doubt if any moving-image record, even one made professionally and well, can stand for a live performance, where the viewer reacts directly to the performer rather than through the intermediary of the camera's eye. So what does the dance historian do?

Essentially it is a process of bricolage. I use this term to identify the concep-tual reconstruction of the dance from whatever is at hand – archival documents, published accounts in books, journals and newspapers, photographs, moving images and memories. In its dictionary definition, bricolage signals the bringing together of unconnected things. It also bears the trace of Claude Lévi-Strauss's ethnographic metaphor for the cultural construction of myth out of reassembled symbolic forms, making new meanings. Although I do not use the term in a strictly Straussian way, it reminds us that my bricolage is an act of meaning-making that can neither resurrect a dance as it was, nor claim to make a definitive interpretation.[35] I adhere to the process of bricolage as one fundamental for dance-history writing. As Susan Manning has written, when introducing her own method of reconstructing the dances of Mary Wigman on the page:

> The dance scholar has no choice except to pursue the elusive and uncertain text of performance. An event bound in space and time, a performance can be read only through its traces – on the page, in memory, on film, in the archive. Each of these traces marks, indeed distorts, the event of performance, and so the scholar pursues what remains elusive as if moving through an endless series of distorting reflections.[36]

The materials of my bricolage are apparent in text or notes and can be used and reinterpreted in other ways. My own interpretations arise as I move between a notional reconstruction of the performance and a placement of it within its historical context.

This narrative proceeds in a generally chronological fashion. In Chapter 1 I discuss the personal histories of Dorothy and Leonard Elmhirst before they came to Dartington.[37] Dorothy's experiences as a philanthropist in early twentieth-century New York, I argue, would have made her aware of the context that was beginning to define modern dance. Leonard experienced dance at Rabindranath Tagore's school and university in Bengal. For both of these, notions of education and dance were entwined. I outline the first years at Dartington Hall but also refer to some historic practical utopias where dance had a place and that fed into the Dartington vision. The first of Dartington's dancers, Leslie Burrowes, began teaching there in 1928 and left for Europe in late 1929.

In the new decade, the Elmhirsts began to look to a much more impressive institutional structure for dance. Two teachers from America, Margaret Barr and Louise Soelberg, came to staff the School of Dance-Mime, the subject of Chapter 2. Here we can note two of the themes that run through this history. The name of the School indicates that the concept of dance was subsumed into a wider notion of performance, something that remained a powerful structuring principle. Dance and performance were in the domain of the adult amateur as well as the professional, but this leads to the beginnings of a controversy about appropriate standards of execution, which continues into the very clearly professional era of Ballets Jooss and the Jooss–Leeder School at Dartington, the subject of Chapter 3. This was a hugely ambitious period for Dartington – perhaps over-ambitious – brought to an end by the onset of World War II. In those last years of peace, I argue, both Kurt Jooss and Margaret Barr (now in London) articulated the crisis of the times in their work.

From the 1940s to the mid-1960s, very little dance happened at Dartington, but the Elmhirsts had a close relationship with the émigré dance theorist Rudolf Laban and Lisa Ullmann, a teacher from the former Jooss–Leeder School. Chapter 4 examines the new national focus on dance as education for children and a renewed focus on the amateur. The Elmhirsts had a hand in this through the Laban Art of Movement Centre Trust that they set up. The parallel narrative to that one is of the development of professional dance after World War II. This includes the funding policies and slow recognition of the needs of dance, coming from the Arts Council of Great Britain. Dartington had a part to play in this too, as a performance centre of the South West region; and in this post-war period the connections with the arts of India brought many exceptional performers in South Asian music and dance.

I carry into Chapter 5 a discussion of dance as education and as art at Dartington College of Arts. The wider development of the study of dance as an academic discipline is reflected there, as is the diversification of the dance field with successive influences from America. Very soon, a homegrown, flourishing dance culture was established, 'British new dance', both at Dartington and elsewhere. But there are questions here about the functioning of a creative artist in an academic setting – how to be simultaneously an artist and an educator. It is important that Dartington's dance culture was embedded in a theatre department, not a department of dance. Once again the symbiosis between dance and other performance genres was taken for granted, as it had been in the 1930s.

In Chapter 6, I return to another topic that runs as a thread from when Dartington was established: that of dance functioning for the good of the community as a whole. The Theatre Department of Dartington College of Arts developed a solid ethic about working with communities in urban and rural areas. We can look at this work in the 1970s and 1980s in the context of a changing social and artistic climate. Notions of community arts and community dance were developing, making possible a different kind of relationship between the professional and the amateur than was envisaged in the 1920s and 1930s. Perhaps that makes the efforts of the earlier pioneers so much more important to celebrate.

These, then, are the themes of this history of dance at Dartington – utopian schemes, important ideas to communicate, and dance as art, in education and out in the community. My detailed analysis must break off at around 1990 for various reasons, not the least of them being the difficulty of bringing the most recent decade into balanced focus. Histories by necessity must always end at an artificial point. As the historian Simon Schama has written:

> Histories never conclude: they just pause their prose. Their stories – like the one just told – are, if they are truthful, resistant to windings-up and sortings-out.[38]

And I would add, be assured that the dance goes on.

Chapter 1

Why Dartington? Why Dance?

We are attempting to build up a community founded on an economic basis of self-support and productive rural enterprises, and at the same time we are trying to develop a more creative life for everybody by offering opportunities for a study of many subjects and for the practice of painting, dancing, singing, and acting.

Dorothy Elmhirst, July 1928[1]

It is April 2001 and I am on a train to Totnes for the first time. Leaving Exeter, it runs alongside the estuary of the River Exe then follows the coast of South Devon, through seaside resorts, Dawlish and Teignmouth, cutting through amazing cliffs of weathered, red rock. Eventually the train starts inland, up the Teign Valley to Newton Abbot and finally south across the countryside to Totnes. This district of Devon, known as South Hams, presents itself as a landscape of tightly packed, rounded little hills. Settlements like Totnes seem to be just inserted into the crannies between them, served by narrow, winding lanes and roads. This is 200 miles south-west of London.

It is really not far from Totnes station to Dartington Hall: two miles at most. The route mounts through fields with views of the River Dart below. There are mossy stone walls and spring flowers in the banks. Just before the top of the hill, the utilitarian buildings of Dartington College of Arts come into view. Further on is Dartington Hall itself, the rather modest gateway arch leading into a rectangular, grassed courtyard almost entirely enclosed by its four wings. Straight ahead, its entrance under the clock tower, is the Great Hall; fixed into the roof of its porch is a boss showing the White Hart on a red rose, the insignia of King Richard II whose half-brother built this place. There is a palpable atmosphere of history and tradition. Descriptions and photographs of Leonard Elmhirst's arrival here in March 1925 show the aspect to have been very different. The Great Hall had no roof, the wings were agricultural buildings, what is now the Barn Theatre (off the gateway arch) was literally a barn and the courtyard was a farmyard, but he immediately recognised it as the place for the 'English experiment' he was planning.[2]

Passing the White Hart bar and restaurant, my explorations continue in the 38 acres of garden. At its centre is the huge flattened area of the tilt-yard, earlier named the open-air theatre (as I will refer to it throughout this book).

Its high terraces are primrose-studded at this time of year. It seems impossible, though, not to be drawn up the pathways and wooded slopes, giving views of the Great Hall and the Private Residence. There are sculptures, too: a reclining figure by Henry Moore celebrating the life of Dartington's first Arts Administrator; a tiny bronze donkey by Willi Soukop, an émigré sculptor of the 1930s who married one of Dartington's dancers. In my mind, the gardens resonate with past moments of Dartington's dancers. Members of Ballets Jooss practised here and posed in their costumes for *A Ball in Old Vienna*, moments preserved in photographs. Backed by landscaped parkland and medieval buildings, the dancers seem to be absorbed into an idealised countryside, utopian in its integration of physical beauty, life, work, dance and nature – the Dartington phenomenon.

I have arrived at Dartington at a beautiful time of year but a time of national crisis. The country is in the grip of an epidemic of foot-and-mouth disease, affecting sheep and cattle. Tourists are being discouraged from the countryside, even from Dartington's gardens, which I can enjoy alone. I seem to be the only occupant of the Conference Centre accommodation in the East Wing of the Courtyard, eating my breakfast in splendid isolation in the dining room that occupies the immense Tudor kitchens. 'Everything here is so beautiful, peaceful, gorgeous, blooming', I write in my diary.

The Founders

The estate was bought by Leonard and Dorothy Elmhirst on the eve of their marriage in 1925.[3] Leonard Elmhirst was born in Yorkshire in 1893. The family's landowning status predicted the course of his education at boarding preparatory and public schools followed by Cambridge University. Although the position of the Elmhirsts in the hierarchy was a comfortable one, they were not particularly wealthy. His father, with a minimum of vocation, took up the calling of a country parson for the usefulness of the stipend, and gave that up as soon as he could inherit the estate. Originally, Leonard too was earmarked for the Church of England ministry. By the time he was ready to leave university, World War I was upon them. Leonard's attitude towards the Church had become gradually more sceptical, but his sense of social service remained strong. He set out for the East, to India and Mesopotamia, working for the YMCA, endeavouring to provide morally uplifting entertainment and education for British troops.

Having finally given up all idea of the Church, and become disillusioned with the YMCA's religiosity, Leonard's future direction was settled when he became secretary to a man whose commitment to the future of India was of a far higher calibre than that of the usual colonial *sahib*. Sam Higginbottom was a missionary who had gained an American agricultural degree in order to help the Indian farmers improve their yields and thereby their nourishment and health. This was the spark that sent Leonard to Cornell University in America in 1919 to get a degree in the most advanced, scientific and businesslike methods of farming. The attachment to India and its political and economic future stayed with him all his life and will be seen as a strong shaping influence on the arts at Dartington.

While at Cornell, Elmhirst met Dorothy Whitney Straight, a widow with three children, and a millionaire in her own right. Their backgrounds could not have been more different. She had been born to every privilege. At the time of her birth in 1887 her father, William Whitney, was serving as Secretary to the Navy in the cabinet of President Grover Cleveland. The First Lady was her godmother. Politics was not Whitney's only calling. Having married a wealthy wife, he set about making his own millions. Dorothy's mother, Flora Payne Whitney, concentrated on a lavish project of entertainment, which would be a factor in ensuring that the family was counted in the ranks of 'The Four Hundred' elite of New York society. (The number was significant only because it was said to be the capacity of the ballroom owned by the undoubted society leader, Mrs Astor, wife of William Backhouse Astor.) One of the mechanisms for keeping the top echelons exclusive was patronage of the boxes at the tiny Academy of Music that acted as an opera house. Whitney was one of those rising stars of New York society who together retaliated by forming a company for the building of the Metropolitan Opera House, which opened in 1883.[4] Whitney's sponsorship of the Met was undertaken for pragmatic reasons. Owning a box amounted to declaring a position in society, but he does also seem to have genuinely loved music, at the opera or in private recitals at home, as would his daughter Dorothy.

In the climate of late nineteenth-century America, there were vast business fortunes to be made. Profits were largely unregulated and untaxed. Business practices were cut-throat and frequently immoral, if not actually illegal. Whitney was one of these so-called 'robber barons', his name counted alongside those of Vanderbilt, Rockefeller and Carnegie. Although he made millions of dollars, his fortune was nevertheless small by Rockefeller standards. However, his acquisition of land was second to none. There were huge estates, some of which housed his successful racehorse stables and racetracks. He travelled between his six homes in his own railroad car. It is said that only the government owned more land in the states of New York and Massachusetts than he did.[5]

William Whitney died in 1904 when Dorothy was seventeen, leaving her an orphan who would inherit about 8 million dollars at twenty-one. She had been brought up to take part in activities suitable to her class: a society debut in the ballroom of her brother's New York mansion (originally built by Whitney senior), the grand tour of Europe and the East, the box at the Met, a little charity work.

The philanthropy of the 'robber barons' such as Rockefeller and Carnegie is legendary. Whitney was not one of the most lavish of them. The next generation of Whitneys was more generous than he, but Dorothy's philanthropy was of a quite different order. Rather than offering a temporary fix for the ills of society, she was to gradually assume the role of reformer. She was intelligent, serious and independent-minded (having her own household at the age of nineteen helped in this respect) and she educated herself through courses and lectures. She was interested in political issues such as women's suffrage and women's trade unions as well as in social projects for New York's poor. She joined the Junior League, volunteer debutantes who took on social service projects, and became its president in 1908.

One reason for the further blossoming of her social conscience lies in her intellectually stimulating marriage in 1911 to Willard Straight, diplomat, financial negotiator in China and political ally of Theodore Roosevelt. They both began to take an interest in the reformist agenda of Herbert Croly, author of *The Promise of American Life* (1909). He believed that the 'promise' of which he wrote had been destroyed by the effects of rapid urbanisation and industrialisation. It could only be restored by strengthening government in order to overcome social and economic problems and to control big business in the interest of the whole nation. Government should defend and extend democracy and lead America out of isolationism to take a full part in international affairs. Croly exemplifies the conscience of the period of turn-of-century America that is commonly now called the Progressive Era. With a particular leadership role assumed by women like Dorothy, social and economic conditions began to change because of the activism of people who set in motion projects for the relief of urban conditions and supported movements for improved democracy, such as the extension of the vote to women and trade union rights. Dorothy was involved in such projects as these and put up the money for a new weekly newspaper, *The New Republic*, first published in 1914, to be edited by Herbert Croly in order to pursue these aims. Dorothy did not simply provide the bankroll: she was active on the editorial board alongside her husband.

The legendary columnist Walter Lippmann, who was assistant editor on the paper, believed that Dorothy felt her inheritance was 'tainted' and she must therefore use it for the public good.[6] This sensitivity may well have been influenced by a public scandal that highlighted the sometimes dubious practices in which her father was involved. Among his diverse business interests was a company with a monopoly of New York utilities – gas, electricity and streetcar lines. Money raised by repeated share issues was not used for modernisation of the infrastructure, and watered the value of the stock. The income raised had gone to enrich Whitney substantially, but had not benefited New York or the shareholders. The collapse of the company in 1908, after his death, with much loss of money to shareholders confirmed how slippery he had been. The company structure was so complicated that it could not be legally traced to him, and the books had been destroyed.

Closely allied with the social projects of Progressive Era America was the notion and theory of progressive education. Its leading theorist was John Dewey. In books such as *The School and Society* (1899) and *Democracy and Education* (1916) he promulgated a child-centred approach, appreciative of the diversity of all humans, and capable of making citizens who could act critically and effectively in a democratic society. In 1904 he joined the faculty at Teachers College, Columbia University. Dorothy was to become enthusiastic about his ideas, and enrolled in some of his classes. Her children (born in 1912, 1914 and 1916) attended the Lincoln School, the demonstration school attached to Teachers College of which she was a Trustee.[7]

By the time that Willard Straight had died in 1918, a victim of the great post-World War I influenza epidemic, it was clear that Dorothy had begun to use her money to sponsor new ways of thought about political and social disadvantage.

Another of Dorothy's New York projects was the founding of the New School for Social Research in 1919 with her money. Some of the radical professors who were to be given a voice there, historian Charles Beard and economist Thorstein Veblen, critics of the social and economic order under American capitalism, were considered with suspicion by established society in New York. (In the 1930s the New School was to be the location of dance recitals by emerging modern dance artists and of lectures by the dance critic John Martin that would help to establish the status of American modern dance.)[8]

Leonard had met Dorothy in 1920 in connection with her contribution towards a building project at Cornell, her late husband's university, but it was to be some years before his courtship of her was to meet with success. Meanwhile there was to be a return to India for a period, which would sow some of the seeds of the ideas that set Dartington in motion.

In the 1920s, the name of Rabindranath Tagore would have been well known to Western intellectuals. From a wealthy, landed and artistically talented family, Tagore had been lionised by English literary society in 1912 when he published his own English translation of his poem collection *Gitanjali*, for which he received the Nobel Prize for Literature in 1913. But this man was simultaneously poet, artist, composer, dramatist and a significant force in the philosophical and political development of India before its independence. To westerners he could be seen both as 'one of us' and as an exotic. He had an impeccable English education that had included studying law in London, and he received a British knighthood in 1915 (which he returned in 1919 as a protest at the Amritsar Massacre). With long flowing hair and robe, always addressed respectfully by associates (including Mahatma Gandhi) as *Gurudev* (Revered Teacher), he was also impressively 'other'.

In 1901 he opened a school at Santiniketan in Bengal. Like the progressive school that the Elmhirsts would open later at Dartington, it was for the children of the moneyed classes, but one where learning should be accomplished through motivating the interest of the child rather than through harsh external discipline. More than this, the school was part *ashram*, with the emphasis on community and spirituality. Nature, the arts and the spiritual were all entwined in his thinking.

> I believe that the vision of paradise is to be seen in the sunlight and the green of the earth, in the beauty of the human face and the wealth of human life, even in objects that are seemingly insignificant and unprepossessing. Everywhere in this earth the spirit of paradise is awake and sending forth its voice. It reaches our inner ear without our knowing it. It tunes our harp of life which sends our aspiration in music beyond the finite, not only in prayers and hopes, but also in temples which are flames of fire in stone, in pictures which are dreams made everlasting, in the dance which is ecstatic meditation in the still center of movement.[9]

At Santiniketan, the singing of Tagore's songs and the performing of his plays and dance dramas were an integral part of school life. In 1921 he founded a university there, Visva Bharati, with departments for the study of the arts of India, but also a point of contact for Eastern and Western culture.

In this charged spiritual environment, nature and culture became metaphors for the developing anti-colonial movement. Mahatma Gandhi visited from 1914, bringing students from South Africa. The young Indira Nehru, later to become Indian Prime Minister as Mrs Indira Gandhi, was a student.

The meeting in America in November 1921 between Leonard and Tagore resulted in a long association that lasted until Tagore's death in 1941. Tagore wanted to expand his educational projects with an Institute of Rural Reconstruction that would train boys from the school to take part in projects in the surrounding countryside. Sam Higginbottom, the mentor who had inspired Leonard to study agriculture at Cornell, suggested him as director. However, Tagore first needed to raise the necessary funds. It was Dorothy who provided the money and who continued to support the Institute until 1947. Tagore named it Sriniketan (The Abode of Plenty) and Leonard directed it until 1923. He also helped Tagore to plan a weekly boarding school, Shiksha-Satra, for the educational needs of the village boys.

The projects in which Leonard was involved were to promote self-help and improvement in the villages; but even in these practical schemes, art was not to be separated from life. He later wrote that Tagore

> would urge us to draw upon all the resources, in music, song, drama and dance, drawing and design at Santiniketan in order to enrich our lives, to liven our aspirations, to inspire our leisure and to increase our delights in every kind of artistic expression, until we and the cultivators could produce a richness and a wealth of cultural life of our own, and a rejuvenation of those ancient art forms that still survived, but so tenuously, in the villages around us.

Leonard himself performed publicly in a dance drama in Calcutta (see page 43).[10]

So in this extraordinary environment, Leonard must have absorbed some of the world view and aesthetic within which Tagore so valued dance. It is important, therefore, to capture some of the flavour of the dance that surrounded him at Santiniketan; but first we should return to the whole notion and phenomenon of utopian dreams of the sort that propelled the Elmhirsts and Tagore.

Utopia and dance

In the Introduction, I broadly outlined some ideas about utopian schemes and their history. Dartington, I suggested, could be placed in the general lineage of practical utopias because they hold things in common – for example, a recourse to the natural environment and a social agenda that includes equitable social relations and promotion of education. Is it possible that dance also has a history in utopia that Dartington draws upon?

In Western culture, the most striking and well-documented historical case of dance in a utopian community is provided by the Shakers, a millenarian cult that began as an offshoot of Quakerism in England in the 1740s. In 1774, a small group under the leadership of a prophetess and visionary, Mother Ann Lee, set off for America, where they founded a string of successful communities based upon strict celibacy, communal holding of property, and an ethic of hard work and self-sufficiency. Shaker furniture design is still considered to represent formal clarity derived from the clear functionality of the object and the moral duty to make a thing well.[11]

Early Shaker worship often seemed chaotic, as individual members were inspired into involuntary singing, dancing and speaking in tongues. But from the late 1780s onwards, danced rituals became more formalised. Songs, tunes and dances (often said to be given to their originators in visions) were written down and circulated between communities. They were rehearsed and perfected and in a sense 'performed', since Shakers welcomed observers from 'the world' at Sabbath meetings. So the dances symbolised to the adherents and to visitors the tenets of Shakerism in the bodies of the dancers, in the actions they performed and in the floor patterns of the massed dances. Simplicity and moral rectitude were embodied in stepping with a straight foot; square or oblong figures meant 'holy order'; and straight ranks facing in opposite directions moved into an endless chain in a 'union dance'. This notion of a physically expressed moral rectitude is verbalised in the words of the Shaker hymn *Simple Gifts*, famously incorporated by Aaron Copland into the music of Martha Graham's *Appalachian Spring* (1944):

When true simplicity is gain'd,
To bow and to bend we shan't be asham'd,
To turn, turn will be our delight,
'Till by turning, turning we come round right.[12]

It seems that the most exciting manifestations of Shaker dancing were in the concentric circular and wheel formations, brothers' and sisters' circles going in opposite directions, with the different circles representing the epochs of Shaker Christianity.[13] In the Shakers we see dance codified and made to function for religious and community purposes. There is also evidence that individuals anticipated dancing meetings with pleasure as an enjoyable diversion from all the strictures of the labouring week.[14]

It would be a mistake to assume that utopias *must* offer complete physical freedom. A community, which a utopia must aspire to become, has to embody some common values. The Shakers are a fascinating case because, in the period of their great rituals, they embodied so closely in dance their communal ethics and cosmology. This was in spite of the individualism implied in the trance-like whirling and wordless singing that was a feature of early worship and continued to some extent even when worship was more formal. Shaking and whirling mortified the flesh and freed the spirit, implying a belief in mind–body dualism,[15] but the massed dances did the reverse. The bodies of the dancers and their spiritual worship were totally subsumed into the symbolic representation of their society as a 'social body'.[16]

So the Shakers start us off on a journey towards a dance utopia. There is no direct link between the Shakers and Dartington, but there is an indirect one through the educational reformer and philanthropist Robert Owen. He was a great admirer of the Shakers and visited them in 1824. The influence of Owen in America fed into the notions of progressive education that made a mark on Dorothy through John Dewey.

At New Lanark in Scotland, Owen set up one of the most successful and influential British utopian experiments of the nineteenth century in order to improve conditions for the workforce of his cotton mill. The key was to be education, and to that end he built The Institution for the Formation of Character, which opened in 1816. Children normally attended the school from toddlerhood up until the age of ten, the legal age at which they could begin work, although he tried to keep them in education for longer. Owen saw that children's bodies must be healthy in order for them to learn, so he believed in outdoor play, physical activity and light clothing. The children, girls and boys, wore white cotton tunics, apparently Roman in shape, which were changed three times a week.[17] In the large, well-lit upper room of the Institution there were dancing lessons for the children – boys and girls together, although they were separated in other classes. Dance and music had a clear function within this vision of education:

> When properly conducted, each of these acquirements becomes a pure and natural source of enjoyment; and it is a well-authenticated fact, that the best method of making a people virtuous, is to begin by rendering their situation comfortable and happy.[18]

This was the Owenite philosophy, a form of utilitarianism in which securing the greatest happiness for the greatest number of people was the course to a better world. The individual's happiness was to be seen as intimately connected with that of the community. Perhaps we should also notice that Owen was intent on what we would now call 'social engineering'. He believed strongly in the power of nurture over nature, which is why he brought children so early into education to remove them from the influence of family lives that he regarded as largely unfit for giving children proper values.

Owen's son, Robert Dale Owen, described the school syllabus.

Dancing

Is taught, as a pleasant, healthful, natural and social exercise, calculated to improve the carriage and deportment, and to raise the spirits and increase the cheerfulness and hilarity of those engaged in it. The dances are varied. Scotch reels, country dances, and quadrilles are danced in succession; and by some of the older pupils with a simple and unaffected ease and elegance, which we have never seen surpassed in children of their age.[19]

The Institution was also available in the evenings for the young workers to continue their education and enjoy recreation together, including music and dancing twice a week.[20] Robert Owen and New Lanark are forerunners to Dartington both in the history of progressive education in a stimulating and non-punitive regime and in the idea that a commercial enterprise could provide a basis for a real sense of community through enriching the lives of workers.

Symbolically expressing higher spiritual values, aiding social cohesion, promoting health and well-being: dancing seems naturally to fulfil these functions. The anthropologist Judith Lynne Hanna has argued that it is a common experience across different cultures that dance should be called into play to express social relationships, political power and the spiritual dimension, and that this has a sociobiological foundation in the evolution of the human brain to enable symbolisation. It is a uniquely human ability to communicate and perceive in simultaneous and mutually reinforcing multi-sensory channels (sight, sound, smell, touch etc.) and dance is particularly effective in bringing all of this into play.[21] Both with the Shakers and in New Lanark we can see notions of community and utopia being served by quite different dance cultures. With both there is a sense of social control, although spontaneity lies just beneath the surface, in the Shakers breaking out into uncontrolled movement and in the 'cheerfulness and hilarity' of the New Lanark children.

I will now examine three examples of early twentieth-century utopias where the experimental life supported innovation in dance as art: Monte Verità in Switzerland, Hellerau in Germany and Santiniketan in Bengal. My discussion may initially seem to take us rather far away from Dartington. I will admit that my first interest in these rather extraordinary places was to find out just how the notion of utopia and dance had worked in some well-known cases. The outcome was much more complex than I had originally considered; for while I knew already how Monte Verità and Santiniketan fitted into Dartington's story, I was unaware of how Hellerau and New Lanark recur in the narrative. Tagore's utopian community has already been discussed, but its dance component will be considered in more depth. The direct line of Monte Verità's influence was carried to Dartington by Rudolf Laban and more indirectly by many other dancers. Hellerau was a short-lived but enormously important component in twentieth-century innovation in dance and theatre, becoming a reference point at Dartington as it would in so many other twentieth-century artistic environments. All three are significant in different ways for the development of twentieth-century dance.

From the late nineteenth century, political and cultural dissidents began to converge on the Swiss village of Ascona, on the shore of Lake Maggiore. In 1900 a small group, led by Henri Oedenkoven and Ida Hofmann, set up a commune and a nature cure sanatorium on a hill outside the village, which they named Monte Verità, Mountain of Truth. This beautiful place, with its view of the lake and with the Alps rising in the background, attracted people whose beliefs set them against the norm: theosophists, healers, pacifists, pagans, anarchists, vegetarians, feminists and followers of vagabondage. This was a pluralist utopia, but there was a dominant ethos: Monte Verità conveyed an alternative lifestyle striking at the materialism and positivism of 'civilised' urban society and the oppressive patriarchal order of family, Church and state. Opposing all of these things was a life lived in freedom and in nature. Light, air, earth and water were the instruments of healing. A harmonious life was expressed in self-sufficiency, homespun 'reformed' dress (loose robes or cut-off trousers, and women went uncorseted), nudity and sexual liberation, ritual and mysticism, physical culture and dancing. The body was central. Martin Green, one of Ascona's main chroniclers, has called it 'The Home of Modern Dance'.[22]

Although separated by hundreds of miles and a national border, the colony had close contacts with Schwabing, the artists' quarter of Munich, famed for its rich carnival culture. Among those who made the journey from Munich to Ascona was, in 1913, Rudolf Laban, already quite prominent in the modern dance developments in Germany. He would much later enter into the last phase of his career at Dartington Hall.[23]

Laban settled in Munich in 1910 (he had also studied art there at the turn of the century), earning a living as a graphic artist. The artistic life of Munich provided a catalyst for the awakening of his latent fascination with movement. Modern dance (also called 'new dance' or 'free dance') was beginning to explore the distinctive expression of modernity and movement was being expounded as the vehicle for improvement of the whole individual (*Körperkultur*). The mass festivals of the Munich carnival season integrated profound symbolism with Dionysian excess.

At the invitation of Henri Oedenkoven, Laban held his first summer school at Monte Verità in 1913. The School for the Arts (*Schule für Kunst*) was not only a way for Laban to continue working with Munich colleagues and attract more students, but also to be a focus for the danced celebration of life and spirituality for the whole artistic community. The syllabus set out courses in movement, sound and speech, reflecting Laban's experimental direction, to free dance from its dependence on music through the integration of all kinds of expressive movement, which he called *Tanz, Ton, Wort* (Dance, Sound, Word). There were also studies in visual and applied arts and physical work that contributed to the subsistence of the community.

It was at this first summer school that Mary Wigman began her training with Laban. Her memories focused on the liberating environment:

How young we were! We moved, we jumped, we ran, we improvised and outlined our first simple solo dances and group sketches. To me it was supposed to be a short summer course, and it turned into a life's direction. And there was always Laban, drum in hand, inventing, experimenting.

Laban the magician, the priest of a unknown religion, the worshiped hero, the lord of a dreamlike and yet ever-so-real kingdom.[24]

How did Monte Verità's dancers live a utopian life? In his memoir *A Life for Dance*, Laban gives a somewhat autocratic and certainly sexist description of how the days commenced. Whether it is an accurate memory or not, it rings true with other things we know about Monte Verità's attempts to shake off material 'progress' and critique the mechanised, urbanised twentieth century:

> Each morning from the veranda of my small house with its overhanging creepers I sounded a gong and everyone turned up for work. Tools were distributed and before breakfast groups went to the various gardens to weed, dig, plant and do other necessary jobs. Groups of women went into the sewing rooms, where they made dance-costumes and sandals. We had a bakery and later even two weaver's looms which produced the fabric we needed.[25]

At the 'dance-farm', dance was embedded in, rather than divorced from, daily life. The heady mountain environment, the free and easy life of the commune, the perception that dance could have a spiritual function, resonated with ideas Laban was already developing. Most of all he was beginning to believe that there must be something that could express the community spirit more genuinely than those Munich carnivals did. Communal festive culture (*Festkultur*) flourished on the mountain in the summer months and became central to the ideas he later put into practice for amateurs dancing together in 'movement choirs'.[26]

Laban's second summer school was disrupted by the declaration of the Great War of 1914–18. For a while he remained at Ascona with Wigman as his sole student, experimenting and creating. He was later able to work in Zurich for the remainder of the war years. He returned to Monte Verità for the summer of 1917, where in addition to the summer school there was to be the 'Anational Congress for Organising the Reconstruction of Society on Practical Cooperative Lines' organised by OTO (Ordo Templi Orientis), the occult order combining aspects of Freemasonry, Rosicrucianism and oriental mysticism of which he became a member. One of the most extraordinary dance events of the twentieth century now took place. *Sun Festival* (*Sonnenfest*) was presented in real time on the hillside between sunset and sunrise, being both a danced ritual and a site-specific dance performance.

The originators of the colony sold up in 1920, but Monte Verità continued to be the site of alternative living and cultish practices, still attractive to artists. In the 1920s, inspired by the exotic dancer Charlotte Bara, the archi-

tect Carl Weidemeyer designed and built a theatre for dance. Dancers continued to be drawn to the hillside. Wigman herself maintained her connection,
visiting regularly until her death. Laban, as the originator of a vigorous
strand of European modern dance, reappears in subsequent chapters as his
work impinges on Dartington.

Hellerau, on the outskirts of Dresden, Germany, was a very different kind
of utopia. Rather than rejecting modernity by retreating from urbanisation
and technology, Hellerau positively embraced it, but within a new blueprint
for the urban environment. Based on the English garden city, with open
spaces and low population density, it was a project of the German Werkbund,
which aimed to promote modern architecture and design alongside better
social conditions. Wolf Dohrn was a member of the Werkbund and one of
the proprietors of the furniture factory in the new community. In 1909 he
saw a demonstration given by the students of Émile Jaques-Dalcroze and was
instantly enthusiastic about what this unification of movement and music
education could bring to the people of Hellerau as a regenerative cultural
activity.

Dalcroze (1865–1950) is an enormously significant personality in the
development of twentieth-century dance, and yet he was neither dancer,
choreographer nor dance educator. He was a Swiss composer and teacher
who developed a series of exercises designed to improve his students' understanding of the components of music, and to develop an easy and immediate
physical response to it. The whole system comprised ear training (*solfège*),
body movement (*gymnastique rythmique*) and piano improvisation, together
known as eurhythmics.[27] Public demonstrations of exercises, such as re-
sponding with whole-body movements to varying, complex and
counterpoint rhythms and singing back tunes after one hearing, could be
very impressive.

Dalcroze insisted that this was not dancing, and yet it was often interpreted as such.[28] There are several reasons for this. His students developed a
spontaneous movement style that was especially attractive in the context of
Isadora Duncan's triumphs, and indeed the influence of Duncan on his
thinking has been observed.[29] The exploration of music in movement terms
was also an exploration of time, space and energy, which are all expressive
components of dance. Dalcroze wanted students not just to understand the
way music was made but to enter into its spirit. They learned to interpret the
music, improvising with a wide vocabulary of expressive gestures. Dalcroze
insisted 'eurhythmics is not an art form ... but a path towards art'.[30] Clearly,
though, the dividing line between the two could be a matter of degree rather
than an absolute. Some of his students' musical interpretations were clearly
dance in a Duncanesque mode, and their so-called *plastique animé* consisted
of choreographed dances. A number of them made their reputations in the

dance world: Suzanne Perrotet, Mary Wigman, Marie Rambert, Michio Ito, for example; and Beryl de Zoete, who will become an important Dartington personality later in this narrative.

In 1906 the theatre designer Adolphe Appia encountered Dalcroze's work, and there followed a period of mutual influence which would culminate in their work together at Hellerau. Appia's design philosophy was strongly contrary to the pervading realism of stage design using painted flats. He worked with solid volumes and levels and the sculptural effects of light. Particularly in the staging of Wagner's operas, he believed that the design should derive directly from the musical expression and not be an attempt to replicate an external reality. Studying with Dalcroze, he was able to see more clearly the correspondences between music, movement and space: the human body in movement as central to stage design. In his turn, he suggested to Dalcroze ways of using the space in a more three-dimensional way, and so staircases and rostra were now incorporated into exercises. It is due to the enthusiasm of Dalcroze that the Hellerau scheme included Appia.

Dalcroze opened his Hellerau school in 1910, at this stage in temporary quarters in Dresden while the Jaques-Dalcroze Cultural Institute (*Bildungsanstalt Jaques-Dalcroze*) was being built as a central cultural space in Hellerau.[31] Appia designed the main hall as a large, rectangular, flexible teaching and performance space with no proscenium to separate performers and audience. Settings could be varied with his modular system to create multiple levels for performance and seating. Diffused lighting, integrating performance and audience areas, came from walls and ceiling, which were lined by stretched linen concealing banks of lights. Other sophisticated lighting effects were available. But this was first and foremost a purpose-built establishment for music and movement education: nothing like it had been seen before in the Western world. There were studios, changing rooms and offices, with nearby student accommodation. The school attracted students from around the world, as well as being a focus for local children and adults. At the cornerstone-laying ceremony, Wolf Dohrn declared the utopian purpose:

> [Hellerau's] people will present celebrations and festivals, for themselves and others, of a type which no other place can offer, because nowhere else will there exist a population so widely and equally educated, and invigorated by such a sense of community.[32]

The full theatrical possibilities of Appia's theatre were seen only in the summer festivals of 1912 and 1913. Act II of Gluck's *Orfeo ed Euridice* was presented in 1912[33] along with some shorter pieces, and the full opera in

1913. In its movement, lighting and staging, it was considered a triumph, 'music made visible'.[34]

As with Laban at Monte Verità, the outbreak of war in 1914 was a blow to all plans, but to Dalcroze and Hellerau it was even more tragic. Dalcroze signed a public letter in 1914 objecting to the shelling of Rheims Cathedral by the Germans. In this charged, nationalistic atmosphere, the public furore made it impossible for him to return to Germany, and in any case the Institute had been commandeered as a hospital. He reopened his school in Geneva. After the war, Hellerau re-opened without him, as a school that included both the training according to Dalcroze's principles and the modern dance that was developing elsewhere in Germany. In 1925 the school moved to Schloss Laxenburg near Vienna, reborn as Hellerau-Laxenburg.

Considered together, Monte Verità and Hellerau attest to the kind of utopia that looked attractive in the context of the early twentieth century. Utopia's reversing mirror reflected back solutions to the effects of modernity and to the problem of discovering real individuality within an authentic sense of community. In both locations the body itself was the subject of reform and the means to freedom from constraints such as clothing and outdated artistic norms. The freed and dancing body was emblematic of this individuality, while dancing with others signified the ideal of an organic community.

In both utopias, dance was an integrative activity, and not only between individuals; Laban and Dalcroze both believed that beyond the body there was something that dance could reach. It might be supernatural or not, but it was beyond words. Dorothy Elmhirst also was looking for a sense of the spiritual through artistic experience. She wrote in 1950 about 'the meaning and function of art' as being the expression of a:

> moment of vision that one longs to express in some form of art. Perhaps you will want to express it through dancing: through a form of movement that unites you with this larger movement in nature; perhaps music will be your form of expression – or painting, or poetry. ... For art is surely a process of extending ourselves, through our sensibilities and our imagination, to something we have not reached before.[35]

If Monte Verità typifies the search for a utopia deep in nature and Hellerau stands for the utopia that must be designed and built from the ground up, it is still true of both places that their buildings spoke in the language of symbols about the nature of the communal practice, whether in Monte Verità's rustic bothies and 'theosophic architecture' or in Hellerau's democratic central space. At Dartington, new buildings that arose out of pragmatic need say much about the Elmhirsts' principles, but there seems to be an architectural tension between tradition, typified by the faithfully restored Hall itself, and modernity, including some large houses in the high modernist style. Dartington's built environment also attests to the internal hierarchy of the place, which was never challenged while the Elmhirsts were there. It is quite easy to see which dwellings were erected for workers and which for managers. While social integration around the symbolic space of the Courtyard was valued, the estate's settlements as a whole lack geographical cohesion, making that difficult to achieve.[36]

Monte Verità and Hellerau together suggest something of the underlying aesthetic climate of Europe in the first two decades of the century. Both centres attracted intellectuals and artists who were open to artistic renewal. We can think of extremely significant literary names who gravitated to dance utopias. For example, from the British theatre, Edward Gordon Craig and George Bernard Shaw were intent on seeing what was happening at Hellerau, as were two sisters from New York, Alice and Irene Lewisohn, and Maurice Browne, an English actor/director with his American wife, all of whom became important to Dartington. Serge Diaghilev went there with Vaslav Nijinsky, a visit that resulted in Marie Rambert being hired to help Nijinsky understand the rhythms of Stravinsky's *Le Sacre du printemps* score. Monte Verità attracted more extreme revolutionaries: Isadora Duncan visited in 1913. It was a great influence on D.H. Lawrence through his wife, Frieda von Richtofen, a Monte Verità regular. The author Hermann Hesse lived a long time in its shadow.

For dance, these names indicate some of the most influential aesthetics of the time. Isadora Duncan was the trailblazer in showing new possibilities for the female body in motion, while Serge Diaghilev's Ballets Russes, representative of an appeal to the influential elite in established society, was also the site of some extraordinary innovations in choreography and theatre design. Experimental efforts in movement cross-fertilised each other, and not only with the example of Hellerau's influence on Diaghilev and Duncan's on nearly everyone. Suzanne Perrotet, a student with Dalcroze since childhood and a teacher at Hellerau, moved over to Laban in 1913 together with a young student, Mary Wigman.

All of this provides a background to the following decade when the Elmhirsts established their own experiment. The cultures of Hellerau and Monte Verità came in due course to show themselves at Dartington, but neither Leonard Elmhirst nor Dorothy Whitney Straight had any direct contact. So what ideas about dance did they bring to the development of their English experiment?

Dance and the Elmhirsts

It is not an easy task to uncover what Dorothy and Leonard believed about dance, since they tell us so little. Clearly they wanted to bring dance to Dartington, as can be seen from Dorothy's letter that heads this chapter, but did they have any models in view? What immediate experience might have shaped their formulation of dance at Dartington? To consider Leonard Elmhirst first, we can locate him very clearly within Tagore's Santiniketan in the years 1921 to 1923.

Tagore's efforts to give dance a place in the curriculum at Santiniketan and to show dance to the public are quite remarkable, considering the low and disreputable status occupied by dance at this time, with both the authorities of the British Raj and the Indian middle class. Dancers were considered low-class individuals, sometimes prostitutes, although the techniques continued to be passed down in villages and temples. Public dance performances were banned in the early twentieth century. Even before the revaluation of the classical dance forms of India that began in the 1930s, spearheaded by dancers such as Uday Shankar and Rukmini Devi, Tagore was preparing the ground.[37] Not only did he have dance taught at his prestigious school and university, but he also asserted its value by himself performing and encouraging members of his family to do so, even the female ones. However, he retained some prejudices: he felt that kathak, (one of the principal dance styles of northern India) was tainted by its association with courtesans. He admired the dances of Manipur in the north-east, where he had seen the *Ras Lila*, a devotional dance that describes the love of Krishna and Radha, and he brought teachers from there to Santiniketan in the early 1920s. Folk dancing with cymbals from Gujarat was introduced and, later in the 1920s, the kathakali dance drama of Kerala. Manipuri and kathakali were the main ingredients of his own dance style (Rabindrik dance or Rabindra nritya), developed for the interpretation of his drama, songs and poetry, and which is still taught at Santiniketan and has disseminated from there.

Tagore also wrote musical plays and dance-dramas. His interest in these two genres probably stems from his reading of ancient Sanskrit texts that describe the hybrid theatrical forms. Because he had travelled widely in Asia, Europe and America, performative experiences from other cultures influenced his writing. Opera in Europe and the native spectacular forms in Bali, Java and Japan fed his ideas on the integrated dance-drama-music theatre. However, he could not fully develop this form until after guest teachers had established dance at Santiniketan. His first dance-drama, *Natir Puja*, the story of a dancing girl who becomes a Buddhist nun, with a cast of girls from the school, was presented in 1926, produced by his daughter-in-law, Protima Devi.

Leonard Elmhirst was present in Santiniketan in the early 1920s when Tagore's enthusiasm for dance as part of an integrated performance was clearly manifest, but when the systematic teaching of dance at Santiniketan was just beginning. Elmhirst joined in the performances of musical plays. The dance content at this time was very simple and often improvised, probably with the influence of the folk dance of the Baul people of Bengal. His description of one of these offers little in terms of dance description, but conveys, if nothing else, Tagore's infectious dedication to art and education being conveyed to Leonard. This was a musical play, *Basanta* (Spring), performed by children, staff and the Tagore family at a Calcutta theatre in February 1923. Tagore took the part of the court poet and Leonard the part of a general in a story about a bored king who would rather enjoy a new play by his court poet than hear about his depleted exchequer.

> There was a rollicking dance tune for the last act he had written, and in the finale the whole cast, court, king, poet, players and generals, Benoit *[another European member of staff]* and myself, went romping round the stage to its exhilarating rhythm.
> For the final circuit of the stage, the court poet, Tagore, seized a general by the waist in each arm and we cavorted around together.[38] *[Explanatory note added]*

Local newspaper reviews were appreciative of the spectacle and respectful towards Tagore, especially of his ability, now in his sixties, to dance with such abandon and enthusiasm.

> Everybody joined in the wild dance and the poet forgot his age, his gravity and his greatness and began to dance (in ecstasy) like a simple child, wild with joy hand-to-hand with Mr. Elm Hirst *[sic]* and the vision arose in our mind of the East and West joining hands in the dance of destruction of the present which forebodes the unknown fruit of the radiant future. [39]

Like Monte Verità, Tagore's utopia was deeply embedded in nature as a moral and spiritual force, which modernity, 'progress' and materialism seemed ready to destroy.[40] As in many other utopias, education was seen as the key to the reform of life. Within that education, the arts were 'the expressions of life', and therefore deeply implicated in the process of communicating with the natural world in order to work productively on the land.[41] The normal experience of school and of twentieth-century modernity repressed the natural movement expression of the body and destroyed the unity between mind and body. Tagore and Leonard talked about this in relation to Leonard's plans for a school, while travelling together in 1924 on a tour of South America, a conversation later written up in the essay *Movement in Education*. Tagore specifically recommended that 'the practice of drama and the histrionic arts' be compulsory in the curriculum.[42] Leonard specifically acknowledged Dartington's debt to Santiniketan – indeed, that Dartington's ethos was a combination of Western economic planning and organisation with Santiniketan's education and arts.[43]

It is perhaps relatively easy to identify the dance influence on Leonard, but what of Dorothy? Direct evidence is much more tenuous, but a consideration of current scholarship on women and dance in the first decades of the twentieth century suggests that her philanthropy and promotion of Progressive Era issues would have given her knowledge of dance in social and educational contexts.

Occupying a position in the moneyed class, she must have been aware from a young age of the very popular movement practices of Delsartism, which fed into so much of the radical dance in America of the early twentieth century. François Delsarte was a French music and drama teacher in the mid-years of the nineteenth century. His system of expressive gesture and harmonious movement was brought to America and further developed. The name most frequently associated with Delsarte in America is that of Genevieve Stebbins, who promoted it as a means of graceful, expressive movement, redolent of the ease of classical Greek statuary and suitable for middle- and upper-class women.[44] Stebbins is a link and an impetus to the twentieth-century American dance pioneers, Ruth St Denis and Isadora Duncan and their peers, who were influenced to some extent by Delsartism. An account from 1891 describes a movement class for the women of the exclusive 'Astor, Vanderbilt, Whitney, and Stuyvesant Fish families' taken by the popular society Delsarte teacher, Henrietta Russell.[45] Certainly Dorothy would not have been included, as she was still a toddler, but the story illustrates the penetration of this particular form of expressive movement into Dorothy's class and family. Delsartism paved the way for upper-class American women to appreciate and be patrons of the emerging concert art of modern dance in the early twentieth century. I will suggest that Dorothy was one of those.

The historian Linda Tomko has discussed in great detail the role of women as reformers in Progressive Era America. They were able to take a leadership role in anything that involved homes, families and health because existing paradigms of separate spheres of influence designated women to the domestic sphere while men dominated the public sphere. Restrictive as it was, female reformers and philanthropists were able to manipulate that position with increased confidence.[46] This is a model that fits very well with what we know of the way Dorothy both typified and challenged her position in the women's sphere, for, although she used her position to support projects with

New York's poor and the development of progressive education, she also challenged the concept of a woman's designated domestic sphere through taking on the role of publisher and offering support for progressive political issues.[47]

Some of Dorothy's interests suggest that she quite understood how dance was developing in New York in new and radical directions. Some of her Junior League colleagues taught dancing, singing and art (their middle-class accomplishments) at the settlement houses they supported. Dorothy also saw the work of Lillian Wald at the Henry Street Settlement in the immigrant tenements of the Lower East Side.[48] Here there were clubs and classes in arts, crafts, physical activities and games and the basic skills needed by recent immigrants to negotiate American urban life. The Lewisohn sisters, Alice and Irene, introduced dance and drama classes for children in about 1905 and began to produce integrated dance, drama and music performances, which often took as their content the significant myths, rituals or legends of Jewish or other cultures, although presenting them within a Western theatrical context. These activities were seen as working on many levels to ease some of the problems of immigrant life in the tenements. On a cultural level, the immigrant heritage was shown as enriching, but in a way that would adapt to American society. For individual improvement this was healthy exercise, and socially it promoted self-confidence, cooperation and creativity, bonding the community together.[49] In 1915 the Lewisohn sisters put up a new building for their production work, the Neighborhood Playhouse, with a full-time programme of classes and production work. Two groups emerged from the community-based workshop activities: the Neighborhood Players, performing as a professional acting company, and the amateur Festival Dancers. With her philanthropic connections, Dorothy must have been aware that dance was playing an important part in settlement house ventures that were simultaneously artistic and promoting social integration.

It is also possible that her children danced at the Lincoln School, associated with Teachers College, Columbia University, where they were educated before coming to England. Dance was on the curriculum at Teachers College and the technique of the dance class changed as the notion of an American modern dance constituency changed. In the first three decades of the twentieth century it ranged from folk dancing, 'aesthetic dancing' and Duncan dance to the influence of Martha Graham's emerging style when her student, Martha Hill, went to teach there in 1929.[50] This does not clearly demonstrate what happened at the Lincoln School; however, it is apparent that the curriculum there, at least up to sixth grade, was governed by 'units of work', a version of what we would now call a project-based curriculum, within which the physical education teacher might be called upon to teach dances, or supervise the children creating their own, around a particular unit theme. A source from 1927 indicates that 'sailors' dances' and 'Indian dances and dance rhythms' came into appropriate units. In connection with a unit on the study of time, children created dances about the revolution of the planets, the 'Spiral Nebula' and a 'Chinese dance' for their dramatisation of the invention of the water clock.[51]

Certainly, Dorothy's daughter, Beatrice Straight, was a young dancer. Her brother Michael Straight recalled of his childhood in New York that she and her best friend, Nina Fonaroff (later to have an influence on contemporary dance in Britain), performed little dances at home as 'wood nymphs' or something similar.[52] All this suggests the climate of dance education of the period and that Dorothy was acquainted with it.

Finally, to what extent was Dorothy aware of the emergence in the 1920s of a generation of American dancer/choreographers, leaders in a self-consciously American modern dance movement? They distanced themselves from the influences of Delsartism and Hellenic dancing, which they perceived as looking back to a European antiquity. They were also rejecting the decorative, often orientalist commercialism of Ruth St Denis and Ted Shawn and their famous Denishawn school and company. For some of them it literally meant breaking a working relationship with St Denis and Shawn. Martha Graham left Denishawn in 1923 to work in the commercial theatre and then to strike out as an independent teacher and choreographer; Doris Humphrey and Charles Weidman left Denishawn in 1928. In penurious circumstances, working on the movement that arose from their own bodies, they strove for new dance vocabularies that were authentically American and of the twentieth century.

Again it is likely that Dorothy knew this. Leaving New York in 1925, she placed responsibility for her local philanthropy in the hands of a committee under her supremely efficient secretary, Anna Bogue. In 1926, Dorothy sent a $500 loan for the American Angna Enters, who then became the first dancer to walk through the gates of Dartington, in December 1927.[53] There is no evidence that she danced at Dartington, but she had been invited to make her base there while arranging London concerts, which took place in February 1928 at St Martin's Theatre. She received further subsidies from the New York committee. In the early 1930s the committee was subsidising Martha Graham on her summer expeditions to Arizona and New Mexico to find inspiration, and Graham wrote to Dorothy expressing her gratitude. In 1938 Dorothy announced herself willing to underwrite a London performance for Graham, but she was unwilling to travel to Europe in the threatening political situation.[54] Michael Straight wrote that the 80-year-old Graham recalled Dorothy giving her a cheque in his presence as a little boy in 1920 and she had taken his hands and done a dance of joy with him.[55] The story must be treated as anecdotal and the date questioned (Graham was performing with Denishawn at this time), but it indicates clearly that Graham felt indebted to Dorothy. Bogue kept Dorothy abreast of developments in New York, in dance as well as in other areas of culture, so she was aware of the emerging dance artists of the 1920s and 1930s and their need for support. In 1930, for example, she wrote to Bogue recommending the Dance Repertory Theater, an amalgamation of the modern dance groups of Martha Graham, Doris Humphrey–Charles Weidman and Helen Tamiris, who were briefly cooperating in order to afford the hire of a New York theatre to present their individual work.[56]

However, funding for dance through the New York committee was erratic, with no consistent policy emerging. Doris Humphrey had little luck in spite of a number of applications. She was successful once, in 1935, after participating in a forum at the Bennington Summer School on the diversity of ideologies and techniques within modern dance. The forum had been partly sponsored by 'Mrs Leonard Elmhirst's Committee'.[57] Although the result of an application for support was unpredictable, reflecting both Dorothy's changing interests and the efforts of the committee to keep within budget, there seems to have been a consistent trend in Dorothy's affairs that shows her as aware and interested in the development of dance in New York, suggesting that this was an element in her thinking that predated her arrival at Dartington.

'The English experiment'

It is possible that the marriage of Dorothy and Leonard might never have taken place had it not been that her reluctance was broken down by the appeal to her philanthropic nature: to transplant herself and her children to England offered the possibility of an exciting project, also utopian in its scope, which they called 'the English experiment' in their correspondence. This was to be a progressive school, building both on Leonard's experience of education in India and Dorothy's knowledge of progressive education in America and rejecting the kind of English boarding school experience Leonard had suffered from as a child. It was taken for granted that there would be a working estate to provide freedom, stimulus and 'learning by doing' for the children. The school was to be something over which they cooperated in the early years, while Leonard worked on building up the Estate: farming, horticulture and forestry.

From 1925, Dartington entered into a period of great activity, to make the Hall habitable, to create new residences for staff, to bring modern conveniences – electricity, running water, sewage and the telephone – and to restore the buildings, some of which originated from the fourteenth century. Dartington Hall School opened in 1926 with nine pupils, including Dorothy's children Whitney, Beatrice and Michael. What was this utopia like? In some respects it was not utopian at all. Dorothy employed a full household staff such as she had been used to: butler, cook, housekeeper, nanny, chauffeurs, gardeners, secretaries and various maids and footmen. This hierarchy was never called into question. However, those first few years demonstrated some very utopian aspects. 'School', when not taking place in the Estate department or gardens, was in the Elmhirst's private residence, an extension of their own home life. The extended family soon included Leonard's brothers Alfred (known as Pom), Richard and Victor, who joined the team. Children and adults were close: all adults were addressed by first names. Work and life were integrated: Dorothy, Leonard and Estate workers participated in the children's project-based learning. There was co-education: questions about sex were answered frankly. The school was a democratic community: there was no head teacher, but instead a management committee of the adults and children met together to take important decisions. This was to be the broad structure of the school until, with enlarged numbers, it moved into a new building, Foxhole, in 1931 under its first headmaster. W.B. (Bill) Curry would continue the progressive school ethos but in a more formalised, more educationally sound manner. Curry was in fact to be 'Director of Education to the Social and Educational Experiment now being carried out at Dartington Hall, Totnes', which entailed responsibility for arts and adult education as well as the school.

Already by 1927, when *News of the Day* (the Estate newsletter) was begun by Leonard, there were numerous cultural events to announce. The Sunday Evening Meeting was enormously significant as an occasion that brought together a cross-section of Estate people to listen to a concert or a talk, either by a resident or a visitor – often someone of the stature of Tagore, Aldous Huxley or Bertrand Russell. Arts activities were inaugurated. Nevison Robson, music teacher to the school, ran the Estate choir. Erica Inman, the school secretary, started a drama club; they met regularly for play reading. There were dancing classes (see page 5). Leonard consulted Bernard Leach, the celebrated potter, who recommended a student, Jane Fox-Strangeways, to be Head of the Art Department. The studio was open to anyone on the Estate at set hours every day. She was passionate about her remit to widen participation, to the extent that the arts and crafts exhibitions she organised would exhibit examples of boot polishing or typing as 'craft'. Perhaps the exhibitors submitted with tongue in cheek. Dartington caught the attention of the Worker's Educational Association (WEA) drama organiser for Devon, F.G. Thomas, as he looked for ways of promoting drama in the villages. Leonard encouraged Dartington people to help with this work, as the principles were in line with 'the general fulfilment of our ideals'.[58] This alliance began to bear fruit in the early 1930s.

As much as Tagore and Santiniketan provided the general shape of

Dartington and the philosophical basis that tied the parts together, it is doubtful whether the performing arts would have assumed the importance they did without the equally influential contact with the actor/director Maurice Browne. The Labour Party M.P. Ellen Wilkinson recommended Browne's performance of the play *The Unknown Warrior.* This led to an invitation to bring it to Dartington for four performances in July 1928. This play was one of those instances of late-1920s and early-1930s arts that were beginning to deal with the shattering experience of World War I. (Others will become apparent in following chapters.) It was a translation from the French of *Le Tombeau sous l'Arc de Triomphe* by Paul Raynal, referring to the Tomb of the Unknown Soldier placed there, as in so many other combatant countries, as a memorial to the many unidentified dead. Deeply moved, Dorothy and Leonard offered to underwrite the production of a new play, and Browne found one almost immediately: *Journey's End* by R.C. Sherriff, a story of soldiers in the Great War trenches. Browne's choice of plays had caught the tenor of the times in a profound way. The select few had enjoyed the briefly 'roaring' twenties, but a new realism, a sense of loss, was being articulated more and more in books, plays and films. The play was appreciated by numerous audiences over the next few years and the Elmhirsts' financial backing was paid back manyfold. For the time being, theatrical enterprises must have seemed relatively safe, and the Elmhirsts went into partnership with Browne to form a production company, Maurice Browne Ltd.

Characteristically, the Elmhirsts were content to follow Browne's advice on the development of performing arts at Dartington. In the early years they would frequently invite reports from experts in the various enterprises in which they were involved, from poultry to education. Dance at Dartington in the next few years was to be directly shaped by Browne and the contacts he introduced. Without the injection of his professional theatrical know-how, it is probable that dance and drama would have remained amateur activities (and none the worse for that) focusing on the kinds of objectives that F.G. Thomas of the WEA was promoting. Perhaps the Elmhirsts were even a little stage-struck.

Browne had worked in America since around 1910, where he married an American actor/director, Ellen Van Volkenburg. (They later divorced, but maintained close professional ties.) They founded the Chicago Little Theatre and set in motion the Little Theatre movement in the USA. Crucially for Dartington, there are two aspects of his work in America that contributed to the value he placed on dance. He was inspired by Edward Gordon Craig, the English theatre designer/director, not only towards the expressionist use of non-illusionary stage settings (including the famous moveable white screens), but also to view classical Greek theatre as the archetype of all theatre, a theatre of poetry, music and movement. Craig's stance in relation to the

revival in classical Greek theatre was, of course, influenced by Isadora
Duncan's aesthetics (and their love affair).

Browne wrote of the Chicago Little Theatre (which existed between 1912
and circa 1917):

> Our theory was simple. Dance – ritual dance – is the basis of drama ... our
> objective, a 'dance' with words, now became more clearly defined as a
> rhythmic fusion of movement, dancing-place (stage and setting), light and
> speech.[59]

John Martin, later to be the first critic to promote American modern
dance, was a member of the company. (He will appear at Dartington in person in the next chapter.)

The other, and even more central, experience he brought to Dartington
was the relationship he and Van Volkenburg had built up with the Cornish
School in Seattle, teaching there periodically from 1917. Nellie Cornish had
founded a music school dedicated to 'the creative spirit in education' in
1914. This was seen:

> not as imitation or invention, but as the spontaneous expression of that
> inner urge which may be awakened by touching the hidden spring of in-
> tuition, making it possible to lead the child to discover and organize
> himself – the prime aim of education.[60]

Gradually, dance, drama, puppetry and visual arts were incorporated,
with the intention of producing all-round artists. Considering the significance of folk dance as an educational tool in American schools (see page 68),
it is interesting that the first of the other arts to be introduced alongside
music was folk dancing, taught by a student of Mary Hinman, a prominent
folk dance educator and researcher.[61] Visitors of the status of Ruth St Denis,
Ted Shawn and Anna Pavlova came to view the facilities. The dance teaching
was eclectic: Dalcroze eurhythmics, Duncan-style dancing, ballet and modern dance as it was then developing. Among the guest teachers were Adolph
Bolm, former principal of Diaghilev's Ballets Russes, and the Japanese modern dancer Michio Ito (with Pauline Koner and Martha Graham's sister
Georgia in his group); and in 1930 Graham herself gave a summer school
with Louis Horst. Dance history tends to remember the Cornish School because of the following decade. It was in the late 1930s that John Cage was
dance accompanist and percussion teacher and Merce Cunningham was a
student, but dance at Cornish also has a rich early history.[62]

The Elmhirsts were enthusiastic about the idea of modelling the arts at
Dartington on the Cornish School. So, with Maurice Browne's influence,

Dartington began to move towards the professionalisation of its artistic vision in relation to dance which would become increasingly apparent in the 1930s. Dorothy wrote to Ellen Van Volkenburg, currently teaching at Cornish (the letter is extracted at the head of this chapter), but the ideas were formulated slowly. Dartington's first teacher of technique and creative dance did not come from America but from London.

In September 1928, Leslie Burrowes, a twenty-year-old student and teacher from the Margaret Morris School in London, began to teach dance at Dartington on Fridays and Saturdays. It seems from comments she made in later life that her engagement came about quite fortuitously through personal rather than professional recommendation.[63]

In the Introduction, I outlined the professional dance culture in 1920s Britain from which the Elmhirsts might have chosen a teacher. It was the era of the Ballets Russes's influence on high society and intellectual Bloomsbury and of early attempts to form British ballet companies. There is no evidence that the Elmhirsts considered bringing a ballet teacher to Dartington.

There were two other groupings of dancers on the contemporary scene that might have offered a fruitful alliance with Dartington. The influence of Isadora Duncan was still felt, as was that of other practitioners of 'free' or Hellenic dance – the Canadian Maud Allan and Duncan's brother Raymond, for example, and the British Hellenic dancers Madge Atkinson, Ruby Ginner and Margaret Morris who created Natural Movement, Revived Greek Dance and Margaret Morris Movement respectively. Another innovation was that, by the late 1920s, there were dancers coming to Britain with a training in European modern dance, either from one of the many Laban Schools, or from Gertrud Bodenwieser's Viennese school. Because of the geographical hub of the techniques, this genre was often labelled 'central European modern dance'.

The Elmhirsts do not appear to have surveyed the British scene to find an appropriate teacher but instead asked their theatre experts for advice. Correspondence between Dorothy and Van Volkenburg reveals that there was some thought of introducing Dalcroze eurhythmics. Van Volkenburg had been in contact with Percy Ingham, director of the London Dalcroze School, and a teacher from Exeter had been suggested.[64] The fact that a Margaret Morris teacher was invited to Dartington may have been no more than a chance suggestion from an acquaintance and may even have been considered as a temporary arrangement until the full fruition of the arrangement with Cornish.

Margaret Morris had been greatly influenced by Raymond Duncan (she incorporated his 'Greek positions' and flattened two-dimensional frieze-like body designs), but she was also inspired by contemporary painting and some orientalising details from Cambodian and Indian sculpture. Her technique had already been developed into progressive levels of exercises (Margaret Morris Movement), still taught internationally today. Unlike the other Hellenic practitioners, Morris had consciously attempted to show her work as universally valid for children, adults, amateurs and professional dancers, and also as physical training for sports and in therapeutic situations. Morris had a high profile amongst intellectuals and other artists. She opened her Chelsea Club in 1914 as a meeting place for artists from all disciplines, a sort of Paris café society in London, where also dance performances, informal and formal, might take place. Through her husband J.D. (John Duncan) Fergusson, one of the four Scottish Colourists who adapted the rich colours of contemporary French art to a national style, she was well connected in the art world. She ran popular Summer Schools, in Harlech in North Wales, in Devon or in the South of France at Cap d'Antibes.

Leslie Burrowes would come down to Dartington every weekend to teach two adult classes, on Friday and Saturday. She also taught the schoolchildren, which she found difficult because of their lack of discipline.[65] She was at this stage working very much in line with the Margaret Morris practice in which she had been trained. In autumn 1929 she added a dance composition class, because creative work was considered important to those who had been studying technique over the past year.[66] Morris's approach to composition was through improvisation, and she developed a number of exercises for structuring improvisation in groups.[67]

Burrowes's expertise in training dancers and in composition was called upon for the first major performance ever put on at Dartington.

Comus

In early 1929, the drama club felt confident enough to propose putting on an open-air production of John Milton's masque *Comus*; this was approved by Van Volkenburg, who had been invited to Dartington to work with the drama group and the school. *Comus* was a particularly appropriate choice on a number of levels. The masque form provided an ideal frame for the integration of all that had and could be achieved at Dartington in the arts of drama, dance, music, singing and design. It is set in a wild rural place and another medieval structure, Ludlow Castle, where it was originally performed in 1634 by members of the Earl of Bridgewater's family. Similarly, the Elmhirst family proved to be committed performers of dance and drama, both in *Comus* and in later productions in the 1930s. The chosen location for the performance was the bowling green at the back of the Elmhirsts' private residence, where a row of ruined arches acted as the background against which Maurice Browne devised the lighting effects. The overall production was by Ellen Van Volkenburg, with Erica Inman and Wyatt Rawson (a teacher and an old university friend of Leonard's) acting as principal directors, since Van Volkenburg was teaching at the Cornish School in the later stages.

The extent to which Dartington's *Comus* is recoverable as a historical performance depends on my imaginative interpretation of sources – my bricolage. In this case, visual evidence is confined to a small collection of photographs, mostly of rehearsals in daylight. There is a script as published, annotated to show cuts, music and some acting notes; there is also a stage-management copy of the script as produced, and a programme.[68] *News of the Day* put on a *Comus* Special Edition.[69] *Comus* was a significant event for Dartington as a community: the time when the four-year-old English Experiment put its arts on public show for the first time. It is also a high point of one version of Dartington's artistic ethos. Dartington accepted gratefully the guidance of professionals and outsiders, but the star of the show was the community that comprised the Elmhirst family, the school and Estate employees. Nevison Robson had brought together an orchestra of fourteen and a twenty-voice chorus, some of them placed at a distance, in the still unrestored Great Hall, for its eerie aural effect. Leslie Burrowes arranged the dances and performed in them. Jane Fox-Strangeways designed the masks and costumes, which were made at Dartington.

Briefly, the narrative proceeds as follows. In the first scene, 'A Drear Wood', the Attendant Spirit (Leonard) in a shining robe proclaims his role as one who would confound Comus in his plot to pollute any virtuous person who comes to this place. Comus, the son of Circe and Bacchus and thus implicated in magic and alcoholic excess, enters with his Crew, and they perform the first dance. This is *Comus' Measure*, supposed to be a round dance and 'a wild, rude and wanton antic', as the script indicates.[70] The Dartington photographs show the Crew, children dressed in tunics and wearing animal-head masks. Comus becomes aware of the approach of the Lady (Dorothy, dressed in white) who has become separated from her two brothers on the journey home to Ludlow Castle. He appears to her in the guise of a shepherd, and guides her to supposed shelter. The Two Brothers (played by Leonard's brother Victor and his wife Helen) enter in search of their sister, and the Attendant Spirit appears to them in the guise of their father's shepherd, Thyrsis, conveying his concerns about their sister's fate and leading them to her rescue.

In the central scene, set in Comus's Palace, Comus attempts to persuade the Lady to drink from his cup. The audience knows that this will turn her into one of his monstrous Crew, and the Lady resists, arguing strongly against all his tempting words. In the Dartington production, here are performed two 'Masques' of dance and song. The Brothers rush in and defeat Comus but cannot release the Lady from the spell that imprisons her, until the Attendant Spirit calls on the assistance of Sabrina Fair, goddess of the

River Severn (Erica Inman). The scene changes to Ludlow, where country dances are performed in expectation of the arrival of the sister and brothers. The Attendant Spirit brings them to their parents (who do not have speaking roles).

Identification of the main cast members suggests that, as in the original Ludlow masque, members of the Elmhirst family captured the moral high ground by personifying the virtuous characters.[71] This is perhaps no more than could be expected, considering how central they were to everything at Dartington. *Comus* is a 'moral' masque in verse proclaiming the power of virtue over evil, self-control over revelling in excess. The Dartington production was a very much abbreviated version of the text, reducing the script from 1023 lines to 593.[72] Perhaps this is not surprising for an amateur production, but it could be argued that the meat of the argument had been excluded. The Lady personifies Virtue but more specifically Chastity, which is her shield against temptation. It was on the lengthy discourse on chastity that the editor's pencil mainly fell. Perhaps it was considered inappropriate, since everyone knew that Dorothy was twice-married and now the mother of five children. (The Elmhirst children, Ruth and William, were born in 1926 and 1929 respectively.) Or perhaps it seemed a bit risqué for a rural audience with children present. Either way, Dartington's *Comus* has a changed meaning, with the emphasis on the dramatic tension of the Lady's capture and release rather than on the moral argument.

The production expanded the role of dance from the two scenes provided for in the script (*Comus' Measure* and the country dances before Ludlow Castle) by interpolating the two masques of dance and song into the central scene in Comus's Palace. Seventeenth-century music was chosen for these (although from late in the century rather than the period of *Comus*) and the majority of the interpolations are by Purcell, who occupies a canonical position in the English musical tradition. The expanded role for dance is matched by the expanded role for choral singing. Dartington was able to show that it had made some progress in both these arts. In the first masque, there is a dance to a gavotte by Corelli. A chorus, 'Come, shepherds, lead up a lively measure', is followed by a dance, both pieces from Purcell's semi-opera *King Arthur*. In the second masque, a sung trio of 'Let us wander not unseen' (from Purcell's *The Indian Queen*) is followed by the trio dance of shepherdesses to 'Shepherd, shepherd, leave decoying' (from *King Arthur*). After more sung solos and duets, the masque ends with a dance and chorus, 'Let us love and to happiness haste' (from *King Arthur*).

These dances and songs, thematically linked by Arcadian images of shepherds and shepherdesses, do not belong with the landscape of the 'drear wood'. They rather celebrate the sunny aspect of pastoralism, where Dartington would wish to be located. There is a link in that Comus is also a character in *King Arthur*, but with a rather different aspect: he leads a chorus of peasants celebrating the harvest with justifiable excess. Perhaps the masques here serve to take the audience outside the Palace where the Lady is captured, give more weight to goodness over evil, and increase the tension while we wait for her release. On the other hand, perhaps looking for a structural meaning in the masques that fits the narrative of Milton's *Comus* is missing the point. For Dartington in 1929 the meaning of the masques was to give an expanded role for the amateur groups of singers and dancers, making them centre-stage in the performance, so to speak.

Uncovering the performance style of this *Comus* is very difficult, considering the small amount and nature of the sources. The fact that the main actors were masked would tend to focus on the whole body in expressing meaning. The extant annotated script and photographs suggest that the performance style used bold, stylized gestures, and Dorothy wrote in a letter about its 'stylized and arrested motion'.[73] The staging after dark on a narrow grass strip in front of the grey, ruined wall, and in the empty door frame, aimed for frieze-like effects. This would have improved visibility and Burrowes would have been able to use some of the Greek statuary-inspired shapes of Margaret Morris Movement to give this effect. There is a photograph of some of Comus's Crew, children standing against the wall in their animal heads, arms in various angular positions.

Another photograph shows the trio of Shepherdesses: Leslie Burrowes with probably her best students, Dorothy's daughter, Beatrice Straight, and Dorothy Carter (a Dartington housekeeper). We can see the strong oppositional movement between upper and lower body and the 'Greek positions' typical of the Margaret Morris vocabulary. Burrowes is poised on one leg, confident and accomplished. The other two young women would continue to be some of the Dartington community's most enthusiastic dancers in the 1930s. The image encapsulates the Dartington ideal: the professional artist working cooperatively with Elmhirst family and community members. Dorothy Carter will appear as Paula Morel in later chapters, an enduring personality in Dartington's dance.

Leslie Burrowes

Burrowes is the first dancer who participated directly in the Dartington project. Like a number of others to be discussed, she was there for only a brief time and then went out into the wider arena of dance developments. In terms of the changing dance ecology of Britain over the next few decades, she is a linking figure moving from the early British modern dance style of Margaret Morris to the influence of the central European dancers. She was an undoubtedly talented student of Margaret Morris. In a report on her work in Dartington Hall School, she strongly defended her methods:

Our form of movement is based on an entirely natural basis, accepting the
best and most useful methods used in the past i.e. Greek Positions; but at
the same time allowing scope for expression and creation ... consequently
lead[ing] to progression.[74]

There is evidence here of her commitment to dance as a holistic mind/
body activity through the development of self-expression and creativity.
Later, she remembered the frustrations of her time teaching at Dartington:
attendance at classes was not compulsory for schoolchildren; and perhaps
because of her experience there, she knew she had to expand beyond Morris's technique, into something that expressed her own identity. Teaching at
Dartington seemed to fuel the sense that she was not totally convinced by
what she was doing. Dorothy was a good listener and a great encourager:
Burrowes remembered that she would say, 'Good for you', when Burrowes
talked about her ambitions. She needed to spread her wings and Europe
beckoned. It is not surprising that this should be so, since modern dance
developments in Europe were regularly being outlined in *The Dancing Times*.
Mary Wigman had performed in London in 1928 and Gertrud Bodenwieser's
company the next year. It would appear from Burrowes's later comments
that the original intention was to explore various schools in Europe. Dorothy
immediately gave her a cheque for £400.[75] By January 1930, she was in
Dresden to train with Wigman, where she stayed. Her letters back to Dorothy,
who continued to subsidise her studies there, were full of excitement.[76]

Burrowes returned to London in the autumn of 1931, the first Briton to be
awarded the full certificate from Wigman's studio. In the following years she
performed in her own recitals, had some commercial stage experience and
opened her own studio. She figures in later chapters.

So, why Dartington and why dance? According to Leonard, Tagore once
said to him:

Choose the most beautiful place that you can find. However deeply men
may immure themselves in cities, remember you have no right to deprive
growing children of a natural beauty in their surroundings. And please
always keep a vacant corner for some lazy do-nothing dreamer or poet, or
singer like myself.[77]

Tagore visited in 1926 and said, 'Elmhirst, it will do'.[78]

In Dartington, Leonard and Dorothy had fulfilled the first part of that
advice and the poetry (understood widely as all the creative arts) was now in
place. The production of *Comus* affirmed this, even for outsiders. Why dance?
Both Dorothy and Leonard had their own ideas, formed by their experiences
in America and India, about the community and educational functions of

dance, but they did not take any immediate steps to expand this into a plan for vocational theatrical training. It was Browne and Van Volkenburg, with their knowledge of professional schools such as the Cornish School, who were able to suggest such an ambitious plan. Dance at Dartington was about to have its first big injection of foreign talent.

Chapter 2

Dance-Mime for the People

Propaganda? – absolutely. The Dance-Mime wants to aid in the clearing away of present problems and a growth away from those mistakes of the past which still exist and influence this age.
And if there is Art? What is it more than something said with all the passion of beauty and thought and 'wanting to say' that a live group of people can give?
Standards? Something more than those of the careerist. In the abstract realm, each idea sets its own standards – born of the community itself – not projected in from the outside.
Margaret Barr, November 1933[1]

Arriving up the hill now, just before reaching Dartington Hall, look over to the left on slightly higher ground and see some of the buildings of Dartington College of Arts, amongst them a rather barn-like gable-end faced with overlapped wooden boards. It looks somewhat out of place in relation to the more modern and utilitarian buildings sprouting from it and hemming it in. (The building group is now called Lower Close.) This is the Dance School, opened in 1932 and still a space for dance.

By January 1929, plans were afoot to put something in place at Dartington to supersede the somewhat ad hoc amateur activities in place up to then. There were reports in the national press that Maurice Browne would soon be involved in an experimental school of drama and theatre 'somewhere in the country'. [2] Dorothy invited Nellie Cornish to lunch in New York in the summer of 1929 and came to an arrangement that would bring some of the Cornish teachers to Dartington. Beatrice Straight and Nina Fonaroff, both later to become Cornish students, were also present.[3] How Miss Cornish was persuaded to lose people who it must be presumed were valued staff members must be a matter of conjecture, but she did so. Dorothy in turn was generous in making grants to Cornish, and a few Cornish students received scholarships to study at Dartington.[4]

First to arrive at Dartington, in autumn 1929, was a puppeteer, Richard Odlin. There, he would be particularly remembered for his puppet of the African-American dancer Josephine Baker, standing nearly as tall as himself, replicating the semi-nude dance for which she was famous in Paris.[5] It was made for the revue *Caviare*, produced by Ellen Van Volkenburg at the Little

Theatre, London. A year later, with Dorothy's financial support, he was off for a period to study the puppet traditions of Indonesia.

In January 1930, at the invitation of Dartington's Education Committee (the school was still under cooperative direction), a small group of dancers arrived to give an initial demonstration and then to take on the teaching schedule, adopted from Burrowes's time, of Friday and Saturday classes for adults plus work with the schoolchildren. Margaret Barr, the leader of this group, was to be the first strong character to mould dance at Dartington. She had an American father and an English mother and had been brought up in India, England and America. A brief part of her eclectic training had been at Cornish, but she had trained very extensively with Browne and Van Volkenburg. She had recently set up a studio in London, 'Workshop of the Modern Dance', and had gathered her little group: Joyce Peters, whom she had met in America, and Rosemary Showler.[6] Another dance teacher, Louise Soelberg, arrived from Cornish in May of that year, and within a few weeks was married to Leonard's brother Richard.

The final immigrant from Cornish was the painter Mark Tobey in autumn 1931. He was to be based at Dartington until 1938, although the time was to be punctuated by frequent world travelling. A spiritual man (a member of the Baha'i Faith) and a charismatic teacher, he is now considered to be a formative abstract expressionist, who began his famous 'white writing' paintings of calligraphic-like white scribblings on a dark background while at Dartington.

These, with Ellen Van Volkenburg, were the main teachers of the School of Dance-Mime, which officially opened in September 1930 with Barr as its director. This was intended to encompass a full-time vocational school, a base for professional performance groups and an outreach organisation for the arts on the Estate and in the surrounding villages.

Barr and Soelberg were responsible for developing dance at Dartington until 1934, but where did they come from? How were they trained and what, if anything, did they bring from the current American practice and ideology of dance to their rural school in Devon? Their training in America was framed by three locations – California, Seattle and New York – but we will see that the European influence was also important.

Barr and Soelberg – locating dance influences

Before embarking on an historical analysis of these two women, I think it is important to reflect on my own reaction to them as I have apprehended them through the sources. Barr becomes immediately apparent as a fiercely dedicated artist who continued to work for dance, virtually to the end of her life: she is represented by a biography, an archive collection in Sydney and a strong presence in the Dartington Hall Trust Archive.[7] Soelberg is more difficult to bring to the page. She does not have a biography or a public archive collection. She did not write much in reports at Dartington as Barr had done, although in the 1940s she published a leaflet that can be seen as a serious contribution to the developing theory of modern dance (see page 139). Fortunately, collections of her letters have been donated to the Dartington archive, including those to her mother-in-law, Leonard's mother (her 'other mother'), and to Paula Morel (the former Dartington housekeeper mentioned in Chapter 1). [8] In contrast with Barr's writing, which reflects on her artistic beliefs, Soelberg's letters give a personal insight into her life, revealing the problems of always trying to balance family, art and economics. Barr's work makes an immediate impact through the sources, while it has taken longer to reach an understanding of Soelberg as an artist. I am conscious that my understanding of both women has been conditioned by the nature of the sources I have had at my disposal.

In her teenage years, Margaret Barr's family lived in Santa Barbara on the Pacific coast of Southern California, which was also the home of Martha Graham's family. Graham later hailed this environment for its liberating lushness: 'No child can develop as a real puritan in a semi-tropical climate. California swung me in the direction of paganism', she is reported to have said.[9] California was also the location of the first of the Denishawn schools, opened by Ruth St Denis and Ted Shawn in Los Angeles in 1915. This was where Martha Graham came in 1916 and her sister Georgia (Geordie) a little later. Until its founders split up in 1931, the name 'Denishawn' identified a network of schools, companies touring nationally and internationally and a notion of dance that was both glamorous, like St Denis herself, and sanctioned by careful marketing as properly artistic. Denishawn dance training drew on eurhythmics, ethnic styled movement and Delsartism, with a freely adapted balletic vocabulary.[10]

In the early 1920s, the Barr sisters, Margaret and Betty, attended Denishawn-style classes in Santa Barbara with Geordie Graham. They were drawn to the theatre in general as well as to dance. In 1923 there was a summer school at Santa Barbara, with drama taught by Maurice Browne and Ellen Van Volkenburg and with additional classes in 'aesthetic dancing'. The Barr sisters followed their drama teachers to theatre school in San Francisco for a period, and in 1924 Margaret attended Browne's summer school at the Theatre of the Golden Bough in Carmel, a purpose-built bohemian and artistic community near Monterey. It included a dance course and recitals by the Denishawn dancer Betty Horst, alongside her pianist husband Louis Horst, who would become so significant in Martha Graham's development. Barr had a role in Browne's play *The Mother of Gregory*.[11] The West Coast environment of Barr's youth, blessed by its climate, attractive to artists, clearly offered opportunities to develop artistically and perhaps also, like Graham, to develop a vivid emotional life.

Margaret Barr also went to Seattle, to the Cornish School, probably for a summer course in 1925. This was almost certainly because of the influence of Browne and Van Volkenburg, who frequently taught there. She took ballet with Adolph Bolm and eurhythmics with Louise Soelberg, a long-time Cornish student and now staff member.[12] The context of Seattle reminds us that there were well-developed centres of dance activity outside of New York. We can also get a snapshot here of modern dance at a time before it had solidified into clearly differentiated techniques, when there was a loosely defined 'free' dance in which the innovations of Duncan, Denishawn and Dalcroze informed each other. Within this mix, the contribution of Bolm, one of the Ballets Russes émigrés long before George Balanchine arrived, does not seem out of place.

Barr and her sister started to teach in Santa Barbara in 1926.[13] Their 'Studio of Dance, Aesthetic, Pantomime and Character' perhaps indicates by its title their twin influences of dance and drama plus the continuity of notions of 'aesthetic dancing' and Delsartism in what was considered appropriate for middle-class girls to perform. Having met Martha Graham in Santa Barbara (evidently home on a visit), Barr was off to New York, to Graham's studio at Carnegie Hall, where she encountered Louis Horst again. This was in autumn 1927,[14] when Graham was in the process of stripping away the decorative features of her Denishawn training. Barr's biography, written by Caryll von Sturmer and relying heavily on Barr's memories towards the end of her life, implies Graham's approval of her as a dancer, choreographer and teacher, citing the facts that Barr was allowed to deputise for Graham's classes, that Barr's first choreography, *Hebridean*, was praised by Graham and that, had she stayed in New York, she would have been included in Graham's first dance group.[15] It is as well to be circumspect with any notion that Barr was a budding Graham dancer who only left New York in order to be free to do her own creative work. The deputising may not have amounted to very much; Graham taught many classes, not always to talented dance students.

Barr was probably with Graham for about a year in 1927–28. The evidence from Graham's students of this period is not precise, but it would appear that the basis of the technique in 'contraction and release' was coming into focus in these years, although the terms may not have been used consistently and their physical expression would not have been identical to the later, codified ones. What is important, however, is that Graham was working for the full involvement of the spine – an internalised sensing of its curving and extension – as a development of breathing exercises. The floor work, a hallmark of Graham technique, was becoming formulated, but there might well be barre exercises as well.[16] A number of accounts from the late 1920s suggest that steps of locomotion were simple – walking, running and leaping, with changes of rhythm and dramatic intensity. There may well already have been some element of the percussive exercises typical of the 1930s, as Graham worked towards the style that would first be demonstrated fully in *Heretic* in April 1929. Her tendency to strip movements back to the most stark and dramatic had already been shown in the choreography for her October 1927 concert, particularly in *Revolt* and later in *Immigrant (Steerage, Strike)* in April 1928, pieces which Barr is likely to have seen. Perhaps Barr took something of the Graham dynamics, the emphasis on the breath and spine, with her to England. Highlighted on her handbill for the Workshop of the Modern Dance is a curriculum for 'The Dynamics of the Body', including 'Working on the Breath' and 'Percussion and Release'.

If Barr took notice of what was going on around her, New York was an exciting place to be. By this time the main Denishawn school was based in New York, the Los Angeles school having closed in 1924. The New York dance recital culture was firmly established. Graham showed choreography with her trio of dancers or as a soloist. Others on the concert dance scene, to take some of the names from *Dance Magazine* reviews of 1927–28, were Helen Tamiris, Angna Enters, Ronny Johansson, Michio Ito, Agnes de Mille, Doris Humphrey and Charles Weidmann. There were European visitors too – Eugen von Grona, Tilly Losch and Harald Kreutzberg.

Irene Lewisohn, one of the founders with her sister Alice of the Neighborhood Playhouse, was turning her attention to large music and dance events now that the Playhouse had changed from production work to being a theatre school. These extravagant productions, which she called 'orchestral dramas', were welcome paid work for the cash-strapped concert dancers. In May 1938 the full evening performance at the Manhattan Opera House, with the Cleveland Orchestra in the pit, was Bloch's choral symphony, *Israel*; Debussy's *Nuages* and *Fêtes*; and *On the Steppes of Central Asia and Dances from Prince Igor*, an interpretation of two pieces by Borodin. Lewisohn was no choreographer but allowed the dancers to make their own movement material, which she would direct and select as necessary. In the Borodin dances, a caravan arrived at a tribal encampment amongst the 'Golden Hordes of Tartary' and the merchants were entertained by dancing. Barr took the part of one of the camel boys. (Her pseudonym Rhys Meredith-Barr appears on the programme.[17]) The camel boys danced the *presto* movement, led by Charles Weidman as a tribesman. In the finale, the impression of wild abandon was to be achieved by all the camel boys doing cartwheels. Barr could not cartwheel, so she was allowed to give the same impression by spinning madly.[18]

The dance culture to which Barr was exposed in the New York of 1927–

28 was diverse and in a state of flux as the new generation of dancers strove to consciously redefine themselves as both modern and American. While their efforts were slowly raising dance onto the pedestal reserved for the 'high arts', the socially committed cause that had motivated dance teaching at the Neighborhood Playhouse for decades would soon be taken into a more radical political direction by the Workers' Dance Movement. It was mainly a 1930s development, but there was a first blast in that direction in Edith Segal's mass dances at the Lenin Memorial Meeting in Madison Square Gardens in January 1928; dance was marching for the politics of the left.

There are two factors in Barr's Dartington work to suggest that formative experiences in California, Seattle and New York influenced her own dance ideology. One is the cross-disciplinary nature of her work, which she titled 'dance-mime' or 'dance drama'. The dramatic idea was central and the material of the work could cross between dance, rhythmic mime and scripted dialogue. There is undoubtedly the influence of Browne and Van Volkenburg to be seen here. The Little Theatre Movement that they spearheaded in America was an alternative to the commercial theatre, inspired alike by Edward Gordon Craig and the ancient Greek drama towards re-envisioning theatre as a fusion of arts, with movement centrally significant. The second factor is the social and political consciousness that she took to Dartington, which suggests something of the New York philanthropic and political dance movements. There is no evidence that Barr had any direct contact with these projects, although she had clearly met Irene Lewisohn.

Louise Soelberg's dance was formed in a very different way. Her training was eclectic but probably much more systematic than Barr's, as she had been associated with the Cornish School since childhood: her father had been one of its financial backers. Although the Cornish School had begun as a music school, Nellie Cornish had quickly broadened the curriculum with folk dancing, eurhythmics, ballet and Isadora Duncan-style free dance, and she remained aware of the new trends in dance as they arose, bringing them onto the curriculum. Soelberg was sent to Geneva to train with Dalcroze for two years, returning to Cornish to teach. She also attended a short course with Elizabeth Duncan, Isadora Duncan's sister, in Germany.[19]

This turning to the current European context of dance would be typical of Soelberg. What she derived from the Duncan style of dancing is unclear. This form certainly does not seem to have persisted in her work, but it is as well to remember that during the 1920s and even into the 1930s, while the modern dancers were beginning to assert themselves as individualistic, innovative denizens of the twentieth century, Duncan dancing still had its followers in America. Some of the first-generation students and adopted daughters of Isadora (the 'Isadorables') were based there – Anna, Maria-Theresa and (later) Irma Duncan taught, gave recitals and toured with their own companies and students.[20] Duncanism offered an expressive, harmonious and exuberant female body (adulterated, in the case of Elizabeth, by the rising tide of racial-hygiene ideology in Germany[21]), but Soelberg found much more interesting role models in the modern concert dancers working in America and Europe.

Amongst these was Michio Ito, who came to the Cornish School in 1929 with a small group, including Geordie Graham, to teach and perform. Ito was also a Dalcrozian, a student of Hellerau. Although he was seen as exotic because of his Japanese origin, and played upon this in some of his recital pieces, he was thoroughly immersed in European and American concert dance as well as being an inspiration to other artists. (He had worked in 1916 with the poet/playwright William Butler Yeats in Dublin on his play in Noh theatre style, *At the Hawk's Well*.) In America he developed his own dance vocabulary and technique and became an influential teacher.[22] Soelberg was greatly impressed and followed the group on the next leg of the tour in order to continue lessons with him.[23] She also listed Doris Humphrey amongst her teachers. It is not clear whether she attended classes in New York before coming to Dartington, but she certainly spent some weeks there in 1932, taking Dalcroze, Graham and Humphrey classes and also private lessons with Humphrey.[24] Perhaps, as a musician herself, Soelberg was impressed by Humphrey's musicality; Humphrey had experimented early on with the idea of musical tone and textures made visual through movement – musical visualisations as in her *Air for the G String* (1928) – but showed later a more sophisticated and varied approach to music–movement relationships.

As much as American modern dancers of the late 1920s wanted to situate themselves as New World people, it could not be denied that dancers of the Old World had advanced modern aesthetics much earlier in the century and were a great stimulus. This was clear not only in the visits of the modern dancers from Germany such as Eugen von Grona and eventually in 1930 Mary Wigman, but also from photographs. It appears that Martha Graham's movement experiments were influenced by books of photographs that Louis Horst had brought back with him from Vienna in 1926.[25] Soelberg had experienced Europe at first hand and was aware of what was happening there in dance, which was dominated now by Rudolf Laban, Mary Wigman and their followers. She attended the Dancers' Congress of 1930 in Munich, where she was deeply impressed by Wigman's memorial for the dead of World War I, *Totenmal*, with its masked figures, dance, speech, sound and light.[26] This was part of a week of dance performances from Germany and abroad that would have given a strong impression of the whole field, both good and bad. Leslie Burrowes was also there, following her teacher, Wigman. This is possibly where Burrowes and Soelberg met. Deciding to deepen her knowledge of European modern dance, Soelberg later attended a summer school in Essen with Laban's former student, Kurt Jooss and his colleague Sigurd Leeder, both of whom would become highly significant to Dartington's future.

The School of Dance-Mime

At its opening in 1930, the School had no suitable premises. The barn at Dartington Hall's entrance gate was earmarked for conversion to a theatre, but this work had not yet begun. The Great Hall was still without a roof. Dance classes took place in the Solar (the small room above the Hall that was used for many community activities such as the Sunday Evening Meetings) or the gymnasium, both unsuitable for dance in size and flooring. Barr set out her ambitious requirements for her 'headquarters' in a letter to Leonard in October 1930.[27] The floor space of the main studio (to be hers, while the smaller studio was to be used by Soelberg) must be very long, 30 by 100 feet or longer. There should also be showers, dressing rooms, offices and facilities for the wardrobe, including for costume making. There must be a sprung floor.

Barr would have to wait until 1932 for the purpose-built Dance School (as it is still known today) to be ready. The main studio was indeed built to her length specifications and with a sprung maple-wood floor. People at Dartington even now say that its length was decided by Barr taking an enormous run-up, a single leap and then running until she had lost momentum: this was to be the length of the studio. The story is amusing and at least perpetuates her name in Dartington's oral history. Barr may also have had in mind some very particular requirements for performance that will become clear later in this chapter.

While the building was still in the future, the Dance-Mime project had to proceed with the facilities available. There was work to be done: amongst the pupils of Dartington Hall School, for employees on the Estate, to build the resident school for performers and to set up professional performance groups. The ambitious and wide-flung nature of the conception perhaps speaks of a poor plan, especially considering the limited experience of Barr as director and the Elmhirsts as funders in the diverging spheres of activity. Regular reports, termly at first and then annually, revealed progress and problems.

As Burrowes had done before, Barr sometimes found issues of discipline when teaching some of the schoolchildren, but she clearly made an impression on them if the school song below is to be believed. Expressive dancing, it appeared, ranked alongside other more practical skills as remarkable and unusual aspects of the curriculum at Dartington Hall School.

We papered walls and lino's cut [sic]
And pranced for Margaret Barr.

Sing ho, my lads, sing ho,
Leap high, my lads, high ho.
The life at Dartington's just great,
Sing ho, my lads, sing ho.[28]

When the School of Dance-Mime opened, Barr found herself taking care
of the dance work alone, as Soelberg had gone for an extended trip to
America with Richard Elmhirst, her new husband, who was studying methods of poultry production to bring back to Dartington. Returning in 1931,
she was pregnant and able only to take over the administration of the School
from Barr, so it was not until 1932 that her influence could really be felt in
teaching and performance.

An undated prospectus from about this period states the purpose of the
School: 'to provide intensive training, both technical and experimental, for
those who wish to make Dancing either a recreation or a profession, and
further, to correlate this training to the allied arts of Music and Drama'.[29]
The syllabus included dance technique and creative work, eurythmics, music, creative design, puppetry, staging, make-up/mask-making and drama
(improvisation and production). Considerable trouble had been taken to find
a musician who could work with the School as teacher, accompanist and
composer. For the first two years this was Donald Pond. Later, Alan
Rawsthorne and Edmund Rubbra joined the staff, both of whom would become significant English composers. Van Volkenburg worked on the drama
side of things when she was able to leave her production work in London. By
the time of the prospectus, with Soelberg now fully involved, some thought
was being given to how the different dance approaches could work together;
but the solution suggests an unsuccessful compromise. After the first year,
students could focus on group and community work with Barr, or on small-
group and solo recital work with Soelberg. This division within the
organisation suggests an unpromising and cliquish fragmentation, later
identified as a weakness in the School. On the other hand it could be seen as a
useful development, in that specific functions and manifestations of dance
were being identified, if only that could be carried through with systematic
thinking.

A few undated photographs show class exercises in the Dance School. In
one, Soelberg is identified leading a class in her studio; in the others, it is not
clear whose studio or whose class is depicted. The dancers are most likely to
be the full-time students of the School. Dressed in leotards (men in trunks)
with bare legs and feet, they exhibit a variety of technical abilities, using the
barre for whole-body swinging movements and stretching exercises. They
use parallel positions of the legs, but not exclusively. This is clearly modern

dance territory: the movement looks strong, percussive, even harsh, dominated by dynamic concepts rather than accurate physical placement.

A tiny clip of film gives further information on the barre exercises seen in the photographs. It shows a children's class just after Dartington Hall School had moved into its new building at Foxhole in 1932.[30] I assume this to be a class taught by Barr, since there is evidence that she taught the children. Facing the barre, they perform whole-body ripples, leading with the pelvis pulling away from the barre and then pressing in towards it. With one hand on the barre, they do leg swings with full involvement of the torso curving forward and back; the sequence includes a sweeping transition of the arm 'over the top' from the backbend to the forward curl. In the centre, there is another swinging sequence with various arm configurations, ending with a double circle of the arms upwards that lifts them onto their toes. Finally they can be seen rolling across the floor using a succession of movement in the upper and lower bodies. The teaching points would appear to be successive movement, rebound, suspension at the top of the swing and a huge investment of energy. If this is Barr's class, it does not resemble Graham work, but its sources could be anywhere in the melting pot of American modern dance encountered by Barr and Soelberg in the 1920s.

With such ambiguous evidence, class style is very difficult to pin down. What, then, can be made of Barr identifying her classes sometimes as 'Martha Graham dancing'? She would not be the first dancer to have exaggerated her relationship with a revered predecessor. Even in the early 1930s there were significant people in Britain (Dorothy, for example) who knew of Graham. Barr's New York background was useful to her and it is clear from sources relating to her later Australian career that she did not actively try to clear up the misapprehension that she taught Graham technique. Perhaps it was also useful for her technique to have a name, since Soelberg could legitimately claim to teach eurhythmics.[31] It is likely that both teachers were creatively adapting what they had learnt before to this new situation. Soelberg also had to adjust as necessary the strictly Dalcrozian methods to the demands of a dance course; according to the School of Dance-Mime prospectus, her course on 'Dance Design' developed the understanding of musical forms as the basis for making dances. By chance, Soelberg was not the only Dalcrozian at Dartington. Winifred Edwards joined the regular teaching staff of Dartington Hall School in 1931 and began to give lessons in eurhythmics to children from the nursery school upwards. These were voluntary classes, but popular by her own account. By 1935 she could report she had fourteen classes per week, including the children and a group of trainee nursery school teachers resident there.[32]

Barr and Soelberg gave amateur classes for the Estate in dance technique, dramatic improvisation and eurhythmics. Classes were given at two levels, but it seems that numbers were not large: Barr mentions a satisfactory class of ten members including one man, but in another 'eight boiled down to four office girls'.[33] The folk dance classes were more popular, under Barr's direction but organised by the participants as a club and visiting other local clubs for social dances; Barr seems to have appreciated the place of the arts in developing the spirit of independence and self-confidence. Developing as she had from the dual influences of dance and drama, Barr brought those two disciplines together, ranging in her work from pure dance to an amalgam she labelled dance-mime or dance drama.

She taught a regular group at the village of Liverton (about ten miles away), where her class combined creative voice and movement. This came under the auspices of the Workers' Educational Association (WEA) whose local representative, F.G. Thomas, was an advocate of drama work in the villages. Rural drama groups such as the one at Liverton were strongly supported in the 1920s and 30s, inspired by the travelling shows of the Arts League of Service and Mary Kelly, founder of the Village Drama Society.[34] Barr readily found a niche in this work, although she would take a rather different course from the pageants and folk plays usually produced. They worked on a theme that was outside their own experience, the dance-mime *Colliery*. Folk dance was brought in as a finale to the class, as a social activity and a release of tension from the creative work. It may be that Barr's use of folk dancing in her amateur classes reflected her school days in America, where it had been a feature of physical education programmes following Mary Hinman. It was also taught for its social value in the settlement house activities that she may have encountered in New York. Here in Devon, the rationale would have been rather different from that expounded for the urban new immigrant cultures of the settlement houses, but Barr does seem to have brought with her some general notion of folk dance as a binding agent within a community.[35]

Both Barr and Soelberg worked creatively with their students. With Barr we can be specific in some cases: with the Liverton group, on the drama end of the dance–drama continuum, she used the creative involvement of participants from the beginning. It appears that creative work for the Estate was undertaken in the class she called 'dramatic improvisation' and her description suggests that, again, creative work was associated with dramatic ideas crossing over into mime and drama:

> Dramatic incidents created on the spot, using the voice in singing, chanting, elemental sounds, the body in every plastic movement necessary to aid the idea.[36]

These had the characteristic of directed group creations and were sometimes shown at formal or informal performances. So, individual creativity was valued and encouraged up to a point, but it is noticeable that dances created by individuals other than Barr and Soelberg rarely appeared on School of Dance-Mime programmes. It is possible to get the sense with Barr that she was pulled in two different directions. On the one hand, particularly later on, she was explicitly committed to cooperative working within the group of equal collaborators she believed had formed by 1934; whereas on the other hand she wrote of herself as an artist of vision who depended on the active cooperation of others to help her refine her own conceptions.[37]

Barr's reports indicate the degree to which the work on and outside the Estate was conceived as socially as well as artistically useful. The purposes served were not just those of the betterment of the individual amateur in the way envisioned in Dorothy's *The Arts at Dartington* but also for the ultimate good of Dartington as a community. There had certainly been local bad feeling between Dartington and its neighbours – partly because of the weirdness of what went on there; partly because Dorothy was American; partly because Dartington's estate workers received the agricultural minimum wage whereas workers on surrounding land were paid less. Now that the idealistic togetherness of the 1920s had passed, there were also splits in the Dartington ranks between the Elmhirst family with its associated upper management and the 'Estate' of manual workers. Barr's mission was to use dance to heal social divisions. She taught at the County Girls' School in Totnes and encouraged some of the girls to come up to the Hall; there was visiting between folk dance teams from Dartington and surrounding areas, and between the Liverton and Estate classes. She integrated people from her amateur classes into performances of the School of Dance-Mime. Entertainments were provided for Estate parties and canteen 'smoking concerts'. Her most successful gesture of local outreach (but not a dance production) was *A Mystery of the Nativity*, produced at the parish church at Staverton in 1931.

How much was this Barr's own vision and how much something pressed upon her by the Elmhirsts? When she was on the verge of leaving Dartington (in the circumstances I describe later) she wrote a rather bitter letter to the Elmhirsts, implying that the development of her creative and performance work had been frustrated because Leonard had wanted her to concentrate on work that would heal the rift between Estate and Courtyard.[38] However, the evidence is also that Barr carried out the community role with enthusiasm and flair. 'They simply worship her at Liverton', wrote F.G. Thomas, describing a moment when Barr was making dances for a village play production of *Peer Gynt*:

Old Mrs. Cox was watching Margaret with the children – she was standing by me. I heard her pull herself up with 'My dear soul, I'm doin' it mysen!'[39]

Perhaps indicative of the way Barr envisioned community in the Dartington context was the Spring Festival that she attempted to mount in both 1931 and 1932 but for which she was unable to get permission. Planned for the gardens at dawn using all the levels of the open-air theatre, it called for a dancing/acting cast of nearly 100, an orchestra of at least 50 plus singing chorus and 26 assorted cattle. The Ancients of Winter were to be defeated by the Adolescents dressed in 'sap green' and a Nature Elemental with a blazing torch. There would be dances to bless crops, motherhood and cattle and a stylised bacchanal to symbolise procreation.[40] She saw the project in terms of a coming together of the disparate social elements from Dartington and beyond for a common cause, and clearly it would have been a way of proving the relationship of arts and agricultural industries one to the other. Further, she was projecting the whole idea of festival as a theme for Dartington's artistic life: Dartington had special attributes to be a festival centre, perhaps even as a centre for a whole network of festival centres.[41] There is no record of why the plan was not taken up. It would, of course, have been very expensive and time-consuming. Its nature as an event would have been of purely ritual significance, to be participated in rather than observed. Could such a pagan manifestation really have captured the imagination of everybody needed to bring it off? Her Staverton *Nativity*, equally ritualistic, had enjoyed universal praise. But this was rural Devon after all, not Monte Verità.

So rather than the great symbolic ritual of a Spring Festival, Dartington's notion of community was presented in rather more pragmatic ways. There was a broad scheme of activities open to all (in itself a ground-breaking idea in a class-segregated rural economy). Amateur dance classes at Dartington took place within an adult education programme that included arts, crafts, sports and other subjects such as history or building construction if there was a current interest in them. In 1933, Dartington's adult education rules and subscriptions were standardised. Five shillings per term (0.25 GBP) was to be the rate for a course. This had always been the rate for dance classes and remained throughout the 1930s.[42]

With the opening of the Dance School building, there were further developments in the community work – tap and ballroom dancing classes taught by Bethene Miller and Beryl de Zoete, informal studio performances from Soelberg's group, public music concerts and performances from outside groups. For a few years the Dance School became a broadcasting centre for music concerts on the West Regional Network of the BBC, including such international stars as pianist Arthur Rubinstein.

The School of Dance-Mime was conceived on two broad fronts: across dance and drama, and across the functions of professional performance training and amateur community work. This distinction between professional and amateur becomes rather important later, so it is worth exploring just a few of the tensions within those two terms that were bandied about rather indiscriminately at this time at Dartington. From our contemporary perspective, the operant term is 'professional', as it defines what the amateur is not. Taken purely from an economic point of view, the professional is worthy of payment. The term also has connotations of accreditation (professional-body membership or training from a recognised 'professional') and/or reputation (critical acclaim or respect), which are associated with notions of standards.

We can, however, observe the grey areas within the concepts. Barr and Soelberg were paid professionals but the work was subsidised, not yet meeting the real economics of the market. With her Dalcroze diploma, Soelberg's claims to accreditation as a teacher to professional standards were better than Barr's (perhaps this is one of the reasons for emphasising her connection to Graham) but neither had a British reputation in teaching or in performing. This could be seen as a disadvantage within the British system, with its established tendency to institutionalise the dance teaching profession through examining bodies such as the Imperial Society of Teachers of Dancing and the Association of Operatic Dancing (established in 1904 and 1920 respectively). As with other concert dancers, the possibility of building a professional performance reputation was frustrated by the limited opportunities. If the outcome was to be professional performance groups arising from Dartington that would be viable in an open cultural market, there would have to be a real push forward from the School of Dance-Mime in terms of the audience it could develop. If this did not happen, it would undermine the aspirations of students in the full-time School as professional performers in the making.

For the amateurs on the Estate and outside it, dance was offered as a leisure activity and an educational and social engagement, with a heightened sense of community as a hoped-for outcome. But a tension arose between these objectives and the expectation that amateurs would be put on show in a substantial public performance programme, in the tradition established by *Comus*. This performance culture blurred the distinction between amateur and professional, integrating amateurs with the aspiring professionals of the full-time school and dancers of professional standard such as Soelberg. I would argue that this was a legitimate representation of the community and had the potential to increase understanding across the various social entities at Dartington, but it is also possible that it hindered the development of professional performance standards that could ensure the continuance of the School of Dance-Mime.

Choreography and performance

The first public performance of the School of Dance-Mime took place in July 1931, in the still unrestored and unroofed Great Hall, since there was as yet no theatre and no dance headquarters.[43] A number of photographs of the production suggest the dramatic effect that the backdrop of weathered stone provided. The music was live, for piano, violin, cello and voice, with a percussion score for one item. Perhaps in the light of concerns that this kind of concert would not be understood, the programme contained a two-page insert by John Langdon-Davies, 'A Note on Modern Dance'. Germany and America are cited as the great leaders of modern dance, which he describes as both a new art and a resurgent form of natural expression:

> One of the great things about Dancing is that almost anyone can be taught to express their feelings through it; and the Dartington School of Dance-Mime aims at showing that here is a recreation or creative activity in which the ordinary man can take part.

He thus frames the performance as a predominantly amateur spectacle. Barr went to great lengths to get her large cast together. Not all were members of the School of Dance-Mime or even from Estate classes. She had to resort to bribery to get schoolboy Michael Young to appear in productions along with his friend, Dorothy's son Michael Straight. The payment Young exacted for each rehearsal was to be allowed to drive her car once up and down the private driveway.[44]

The cast list for the first production shows the integration of the different functional entities of the Dartington community. Michael Straight and Michael Young were in the cast of men that also included Rex Gardner (architect and builder on the Estate), John Langdon-Davies (Betty Barr's husband, a journalist), John Wales (agriculturalist and teacher) and Gustav Baumann, who worked in the sawmill. Among the women were Barr and her sister Betty, Paula Morel and Leonard's sister Irene. There were also children from Dartington Hall School.

Apart from two dances choreographed by Soelberg and one by Joyce Peters, *Stella Maris*, the choreography was all by Barr. A number of these items are built on the theme of the cycle of life. In *Skizzen (Sketches)*, as the programme note describes, 'Three peasant women, mother, young girl and grandmother, portray the emotions aroused in them by a young child in its cradle and by its death.' In *The Child* there are again three generations of a peasant family and the suggestion that the child is a sanctified representation of continuity. Photographs show a tableau of the child standing between seated parents and grandparents, the parents characterised with straight back, the grandparents bent. A percussion score accompanied *Earth Mother*,

a birth-to-death cycle for 'Man and Woman'; and *Funeral and Wedding* depicted the mingling of funeral and wedding parties on stage as if they were
taking place in different dimensions. This repetitive thematic material might
indicate an obsession on Barr's part, but there might have been other reasons. Perhaps she considered this a suitable topic for a rural enterprise, one
with which the community could readily identify, or perhaps she needed
themes that would easily incorporate a range of age groups. It is further
possible that the Dartington ideology had, for the time being, trapped her
into monumental themes that appeared to validate dance-mime as 'natural'
and universal.

The representation of work through audible group rhythms is another
recurring factor in her movement material. In *The Factory*, performed by
Barr's Estate dramatic improvisation group, movement, voice and sound-
making evoked 'Clocking in, idle chatter, levers, clattering machinery, the
accident, back to work again'. Langdon-Davies described 'a row of girls beat-
ing out complicated rhythms with their hands and men swaying to and fro
by their sides'. In *The Child* also, the beating-out of rhythms rather than
realistic mime represented the universal experience of work.

Maurice Browne reviewed the production for *Theatre Arts Monthly*.[45] Because of his connection with the Elmhirsts and Barr, he cannot be seen as a
totally disinterested observer, but he took care to balance praise with criticism. He found the music badly under-rehearsed and much preferred the
group 'dance-mimes' of the second half of the programme to the solos and
trios of the first half, which he found 'somewhat arty' and pretentious. His
preference was surely in a good part due to the introduction of sophisticated
staging, which reminded him of Hellerau. During the interval, the stage was
rebuilt with different ramped levels, one of which passed out through the
empty window aperture of the Hall and provided the spectacular finale to
Funeral and Wedding and the conclusion of the whole performance. The bride
was carried on the shoulder of the groom high up the ramp and out through
the window. Browne and Van Volkenburg had visited Hellerau in 1914 and
been deeply impressed by Appia's three-dimensional and flexible setting and
lighting and then by Dalcroze's lakeside staging of *La Fête de juin* in Geneva.[46]
It can well be imagined that the stagecraft training Barr received with them
in the little theatres of California would have included appreciation of Appia.
Browne was clearly excited to see these ideas given fresh life at Dartington
and seems also to have responded to the overall theatricality of design and
staging, comparing it to his experience of the Geneva pageant and
Diaghilev's Ballets Russes.

In the following summer it was possible to perform in the main studio of
the Dance School, completed at last. A stage setting of successive stepped
levels had been devised, again reminiscent of the modular system at

Hellerau, and we can speculate that Barr's original intention in stipulating the size of the studio was based to some extent on what she knew of Dalcroze and Appia's large, rectangular teaching and performance space. A visiting critic also thought of Hellerau and described the atmosphere of the first entrance:

> On the curtainless stage a flight of fifteen or twenty steps stretching from wall to wall leads from an ample lower level to a shallow platform at the back. Upon this the dancers make their entrance up unseen steps beyond two doors in the corners. Few rises of curtains could be as effective as the sight of Louise Soelberg, the solo dancer of the evening, mounting in the half light to the platform and descending the broad stairs to the position she desired. A raising of lights – white in complete harmony with the whiteness of the unfinished wooden walls – a few notes from the piano and the dance begins.[47]

The writer was none other than John Martin, America's first dance critic, writing for *The New York Times* since 1927 and a staunch supporter of the modern dance culture in New York. It will be remembered that he had been an associate of Maurice Browne in Chicago, so he would have been interested in what was brewing here and Dartington was keen for his judgement. He was not in Britain solely for this event: his summer progress of 1932 would allow him to assess dance in other European contexts.

Soelberg's suite of dances at the start of this performance were mainly solos performed to music by Bach, Debussy, Dalcroze and Tcherepnine. Martin commended her 'purity of line and simplicity of style', comparing her to the Swedish dancer working in America, Ronny Johansson. Soelberg's choreography was strongly influenced by her Dalcroze training, 'aiming for the interpretation of music using its architectural form and content'. In the Bach *Sarabande*, she represented two distinct 'voices' in the music through simultaneous and contrasting movement patterns in feet and arms – a skill that came with Dalcroze training.[48] In another piece, *Bagatelle No. 4* by Tcherepnine, subtitled *Hunger of a soul defeated by fear*, she performed in a mask in front of a chorus of dancers. For Martin, this one 'entered the outskirts of Martha Graham's domain'. Perhaps the 'domain' he is thinking of is most clearly summed up in Graham's *Lamentation* (1930). Photographs of Soelberg in *Bagatelle No. 4* show her completely covered in dark robes, starkly contrasting the white mask with its prominent cheekbones and chin. The chorus behind stands silhouetted by the lighting: dark, threatening figures with hooked arms lifted, hands clenched into fists. As much as Graham's swathed body and white mask-like face of *Lamentation* is suggested, the territory is clearly also that of Mary Wigman.

Martin was appreciative of Soelberg as a solo recitalist ('unfortunately not known in New York. She is an artist of quality') but of Barr's choreography he was more reserved. Her main work of the evening was *The People*, an ideological dance drama with a heavy and literal scenario. Martin complained that the theme gave little opportunity for pure dance. He preferred another piece, *The Song of Young Women*, in which 'Song, Sewing, Washing, Dance, Mowing and Reaping, Gathering Apples' were translated into movement motifs. Motifs such as these could be seen in other Barr works: in *Hebridean*, for example, the actions of mending nets were abstracted into a tracery that the three dancers made with their arms, backs to the audience. Overall he considered that Barr had potential but was not yet formed as a choreographer:

> In her compositions as well as in her personal dancing she involves movements of excellent design and moments of intense feeling, but she has not yet found a way to combine them so that one flows out of the other. The result is that we are faced with many incomplete phrases, alternating with and even interrupted by over-emotionalized passages of pantomime.

He thus recognised Barr's emotional engagement; but when her material moved from dance into drama, he must have experienced a great gulf between her work and the concert dancers he was championing in New York. And she was certainly not cultivating Graham's mask-like and detached facial expression. She could refine and pattern mundane movements and everyday experience into satisfying dance material, but it seems that her foregrounding of content would not allow her to take the abstraction process further in the direction of pure dance. Soelberg, on the other hand, was crafting dances using the formal qualities of music. Nevertheless, Martin concluded that it was possible for Barr to develop 'a finely romantic style to balance the classic approach of Miss Soelberg'. This contrast between the choreographic and performance styles of the two, expressed in another review as Barr's predominant appeal to the emotions (or, to make this a negative comment, 'a tendency to over-act') as opposed to Soelberg's appeal to 'pure intellect',[49] might have been the basis for a genuinely productive, broadly based dance curriculum in the dance school if more cooperation had been possible.

The People

I want to analyse *The People* in more depth because it is such a clear ideological statement emanating from Barr. There are also tensions and ironies between the work and its Dartington context that may indicate some of the ways in which Barr would fall out of favour in the following year. There are a number of sources that make it possible to consider *The People* in more depth and a number of reasons for doing so. We have the evidence of the original scenario, the programme, several reviews, and a series of photographs that were annotated to indicate their place in the action. From these it is possible to hypothesise the movement and production style.

The People are initially seen as deluded by a version of nationalism, which is represented by a golden flag and sanctioned by a figure representing The Church. The Visionary challenges The Patriot, tears down the flag but is beaten by the crowd. In the next scene, the people toil and children die under the strain; The Capitalist shows little sympathy. The Visionary manages to foment a small rebellion, but the men are taken to prison by Representatives of the Law and some are executed. Now there is a scene of The Nation at War. It would appear from the scenario that the stepped levels were used to represent simultaneous scenes: the trenches, women at prayer, The Visionary confronting The Capitalist, and a wife in a vision seeing her husband shot. There is a trudging and deflated homecoming from war. Finally, The Visionary persuades The People to stand together, defeat The Capitalist and tear down the flag.

There were some powerful images, visual and aural. Donald Pond's music included percussion and chanting – 'the reedy wordless voice of the church'.[50] The lighting, which impressed reviewers, and can be seen from photographs to have achieved sophisticated effects of depth and shadow, was by Peter Goffin, who would become a close associate of Barr in the next few years. A local newspaper wrote of 'colour, chanting, resounding symbolism and "noises off"'.[51] F.G. Thomas, who submitted a review to *The Dancing Times*, reported 'no one in the audience was left unmoved', whether to immediate dislike or to call out approval, as some local villagers had apparently done.[52] The photographs show how Barr aimed for strong visual effects. Groupings were simple and clearly defined, including linear patterns and tight clusters of people. 'Mass' and 'moulding' were words Thomas used for her manipulation of the cast.[53] The placing and costumes of her personifications of power on the uppermost levels of the stage space provided the focus of an often symmetrical and pyramidal stage picture and emphasised the theme of hierarchy. The Church was a masked figure in a tall headdress (designed by Mark Tobey) suggesting priestliness in general rather than anything particularly Anglican. In contrast, The Capitalist was characterised with crude realism in a top hat, smoking a cigar.

As with works discussed previously, we can observe Barr's transformation of functional movements several stages away from their source but maintaining the visual reference to the original. In the scene where the people toiled, the women themselves made the links of a chain standing in an ascending row on the stepped levels, suggesting both an industrial process and a wage-slave existence. In this and other examples, stylised, unison gestural motifs, repeated within a simple grouping, a line or a cluster, produced both meaning and pattern. This may or may not have been the consequence of working with amateurs, but it appears to be an accessible and effective vocabulary for such a group.

Amongst The People (including The Visionary and The Patriot) the groups of men and women were clearly gendered in dress and movement. The men, in trousers with bare chests, gripped their hands into fists and flexed and expanded their torsos; their movements tended towards simple gestures, whereas the women, in long dresses emphasising body shape, showed a more fluid, twisting use of torso. As Barr later said, the long jersey dresses she adopted from Graham 'showed off the body beautifully'.[54] In general the women can be seen as more assured in movement; they would have been more likely to be regular amateur class attenders or School of Dance-Mime students. It was not usual for Barr to make men so exclusively the protagonists as was done in *The People*, where there was only one solo female role, that of a wife. Her themes more often revolved around couples (as in *The Child*) or an all-female group (as in *Song of Young Women*). A number of issues must have collided in her choreographic choices here. Although her regular groups were mainly female, her emphasis on the dramatic idea was rooted in characterisation and explicit reference to the real world. Even working with the female group, her dances often depicted women's work as gender-specific (*Hebridean, Song of Young Women*) and did not critique that situation (although she would do so later in her career). So in *The People* the power to preserve the status quo, and to change it, is in the hands of men. She may have seen this as the most realistic way to present her narrative forcefully. On another level, however, *The People*, like *Comus*, needed to represent the ethos of the arts at Dartington with a large cast of men as well as women.

As in Kurt Jooss's *The Green Table* (also 1932; see page 81), war, nationalism, greed and death are conflated in *The People*. Barr did see *The Green Table* in Paris at the insistence of a friend of the Elmhirsts, Beryl de Zoete, although it is not clear whether this was at its premiere in July, when it won the choreographic competition organised by the Archives Internationales de la Danse, or at the later season in October.[55] Even if it was on the earlier date, it would have been too late to substantially alter her own work, which would already have been in production. Rather, it would seem that both *The People* and *The Green Table* indicate something of the mentality of the late 1920s and early 1930s. It had taken some time for the appalling experience of World War I to emerge as a strongly articulated cultural theme: there needed to be a distance of time before it could be articulated with sufficient restraint. A key work was the German writer Eric Maria Remarque's *All Quiet on the Western*

Front (1929), which resonated for all nations that had been involved in the conflict, became an international best seller and was filmed in Hollywood in 1930. Maurice Browne's huge international success with *Journey's End* comes into the same category. Although *The Green Table* is often seen as a work of prescience in the light of the rise of Nazism and the build-up to World War II, its spirit is that of the revulsion at the militarism that stoked the fires of World War I and contributed towards the strong pacifist movement of the 1930s. At the same time, after the hedonistic excess (for some) of the early 1920s, the age of jazz and Art Deco which tried to throw off the memory of the wartime experience, there was a strong underlying pessimism.

The Wall Street Crash of 1929 had proved the fragility of capitalism: the consequences resounded around Europe. The battle lines between fascism and communism were already drawn up and Barr had clearly staked out her place in the phalanx of the Left. Her scenario was uncompromising in its rhetoric, even down to characters who surely could not be adequately depicted in the staging. The Visionary's first converts were to be an Intellectual, a Peasant and a Student, a classic representation of a Marxist revolutionary movement drawn from all classes. Wisely, she seems to have dropped these characters from her production.

But here was the Elmhirst family strongly in evidence in the cast list. Leonard was a masked and imposing figure representing The Church as authoritarian and socially uncaring – not an unnatural role for him since, although the son of a cleric, he was himself critical of organised religion, and Dartington's strange ideas had earned the hostility of the Dartington parish rector.[56] Michael Straight took on the role of The Visionary, with gold-dusted hair,[57] while Leonard's brother Vic Elmhirst was The Patriot. Dorothy and Beatrice were also in the cast. Did they discern the paradox of taking part in a dance-mime that grotesquely represented the kind of capitalism from which the Whitney money was derived? Was Barr implicating them in an ideology that just went too far? This does seem to have been the high point of family involvement in Barr's productions: by the summer of 1934, only Beatrice Straight was in evidence as a performer. But in 1932, Barr's statement of Leftist belief needed to be put on stage with a large cast of about thirty, ranging across the different entities of the community, inevitably clustering around the Elmhirst family. True, the roles taken by the resident authority were now more ambiguous in challenging pre-conceptions than they had been in *Comus*. Leonard was defeated, while the young Michael Straight was ultimate victor both in his scripted role of leader of the people and in his performance. Michael Young commented on the 'oddity' of casting a millionaire's son in this role, although he thought Michael Straight was 'rather good'.[58]

Interestingly, John Martin's review had raised the possibility that there was an underlying tension. Although the performance was 'a model of ensemble playing', he was not sure there was a common understanding amongst the performers of what the School of Dance-Mime was about. He did not expand on this comment, but perhaps his use of the word 'ensemble' is indicative of more than the ability to work together in performance. Perhaps the community spirit expressed in a largely amateur dance-drama production seemed to him to be essentially at odds with the professional aspirations of Barr and Soelberg.

John Martin's European journey, 1932

As Martin told his readers in July, there were two important events scheduled for Europe that summer: the month-long dance summer school in Buxton, a spa town in Derbyshire, England, and the choreographic competition in Paris. Although he had missed the latter, he set out to discover as much about the entrants as possible, culminating in a viewing of *The Green Table* in Essen; but first there was Buxton.

Billed as 'The First International Summer School', it was the brainchild of Sali Löbel, a Romanian-born dance teacher based in Manchester.[59] Her idea was to bring together internationally known teachers, performers and speakers experienced in a variety of techniques, from America, Britain and the Continent. While she was undoubtedly working from the well-established dance summer school culture already in existence at places like the Cornish School and in the studios of modern dancers in Europe, she saw the scope as being much wider in the range of stage and social dance techniques available and in other activities that spanned classes, recitals and lectures. Amongst the artists/teachers were the Russian ballerina Vera Trefilova, Friderica Derra de Moroda (specialising in national dances), Yeichi Nimura (a Japanese dancer working in America), Anton Dolin and Alicia Markova. Evelyn de la Tour (a Denishawn company member and teacher) came to teach tap. Leslie Burrowes (now based in London) attended as Mary Wigman's official representative. Amongst the speakers were P.J.S. Richardson, editor of *The Dancing Times*, and John Martin, who made his journey to Dartington between the two lectures he gave on the development of dance in America.

Unfortunately, it was the first and last event of this nature. Attendance did not add up to expectations. Perhaps the summer-school culture had not spread to Britain sufficiently to ensure enrolment. Perhaps Löbel did not take into account the common British belief that nothing of importance in culture happens outside London. In modern dance, the very top names did not attend, concerned as they were with their own summer schools, and Wigman, for one, was not at all impressed by Löbel's organisation.[60] Martin was scathing about most of it: 'arranged according to the stodgiest type of English formula, and the whole affair is markedly provincial in its outlook'.[61] He cast a disparaging transatlantic eye on 'the famous English ballroom dancing' ('stiff and stereotyped') and the Operatic (ballet) dancing and Revived Greek Dance emanating from the established dance-teaching institutions. His mission, to explain American dance and its theories, was severely subverted by his being scheduled in front of an audience largely consisting of the spa's usual assembly of health tourists. The recital by Alicia Markova and Anton Dolin, which was supposed to be the highlight of the month, gave him a great deal of material for complaint. To him it seemed that, especially in the case of Dolin, there was little artistry and far too much emphasis on 'tricks', while the programme consisted of unrelated dances extracted from the repertoire and some pieces of frankly bad choreography. Perhaps his prejudice against ballet comes to the fore here. He was interested in the extracts from the Camargo Society repertoire, from Ninette de Valois's *The Origin of Design* and the Polka from Frederick Ashton's *Façade* and could see their worth, but the impression of the whole recital led him to conclude that 'the much heralded revival of the ballet in England requires some careful examination'.[62]

The only British artist for whom he had any praise was Leslie Burrowes. She presented some dances on the opening night that were 'exuberant, strong and beautiful' and well appreciated by the audience. On another occasion she and her pianist Victor Swinghammer (originally of Wigman's Dresden School but then at Hanya Holm's New York Wigman School) improvised dances that appeared to be 'models of form and design'. As with Louise Soelberg, he saw her as a dancer who could fit into the New York recital scene.

Martin was perhaps glad to get to France, which offered the opportunity to admire the Indian dancer Uday Shankar whose Paris-based company was already receiving much attention in Europe and was on the brink of conquering America. Like Tagore, Shankar was to be an important figure in the renaissance of Indian culture and of dance in particular that was taking place in the 1930s in the light of the Independence Movement; again like Tagore before him, he would also become part of Dartington's story. Martin praised the visual appeal of the performance: 'The dancers are personally beautiful, the costumes are rich and even the musical instruments are pictorial', all of which enhanced his appreciation of the clarity of the dance forms and the absolute perfection of the dancers' technique.[63]

More important as far as Martin was concerned, and indeed as it would prove for Dartington, were the repercussions of the choreographic competition of the Archives Internationales de la Danse, held earlier in the summer. Not only had the clear winner been *The Green Table* by Laban's former student, Kurt Jooss, but all of the prizes went to modern dance practitioners from central Europe over a lacklustre representation from ballet and Paris-based dancers.[64]

Martin's attempt to catch up with all the Paris competition prizewinners was only partially successful because of holidays. His route now took him deep into the territory of central European modern dance. At the Salzburg Festival, he was not impressed with the dance drama presented by Margarete Wallmann, a former Wigman student. At her school in Schloss Laxenburg near Vienna, he was fascinated to have Rosalia Chladek, without her dancers, explain her second-prize-winning composition, *Contrasts*, a dance based around abstract forms, representing an old and new approach to classicism. This school, known as Hellerau-Laxenburg, was the successor to the Dalcroze Institute at Hellerau to which Dalcroze had never returned after 1914. Chladek had received her own training there in the 1920s when eurhythmics and central European modern dance were being taught side by side and had become director at Schloss Laxenburg in 1930. Martin admired her vigour, dynamism and virtuosity when she performed some solos for him. Finally, in Essen, he caught up with a performance of *The Green Table* with which he could find very little fault, reporting both his own enthusiasm and that of the public.[65]

The Green Table, sub-titled 'A Dance of Death in Eight Scenes', drew on the images, which were common in European mediaeval churches, of a skeletal figure of Death dancing away his victims. This dance of death, however, was positioned in a world dominated by The Gentlemen in Black who begin and end the whole work. Who are they? They could be politicians, diplomats, industrialists or the ineffective delegates to the League of Nations set up in the aftermath of World War I. Their simultaneous gunshots unleash Death to take, in successive scenes, Young and Old Soldiers, an Old Mother who has become a refugee, a Partisan woman and the Young Girl procured into a brothel. The only winners are the Gentlemen in Black and the Profiteer. Their final scene repeats their first scene and it ends where it began, the whole cycle ready to start again.[66] *The Green Table*, as I have argued in relation to *The People*, captured the tenor of its time, but it has also been the world's misfortune that, right into the twenty-first century, its message has never gone out of date.

From Britain to Paris to Germany, a theme of Martin's observations was the current state of modern dance in Europe, including its polarisation in relation to ballet. There are no surprises in his leaning towards the side of modern dance in all its forms. In Germany, he noted the renewed dispute between the rival camps and a tendency for ballet training to come back into fashion, yet he also recognised that larger political issues were stoking the flames. Within the climate of social and political unrest (these were to be the

final months of the Weimar Republic) and economic hardship and unemployment following the Wall Street Crash, he maintained that the issue had
as much to do with the discontent with everything associated with Germany's post-war condition, including the ascendancy of modern dance, as it
had to do with aesthetic preferences for ballet. The furore within dance was
the 'social barometer' telling of deeper ills in the body politic.[67]

Tensions in Utopia

Dartington was now a more complicated undertaking than it had been in the
1920s, and gradually through the following decade the reins of power would
shift from the Elmhirsts themselves to the people they employed to keep
things running for them. Utopia was acquiring a bureaucracy, although
there would be occasions when the Elmhirsts might forget that fact and do
things their own way.

The most significant step was the formation, in two stages, of the
Dartington Hall Trust in 1931–32. The Trust received into its care the properties and land, the shares of Dartington Hall Ltd, formed in 1929 to head up
all the business enterprises on the Estate, and £1 million of Dorothy's money.
It was responsible for the administration of all aspects of Dartington's work,
agricultural, industrial, educational and artistic. The forming of the Trust
was essential to the long-term prospects for Dartington's continuance after
the deaths of the founders, when death duties would be crippling. After a
legal tussle with the Inland Revenue, it was accepted as a charitable trust,
exempt from income tax.

Now the affairs of Dartington were headed by a Board of Trustees rather
than the Elmhirsts themselves, although Leonard was Chairman and
Dorothy, Fred Gwatkin (their legal adviser) and Leonard's brother 'Pom' (Alfred) were the others. There would continue to be no decisions without
Elmhirst concurrence. This was, nevertheless, part of the process that put a
distance between the Elmhirsts and the Estate in a way that went against the
inclusive spirit of the 1920s. Further to the distancing process, and standing
between the Trustees and the workforce, was the upper management level,
whose interpretation of what finances would allow was frequently stricter
than that of the Elmhirsts themselves.

Bill Curry, who arrived in 1931 as head of all the adult education and arts
activities as well as the progressive school, attempted to bring Dance School
expenditure under control. The School could not be self-financing with so
few students, a number of whom were on scholarships. In the academic year
1932–33 there were only ten students.[68] Although numbers rose slightly the
next year, the aim of getting twenty full-fee-paying students did not meet
with success. The School was kept afloat by a monthly and a yearly subsidy
from the Trust, which amounted to £194 and £2480 respectively in the year

1932–33.[69] Productions were expected to be self-financing, although they usually went over budget. The programme of frequent recitals outside Dartington, which should have provided an income for the School, did not materialise, causing Barr's two original dancers to leave her. In May 1932 Soelberg resigned as administrator and her place was taken by the seventeen-year-old Beatrice Straight, too young and inexperienced to excel in the role of Executive Secretary. Curry was in frequent contact with her, complaining about her accounting procedures and the Dance School's 'extravagant' use of electricity. In a letter to Dorothy in August 1933, he was concerned about 'the impression (which is quite prevalent on the Estate) that in the Dance School it is possible to be less efficient with impunity than elsewhere at Dartington'.[70] By 1934 it was clear that Curry could not fully engage with the development of the arts at Dartington because of his other responsibilities, so an Arts Department was set up in May of that year with a full-time administrator, Christopher Martin.

Mark Tobey had tried to indicate some of the issues in a letter to Leonard in July 1933.[71] The differences of approach and sometimes frictions between Barr and Soelberg were a divisive influence. He listed their strengths and weaknesses as he saw them. Barr was 'creative, forceful, ... slow to change. Revolutionary in spirit (both good and bad).... Doesn't particularly need encouragement so much as education.' Soelberg was 'Quite technically and musically sound. Needs stimulation and more personal attention to bring her out.... Her solo work should be more encouraged. Must be made to realize her own talent. Apt to be more imitative.' In general he felt the school to have been badly conceived.

The fissure in choreographic approach and ideology extended to the musicians, Rawsthorne working more with Soelberg and Rubbra with Barr. A memoir by Basil Langton (a student at the School and later to be Soelberg's second husband) brings to light some of this friction. He writes about the 'vast aesthetic distance' between Barr and Soelberg, between the former's 'political mission' and the latter's 'mission to celebrate the aesthetics of dance art', which was what also interested Rawsthorne and Langton:

> and as we listened to the pounding of [Barr's] rehearsals in the upstairs studio, Alan would make one of his sly, dry remarks such as: 'Oh dear, there they go again, one-two-three-four, one-two-three-four. Must it always be in common time?'[72]

It appears that Soelberg was not able to show her work outside Dartington until the spring of 1934 when she attempted a tour of her recital programme with two other former Cornish students, Bethene Miller and Edward Harrington, plus Paula Morel. The tour opened in York but then came to grief in a car accident, causing injuries that made it necessary to cancel other concerts.

Barr may have caused a little offence to her patrons with her summer 1934 production for the Estate Festival, written by her lighting and production colleague, Peter Goffin. The 'musical burlesque', *Subject to Alteration*, was certainly a satire, with many digs at the whole Dartington set-up. Using music, movement and spoken verse, it held up to ridicule the opening of a building on the historic country seat of 'Lord and Lady Boric', a building whose function was totally unclear. In the text, builders and architects make pretentious claims for their skills ('Anything odd, anything queer/may be used in our career.') and experts of every sort offer their advice. New building, in a variety of architectural styles, was a continuing aspect of the Dartington experiment. The opening of Barr's mythical building is attended by upper-class English and American types, a little like a weekend house party at Dartington Hall, and references to progressive education could be taken as rather too close to home. ('Such dreadful tales are told/of modern education/of unrestrained freedom.') Perhaps these comments were taken in bad part by the Trustees (Christopher Martin thought the whole thing was in poor taste[73]), but it could not seriously have affected the outcome, since strategic decisions about the School of Dance-Mime had already been made.[74]

Impressed by Jooss

Against the background of the problems of the School of Dance-Mime, the Elmhirst's own feelings about the kind of dance they wanted to sponsor were once more undergoing a slow transformation. This was in part due to changes in the personalities having an influence on them, but world events would also play a major role.

With the success of *Journey's End*, in which the Elmhirsts had originally invested £2000, a London-based production company was set up, Maurice Browne Ltd, with the Elmhirsts both being directors. With the income from presenting the play and the English-speaking rights topping £80,000, all seemed safe. Ellen Van Volkenburg was brought to London as Director of Productions. She was innovative but not very successful. It was she who presented Wigman in 1932 and directed the now-famous *Othello* with Paul Robeson, rehearsed at Dartington and including dances choreographed by Margaret Barr. Neither was successful financially or critically. By 1932 it became clear that the company was in deep financial trouble. Relationships between the Elmhirsts and Browne became distanced, but this was not sufficient to turn the Elmhirsts against the professional theatre, although they would turn to new advisers.[75]

From about 1933, Arthur Waley, celebrated translator of Chinese and Japanese poetry, was a frequent visitor to Dartington, becoming what

Michael Young has termed one of Dorothy's 'familiars' – those who shared her spiritual wavelength.[76] Along with him came his companion, Beryl de Zoete. Like Soelberg, she was a Dalcroze graduate and knowledgeable about dance developments on the Continent. She was also a devotee of British ballet and a researcher/writer on dance in South-East Asia.[77]

De Zoete took the Elmhirsts to see Ballets Jooss during its first London theatre season in June 1933 and afterwards to meet Jooss in his dressing room. Besides *The Green Table*, the programme offered three other works that would likewise become staples of its repertoire. *Big City*, like *The Green Table*, expresses a modernist concern with the juggernaut of the twentieth century rolling over common humanity. The target here is the modern city with its strict class demarcations. The two worlds of the rich and poor are shown existing in parallel, with little connection beyond exploitation: the central narrative is of a working-class girl (The Young Girl) being tempted away from a young man of her own class (The Young Workman) by a rich man (The Libertine). On a deeper level it is the segregated, frenetic condition of the city itself that separates the working-class lovers and prevents them from finding each other again. Jooss's choreography and his novel use of lighting employ a cinematic segue device to merge back and forth between the charlestoning rich and the poor, waltzing in their *bal musette*.[78] Towards the end, all the dancers appear reduced to the level of automata; they dance robotically with imaginary partners, the very expression of the twentieth-century urban anomie to which Dartington stood in opposition. In *Pavane*, a condensed, miniature piece to Ravel's music evoking the world of Velasquez, the dead hand of courtly formality is seen to crush the spirit of a young Infanta who expires, her spirit crushed.[79] It is also a profound illustration of Jooss's common theme of the individual against extreme social and political forces. *A Ball in Old Vienna*, however, casts aside all pessimism. With a slight narrative about a Debutante evading the partner chosen by her chaperoning Aunts in favour of another man, its essence lies in Jooss's gloriously prolific variations on steps in triple time.[80] While the little vignette of relationships is played out, the dancers joyously swoop around the stage, the very embodiment of the age of the waltz.[81]

The Elmhirsts could not fail to be impressed. Here was choreography that reflected their own social responsibility and yet was manifestly of a high artistic standard. Perhaps the germ of the idea for Jooss to take up residency at Dartington was already taking shape; however, their suggestion that Jooss and his wife Aino should visit them at Dartington was not taken up, Aino particularly feeling uncomfortable about accepting such an invitation from strangers.[82]

At that moment, Jooss thought he had no reason to leave Essen. True, Adolf Hitler had become Chancellor of Germany in January of that year. The

Reichstag fire in February gave Hitler the occasion for demanding and getting full powers, and the elections of the following month yielded control of the majority of Reichstag seats through a raised National Socialist vote, combined with coalition and intimidation. Now there was a speedy process of expunging all non-Nazi organisations, bringing every function of society under Nazi control and Aryanising all public bodies. The media and local authorities of Essen began a campaign against Jooss when he refused to dismiss Jewish members of his company, including his composer and close collaborator, Fritz Cohen. Over the summer a serious situation arose, but de Zoete, the catalyst, was at hand at summer school in Essen and was following the company on tour. It was not just Jooss she wanted for Dartington. She wrote enthusiastically of Sigurd Leeder as an inspiring teacher: 'Any school at which he worked – wherever in the world – *must* become a very important centre.'[83] Perhaps this promise of a starry international role for Dartington was too much for the Elmhirsts to resist. Jooss narrowly avoided arrest by leaving earlier than expected for a company tour. It was no easy matter for Jooss or for Leeder to contemplate a permanent end to their activities in Essen, where they had established a strong reputation.[84] Leeder journeyed to Dartington in October and returned to Essen enthusiastic about the place: 'a kind of paradise' was what he described, according to his colleague Lisa Ullmann.[85] Late in 1933 Jooss wrote to the Elmhirsts from New York, 'We are ready to bring our work to Dartington.'[86] Leeder remained in Essen until the following spring, at which time around twenty students and three teachers moved the school as a going concern into the Dance School at Dartington.

It is easy to imagine how Barr felt about this turn of events. She was now expelled from the studios that had been built to her own specifications and where, poignantly, Mark Tobey had recently completed a mural inspired by one of her dances, *The Three Marys*.[87] From the perspective of the Dartington Trustees, the situation looked fairly simple: Barr could be given responsibility for community work under the overall control of Jooss but relinquish her performance group and choreography. Students of the School of Dance-Mime would transfer to the Jooss–Leeder School. In spite of Jooss's greater celebrity, Barr was not prepared to give up her independence, unlike Soelberg and the other former Cornish students who were happy to put themselves under the great masters from Essen.

It is clear that any attempts to facilitate an easy transfer of power were ineffective, and probably complicated by the Elmhirst's reluctance to confront an awkward situation personally. There is a paper in the Dartington archive that may indicate an attempt by Leonard in early 1934 to be persuasive. It would be surprising if these notes, headed 'To Dance School, Sat[urday] Feb. 10th 1934', were delivered as a speech to Barr and her associates, but it is fascinating as evidence of a nascent rationale for dance and an attempt to establish some principles for its development at Dartington:

> *Dance* – Oldest and Newest of all Languages. – Not only the basis of [the] structure of matter but among birds at any rate still the prelude to the great annual festival of marriage.[88]

This equating of movement (of atoms and of birds) with dance seems strange to us today when it is accepted that artistic creation is a uniquely human ability. For Leonard, dance was a universal experience, organic in origin and unifying. At this difficult moment, with the prospect of both Barr's and Jooss's work inhabiting Dartington, he made this the somewhat romanticised basis of an argument to distinguish between the expressive abilities of amateur and professional dancers' bodies. For the professional the training had to be comprehensive so that the dancer could reach out to the audience. For the amateur, comprehensive training was less important than the 'age old' group involvement, founded in such things as marching to war and religious rites but, in the context of Dartington, clearly conceived on a more civilised level. Was he using this comparison to argue for the complete separation of amateur and professional spheres? That is not what he wrote, but he seemed to be turning away from amateur performance. His main concern was for professional standards. The School of Dance-Mime had not delivered expectations in levels of dance technique and the allied arts. Furthermore, and seemingly this was a crucial point, Barr resisted offering a diploma. This she always attributed to Martha Graham's antipathy to giving diplomas at this time; but in terms of those paradigms of professionalism discussed earlier (see page 71), Leonard clearly believed that this was standing in the way of the professional accreditation that Dartington students must have. At this point, Leonard's vision may be seen as prophetic, since he linked the diploma issue to his belief that there was a future for dance throughout the educational system right up to university level. Dartington's part in the trajectory of dance as education in twentieth-century Britain will be examined in Chapters 4 and 5.

Documentary evidence of Barr's reaction cannot be found until July 1934. Asked by the Trustees to put forward her plans in the light of the presence of the Jooss–Leeder School and company, she replied with a 'Manifesto' that reaffirmed the relevance of her Little Theatre training. Members of the group had 'no faith in the commercial Theatre System and visualize a new Theatre-form springing from movement, sound, form. Light and colour unified to express their ideas [*capital letters as in the original*].' Characteristically, having been told to restrict her operations, she now put forward an expanded plan for more Estate and village work. This seemed possible because numbers for Estate and village classes had risen and there was the prospect of more outreach work under the auspices of the Workers' Educational Association (WEA) and University Extension Classes being developed from Exeter. Crucially, though, Barr could not give up the idea of her own professional group, which she wanted to boost to ten members.[89] Barr's community work was consistent and dedicated, but she did not conceive of it as separated from a performance culture, as her Dance-Mime productions show. Perhaps most important was her own sense that she had finally arrived at a cohesive group of collaborators. She had Peter Goffin for lighting design and Edmund Rubbra as composer. Among her dancers were Bridget d'Oyly Carte (heir to the internationally renowned opera company, sole producers of the Gilbert and Sullivan light operas), Teda de Moor and Paula Morel.[90]

The result was something of a stalemate. On arriving in 1934, Jooss expressed his horror at finding Barr and her work still ensconced in a corner of the courtyard. He might, on understanding the reality of her feelings, have agreed to her remaining. This was acceptable neither to Christopher Martin in the Arts Department nor to Barr herself.[91] Finally, an agreement was reached whereby Barr and her group would receive a subsidy of £1000 for the coming year to enable them to set up in London.

The newly named Dance-Drama Group's London life began with great hopes. They opened a studio in Soho, the Dance Gymnasium, and Barr began to work with like-minded artists in the Left Theatre Movement. It appears that neither the economics of the studio nor a regular recital programme worked out and they had to change their base a number of times. The political context and content of this London work will be discussed in Chapter 3, where the creative lives of Jooss and of Barr in the late 1930s will characterise alternative ways of reflecting the polarised political climate.

The amateur and the professional

It would be easy to over-romanticise the efforts in the School of Dance-Mime to make dance accessible and relevant to all – Estate workers, managers, Elmhirsts and schoolchildren. Evidence of her written reports suggests that it was when Barr's work veered towards drama, as with the Liverton group and her Estate dramatic improvisation class, that there was a more credible outreach based upon a creative process with participants. There are no extant registers from the regular Estate classes, but if dance and dance-drama works presented in main productions are taken as a guide, performers tended to be of managerial status, particularly amongst the men, and included the Elmhirst family members.

Perhaps it is more worthwhile to particularise than to generalise. Individual people were given extraordinary experiences – Paula Morel was a case in point. If we take her as the embodiment of Dartington's amateur dancers,

SUPPLEMENT . . .

TO THE 500TH NUMBER

TUESDAY, MARCH 13TH, 1934

Dance drama as a segment of the Dartington ideal, as drawn by the architect and designer Rex Gardner. [© Dartington Hall Trust Archive]

Dorothy and Leonard Elmhirst, a photograph taken at Dartington Hall at around the time they purchased the estate. [Dartington Hall Trust Archive]

Leonard Elmhirst and Rabindranath Tagore on the Private Lawn at Dartington Hall. The children are Polly Church and Diana Crisp. [Dartington Hall Trust Archive]

Leslie Burrowes posed in the ruined
arches on the Private Lawn, the still
unrestored Great Hall in the background.
[© Dartington Hall Trust Archive]

Left to right, Paula Morel, Beatrice Straight
and Leslie Burrowes as three shepherdesses
in *Comus*, 1929.
[© Dartington Hall Trust Archive]

Margaret Barr at Dartington.
[© Dartington Hall Trust Archive

Joyce Peters in her
choreography, *Stella Maris*,
c.1931. The roof of the Dance
School is visible in the
background. Photo: Dinham
and Sons, Torquay.
[Dartington Hall Trust Archive]

Hebridean, choreography by Margaret Barr. Left to right: Paula Morel, Magda Baumann, Margaret Barr. Photo: Stuart Black. [Dartington Hall Trust Archive]

Bridget d'Oyly Carte and the Liverton group in *Colliery*. Photo: Stuart Black. [Dartington Hall Trust Archive]

Left and below: School of Dance-Mime students in class in the Dance School.

Right to left: Teda de Moor, Deirdre Hurst, Bridget d'Oyly Carte , Betty Fitzpatrick.
Fox Photos [© by permission of Getty Images; repository Dartington Hall Trust Archive]

Left to right: Louise Soelberg, Betty Fitzpatrick, Basil Langton, Paula Morel, Bethene Miller, unidentified. The pianist is Alan Rawsthorne.
Photo: Planet News. [Dartington Hall Trust Archive]

The exterior of the Dance School at Dartington when completed in 1932, architect Oswald Milne.
[© Dartington Hall Trust Archive]

Teda de Moor dancing on the stepped-level staging for the 1932 summer performance of the School of Dance-Mime in the Dance School.
[© Dartington Hall Trust Archive]

Louise Soelberg in her choreography, *Bagatelle no. 4: Hunger of a soul defeated by fear,* 1932. Photo: Stuart Black
[Dartington Hall Trust Archive]

The Capitalist watches the chained wage slaves, *The People*, choreography by Margaret Barr, 1932. Photo: Stuart Black. [Dartington Hall Trust Archive]

Margaret Barr's *Red White and Blue*, late 1930s, London. Barr is on the far left.
[by permission of the Margaret Barr Collection, Mitchell Library, State Library of New South Wales]

Uday Shankar talking to children at Aller Park, the junior department of Dartington Hall School. [Dartington Hall Trust Archive]

Kurt Jooss rehearsing the Gentlemen in Black in *The Green Table*, 1935. Photo: Sasha. [© Hulton Archive/ Getty Images]

Jooss-Leeder dancers at Dartington, summer 1934, Lisa Ullmann in the centre.
[© Lisa Ullmann Archive, National Resource Centre for Dance, LU/F/3/42]

Lisa Ullmann teaching 'Script' (Kinetography Laban) at Dartington, c.1936.
[© Lisa Ullmann Archive, National Resource Centre for Dance, LU/F/3/54]

Jooss-Leeder School students on the terrace of the Dance School. Centre row: 2nd from left, Ann Hutchinson; 3rd, Joy Bolton-Carter; Birgit Cullberg behind wall. Top row: 2nd from left Yoma Sasburg; 4th and 5th, Annetje Wijnberg and Pem Becker. [Dartington Hall Trust Archive]

Students of the Jooss-Leeder School rehearse *Danse Macabre* in the Dance School, choreography by Sigurd Leeder. [© Rudolf Laban Archive, National Resource Centre for Dance, L/F/1/112]

Dancers of Ballets Jooss in costume for *A Ball in Old Vienna* outside the gardeners' office in the grounds of Dartington Hall. Photo: Sasha. [Dartington Hall Trust Archive]

Sigurd Leeder and students of the Jooss-Leeder School in the open air theatre, the Great Hall in the Background, c. 1935. Photo: Charles E Brown. [Deutsches Tanzarchiv Köln]

Louise Soelberg as The Queen in
Ballade, choreography by Kurt Jooss.
Photo: Gordon Anthony.
[© V&A Images/ Victoria and Albert
Museum, London]

Members of Ballets Jooss gathered
around Fritz Cohen, USA tour, 1937–
38. Photo: Fritz Henle.
[© by permission of the Fritz Henle
Archive]

Ulla Soederbaum as the Princess in *A Spring Tale*, with Snake and Wondrous Hermit, choreography by Kurt Jooss. Photo: Gordon Anthony.
[© V&A Images/ Victoria and Albert Museum, London]

Hans Züllig, Elsa Kahl and Ulla Soederbaum as Prince, Queen and Princess in *A Spring Tale*. Photo: Gordon Anthony.
[© V&A Images/ Victoria and Albert Museum, London]

Chronica, choreography Kurt Jooss. Andrea (Rolf Alexander) begs Fortunato (Rudolf Pescht) to be less harsh. Photo: Gordon Anthony.
[© V&A Images/ Victoria and Albert Museum, London]

The climax of *Chronica*, left to right, Noelle de Mosa (Clarissa), Elsa Kahl (her mother), Rolf Alexander (Andrea), Rudolf Pescht (Fortunato). Photo: Gordon Anthony.
[© V&A Images/ Victoria and Albert Museum, London]

The 'Arts Council' at Dartington. Left to right, Hein Heckroth, Sigurd Leeder and Hans Oppenheim meeting with Christopher Martin, late 1930s. [Dartington Hall Trust Archive]

Left to right, Rudolf Laban, Aino and Anna Jooss, and Lisa Ullmann, at Dartington 1938. The photograph was taken behind the Jooss house, and other modernist houses in Warren Lane can be seen in the background. Photo: Kurt Jooss. [© by permission of Anna Markard; Rudolf Laban Archive, National Resource Centre for Dance, L/F/1/48]

both the fascination of individual lives and the contradictions within Dartington's amateur project are apparent. When she came to Dartington in the 1920s as a housekeeper, her name was Dorothy Carter. She changed her first name to avoid confusion with Dorothy Elmhirst, first names having been decreed as the normal way of address, and became Paula Morel later on her marriage to the orchards manager, Roger Morel. Dartington gave her the opportunity to dance with Leslie Burrowes, a scholarship to the School of Dance-Mime and performances with both Barr and Soelberg. When Barr left for London, Morel went with the group for about a year, leaving husband and child at Dartington. Although her artistic interest in the later 1930s was mainly absorbed in the drama studio under Michael Chekhov, she did rejoin Barr for specific projects from time to time. Photographs suggest a strong stage presence with a refined and subtle ability in characterisation. In her role of The Spinster in Barr's *The Three Sisters*:

> there was more movement and emotion in this player's moments of still-ness (broken only by a tapping of fingers on the table, counting the years gone and hopes defeated) than in many whirling figures of ballet ...

In another role: 'Her performance was really terrifying in its suggestion of malice and powerful meanness'.[92]

For Morel, the arts at Dartington meant an opportunity to train in dance and drama and to perform. It also meant an absolute dedication to Dartington, which she served throughout her lifetime in various capacities. After Word War II she was known successively as amateur actor, wardrobe mistress and flower arranger. But this is not quite the story it might seem, of latent and undiscovered talent allowed to bloom because of Dartington's enlightened community (although there is something of that in it). Morel did not come to Dartington by accident and she was not a housekeeper by trade but a middle-class young woman who had already moved in artistic circles and had modelled for Eric Gill. Her childhood dance experience had been under Mrs Wordsworth[93], a well-known teacher of 'fancy dancing' who had also been the teacher of Ninette de Valois. She came to Dartington because one of her former schoolteachers had been appointed to the progressive school and immediately saw how Morel and Dartington were suited to each other. So the Dartington project became Morel's own project, as a participant and prime mover in its arts and as a resident throughout her life. The tensions within this are clear when she had to choose between different loyalties, to her family and to her artistic vocation.

To try to pigeonhole Morel exposes some of those grey areas between the professional and non-professional performer. Artists such as Barr and Soelberg, or even Martha Graham, must often work within a system of personal or state patronage in order to survive; often critical reputation eludes them. Morel's position is even more equivocal, not demanding anything beyond the chance to display her own expressive potential but always 'the professional' in her devotion to the ideals of performance discipline.

By the autumn of 1934 we can observe a souring in the utopian ideal at Dartington. In his first Report to the Trustees in July 1934, Christopher Martin attempted to draw the distinction between professional and amateur standards in order to define a strategy towards the 'Ultimate Aim' for the arts at Dartington. He had not been impressed by the work of Barr or of Soelberg.

> Is the Arts Department to be primarily a professional undertaking having amateur work with the Estate as an offshoot of its professional activities, or is the Department to be primarily amateur and dilettante with professionalism only a chance consideration.[94]

From what happened in the following years, it would appear that he and the Trustees decided for the professional option. The experiment of 1930–34 had been overly optimistic, not worked out in all respects but not necessarily impossible. Barr and Soelberg's lack of professional performing experience and the ramshackle organisation of those years must have contributed to failure, but it cannot have helped matters that there was no clear agreement on the definitions of dance for 'amateur' and 'professional', which as I have pointed out have grey areas. Between Barr's scoffing at the 'careerist' professional (in the quotation heading this chapter) and Martin's condemnation of amateurism as dilettantism or uncontrolled self-expression there is a vast gulf, which might have been bridged by Leonard's more intuitive approach on the nature of dance expression in amateurs and professionals. The one point on which all would agree was that the arts at Dartington were there to enrich the lives of the people of the Estate, but how exactly were they to participate? Were they to become passive consumers of the professional work or to be active in making performances that could be shown in public? For Barr, the answer was the latter for a variety of reasons. She saw the art of dance in terms of its product on stage, as a complete communication of an important idea. With such a small group enrolled in the School of Dance-Mime, non-professional dancers from the community were essential to her choreographic experiments. With the Elmhirsts needing the Dartington phenomenon to be put on public show, there was every encouragement for Barr to indulge her penchant for spectacle.

Perhaps, too, the dance area of the amateur arts at Dartington was in an intrinsically disadvantaged position in relation to the other arts. All performing arts expose the body of the executant to critical view; this is even more the case in dance, where the body itself is the prime instrument of communication. For the amateur dancer, where the 'instrument' may be undeveloped, the position is even more exposing unless the coherence of the message and the form in which it is expressed lend it authority. At Dartington, dance on stage was held up to scrutiny in all its aspects, in choreography, production and execution. The drama group and the choral society could perform existing plays and music without the whole enterprise being held up to judgement in quite the same way.

Christopher Martin insisted on the highest standards for the Arts Department, but how could those standards be applied to the amateur in dance? If stage performance was to be an outcome, by what standards was it to be judged? How could the amateur and professional spheres mesh together? Did the amateur dancers have their own creativity to offer? For Leonard, in the document quoted previously, the amateur clearly could have 'something to say' and often it could be more personal and more profound than from the professional. Understandably, Leonard had no practical suggestions on how to carry this out. The policy line from the School of Dance-Mime was also a little ambiguous, with the principals more interested in developing their creative work than in theorising the amateur field.

Were such questions being addressed seriously elsewhere in Britain at this time? True, Margaret Morris had been writing for many years about the application of her own technique across the amateur, professional and therapeutic fields. It often seemed, though, that her main justification for amateur dance was the improvement of physical health and mental well-being, rather than for its expressive content.[95] And yet the country could boast a wealth of activity in the amateur performing arts, in little theatres and amateur dramatic and operatic societies. A massive, two-volume tome published in 1934 – *Theatre and Stage: a Modern Guide to the Performance of all Classes of Amateur Dramatic, Operatic, and Theatrical Work* – is a literally 'weighty' affirmation of this, but it is interesting to notice how the scores of practical essays on all aspects of amateur staging frame amateur work as a reflection of the professional stage. For the most part, the performance that amateurs were expected to work towards was a version of an existing script or score. Dance sits rather awkwardly within this set of assumptions. This is even more striking when one considers the choice of writers for the dance articles. There is no Margaret Morris writing here, but Arnold Haskell, *aficionado* of Russian ballet and the developing Vic-Wells Ballet in London, and P.J.S. Richardson, editor of *The Dancing Times*. These were certainly two of the handful of serious British dance writers of the time, but they were not qualified to give practical advice or even support for amateur dance performance. Haskell focused eight essays on describing the history of ballet and its handful of 'greats', partly to dissuade any amateur from attempting it. He also expressed his disdain for barefoot 'expressive' dancing, and his best advice for anyone intent on putting dance on the amateur stage was to keep it short and not to attempt anything ambitious.[96] This suggests something of the critical context within which Dartington was working.

The absence of a serious theory or rationale behind dance for the amateur can be contrasted with the contemporaneous German dance scene in which the amateur, or 'lay dancer', was a specific concern, not only in practice but in writing and debate. The special domain of the amateur was the 'movement choir', developed from Rudolf Laban's work and becoming a feature of many cities as his influence increased in the 1920s. The movement material used by the movement choir was simple and the dance could be semi-improvisational. Groups were often brought together in festivals and mass dances many hundred strong, but the main rationale for the dance was not its exterior effect but the experience within the group. (Leonard's intuition resonates with this.) To Laban, this was an almost mystical blending of the individual with the community, 'experiencing in ourselves and in togetherness the increased vigour of the spiritual-emotional-physical forces which are united in dance'.[97] This sense of communality was a specific of the concept of the social community (*Gemeinschaft*) prevalent in Weimar culture, suffused with nationalism and nostalgia for a pre-industrial society.[98] In Germany, amateurs had their own dance form and a technique specific to its practice, whereas in Britain the whole amateur field was skewed towards the already existing forms of the professional stage. Community dance in contemporary Germany shows that a cogent position for non-professional dancers was possible; but clearly the social and ideological climate of Britain and Germany were totally different, and the German community dance form was no universal panacea. In the future, there would be some attempt at bringing about a translation suitable for a British community dance, as we will see in later chapters.

Chapter 3

Dancing on the World's Stage

The international aspect of Dartington Hall is one of its distinctions. Mr. and Mrs. Elmhirst, both great travellers, are quick to incorporate in their own plan anything of value from other countries. Here is no British insularity, but rather, perhaps, a new aspect of British imperialism, extending the boundaries of the mind to include methods of work of other countries. Hallie Flanagan, May 1934[1]

At nine o'clock one night in May 1934, bonfires blazed in the open-air theatre behind the Great Hall. By their light, 'Uday Shan-kar and his Company of Hindu Musicians and Dancers'[2] performed to a large, fascinated audience. He was the first Indian dancer to beat the West in its own invented field of 'oriental' dances in the manner of Ruth St Denis and Anna Pavlova (with whom he had performed). Unlike theirs, Shankar's dances were positioned as authentically Indian, although he had no consistent training in any of its dance forms until later. Like Tagore, Shankar was a cosmopolitan whose culture and education were steeped in the West as well as in India, but at this crucial moment in the development of Indian national consciousness both were engaged in developing the indigenous arts as symbolic carriers of nationhood. He drew on his knowledge of the dances he saw and imitated as a child, and assimilated into his choreography stylised gestures and movements that gave the impression of being authentic although not specific to any of the indigenous dance forms. Dancing an acceptable version of the real India while framing it in the Western form of a theatrical dance concert, Shankar's performances were to form a bridge to later, more knowledgeable, audiences for the classical dance forms. Now on a roll of acclaim following tours in America and Europe, what could be more appropriate than that he should come to Dartington, where Tagore and other notable Indians were frequent guests?

There may have been some vague idea on Dartington's part that the arts of the sub-continent could become a regular part of its programme: in January 1934 Tagore was recommending Haimanti, a dancer from his group, who could take charge of an 'Indian Dancing section' and teach crafts.[3] Nothing came of this idea, but Tagore's niece, the dancer Srimati Tagore, may have spent some time at Dartington in the late 1930s; and Tagore's daughter-in-law, Protima Devi, also a dancer, recorded a visit in 1935 when she observed and was apparently influenced by Kurt Jooss and his manner of working with groups.[4] Shankar made several visits to Dartington after 1934. The 1936 visit was for several months of performing, giving workshops and sharing artistic visions with the European émigrés. Uday Shankar's younger brother Ravi was in the troupe, as he had been in 1934, performing on sitar (later his virtuoso instrument) but also dancing and involved in the whole residency experience.[5] Later in the decade, Uday would become even more closely linked to the Elmhirsts in the furtherance of his work. The connection between the arts of India and Dartington was to remain important right into the 1990s.

Although, with a twenty-first-century sensibility, we might find Flanagan's use of the word 'imperialism' strangely uncritical, it is as well to remember that Britain was indeed at this moment an unashamed imperial power. Against this mainstream, Leonard Elmhirst was a firm supporter of a speedy programme towards Indian independence. Perhaps Flanagan was suggesting that Dartington's open window on the world was in part founded on an imperial power's confident tendency to absorb and appropriate. Dartington's cultural programme from 1934 until the outbreak of war did just this, supporting not only Shankar but also a number of European artists displaced by political events. At the same time, Dartington had its own dance company, Ballets Jooss, touring Dartington's name to three continents.

Laban, Jooss and Leeder

The dominant dance influence in Dartington from 1934 was to be the thread that runs from Rudolf Laban and his utopian activities on Monte Verità, through the following two decades up to the cultural dominance and diversity of *Ausdruckstanz* (translated as 'dance of expression'), the modern dance chiefly associated with Germany and Austria.[6] During the years of the Weimar Republic in Germany (1919–33) there was an explosion of dance activity. Political unrest and economic problems including hyperinflation forced artists in all fields to seek and express answers to Germany's problems. This is the period of Berthold Brecht and Ernst Toller in the theatre and Otto Dix and George Grosz in painting, to name a few of the socially critical artists.

The body had been a site of reform and even revolution in Germany during most of the nineteenth century. Friedrich Ludwig Jahn had developed and popularised *Turnen* (gymnastics using apparatus) in the early part of the century with an explicit nationalistic agenda – the strong and healthy body prepared to fight against foreign domination. In the latter part of the century the *Turnen* movement was associated with other political aims – German unification (the German Empire was created in 1871) and democracy. So by the twentieth century the healthy body in German culture had connotations of national pride. The rising popularity of body culture (*Körperkultur*) fed into a fascination with dance and a range of manifestations. The communal festive culture (*Festkultur*) brought out amateur dancers in open-air parades and mass dances. There was a proliferation of professional solo dancers and dance groups, amateur movement choirs, groups performing radical politics and satirical dancers in cabaret. In a unique genre of his own making, Bauhaus artist Oscar Schlemmer composed geometric and spatial dances of bodies abstracted or dehumanised by costumes emphasising the pure forms of colour and shape.

Laban had embarked upon the theoretical and practical exploration of the principles governing human movement. Fundamental to his whole concept was the idea of the human being as a holistic entity of body, mind and spirit. The dancer's motivation and its expression in movement were inextricable, and this shared understanding made dance decipherable to the observer. Movement and meaning, inner impulse and outward manifestation existed in a reciprocal, reflexive relationship. His movement exploration led him towards developing two main groups of theories, those of spatial forms (choreutics) and of the expressive dynamics of movement (eukinetics). Choreutics explained human movement as shaping its own spatial environment: expanding, contracting, elevating and lowering, designing the body as a mass and leaving virtual trace forms in the surrounding space. The main proposition within eukinetics was that force (later named weight), time, space and flux (later called flow) were the dynamic components of movement, each ranging on its own continuum between extreme polarities but normally seen when fused in different combinations, giving movement its expressive character.[7] The Laban dancer's technique lay in the ability to use choreutic form and clearly articulated eukinetics for expression rather than employing a set vocabulary of movements, as in ballet, for example. Laban's third important technical development was the written notation system, Kinetography Laban or Labanotation.[8]

In the 1920s, Laban's star rose rapidly in the firmament of German dance. Through his choreography, teaching and published theoretical texts, he became recognised as the central figure of German dance, with a vision of a new place for dance in education, theatre and society, although his fame in performance was exceeded by his former student, Mary Wigman. His students spread out through Germany and into Switzerland, Austria and eastern Europe, forming their own movement choirs and schools. By 1927, when he organised the first German Dancers' Congress, he was at the centre of a network of twenty-one Laban Schools, whose directors had to be in possession of his diploma and have their expertise revalidated annually.[9] This number continued to rise; German modern dancers knew the importance of accreditation in validating their professional status.

Kurt Jooss first encountered Laban in Stuttgart in 1920 and swiftly be-

came a leading member of his performing group and a teaching assistant. As
he later wrote, 'At that time for the "Expressionistic Dance" in Germany one
did not need great proficiency: strong intensity was all convincing.'[10] In
1924, while working with Laban in Hamburg, Jooss met Sigurd Leeder, who
had been trained by a former Laban student and had performed as an actor
and recital dancer since 1920, and with Laban since 1923. The Jooss–Leeder
artistic association would last for more than twenty years. Its immediate
product was their own recital tour of solos and duets. In 1926 Jooss was
invited to become movement director at the opera house in Münster, where
he set up his own company, possibly the first encroachment of the modern
dancers onto the ballet dancers' territory of the opera house. Also in
Münster, the Westphalian Academy of Movement, Speech and Music
opened, where Jooss and Leeder began developing their own dance pedagogy,
which would become so significant a factor at Dartington. In 1927 the group
moved to the Essen Opera House, Jooss and Leeder directing dance at the
newly opened Folkwangschule. Alongside the pedagogic work, Jooss was developing his choreography. He formed a new group and consolidated the
collaborative relationship with composer Fritz Cohen and designer Hein
Heckroth. These were the artists who created *The Green Table*, and following
the competition prize of 1932 they toured as Ballets Jooss.

Laban's experimental work challenged all the norms of theatre dance, but
in significant ways Jooss moved away from Laban's approach. Whereas
Laban had tried to break the 'natural' link between dance and music in order
to give dance autonomy, Jooss's collaboration with Fritz Cohen cultivated an
affinity between choreography and music. In contrast with Laban's emphasis on expression, Jooss aimed for clarity in choreographic form and precision
in movement style. While theatre directors such as Erwin Piscator, Leopold
Jessner, Max Reinhardt and indeed Laban himself were envisioning new
kinds of theatrical spaces for new audiences, Jooss was concerned with a
middle way within the existing opera house and theatre system. His form was
'dance theatre' (*Tanztheater*), springing from dramatic ideas, specifically for
the communication of contemporary themes within a mainstream theatrical setting. He was in effect using the advantages of the subsidised German
theatre – a system that did not exist at that time in Britain.

Jooss also reassessed the older dance forms. He did not exhibit the same
antagonism towards ballet as had most other modern dancers, going to Paris
and Vienna with Leeder in 1926/1927 in order to discover what ballet training
could offer in choreography and teaching. In 1928, at the Second Dancers'
Congress held in Essen, the same event at which Laban's notation system
was introduced, Jooss read a paper advocating the incorporation of some
aspects of ballet training into that of modern dance. This was not a popular
opinion with the other modern dancers at this time, who saw ballet as a

highly restricted movement vocabulary that would not allow a full range of expression and as the outmoded representative of discredited aristocratic values.

Jooss and Leeder were both working towards a clear language of movement and teaching techniques that would make modern dance a flexible instrument for the communication of ideas. This would mean a change in their choreographic aesthetic from the late 1920s. Laban and his followers were associated with German expressionism, a diffused artistic trend in literature and the visual and performing arts in the early twentieth century, and which became particularly influential during the turmoil of World War I and the Weimar Republic but was expunged by the rise of fascism. It is hard to bring all the salient issues within expressionism into a simple statement that is true for all the art forms, but it is useful to fill in something of this background in order to explain how Ballets Jooss and the Jooss–Leeder School diverged from it.

Laban's work exemplified the central strategy of expressionism, to make the abstract properties of the art form (or a synthesis between art forms) the means and conduit of expression. This led towards abstraction, distortion and extremes of theatricality that challenged forms of art that were merely representational of exterior reality. Artists wanted to express a profound level of disillusion with the life they knew, so works were often shocking, metaphysical, political, passionate, rebellious, personally intense. But from the middle of the 1920s there was a discernable trend in artistic and social thought that brought a more realistic and diagnostic attention to the ills of Weimar society than that afforded by high expressionism. The so-called New Objectivity (*Die Neue Sachlichkeit*) or New Sobriety allowed a turn back towards realism and representation to show society how to reform. For Jooss and Leeder, expressive forms, still embodied in Laban's eukinetics and choreutics, must be clarified through body training. Personal intensity was replaced by a more detached performance style and sensitive attention to the depiction of human relationships. This is apparent in the Jooss works such as *The Green Table* that have entered into the repertoire.[11]

The culture of the Courtyard

On most of my visits to the Courtyard in researching this book, I have been impressed by its calming and traditional atmosphere. It seems to belong out of time; it does not pulsate with activity. There are exceptions, of course. During the month-long International Summer School of Music, the Courtyard becomes the hub of artistic life. That was the atmosphere at the institution of Dartington's Arts Department in 1934, when the buildings of the medieval Courtyard became its domain. The East Wing was turned into accommodation for the dance students. The Dance School, now home to the

Jooss–Leeder School, was just a few minutes' walk away, and during the 1930s it was extended twice so that by 1938 there were five studios. A further conspicuous new structure close to the Courtyard was a house built for Kurt Jooss. Warren House was designed by the Swiss-American architect William Lescaze to include a small dance studio. The house had the white, stark lines and open balconies he had just produced at High Cross House for the headmaster, Bill Curry. The financial status of Curry and Jooss was equal at Dartington, and that status was solidly in the British middle class of the day, with homes built to accommodate a servant.

Back in the Courtyard, in the gateway block and West Wing there were rooms for music and before long there were studios for artists – painters Mark Tobey (the only retention from the School of Dance-Mime) and Cecil Collins, potter Bernard Leach, sculptor Willi Soukop, and the Ballets Jooss designer, Hein Heckroth. The latter two were refugees from the political situation in Europe, from Austria and Germany respectively. Aliens made a major contribution to Courtyard culture in the late 1930s.

In 1935 a refugee from a different political arena arrived. For some time the Elmhirsts had wanted to counterbalance their dance school with a drama school. The combined School of Dance-Mime had not worked well, but the notion of dance and drama being developed side by side remained. They were originally in favour of inviting Hallie Flanagan, director of the Experimental Theatre at Vassar College[12], but in America Beatrice Straight met a refugee from the Soviet Union, Michael Chekhov, formerly of the Moscow Art Theatre and nephew of the playwright Anton Chekhov. He had developed his own psychophysical approach to acting, and both Beatrice and Dorothy found him inspirational as a performer and as a teacher. The young Ravi Shankar, visiting Dartington with his brother's music and dance troupe, remembered Chekhov as being one of those performers, like the kathakali artists of south India, who could seemingly transform themselves physically on stage.[13] The Chekhov Theatre Studio at Dartington opened in 1936. Former Dance-Mime students Beatrice Straight, Paula Morel and Deirdre Hurst transferred their performing aspirations to this Studio; Dorothy was perhaps the most devoted of the Chekhov students. The Studio was active at Dartington until 1938, when it relocated to Ridgefield, Connecticut, because of the growing European crisis.

The Courtyard must have had an extraordinary atmosphere. There were American and Canadian drama students wearing their long blue uniform gowns; dance students in their black tights and white tops; a whole range of European languages being spoken; and, when the ballet was in residence, a wondrous array of beautiful bodies and faces. Artists and students ate together in the White Hart dining room in the huge Tudor kitchen. In the bar of the White Hart Club there was debate, conviviality and a political climate shared by some that was 'rationalist, cosmopolitan and politically "Left of Centre"'.[14] By any country's standards, this was a remarkable assembly in a remarkable setting. It was not only the dance and drama students who benefited from the various art and music studios but also the artists and musicians who shared skills and thoughts with each other. Bernard Leach told a story of Mark Tobey forcing his class, including Leach himself, to release their inhibitions by dancing around to music provided by a Jooss–Leeder School musician, also in the class.[15]

The culture of the Courtyard, and the Jooss–Leeder organisation in particular, generously put itself on show to the Estate. Visitors were welcome to watch a Monday morning technique class in the School (a very inconvenient time for workers). There were open School performances, especially at end-of-term concerts of student choreography. Ballets Jooss showed its repertoire in the Barn Theatre before tours. At Arts Balls the School performed light entertainment. The Jooss–Leeder musicians gave concerts (there were four accomplished pianists when the company was in residence). In March 1935, the Arts Department was displayed in the Great Hall with 'The Three Arts Show' (*Music and Dance in the Elizabethan Age, XVIII Century and the reign of Victoria*).[16] Genuine attempts were made to communicate the nature of the work and some historical context. Friderica Derra de Moroda gave public lectures on dance history and Kurt Jooss spoke at more than one Sunday Evening Meeting, 'Why do we dance and why do we go on tour?' being one of his subjects.

From 1934 to the outbreak of war in 1939, the community of the Courtyard became a beautiful thing in itself, open to any who cared to be involved. The professionals arranged amateur activities – a dance class, artists' studios, music. The Arts Department cooperated in bringing teachers from outside Dartington to the Courtyard for tap, ballroom and folk dance. Members of the Estate were given a preferential booking period for performances.

The Estate was welcomed to the Courtyard but the Courtyard did not go out to the Estate and beyond, actively seeking involvement by breaking down the barriers that persuade some social groups that they do not have the cultural competence to be part of an artistic endeavour, especially a strange and hardly understood one like dance. Dance performance by amateurs was no longer on the agenda. A split between Estate and Courtyard remained. It could seem to the average Estate worker that the Courtyard was doubly alien. While the whole financial enterprise of Dartington faced severe financial problems in the 1930s and the early months of 1939 promised a major crisis,[17] the Courtyard represented an alien kind of life, unproductive and certainly squandering the money desperately needed elsewhere. And there were aliens in fact, foreigners whose comings and going were inscribed in an Aliens Register as required by the Home Office.

The Jooss–Leeder School of Dance

It is some time in the late 1930s and a silent, black-and-white film camera is documenting the work in the dance school.[18] Shots of the surrounding countryside and the Courtyard set the scene and students look out of their bedroom windows in the East Wing. Inside the main studio we see Jooss and Leeder and second-year teacher Lisa Ullmann. There is footage of some of the famous Jooss waltzing exercises – a waltz lifting the female partner on every other bar and the 'dotted waltz' with a hop to add rhythmic interest. In the main studio of the Dance School there is a spatial study: the movements advance and raise the body, open to one side, lower and narrow the body, then an impulse opens outwards into a turn. Sections of two other studies are shown, emphasising the coordination of upper and lower body movement with smooth transitions and legato phrasing. Masked dancers in black dresses perform a restrained, courtly scene in Jooss style. Throughout it is possible to recognise professional dancers of the future – Birgit Cullberg, Lucas Hoving, Simone Michelle, Ann Hutchinson.

When the School moved to Dartington in April 1934, it was shifting a mainland European institution into the English countryside. Its technique and ethos were already formed out of the Jooss–Leeder development of Laban's work. In some senses this was a foreign graft onto Dartington's stem and not one growing from seed as the School of Dance-Mime had done. It had to establish itself in a new habitat.

The Jooss–Leeder dance technique was the product of the pedagogic experiments Jooss and Leeder had undertaken together in their previous schools, founded and developing upon the Laban work in choreutics and eukinetics they had experienced and helped to elaborate in the 1920s but with a view to creating the kind of dancer needed for the Jooss repertory. It was successful in this: by 1937 fourteen of the Ballets Jooss dancers had graduated from the school at Dartington.[19] Jooss was often away with the company, so Leeder was the School's main teacher, instructing the most advanced class of the three-year course. It gives some flavour of the style to remember that the students were not barefoot like most American and European modern dancers at this time but wore soft ballet shoes, giving a different kind of relationship to the floor and suggesting something of the rapprochement with ballet. The training was systematic but aimed at an internalised understanding of movement in all its dynamic, spatial and expressive complexity, rather than focusing on the mechanical aspects of the dancing body such as strength, flexibility, placing and a set vocabulary of movements.[20] This meant that the outcome for individuals could be quite variable, and often more advantageous if there was a previously sound training.

Dance technique classes, as Ann Hutchinson Guest has written,[21] started with simple movements, mainly based on swings, some using the barre, but these swings were different from the ones seen in the School of Dance-Mime. Both groups of exercises aimed for the integration of the whole body into the movement, but the Laban and Jooss–Leeder approaches had developed detailed ways of analysing the dynamic qualities of a swing, or of any movement, in terms of its changing relationship to gravity and the contrasts of energy within it.

The essential difference in the structure of classes at the Jooss–Leeder School compared with other methods was the part played by Leeder's own system of studies, which were the central part of the class. A study was comparable to a musical *étude*. It was created for a specific technical purpose but it was also a little choreography in its own right, albeit one not intended for an audience. It developed gradually class by class from exploring a simple movement, adding phrases, and then being brought to performance standard for end-of-term exams. There were studies developed in the technique class, and in the separate eukinetic and choreutic classes, but all were rich in dynamic and spatial elements and enlivened by Leeder's superb talent for verbal imagery.[22] Ann Hutchinson Guest has vivid memories of these, informed by the notation she made of them at the time. Studies had names that were often evocative of their purpose and content – for example, *Horse Waltz*, *Laufen* (Running), *Russian Foot Study*. Some were a regular feature of each year's work, but Leeder had a great facility for composing new ones to meet the specific needs of the class.

Students also learned 'Script', the term used at the School for Laban's dance notation and reflecting one of the German terms used in the 1920s, *Tanzschrift*. They practised by writing down their classroom exercises. There was no reconstruction from existing scores: these were still the early years in the development of the system. There were additional studies: improvisation; dance styles of different periods and geographical locations, taught by Derra de Moroda when she visited; music from the School's own pianists; and design, taught by Hein Heckroth.

Dance composition was an essential part of the syllabus but was encouraged and allowed to develop through practice, rather than through a composition course. Every term each student choreographed a dance, advancing from solos to group dances, working with one of the School musicians who would suggest or even compose the music. The School always had at least two musicians of its own, including at one time the American Dalcrozian, John Colman. According to Beryl de Zoete, his piano accompaniments for Leeder's studies 'were musical studies in their own right'.[23] At the end of term, all the classroom studies and individual choreographies were shown and evaluated by the staff.

Gertrud Heller, who had performed in Germany in a duo with her sister (as

Ursula and Gertrud Falke), was a teacher with a specialist field. She had been a student of Elsa Gindler in a technique now called Sensory Awareness, concerned with becoming conscious of every part of the body and not blocking spontaneous movement.[24] Lucas Hoving recalled how the work increased the awareness of the body. He remembered standing and lying on poles and feeling the body relax and adjust rather than reacting against them.[25] These classes were in German, which caused problems for some of the students but not generally for the large Dutch contingent.

Jooss–Leeder School performances were very different from those of the School of Dance-Mime, which had been dominated by Margaret Barr's symbolic, cycle-of-life or political dance-dramas. Gone, too, were the integrated amateurs, tapped-out rhythms and Hellerau-influenced staging. Jooss–Leeder School programmes were less experimental but were clearly formulated as part of the training process of, and a showcase for, a professional dance school. There was always a selection of the students' own choreographies, usually solos, while group dances by Leeder gave experience in different aspects of staged dance performance – small- and large-group pieces, pure dance and character-based narrative. One of these was *Danse Macabre* to the music of Saint-Saëns, ghostly, veiled figures rising from the grave. [26]

In September 1937, the Studio Group was instituted for advanced students preparing for professional work. That first group consisted of five women, including the English former Wigman student, Joy Bolton-Carter, and the Swedish Birgit Cullberg. This was the opportunity to spend more time choreographing and to mount their own productions. From the available programmes, Studio Group performances seemed to have been recital performances mixing solo, duet and group works but with no attempt to work on extended choreographies. In March 1939, Birgit Cullberg and Barbro Thiel gave their farewell performance before they went off to form their own group in Sweden, as they hoped. Of the sixteen items on the programme – solos, duets and small group pieces – ten were by Cullberg, clearly already coming to grips with the business of choreography.[27] One of her solos, *Cleopatra*, appears in the film described above. We can see in this her personal flair for performing comic and satirical roles. Ann Hutchinson Guest recalled that she had a manner of movement that made it difficult to take her seriously when she performed a serious dance. Jooss advised her to choreograph her serious dances but to give them to others to perform.[28]

One of the great advantages of this school over the School of Dance-Mime as far as the Trustees were concerned was its structured three-year system with examinations, certificates and diplomas, the lack of which had been a real point of contention with the School of Dance-Mime. In the third year, students took the examination for the Teacher's Certificate, which was a qualification to teach amateurs, while the Jooss–Leeder Diploma to teach professional dancers could be obtained after undertaking a period of independent teaching and then returning for special courses. Instruction in teaching amateurs was a third-year subject taught by Leeder. Students preparing for examination could observe the weekly open class for amateurs, taught by a member of the School staff, could participate in it and perhaps occasionally lead it, but their practical test was to demonstrate teaching on fellow students.

The whole concept of arts provision for the Estate was central to the Dartington ideal, and the certifying of dance teachers for amateurs was, if not central to the Jooss–Leeder School, at least its second objective ('The Jooss–Leeder School trains dancers and dance teachers', the prospectus announced). In view of these facts, it seems an inconsistency that amateur work did not advance during the Jooss–Leeder period. A register for an amateur class survives from 1938/39. The frequency of attendance varied as all evening classes do, with a maximum of twenty students, including Elizabeth Collins, wife of the painter Cecil Collins. Although there was a suggestion at one time that the class should be given twice a week, this does not seem to have been followed through, perhaps for lack of interest. So the class was a fixture but not an expanding activity. In one documented case it facilitated a professional career. David Walker, who originally came to Dartington as a weaving apprentice in the textile mill, progressed from the amateur class into the full-time Jooss–Leeder School on a scholarship and was to have a long professional career in dance.[29]

The class was the only expressive outlet for the amateur dancer: performance and creative work were no longer encouraged, and outreach to the surrounding countryside had ceased. From the perspective of today, it seems a lost opportunity that these areas were not expanded in parallel with the training of the students as teachers. Considering how alive the experience and ideology of amateur work was within *Ausdruckstanz*, the fact that there was no further development at Dartington strongly suggests how much Jooss and Leeder focused on the needs of the professional dancer. Licensing of teachers by examination for amateur and professional work was a reflection of the current system in the Laban Schools and Wigman Schools on the Continent. For Dartington students who did not become company members, a qualification to teach amateurs would be the most likely outcome; and yet there were too few examples available to them of what could be achieved with creative thinking and commitment in the amateur field.

A prime example of amateur dance development was close at hand. From 1934 the Jooss–Leeder School's second-year teacher, Lisa Ullmann, had started to develop movement classes for women and girls in Plymouth, the nearest industrial and port town 25 miles away.[30] As had been the case with

Barr, these classes were under the umbrella of the Workers' Educational Association (WEA); and as Barr had done, Ullmann used the connection to bring outsiders up to Dartington for performances and events. Quite early on she was able to move the class from the exercise format with which she had begun towards a more creative use of movement and towards dance making. But her work was a splinter from Dartington rather than being part of a conscious Arts Department policy on creative and expressive movement for amateurs. As the Elmhirsts and Christopher Martin had wanted, the emphasis had moved back to the professionals. There is no evidence that Dartington students were able to see the results of Ullmann's Plymouth classes. Perhaps this is another aspect of the culture of the Courtyard: that, being so absorbed in its own artistic flowering, it became quite inward-looking. The London dance scene was seemingly ignored, even though there were two Laban Schools operating there and there was a small but interesting growth in dance for workers, allied to the political Left (coming into focus later in this chapter).

A question-mark hangs over the possibility that the Jooss–Leeder School could have become a truly British institution. In terms of the student body, it continued to attract northern Europeans, partly as a consequence of the company's touring schedule. In autumn 1936, the first term for which the Aliens Register was kept, there were 32 foreign students: Dutch (12), Swedish (5), German (5), American (2), Swiss (2), Polish (2), Danish (1), Romanian (1), French (1) and stateless Russian (1).[31] By this time, a number of the students who had come from Essen had moved into the company. It is not surprising that there were fewer German students now, since the company could not tour there and it was impossible to transfer money out to pay fees. Ballets Jooss was popular in the Netherlands and this is reflected in the student body. Could a British tour in spring 1938 (the first extensive one) encourage recruitment to the School? Perhaps; but outside London, British audiences were unfamiliar with the Jooss name, and audience numbers would only build slowly at each venue. Numbers of British students rose, but not startlingly so. They needed fifty students for the School to break even. Expanding the British student body was the logical way to do this. By May 1939, of thirty-three students on the register, seven were British.[32] Any progress here was slow and was cut short, as was much else, by the outbreak of war.

There was also the potential for the annual Summer Schools to become a method of reaching out to a new body of dancers from Britain, for the work to be better known and better embedded in British dance culture. Unfortunately, no Summer School registers seem to have survived; but existing mailing lists show that information was probably sent to a large number of British dancers and teachers of all genres, not just modern dance, as well as to European dancers whose names can be recognised as practising *Ausdruckstanz*. British names on those lists include Anita Heyworth and Mary Skeaping. Heyworth was a leading figure in 'Natural Movement', a British style of Hellenic-influenced dance. Mary Skeaping had danced with a number of ballet companies, including with Anna Pavlova and Marie Rambert's Ballet Club. It is not known whether Heyworth attended, but it is a matter of record that Skeaping did, and it does appear that this connection was a fruitful one, as will be seen later. Summer Schools seem to have been well attended and profitable, although there is no firm evidence of how well they worked in the interest of British recruitment for the Jooss–Leeder School.

Ballets Jooss – of Dartington Hall, England

The company that began rehearsals at Dartington in June 1935 was not the one that had disbanded a year previously. Of the original dancers, only Elsa Kahl (Fritz Cohen's wife), Rudolf Pescht and Ernst Uthoff remained, with Jooss's wife Aino Siimola as his choreographic assistant. Some, like the Swiss dancer Hans Züllig (from the original *Green Table* cast), rejoined the company after the intervening period spent studying in the Jooss–Leeder School. New dancers from the School replenished the ranks: amongst them the three American ex-Cornish students, Louise Soelberg, Bethene Miller and Edward Harrington; and the Dutch dancer Noelle de Mosa. For the rest of the decade, Ballets Jooss would be Dartington's exotic export.

What was to be the legal relationship between Ballets Jooss and Dartington? The Dartington Trustees bought Ballets Jooss. The agreement of October 1935 was for the sale of the company and its goodwill for £1750 and all costumes and properties for £250. Jooss and Leeder became salaried employees of the Trust. Jooss had a five-year contract giving him a percentage of the profits but not of the losses. Why enter into such an agreement? From Jooss's point of view, having spent some time in the German subsidised theatre, it might not have seemed an unusual arrangement, although Ballets Jooss had been independent of the Essen opera house for the year after the 1932 competition prize. The legal arrangement with Dartington certainly gave him security and a working base, and the dancers had permanent contracts covering them for holiday periods – luxuries in comparison with the commercial theatre. For the Dartington Trustees it was necessary to clear up a confusing situation, with varying percentages on profits claimable by Jooss and the Paris-based impresarios with whom he already had contracts. One of these, Leon Greanin, became General Manager. It seems possible that Jooss did not altogether understand the terms of the agreement, since he complained later about his loss of overall control.[33] At all events, considering its large financial commitment, Ballets Jooss had to be tied firmly to Dartington.

The first tour as a Dartington concern began in Manchester and then proceeded to the Gaiety Theatre, London, to open on 30 September 1935. Dorothy, doing her best to fill the house (there were last-minute concerns about poor publicity), wrote to many people in her address book urging them to attend with a party. The Elmhirsts' own theatre party for that evening is interesting: Arthur Waley and Beryl de Zoete, Mr and Mrs Ashley Dukes, and Mr and Mrs John Maynard Keynes. The presence of Marie Rambert (Mrs Dukes) and Lydia Lopokova (Mrs Keynes) may give the impression that the Elmhirsts were not totally opposed to the world of the 'Russian Ballet', since both those women had worked with Diaghilev. While Lopokova was unquestionably a fine ballerina, Rambert's performing ability was far outshone by her tenaciousness in developing her own dancers and directing her own company. Yet it may be that the husbands were the weighty presence at this supper party. Dukes, playwright and proprietor of the Mercury Theatre where Rambert's 'Ballet Club' (soon to be Ballet Rambert) performed, was also translator of the German expressionist playwright Ernst Toller, and British correspondent of *Theatre Arts Monthly* where he was a fierce advocate of the non-naturalist theatre, including dance. Keynes was one of the century's most influential economic theorists and a financial advisor to the British Government, as well as being a patron of the arts and a member of the Bloomsbury Group of artists and writers. In later years he would become one of the founders of the state-subsidised arts in Britain and decisive in the future of Ballets Jooss. In 1935 he was soon to open his own theatre in Cambridge. We could see the Dukes and the Keynes as representing the marriage between dance and drama, which were the twin poles of Dartington's theatre arts project. In a postscript to her letter to Rambert, Dorothy announced that they had exciting things to discuss about the Chekhov Theatre Studio.[34]

The Ballets Jooss touring schedule then took in the USA up until March 1936. After a few weeks' rest, they were off again to Holland and Scandinavia, finishing in Paris in July to begin their next tour in September 1936. In that first year, they were touring for nine months; this was to be the pattern. Compared with the Ballets Russes companies of the 1930s, Ballets Jooss was lucky: Dartington provided a peaceful, unpressured home base for months of holiday and preparation between tours. But in other respects they shared the lot of the itinerant company: everything had to be flexible; changes and setbacks had repercussions months down the line; the cost and wear-and-tear of being constantly on the road were not always predictable, in spite of having managers one or two laps ahead to smooth the way. The tours were long and exhausting, to small and large venues, enthusiastic and frosty audiences, often 'for one night only'. For the 1936–37 tour the expected dates in Tokyo and Russia fell through, causing a financial crisis. The dancers agreed to postpone payment of salaries until the money could be recouped on the next American tour. Even so, from October 1936 to June 1937 they toured America coast to coast, then northern and eastern Europe, finishing in Paris in June: a total of 192 performances.[35]

In a real sense, the tours of Ballets Jooss took Dartington's name with them, with the words 'Dance Theatre – Dartington Hall' appended to the company's name on programmes and letterheads. Souvenir programmes included an article by Leonard explaining the whole Dartington venture, as well as advertising for the Jooss–Leeder School. Yet the connection was not without its tensions. Could a company that was around so little be truly part of the Dartington community? For Christopher Martin the problem was more that Jooss had been absent so much that he did not understand the internal workings of Dartington and, more to the point, that his expectations of what finances would allow were unrealistic because he did not know what else was at stake.[36] But to what extent was the lack of understanding mutual? Could the people who mattered – Christopher Martin, Dorothy and Leonard – really understand the lot of dancers on tour, faced with the daily reality of material, physical, artistic and personal challenges? Did they understand the process that brought the dance to the stage, the efforts needed to keep it fresh on tour, or the prosaic facts of touring – costumes falling apart, sickness, substitution, exhaustion? Even less so might they understand how an artist like Jooss, with issues on his mind, could feel it legitimate to push the financial boundaries to bring the work to fruition.

Perhaps there was too much tension in the company's position between belonging and not belonging to Dartington. That this may have been the case is hinted in a letter written by Fritz Cohen, directing the company on tour in Jooss's absence. Over Christmas and New Year 1937–38, the company's stay in Santa Monica, California, was documented, pictorially in an album of photographs later presented to the Elmhirsts and in writing in Cohen's letter. The photographs show the company enjoying life socially, dancing on the beach and in the normal business of touring – class, performance and travel. An imaginative reading of these photographs could pose questions about the way in which such a close community might also harbour internal frictions but also appear closed and defensive to anyone on the outside. This remains only a question, but is posed here in order to suggest the messy human level at which Dartington's dance theatre company must by nature have operated, a level that is never really considered in official documents.

Cohen's letter reveals how much he worried about the dynamics of the group, trying to integrate the new dancers from the School, trying to improve morale and setting exercises to keep their thinking fresh. He considered it a small victory that the group came together spontaneously to listen to

Toscanini's Christmas Day concert on the radio – just the sort of expansion in artistic horizons he had been trying to achieve. Another event with an excellent psychological result was when the dancers pooled their spare cash for some classes from a local teacher in the big ballroom-dance rage of the time, 'The Big Apple'. There is a deep underlying problem, though, in the relationship with Dartington that he struggles to articulate:

> I am convinced that the present spirit of the group belongs to Dartington Hall and its attitude towards life and art but the spirit alone is not enough; it has to work in flesh and blood not only within our small group but within the much wider order of the Arts Department and the entire estate.[37]

Perhaps it is in order to achieve this flesh-and-blood interface that he suggests Dorothy and Leonard should travel with the company (which they never did). There are hints of tensions 'financial, economical, mental and personal'. But Dartington is still a 'wonderful and miraculous creation'. It seems at least a viable hypothesis that Ballets Jooss sat uncomfortably within the Dartington ethos, a transient and expensive phenomenon, its internal dynamics remaining incomprehensible to those who held the purse strings.

Choreography at a time of crisis

Jooss choreographed several new works for the company while based at Dartington. In 1935, before the first tour, he made *Ballade*, another piece in the manner of *Pavane*, exploring the brutal reality behind the facade of courtly life. *The Mirror* dealt with the aftermath of war – unemployment and class struggle such as were experienced in Germany throughout the 1920s. In complete contrast, *Johann Strauss, To-night!* was one of the light works that balanced the social and psychological themes of Ballets Jooss programmes.

The next major period of creativity was in 1938 when Jooss embarked upon two new works, one light, one dark, both linked thematically with others. (At the same time, he was restaging his 1933 work, *The Prodigal Son*.) The fairy-story ballet, *A Spring Tale*, was a reworking of *Die Brautfahrt* (The Bride-Quest), premiered in Münster in 1925. *Chronica* was one of the works, stretching from *The Green Table* (1932) to *Journey in the Fog* (1952) and including *The Mirror*, in which Jooss explored the relationship between personal lives and political events before, during and after war. *Chronica* was an episodic drama in which a charismatic newcomer to a city became a dictator provoking civil war, then sacrificed himself to prevent further bloodshed.

In creating these two works, Jooss was departing from his previously concise format, which made a virtue of extreme brevity. (*Big City*, for example, was 12 minutes long, and *Pavane* only 8). *A Spring Tale* was approximately 45 minutes long and *Chronica* nearly an hour. These are 'lost' works, never notated, their traces evident only from photographs, programme notes, contemporary reviews and occasionally detailed references in books. (There is one tiny fragment of amateur film.)[38] Here, I will be suggesting that these should best be understood as works of European crisis years.[39]

A Spring Tale

A Prince and a Princess inhabit different worlds, defined and separated by gender. The Prince is first seen moving in a confident, outdoor world of manly pursuits with his friends, a Huntsman and a Knight. The Princess, in contrast, is smothered in the routine of the Women's Court, where movement is stilted, the Mistress of Ceremonies keeps a fussy command of etiquette and the grotesque Butler is the only male resident. The women are not only restrained in action but seem puffed up and pompous, gowns ballooning out around them. The three men set out on their journey to the Women's Court but the reception is cold and the Princess unresponsive to her suitor. Tiny clips of film show the prince (Hans Züllig) in virtuoso attempts to get her interest, with multiple *pirouettes* and turning jumps. When the Court goes to sleep, swathed in white bed-robes and with the Queen still clutching her orb and sceptre, a Wondrous Hermit in a blue cloak takes the Princess away into 'A stormy night in the woods', full of frightening phenomena – a Bogey Man, a Snake, Storm-Witches and Wood-Witches, a Tree-Sprite and Leaf-Maidens. There are some extraordinary visualisations of tree costumes that make the dancers as much scenery as character parts. The Hermit brings the Prince to her rescue and he takes her to his castle to rest. Here he fights a mock duel and pretends that he is fatally wounded, in order for her to 'discover her heart', as the programme note says.

Perhaps this has all been a dream, but a potent one. When the Prince visits the Women's Court again, much has changed. The women are dressed in yellows and greens, and their emotions, too, seem to have been unlocked by the warmth of spring. The Prince and the Princess are united in a dance together. So love is found in the forest, in Nature. The Prince and Princess 'discover their natural selves and mate in happiness', as one newspaper wrote.[40] The resolution of the narrative proposes that nature demands the balanced world of male and female principles combined and, in utopian fashion, it can unpick the effects of the repressions and conventions of modernity.[41]

As Jooss wrote in his programme note, 'This ballet is a fairy-tale. And like all real fairy-tales, it has a two-fold meaning: one for children, another for grown-ups.' The 'grown-up' meanings that Jooss went on to suggest were simple personifications of Youth, Bitterness and the Good in Creation, but it is hard to ignore the romanticism of his theme in its almost nineteenth-century imagining of a natural world that is at once sinister, benevolent and reflective of human relationships.

In this respect, *A Spring Tale* can be considered to share characteristics with the contemporary British neo-romanticism of an artist such as Cecil Collins, with whom Jooss shared the experience of Courtyard culture at Dartington. The neo-romantic sensibility is discernable in arts and letters before, during and after World War II, amalgamating apocalyptic visions engendered by the European political situation with a resurgence of the belief in the artist's moral leadership and a nostalgic attachment to the landscape of Britain. The art historian David Mellor has suggested that Dartington was a major location for the neo-romantic aesthetic and Ballets Jooss had a part in its construction.[42] Collins was interested in the Jooss works and also spent time in discussion with Laban. It appears that Dorothy's art acquisitions at this time favoured neo-romantic artists, including Collins, John Piper and Graham Sutherland.[43] The culture of the Courtyard was that of an artistic colony drawing on a rich brew – a sympathetic patron, an ancient edifice, the Devon landscape, an uncertain future – all of which might fuel this neo-romantic tendency.

Chronica

Chronica has a complex plot and a cast of named characters. (Here Jooss went against his normal practice of identifying his characters as types, such as the Prince and Princess in *A Spring Tale*.) It is supposedly set in a city-state in fifteenth-century Italy. The chief inhabitants of the city are Andrea, a Nobleman; Filippo, the unpopular Town Clerk; and Ferrone, a bellicose Condottiere (mercenary captain).

A Stranger, Fortunato, arrives, and promptly demonstrates the ability to bring order to the carnivalesque and quarrelsome streets. Ferrone, Filippo and Andrea become his followers. Andrea's sister, Clarissa, and their mother are equally impressed and a love affair begins between Clarissa and Fortunato. The women of the city, all captivated by Fortunato, break down the resistance of their menfolk and Fortunato is adopted as ruler.

In Act II, the new regime, headed by Fortunato and his followers, establishes its authority, the Condottiere leading the military and Filippo enforcing rules of behaviour. This becomes an oppressive requirement for conformity in private as well as public life, in manners of dancing, love and clothing. Gloom descends on the community. Fortunato loses Andrea's support but remains resolute.

In Act III, the actions of Andrea and friends in liberating themselves from their hated uniforms are interpreted as a revolt that must be crushed. Filippo is murdered as a traitor. Clarissa attempts to persuade Fortunato to stand down his troops, but despair leads to her madness. Fortunato is moved by this and falls into a trance in which he sees a suffering and masked individual who makes him understand that he has created misery instead of happiness. His change of heart is too late: Ferrone refuses to recall the troops. Fortunato kills him in a fight but thoughtless regimentation has taken hold of the men. Clarissa is trampled to death by the relentlessly advancing soldiers. Fortunato now sacrifices himself to his own men to bring the conflict to an end.

Chronica suffered from its complicated plot, its confusingly named cast and its length (there is evidence that it was considerably shortened while on tour). Clearly, when narrated like this, some of its plot turns are unconvincing and the symbolism awkward and overly explicit.[44] However, its resonances of the then-current political state of Europe could not be denied. It was not only that there were fascist dictators in Italy and Germany: most of Europe fell under the power of dictatorships in the inter-war period. By 1939 there were only twelve democracies remaining, almost exclusively in Scandinavia and western Europe, with the exception of Czechoslovakia and Hungary in the East. The Italian invasion and annexation of Ethiopia in 1935 and Italian, German and Soviet intervention in the Spanish Civil War (1936–39) were outward manifestations of the growing crisis. While Jooss was making the work in 1938, the international crisis over German demands to annex part of western Czechoslovakia had resulted in the Munich Agreement in which Britain and France appeased Hitler's expansionism. Some critics read the work in the context of the times, for example seeing Ferrone and Filippo as Fortunato's Field Marshall and Minister of Propaganda in parallel with the current German political hierarchy.[45] Jooss must have had contemporary fascism in mind when creating the work, but by placing it in a past century it was possible for him to effect an ending in which, unlike in *The Green Table*, the community could be returned to a balance – a state that seemed increasingly unlikely for contemporary Europe. At the same time, there is reflection here upon some of the issues that Jooss, as a German with family in Germany, must have been considering deeply. How are good people acclimatised to tyranny by its very welcome efficiency? What is this idolatry of the people for their dictator? Could it be something sexual? Will the charismatic ruler's power eventually rot himself and those around him to the core? In order to achieve the balance envisaged at the end of *Chronica*, what would Europe have to undergo?

Watching these works in rehearsal was Jooss's old master, Rudolf Laban, who had become another of Dartington's refugees in 1938. How interesting it would be to know how he interpreted *Chronica*. Between 1930 and 1936

Laban had been at the peak of his influence, first as movement director of the State Theatres in Berlin and then, from 1934, as head of the *Deutsche Tanzbühne* (German Dance Theatre), an organisation under Josef Goebbels's Ministry for Popular Enlightenment and Propaganda. It promoted the performance and employment of German dancers; its training wing was the Master Workshops for Dance. The truth is that many artists, including dancers, were seduced by the opportunities presented to them by the new cultural bureaucracy, and Laban was one of them. He must have felt the need to consolidate his work for dance, but acceptance of Nazi ideology was implicit in setting up training and employment structures only available to 'Aryans' and with curricula that included ideological studies in racial hygiene and in conceptualising modern dance on racial lines as 'German dance'.[46]

In 1936 Laban's career began a downturn when Goebbels banned his dance pageant for the opening of the Dietrich Eckart Stadium as part of the celebrations surrounding the Berlin Olympic Games, finding it insufficiently National Socialist in spirit.[47] Laban was now on a downward spiral of allegations, lost influence and illness, but it was not until late 1937 that he was dismissed and left Germany for Paris. With the help of Lisa Ullmann and Kurt Jooss, he was able to come to Dartington as a guest, on a succession of short-term visas. Is it surprising that those victims of the Third Reich who had gathered at Dartington accepted his presence in spite of his collaboration? Perhaps it was that his poor health evinced sympathy or that his artistic reputation of decades could not be sullied by four years under the Nazis. Perhaps they perceived from the actions of their own families and friends still in Germany that there are always constraints on choosing the totally ethical path. There are signs that Laban himself could be economic with the truth about his past (see page 117), but it does not appear that anyone said anything to the Elmhirsts that would make them doubt his victim status. The development of his work in the following decades with Dartington's support will be followed up in Chapter 4.

Dance in London Left politics

Jooss expressed the political moment in an oblique way while Margaret Barr, displaced from Dartington, chose another path. Perhaps it is no surprise that the choreographer of *The People* should very quickly ally herself with left-wing political theatre groups when she moved to London in 1934; indeed, there is some evidence that she had already made these connections. Right from the nineteenth century, the political parties and organisations of the Left had generated strong amateur cultural programmes, including play production and music. From the late 1920s some of this activity moved into a more overtly propagandist mode. The broad socialist agenda of the period was anti-militaristic and pacifist (still drawing on the experience of World

War I), anti-capitalist (the General Strike of 1926 and the Wall Street Crash of 1929 are key events here) and, as the 1930s progressed, increasingly anti-fascist. From far on the Left, various groups of the Workers' Theatre Movement used agitprop (agitation and propaganda), a highly stylised, epi-sodic performance style intended to press home the political message and incite the audience to action. There was also a socialist tendency in profes-sional theatre, a key figure being André van Gyseghem, a director at the Embassy Theatre, a 'little theatre' at Swiss Cottage, North London.

When Barr came upon the scene, van Gyseghem had recently left the Embassy in order to set up an experimental theatre with the writer Aubrey Menon.[48] They put on plays based on current news events, on an open, two-level constructivist stage. Barr and her Dance-Drama Group were involved as well. Van Gyseghem later wrote, 'We were trying to perform immediately relevant material, welding together dance, drama and music, writing new plays for a new kind of stage.'[49] In November, the play was Aubrey Menon's *Pacific*, about race relations in a Pacific colony, preceded by three of Barr's dance-mimes under the collective title of 'News Reel' to point out their con-temporary relevance. All were originally from Dartington days. *The Three Sisters* used the archetypes of Prostitute, Young Girl and Spinster to proclaim an anti-war message. *Breadline* was about the hardness of charity at a time of unemployment and hunger. The rhythmic mime *Factory* was described previ-ously in Chapter 2, but the press comments at this production suggest that it had moved towards agitprop style, depicting a fatal accident and with shouted words: 'Swine!', 'Slaves!', 'Unite!'.[50] It ends in a strike. The experi-mental theatre did not last long, but Barr continued to be associated with van Gyseghem. The Dance-Drama Group appeared at the opening perform-ance of the New Theatre League in January 1936 and the League also presented its February 1936 recital at Rudolf Steiner Hall, implying that the Dance-Drama Group was affiliated to this intended (albeit short-lasting) um-brella organisation for all the left-wing theatre groups.

Left-wing theatre in the late 1930s was dominated, at least in the eyes of the Communist Party, by the Popular Front, a broad anti-fascist coalition uniting all complexions of socialism. Out of this, Unity Theatre was born, presenting a spectrum of plays, 'living newspapers', revues and mass decla-mations in their own 'little theatre'.[51] These were largely amateur performers, directed by professionals (André van Gyseghem among them), and the purpose was political. 'There was no nonsense about "art for art's sake" at Unity Theatre.'[52] The Dance-Drama Group performed at the opening ceremony in February 1936 and frequently thereafter. In 1937–38, the Group performed monthly at Unity's old premises in Britannia Street, King's Cross (Unity had moved to larger premises). Barr also developed the Workers' Dance-Drama Group as an offshoot of her main group – workers dancing workers' themes to worker audiences. *Nothing to Do* was an example, a piece contrasting the idleness of the rich with the idleness of the unemployed.

The highly developed cultural, social and educational schemes of the Co-operative Societies provided another fruitful (or potential) platform for Barr to develop her work. Inspired by the utopian vision of Robert Owen (see Chapter 1), these were practical democracies of producers and consumers, their most obvious presence being the 'Co-op' shops up and down the country where the members (customers) collected a dividend on their purchases. In the 1930s, co-operators were also part of the Popular Front: the Co-operative Party had been fielding a few parliamentary candidates since 1918, but in general its political stance was to be a close ally of the Labour Party. Co-operative cultural events offered a stage to a spectrum of opinion on the Left.

In 1938, Barr choreographed and performed in the massive Pageant of Co-operation, *Towards Tomorrow*, at Wembley Stadium, directed by van Gyseghem, who was, together with writer Montagu Slater and composer Alan Bush, a member of the Communist Party.[53] A huge stage was created in the middle of the stadium with steps on four sides and three central levels. In music, song, declamation, movement and dance, the pageant celebrated International Co-operation Day and depicted the history of the working-class movement – maypole dancing in a utopian 'Merrie England'; slaving and dying factory children of the industrial revolution contrasted with Robert Owen's healthy schoolchildren dancing in their Roman tunics; the top-hatted capitalists planning war. A film of this pageant still exists. As the smoke of war dies down, Barr's Workers' Group climbs the platform to perform the Dance of Mourning Women, in long grey dresses and black cloaks, movements coordinated with the intoned words. The commentator changes the mood, speaking of international co-operation as the effective remedy to war and introducing a procession representing the co-operators of many lands. A group of 'Young Workers' runs in, dressed in white dungarees, each with a large red scarf. (This was the Dance-Drama Group from Well Hall, south-east London, trained by Barr's assistant Teda de Moor.) They take the cloaks from the Mourning Women and use them to overthrow the Capitalists. The different levels of the stage come alive with all the dancers moving and tossing their red scarves. Barr herself enters the arena at the finale, on a massive float, crowned and clothed in white as the figure of Peace, and ascends to the topmost level of the platform with another actor representing Democracy. But the enduring image of Barr is the one published in *Co-operative News*, entitled 'The Spirit of Co-operation'. With hair flowing, she sweeps down from the platform, giving the clenched fist salute of the Left. This moment was not captured in the film.[54]

A number of articles appeared in the Co-operative Movement's journals, especially after the Pageant, and on the evidence of these it was possible to start up Co-operative dance-drama groups in London and Manchester, although, considering the trend of international events and that Barr would leave for New Zealand in 1939, these could not have lasted long.[55]

Was Barr the sole originator of dancing on the Left in London? It would appear not. Groups had already been formed before she set up in London, in particular one instigated and organised by the composer Alan Bush, taking the name of the Workers' Propaganda Dance Group. From 1935 Käte Eisenstädt, a student of Laban and now a Jewish refugee from Germany, took over the choreography. (This group also performed in the 1938 Pageant.) Bush continued to play a major role in shaping the work at rehearsals and composed dances for them.[56]

Leftist dancers in London? Dance historians have been silent on this up to now.[57] True, the scene was not as substantial and vibrant as the equivalent one in America and perhaps has been additionally hidden because groups were usually performing as an adjunct to the main Left theatre and music groupings rather than developing their own organisations like the Workers' Dance League in America.[58] In Britain, dancers' groups could federate with the Workers' Theatre League, which became the Left Book Club Theatre League – very suggestive of the dominance of literary culture.

Barr was not exclusively concerned with overtly propagandist performance for the cause of the Left. Up until 1938 she continued to give recital programmes of her group under the auspices of the Little Theatre Movement, including a joint performance with Leslie Burrowes and their respective associates. Taken as a whole, her recital programmes could be seen as socially concerned in broad terms, as they had been at Dartington, but including items that strongly articulated the political themes of the day. When the latter were selected for a particularly propagandist event, the political message would be amplified by the context, as in the 'News Reels' preceding Aubrey Menon's *Pacific* at the experimental theatre. Another propaganda item was *Red, White and Blue*. The three colours of the Union Flag were used to depict (in reverse order) Imperialism, Pacifism and Militant Labour. It was popular for Communist Party meetings, for example in an Epsom and Ewell Branch Political and Social Evening where it shared the programme with political sketches, a mass recitation and an address on 'The Role of the Communist Party'. In 1939 it was shown at a party to celebrate the birthday of Tom Mann, Chairman of the Communist Party of Great Britain.[59]

Barr was politically committed in London and politically active both in culture and in direct action, engaging with workers' issues and anti-fascism[60], but it is hard to see a fresh development in her choreographic style and themes. New pieces, such as *Saturday Night* and *Means Test*, tended to comment on the real issues of the day, using a naturalistic gestural vocabulary. When she departed from this style to attempt a greater level of abstraction, it seems that she was less successful, at least according to the dance critic and Unity Theatre actor Fernau Hall.[61]

Even by 1936, the Dance-Drama Group that had come from Dartington was splitting up. Peter Goffin and Edmund Rubbra decided that Barr's increased political involvement was adversely affecting the quality of the work and that she was no longer interested in engaging with them in true collaboration.[62] Others of her Dartington group also left, and it appears that the Dance-Drama Group was disbanded in 1938, leaving Barr to concentrate on amateur groups until she left Britain permanently.[63] In 1939, at the outbreak of war, and now married to a communist and conscientious objector, Barr left Britain permanently for New Zealand and then Australia, where her work continued in the same uncompromising manner and is now considered to be an important element in the development of an indigenous Australian modern dance.[64]

Looking at the works of Barr and Jooss at the same historical period raises the question of how an artist should reflect a political moment as intense as this one. Jooss himself denied setting out to propagate a political message even in *The Green Table*, but his definition of 'political' was quite specifically something aiming to change the opinions of the viewer, as with agitprop.[65] Clearly Barr was in the opposite, polemical camp, absorbed in the need to communicate the political message, frequently resorting to words within her dance-dramas in order to clarify content, and using direct, sometimes unsubtle, material. If we take a broader definition than the one he used, there is clearly a way in which Jooss's work can be seen as political, dealing as he frequently did with power relations in society. *Chronica* is an example, but, as we have seen, the references to the current European situation were oblique. Interpretations of the works in line with current events could only result from the reflective participation of the audience. Both *Chronica* and *A Spring Tale* were premiered in February 1939 on tour in England at a time of international tension, which could be, and was, the preamble to war. Even in *A Spring Tale*, fairy tale though it was, perhaps the hope that continuance and balance could prevail made special sense in light of the fears of the moment. Jooss left his audience to make these connections for themselves: in the opposite camp of Barr and her associates, that would have seemed an indulgence because clarity of the ideological position was everything.

Dartington's dancers in wartime

War was declared on 3 September 1939, but the following months were marked by the relative military inactivity known as the 'phoney war'. There were, of course, immediate consequences for Dartington, including the billeting of evacuated children from London in the Dance School. After they were moved to better quarters, the army took it over. On the day war was declared, Christopher Martin interviewed all the Germans in the Arts Department in order to collect the information on nationality status and political stance towards the Nazi regime that the police might require. Laban's statement as recorded in the transcript avoided mention of his post in the administration of German dance established under Goebbels's Ministry for Popular Enlightenment and Propaganda, so that it could be interpreted that the post that he left under a cloud in 1936 was that of ballet director of the Berlin State Theatres.[66] The same is true of the Arts Department's dossier on the aliens for the use of the police. The statement is vague enough to allow assumptions to be made about his relative distance from the Nazi cultural hierarchy.[67]

The 'enemy aliens' had to give up their cameras and cars and were restricted to a five-mile radius of Dartington. Although the legal opinion of Gwatkin was that the company should be disbanded, Martin, who had previously had strong doubts about retaining it, now saw that the arts had a responsibility in wartime, which Dartington, with its special history, should be leading. Ballets Jooss, touring Britain in 1939 before embarking on the pre-arranged American tour, seemed to be both an exceptional and an exemplary case.

> This must be the first time in history that a group alien in conception and very largely alien in personnel, has travelled throughout England while England was at war with its country of origin.[68]

For the time being, the Jooss–Leeder School continued as normal with reduced numbers. Jooss stayed at Dartington rather than crossing the Atlantic with the company in December, perhaps as part of the Arts Department's strategy to reform the relationship between the two. But the war turned against Britain in May 1940 with the invasion of Holland, Belgium and France. The British Expeditionary Force fell back on Dunkirk and the enemy forces were within easy invasion distance on the other side of the English Channel. South Devon was declared a Restricted Area because of its coastline; enemy aliens had to leave and the men were interned.

This was not a glorious episode in British history. It meant that men such as Jooss, Leeder and Heckroth, who had left Germany because they were opposed to the Nazi regime, were in effect locked up, in some cases under harsh conditions and always, especially considering that these were intellectuals and artists, without the mental stimulation of their work. Jooss and Leeder were sent to the Isle of Man; Heckroth was one of the least fortunate, transported to a prisoner-of-war camp in New South Wales, Australia. Laban was able to escape internment on grounds of his ill health, although he and

Ullmann were tightly controlled in their movements. At least Dartington's aliens had powerful friends; the Elmhirsts lobbied for the internees' release through their network of contacts in high places. Without Jooss and Leeder, the remaining fifteen dance students were determined to stay on, taught in the former art studio by Pem Becker and Annetje Wijnberg, two of the Dutch Studio Group members.[69]

Following through his belief in the role of the arts in wartime, and in part because he believed the army would attempt to commandeer more buildings if the Courtyard appeared inactive, Christopher Martin planned new projects for the Arts Department. Beryl de Zoete's hand can again be seen in the decision to invite the Sadler's Wells Ballet to spend nearly a month over Christmas 1940 to rehearse Frederick Ashton's new ballet *The Wanderer*. Set and costume designs were by Graham Sutherland, who came down to Dartington in December with his sketches. The company was in urgent need of a respite; there had been the notorious escape from Holland during the invasion in May, the Blitz on London was in full force and their base at Sadler's Wells Theatre had been taken for air-raid victims. At Dartington, they let their hair down.[70] It was not the full company that went to Dartington but only the members involved in this production, about eighteen in all plus pianists. It appears that there was some sort of showing of *The Wanderer* in rehearsal dress. More significant for the Arts Department was that any financial expenditure on the dancers' keep was offset by six sold-out performances of some of their repertoire in the Barn Theatre.[71] This was achieved with a good deal of doubling-up in roles, but nevertheless the programme was a satisfying mixture of Ashton's light works *Les Patineurs* and *Façade* with canonical pieces from the ballet tradition – a special 'cut-down' version of Michel Fokine's *Les Sylphides* and the *pas de deux* from *The Sleeping Princess* performed by stars of 'the Wells', Margot Fonteyn and Robert Helpmann. Christopher Martin was pleased with the result of the residency, but no permanent connection was made with Dartington.

The position of Ballets Jooss in America was very grave. Fritz Cohen was officially director in the absence of Jooss, but his judgement was under attack from both Jooss and the Trustees. Without first alerting Jooss or the Trustees, there had been preliminary negotiations to amalgamate with other performers – Trudi Schoop, Paul Draper (who specialised in tap dancing to classical music) and Agnes de Mille – for tours of America and Australia. Jooss was particularly anxious that Schoop's genre of pantomime-cabaret would be antithetical to the Jooss style and reputation.[72] Clearly, Cohen's imperative was the survival of the group in his charge. From the other side of the Atlantic, however, the greater danger seemed to be that he was misrepresenting Ballets Jooss as independent of Dartington, or undermining the artistic credibility of the Jooss and Dartington names. Faced with the problems of wartime conditions and all that they meant financially, with the internment of Jooss, Leeder and Heckroth, and with the fact that the Trust could be left with untold financial liabilities, the strings were legally cut in August 1940 with a Form of Release by which the Trust relinquished all interest in the company.[73]

Still, the bonds with Dartington were strong. Elsa Kahl Cohen wrote in great detail to Dorothy from the gruelling South American tour. They suffered from the climate, had terrible journeys (including eight days on a bus through Colombia and Venezuela) and, chillingly for the Cohens, saw the spread of Nazi influence. Finally they reached Caracas, where the group settled together in a house, living on 'rice and bananas and bananas and rice', while they awaited visas for return to the USA.[74] Even in this condition they put on charity performances to raise funds for blitzed Plymouth.

For most of the dancers, the uncertainty of their financial position and fear of becoming stateless could only compound their frustration about the fate of their home countries, while able to fight the war only on stage in their performances of *The Green Table*, as Dutch dancer Lucas Hoving recalled.[75]

There was a brief alliance with Agnes de Mille, who choreographed *Drums Sound in Hackensack* for them, an 'Americana' piece about early Dutch settlers and Native Americans. When disbanding became inevitable for the company in New York in 1942, there was little else to do but for each person to fend for themselves. Ernst Uthoff and Rudolf Pescht, with the company since Essen days, and Uthoff's wife Lola Botka had previously departed, going to Chile to found what was to become the Chilean National Ballet. Lucas Hoving and others danced with a circus. Joy Bolton-Carter and Jack Skinner found lodgings in New York, where they could keep house and do secretarial work.[76]

Jooss and Leeder were released from internment in late 1940. Now with the support of John Maynard Keynes and with some continued support from Dartington, the Jooss–Leeder School reassembled in Cambridge, but this was not a happy time, as if the strains and frustrations since 1939 were allowed to come to the surface on being expelled from their utopia. From students' letters back to Dorothy we can get some impression of how it was: Jooss insisting they go back to basic technique and demanding more of them than they felt they could give; the cold and bad lodgings when they had been used to the comfort and freedom of Dartington. There were quarrels and departures in the heat of the moment. Some of the dancers put together an Anglo-Dutch recital group, the Modern Dance Quintet, and auditioned for commercial work.[77]

The uncertainty of the position for Jooss and Leeder must have compounded their frustrations. In March 1941 Jooss wrote movingly to Dorothy about the tensions that had arisen in their relationships with Dartington. That all-important symbol of his permanent place at Dartington, Warren

House, had been let without his knowledge. What about his belongings? He wanted a clear statement: could they return to Dartington after the war?[78] There was no clear answer at that moment because Dartington's arts policy was being realigned.

When it became clear that Keynes, now chairman of the Council for the Encouragement of Music and the Arts (CEMA), would support the re-forming of the company, some of the dancers agreed to return in spite of the dangers of crossing the Atlantic by ship. For the Cohens, however, the relationship with Jooss, which had depended on a close collaboration, had been poisoned, and there could be no return, even though they felt it their duty to help revive the repertory.[79] The company reformed at Cambridge and was able to tour Britain again, funded by CEMA and then the Arts Council of Great Britain, from 1943 until dissolution in 1947.

The balance sheet

The departure of company and School from Dartington was a final act: there was to be no return. Political events had brought about an outcome that was probably inevitable. The Arts Department's annual budget from the Trustees to fund all its activities was £10,000 plus a £5000 reserve.[80] A considerable amount of this had to be spent on the Jooss–Leeder School and Ballets Jooss. In 1937 the School's cost to the Arts Department (that is, its shortfall of income to expenditure) was £2830, which was increased to £3330 when the Studio Group was added. The situation with Ballets Jooss was even worse; from autumn 1938 to December 1939 the company lost nearly £8000. There were regular reports of the company's accounts being in overdraft, with sums paid in from the Trust as a loan. The average annual cost of School and company to the Arts Department over the six years 1934–40 was over £10,000.[81]

The two new works begun in 1938, long works with a number of costume changes, were estimated to cost £6000, which had to be largely met from the Reserve.[82] Was the company living beyond its means? This was the view of Christopher Martin and the Trust's legal adviser, Fred Gwatkin, who was looking at the idea of making Ballets Jooss into a limited-liability company, forced to sink or swim financially with a monetary advance and nothing else. Clearly Gwatkin thought that Jooss had no incentive to work within budget limits while he was drawing a steady salary and the Trust picked up all debts.[83]

By May 1938 the separation of the company from the Trust, or its closing down, were being discussed.[84] The war made the situation clearer. The remnants of the Jooss–Leeder School, refusing to leave Dartington, hoping clearly for the return of Jooss and Leeder, became an embarrassment. To Christopher Martin, this hanging on with nothing to show for it was intolerable and he was glad to be rid of them to Cambridge.[85] In spite of the financial and institutional realities, the personal bonds between the dancers and the Elmhirsts, particularly Dorothy, remained strong. They wrote warmly to her revealing the tensions of the new situation and their attachment to the Dartington they had left. In the Elmhirsts' case, the patron–artist relationship existed on more than the functionally institutional level.

Dartington's diaspora

I have argued that the Jooss–Leeder School had its main focus on the professional performance of dance. Its success in this can be measured by the flow of students into the company and also the distinguished contributions of many of those dancers in professional performance, choreography, dance pedagogy and dance notation in the decades following the 1930s. Dartington's former students moved on to North and South America, Asia, several European countries and Britain itself. I have included just a few indicative biographies here, chosen because these careers are differentiated by their unique individual creativity, but showing clearly within them the kernel of what they took from Dartington.

Birgit Cullberg left Dartington in spring 1939, preparing to create a little group of her own in Sweden with fellow students. During the 1940s she performed and choreographed and returned to ballet, which she had studied before Dartington. (She also trained later in Graham technique.) Lillian Karina, a ballet teacher in Sweden and refugee from Germany, describes her in wartime:

> One of her dance evenings awakened new hope in me, for in it I saw a dancer who recognized the danger of National Socialism and gave that anger expression in dance. An antifascist and pacifist, Birgit Cullberg brilliantly embodied Swedish humanism.[86]

As she gained experience, Cullberg went further in the integration of ballet technique into a modern dance sensibility than Jooss had done, and the works with which she made her early impact as a choreographer – *Miss Julie*, *Medea* (both 1950), *Moon Reindeer* (1957) – could best be classified as modern ballet, using the full range of balletic technique, broadened by modern dance movement material and with the advanced understanding of choreutics and eukinetics she received at Dartington. When Mary Skeaping became director of the Royal Swedish Ballet in 1953, she brought Sweden's innovative modern dance choreographers into the fold to choreograph for the national ballet company, including Cullberg as choreographer in residence for several years.[87] Skeaping's ability to see the dance world as integrated rather than fragmented by genres and techniques may at least in some part have been generated or confirmed by summer-school experience at Dartington. Like Jooss, Cullberg produced choreography emphasising dramatic content, with meaning embedded in eloquent dance images. Her name continues through the medium of the Cullberg Ballet (one of the companies Jooss allowed to perform *The Green Table*), now one of Europe's major dance companies.

Amongst the dancers scattered by war were two women who have been instrumental in the international spread of Labanotation, Ann Hutchinson and Dai Ailian.[88] Ann Hutchinson (now Ann Hutchinson Guest) arrived at Dartington at the age of seventeen in 1936, an American who had been brought up in Britain. She developed a particular strength in 'Script' and when her course was over she was retained, nominally as a member of the Studio Group, but principally to make the first notations of *The Green Table*. This she completed, as well as *Big City*, *A Ball in Old Vienna* and *Pavane* (with tears dripping down her cheeks, she still insists, because she really wanted to be a dancer).[89] The international crisis resulted in her taking the ship to New York in December 1939, alongside the company. The Jooss–Leeder training had not developed her body as a technical instrument to the degree necessary for commercial work; but training intensively in ballet, Graham and other modern dance techniques enabled her to work professionally on Broadway for eight years, including in Hanya Holm's choreography of *Kiss Me Kate*, which she also notated and with which she returned to Britain as Holm's assistant in 1951. Meanwhile she had co-founded the Dance Notation Bureau in New York and introduced Labanotation in the Dance Department of the Juilliard School, New York, where Fritz Cohen was head of opera. Since her earliest dance scores for Jooss, Hutchinson Guest has become an internationally recognised notation expert. Based in London again since 1962, she published prolifically on notation and founded the Language of Dance Centre, promoting her own development of dance pedagogy, integrating the creative study of movement with the learning of notation symbols.

Dai Ailian was from a Chinese family resident in Trinidad for three generations. As a middle-class child, she had learnt ballet at home, and continued to train in ballet when the family moved to London. There she also found that modern dance gave her a wider means of expression; she studied with Leslie Burrowes and performed in recitals with Ernest Berk, another Wigman trained dancer/teacher, although she was often typecast as an 'oriental'. Seeing Ballets Jooss convinced her that she wanted to be able to dance with the company. She came to Dartington for Summer School 1939 and stayed on to join the regular classes. Here she found a much more profound way of analysing dynamics and space than she had found with the Wigman technique – and she also discovered notation.

Paradoxically, the war gave her the opportunity to travel even while movement restrictions were happening all around her. Feeling the call of the
motherland she had never seen and whose languages she could not speak,
Dai was able to get transport to China through a charity repatriating Chinese
students. This placed her in the midst of the Sino-Japanese War and subsequently the civil war between nationalists and communists. Her ability to
notate and disseminate national dances was used by the communist authorities to establish the Chinese cultural identity of their revolution. She became
the director of the new Beijing Academy of Dance in 1954, which included
ballet and indigenous dance forms in its syllabus. With difficulty, she survived the Cultural Revolution, when everything intellectual or Western was
condemned as counter-revolutionary; she was sent to the countryside to perform manual work. After 1976 she was able to re-establish ballet and
Labanotation in China.[90]

The Dutch dancer, Lucas Hoving, came to the Jooss–Leeder School in
1937, having already danced in recitals in Holland and Belgium with the
radical Florrie Rodrigo and with Yvonne Georgi (who had been in Jooss's
company in Münster). He was taken into Ballets Jooss in 1939, but disband-
ment in New York offered up new opportunities, including training at the
Graham studio and performing with her company in *Letter to the World*
(1940). He joined the Dutch Army in exile and danced for his living while
awaiting D-Day. After the war, he had a significant performing career in the
USA, especially with José Limón's company and as a choreographer, subsequently with a company of his own. He also became an inspiring teacher,
using some of the Laban-based concepts from the Jooss–Leeder School in his
own pedagogy. Some of Dartington's later dancers gravitated to the Rotterdam Dance Academy (see page 181) when he was its director (1971–78).
Returning to America, this time to to the West Coast, he created the Lucas
Hoving Performance Group, a group of San Francisco dancers, both amateur
and professional.[91]

Even in these few names it can be demonstrated that the Jooss–Leeder
influence from Dartington became a far-flung and significant phenomenon.
Far afield also, the Elmhirsts were involved in a dance project in India, quite
separate from the Arts Department. Uday Shankar's visits to Dartington,
with which this chapter began, took place at a time when his fame was at its
height outside India; at the same time, within India, dance was being re-
claimed from its former disreputable associations, the classical dance forms
becoming the gold standard of India's heritage and future identity. Dance
training at respected institutions was the key. It was happening at Tagore's
university, Visva Bharati, and at the dancer Rukmini Devi's Kalakshetra,
opened in 1936.

Passing on the dance was a priority for Shankar too. This was brought to fruition in good part because Beatrice Straight was so impressed by him, both as man and artist. She had imbibed her mother's instinct about the intersection of money and art. Coming into her own trust fund in 1931 at the age of seventeen, she instantly become a patron in her own right, endowing scholarships at the Cornish School. After Shankar's first appearance at Dartington, she went travelling with him in India. In spite of later enthusiasms such as the Chekhov Theatre Studio at Dartington, for which she paid running costs, she continued to support his vision of establishing his own training centre in India. The Uday Shankar India Culture Centre opened in 1938, supported by a Trust, with Beatrice, Dorothy and Leonard as trustees and part of the endowment coming from Beatrice's own money. The curriculum included the classical dance forms, bharata natyam, kathakali and manipuri. In line with Shankar's own aesthetic, crafts and music were also an essential part of the development of the complete Indian dancer.

Unfortunately, the Centre was another victim of wartime conditions, falling foul of financial problems, price increases in India and the restriction on money-making tours for Shankar. Naively perhaps, the chosen place was at Simtola in Almora, a beautiful, mountainous area, but impractical in the long term because of the cost of bringing in services including water, of which there was no natural source, and it was difficult to build communications to the outside world. With all these problems, the Centre closed down in 1944, with the trustees' encouragement that it should be reopened as soon as possible in or near a major city. This never happened.

Shankar became immersed in writing and directing a major film project, *Kalpana* (1948). It reflected on problems of the new India being born in the fight for independence. His narrative critically depicted the pretensions of urban Indian businessmen. A model of a projected new factory dissolved into Shankar's danced dream sequence, *Labour and Machinery*, a dystopic vision of workers enslaved by machinery that bears some resemblance to movement sequences in Fritz Lang's *Metropolis* (1927). There is also perhaps a flavour here of Jooss's modernist rejection of the socially divided and mechanistic modern city in *Big City* (see page 85).[92] Shankar is more than likely to have seen it during his time at Dartington, but we should not be too hasty in assuming a direct connection. Such ideas were part of the European culture in which he was moving as an art student and dancer in the 1920s and 1930s. Indeed, this whole topic must also have resonated with Gandhi's rejection of Indian urbanisation and industrialisation in favour of village life, homespun clothing and self-sufficiency.

Although the Almora Centre had a brief history, it was significant as an instance, like Santiniketan, of the personalised endeavours of Indian artists towards the revival of a national culture and its reintegration into Indian consciousness. Almora's students went out to populate the first post-Independence generation of dance artists, and Shankar's reputation remains secure as one of the pioneers of twentieth-century dance in India. In 1955 he became the first Dean of Dance in the Academy for Dance, Drama and Music in Calcutta.

So Dartington's patronage of dance had widespread geographical consequences; but did all that activity and financial commitment kick-start modern dance on the concert stage in Britain? Even while Jooss and Leeder seemed quite secure at Dartington in the 1930s, the previous waves of Dartington dance were busy in London. For most of the 1930s, London had a potential for modern dance development. The Laban, Wigman and Bodenwieser strands of European modern dance were represented in independent studios (including that of Leslie Burrowes) and even in mainstream dancing schools. If the pages of *The Dancing Times* are any indication, this interest had declined markedly by the end of the decade; this style of dance was no longer a novelty and the connections with Germany could not have helped.[93] Margaret Barr's activities have already been noted. Louise Soelberg went to London on leaving Ballets Jooss in 1937, teaching at the London School of Dalcroze Eurhythmics and in her own studio. In 1938 Soelberg and Burrowes teamed up to open a joint studio, The Dance Centre, where alongside classes they rehearsed a dance group and instituted a programme of lectures, which included Douglas Kennedy of the English Folk Dance and Song Society and Kurt Jooss. This initiative, too, was cut short by the war. Soelberg also worked with the actors of Unity Theatre, a 'speed-up' section at the beginning of the 'living newspaper', *Busmen* (1938), and an impressive choreographed finale to *The Star Turns Red* (1940), depicting Red Guards in combat to the music of Alan Bush.[94] Her wartime work would mainly be devoted to movement with actors in Basil Langton's Travelling Repertory Theatre, as well as dancing her recital pieces in their lunchtime concerts.

The two directors of the Jooss–Leeder School continued to have a tangible effect on British dance but were ultimately to return to Europe. The reformed Ballets Jooss performed with CEMA and Arts Council funding from 1943, but it was too much a conception of the wider world and perhaps also the pre-war world to become an established British company, and disbanded in 1947. After a time in Chile, working with his former dancers the Uthoffs and Pescht, Jooss returned to Essen and a long career as a choreographer and particularly as a pedagogue, forming a new generation of German modern dancers: this is where his influence is felt most strongly today.

Leeder remained longer in Britain. The Sigurd Leeder Studio in London attracted British students much more successfully than the Dartington school had done, but there was now no Ballets Jooss or similar company for graduates to join. There was teaching, commercial work and a limited dance recital culture. Dancers such as Yoma Sasburgh and Annetje Wijnberg, Jooss–Leeder School students who had stayed on at Dartington and rejoined Jooss at Cambridge, had a patchwork career after Ballets Jooss, on the commercial stage and in their own occasional recitals. When Leeder left his school in 1959 to work in Chile and finally Switzerland, a former Dartington student, Simone Michelle, became one of the directors. The school was to close in 1967; the centre of Leeder's work was now in Switzerland and the focus of attention in modern dance, both in London and Dartington, had turned to American dance techniques.

The remnants of Dartington's vibrant dance of the 1930s struggled on in the fragmented and largely self-motivated concert dance performance scene in the 1940s and 1950s, but was formative and preparatory for the explosion of modern dance in the 1960s, which will be discussed in Chapter 5.[95]

Patronage, community and art

The Jooss–Leeder period corresponds to the early years of the Arts Department and of the Dartington Hall Trust that endowed it, when Dartington was moving from a personal patronage of the arts, supplied by the Elmhirsts, to an institutional one centred on the Arts Department. However, there was not a sharp transition from the personal to the institutional and there were both official and unofficial channels through which artists could be supported with Dorothy's money. Her New York grant-giving committee headed by Anna Bogue was later institutionalised under the name of the William C. Whitney Foundation. In Britain, the Dartington Hall Trust became the financial organ for the estate and its activities, including the subsidised Arts Department. Elmgrant was the trust for awarding other grants in Britain. However, none of this stopped Dorothy giving money as an independent patron when she felt moved to do so. One documented example is the £1000 she promised to Marie Rambert in 1947 in order to tide over the period between Ballet Rambert's Sadler's Wells season and their long tour to Australia.[96]

The Arts Department at Dartington was set up as a way of institutionalising the policy and finance of arts activities. In order to work properly, institutions must be able to act independently and establish constraints and rules within their remit. This was what Christopher Martin was trying to do, but he had to remain cautious in the light of what the Elmhirsts wanted or else to persuade them as Trustees to support his views. The signs are that Dorothy, with her instincts as an independent patron, was inclined to undermine the authority of the Arts Department as an institution, and was open to direct appeals over the head of the Arts Department's administrator. She was, according to Jooss, always ready to take his part, inviting him in 1938 to indicate anything he needed. This resulted in a further enlargement of the

Dance School.[97] It was not until 1944 that the Arts Department's then acting administrator, Peter Cox, confronted her about her tendency to make her own arrangements and expect someone else to tidy up the consequences.[98] He won the day and it could be said that this was when the Arts Department began to acquire its independent institutional identity and authority.

I have argued above that the end of Dartington's patronage of the Jooss–Leeder organisation was probably inevitable on financial grounds, even had it not been for the outbreak of war. Support for Jooss and Leeder had been pushed forward by the enthusiasm of the Elmhirsts: they wanted to support the Jooss work, which they believed to be artistically important, articulating significant issues of the decade. At the same time, they were looking for a professional arts community of high artistic merit – Mark Tobey, Cecil Collins, Michael Chekhov, Bernard Leach, Jooss and Leeder were equal elements of that ideal community. The dance components, however, had turned out to be hugely expensive. As Trustees, the Elmhirsts were fully aware of the financial implications. It is less certain how strongly they felt that their initial vision of community engagement had not been served. Perhaps they had turned away from dance to some extent, since Dorothy had become so involved with Chekhov.

In spite of these concerns, the Jooss-Leeder organisation was still very much to the fore when, in early 1939, the Arts Department went through another reshaping, partly as a result of the departure of the Chekhov Studio. Jooss's suggestion of employing Hans Oppenheim, a German opera conductor, as director of music for the Arts Department had been followed up. There was now an 'Arts Council' of principals in the Department, meeting monthly to discuss financial needs and the equal sharing of resources, consisting of Jooss, Leeder, Heckroth, Fritz Cohen, Oppenheim and Martin. Heckroth was now director of the Art Studios just officially set up and was looking to take on students to work with him, as well as Cecil Collins and Willi Soukop. (Dorothy seems to have been very keen to develop the visual arts at this point.) Oppenheim was to head an opera studio, and its first production, of Handel's *Rodelinda*, produced by Fritz Cohen, choreographed by Jooss and designed by Heckroth, was premiered at the Old Vic to encourage interest in the new venture. Was this a new beginning full of possibility, or a haven for the vestiges of Weimar theatre to continue along previous lines? Evidently, Christopher Martin felt he needed to counter this criticism in his administrator's report of May 1939, the last of peacetime. Referring both to *Rodelinda* and to Jooss's new works *Chronica* and *A Spring Tale*, he contended that Dartington was bringing forth something new, 'which is neither German nor English'.[99] That ideal could not last more than a few months.[100]

So in early 1939 there was a resurgence of the culture of the Courtyard. Moreover, this seems to have been a moment when engagement of the professional artists at community level was gaining a high priority once more. From the artists' studios, where Mark Tobey had long set an example in his belief that creativity could be drawn out of everybody, came Heckroth's exhortation for everyone to become involved in art, and that the boundaries between professional and amateur were breaking down.[101]

At the same time, Rudolf Laban was attempting to get Leonard's attention about a plan for achieving a community arts culture in dance. Laban wrote to Leonard in March 1939 at Jooss's suggestion; Leonard had apparently expressed some interest in 'modern community dance ... the new way of our body-mind training for laymen'.[102] Laban's letter was accompanied by some essays relating to the lay dance movement in Germany and Ullmann's work in Plymouth and by a document by Laban laying out 'The Practical Outlook' – a plan for an 'Educational centre for layman dance' to exist alongside the current Jooss–Leeder School, to train 'teachers and leaders of movement choruses and community dance groups'. The teachers of this centre and their students would give classes for amateurs and form community dance groups in Dartington, the surrounding countryside and neighbouring towns. Clearly this was not an opportune moment for such a new establishment to be contemplated. I will take up Laban's ideas more thoroughly in the next chapter.

Wartime brought upon Dartington a time to reassess its future in the arts and in dance. Martin put a paper before the Trustees in 1941, outlining a new direction for Dartington to follow. The most startling aspect of his plan was that it drew a line under the past and presented a volte-face compared with his report of 1934. There could be no more grandiose schemes for performing companies bearing the name of Dartington. As a rural location, it was impractical because first-rate artists needed to be based in London, and furthermore there was too much of a financial gamble involved. The artistic life of the region had not been served either, because great artists were not necessarily good at communicating with amateurs. He recognised now that work with the local community was a speciality in its own right and his previous notion of it being a natural fallout from the professional work was discounted, although not in so many words.

The alternative to the past was in its way quite revolutionary: the arts could best be served at Dartington by building the Arts Department into an educational centre that could train the teachers who would be needed to take the arts to the countryside around. He envisioned four schools, in dance, drama, music and painting. The first three would have a small performing group, giving experience to the students and serving the local area. Crucially, students would work as teachers in the community. It may have been coincidence or linked to a memory of Laban's documents, but Martin's new arts policy made some similar points. As Laban had done, he stated that teachers of amateurs and professionals needed a different training and outlook, and that students should work in outreach activities in amateur arts. Although the ideas did not come to fruition quite as he imagined, especially not in dance, this plan set in train the development of the Arts Centre, which would blossom into Dartington College of Arts and the integration of dance into higher education that Leonard had seen as a possibility in 1934.

Now that the most ambitious period of the arts in Courtyard culture was over, was it a major disappointment to the Elmhirsts after all the planning and the high hopes, not to mention the expenditure? It does not appear so. According to some, Leonard had a 'fatalistic' attitude to the results of experiment. Apparently this was rooted in a visit from a scientific consultant who had encouraged him to see agricultural experiments, not in terms of success or failure, but in terms of positive and negative results from which he could learn.[103] It was also an aspect of the Elmhirsts' patronage that the programme and people they supported at any one time were of less importance than Dartington itself as the idealisation of core standards – a sound rural economy, a sense of community, liberal education for life. The means to these ends were flexible. Dartington passed easily on to new projects.

Chapter 4

Spreading the Art of Movement, Raising the Art of Dance

In movement we shall have to create a demand, since an understanding of
the place movement and dance ought to play has hardly begun. There are
isolated examples – the success of Miss Ullmann's work is one; the L.C.C.
and the Leicester L.E.A. are others. Even our own Authority in Devon is
beginning to be interested.
Christopher Martin, 1941[1]

By the end of the 1930s, Dartington's dance was poised at a historically
interesting point. Almost by default, the Trust had acquired a front-line set of
dance practitioners representing several strands of European modern dance.
The theatrical and pedagogic strand of Jooss and Leeder, well established at
Dartington by then, was nevertheless, as I have argued, in danger on
grounds of cost. They may have been quite unaware of this, focused as they
were on the artistic work in hand. Lisa Ullmann, who was also part of their
professional dance training team, had been developing amateur dance work
in Plymouth based upon the layman dance methods of the Laban Schools in
central Europe. The arrival of Rudolf Laban as a guest in 1938 represented
the fountainhead of all this work, but most particularly his personal drive to
uncover and document the principles of movement expression was present
in ongoing research at Dartington. He worked practically with Ullmann in
the small studio at Warren House and elsewhere and was given a workshop,
where he drew and modelled the dynamic space of the moving body. As
previously recounted (see page 128), Laban and Ullmann put their heads
together, so to speak, in order to try to persuade Leonard, and through him
the Trust, to open a school for training practitioners in the lay dance work.

It could be said that, in early 1939, several different futures for
Dartington's dance were on the table. Would Jooss and Leeder, Laban and
Ullmann carry on as before or would hard economic decisions have to be
made? Would the axe fall and, if so, where? Would a place be found for the
Laban/Ullmann proposal?

Here speculation must cease, since we know that the impending war created specific constraints; but it does nevertheless indicate what possibilities
existed for Dartington at this time. The future of Jooss and Leeder, the company and school, was sketched out in the previous chapter. Now the present
chapter turns attention towards Laban and Ullmann within the climate of
post-war Britain and a new role for Dartington. The war years also brought
about a change of leadership in the Arts Department that would be highly

significant for the future. Peter Cox came originally to Dartington as Christopher Martin's guest to recuperate from the stress of appearing before a tribunal as a conscientious objector to service in the armed forces. Soon he was helping Christopher Martin, who was in poor health. When Martin died of tuberculosis in 1944, Cox became the Arts Administrator and would remain in place over the next four decades, providing a remarkable continuity of purpose and a bridge between the world of the Elmhirst founders and the harsher economics of the 1980s.

In this chapter, through the lens of Dartington, I will link together two of the issues that structured the dance of the post-war period. The first is the development of educational and amateur (lay) dance based on the work of Rudolf Laban; the second is the coming of state-funded, subsidised dance in the theatre through the Arts Council of Great Britain. These represent diametrically opposed notions of the function of dance in society. In the first, dance is an instinctual expression within the abilities of every human and exists for the satisfaction of the individual's need for expression and communication. In the second, dance has to satisfy the highest standards of spectacle and execution; it exists for the admiration of the public. My chapter title is taken from the 'Raise or Spread' debate within the Arts Council in the early 1950s. That argument reflected the perceived polarity between providing the arts for all as a right (to 'Spread'), both as amateur arts and as the geographical spread of the professional arts, and its opposite (to 'Raise') focusing money on metropolitan 'powerhouse' institutions such as opera houses in order to advance the standard of presentation generally through example. I suggest it as both a context and an analogy for what was happening at Dartington during the 1930s and after.

The notion that these two, Raising and Spreading, are inimical was embedded in the controversies around the School of Dance-Mime and the Jooss–Leeder School. Spreading dance to the community of amateur participants catered for by the School of Dance-Mime seemed to preclude high standards when that work was put on as public performance, while raising professional standards at the Jooss-Leeder School had taken the focus away from widespread access and participation and put up barriers against the community expressing itself through dance performance. But there was the possibility of a middle way. In 1941, when he suggested that small schools for visual arts, drama, dance and music professionals could also enliven the amateur arts locally, Christopher Martin had some idea that successful blending of the two was possible. The Arts Council's policies on 'Raise or Spread' would also have a direct impact on the development of Dartington as a regional performance centre from the 1950s onwards.

To understand the 'Raise or Spread' debate, we need to go back to the Arts Council's origins in the early 1940s.[2] The Council for the Encouragement of

Music and the Arts (CEMA) was created in 1940 as an organisation to bring recreation through the arts to the civilian population. The initial decision to fund such a measure came from the Pilgrim Trust, a grant-giving body dispensing money originally endowed by an American millionaire for the support of British heritage and culture. That grant was matched by the Treasury via the Ministry of Education budget. This is the first example of central government subsidising 'the arts' in Britain, although there had previously been individual high-profile expenditures – on the collections and buildings of the National Gallery and British Museum, for example – and the British Council had been set up in 1934 to showcase British language and culture abroad. The Pilgrim Trust's subsidy was only for the first two years. When it withdrew, the Government was left as sole provider for the national arts funding body.

During the war years, the British population was badly in need of distraction from reality. CEMA's original policy was to encourage amateur music and drama, as well as offering professional concerts, plays and exhibitions, often in places of work or factory workers' hostels. 'Music Travellers' and drama organisers were appointed to facilitate the development of local instrumental groups, choirs and drama groups. Although beginning in this populist mode of laying great emphasis on participation, CEMA's nature changed during its first few years as other views became more prominent. It was argued that the Government's funds, which were not lavish, would be better used in upholding standards of execution and by introducing as many of the public as possible to the best in professional arts. This was certainly the view of John Maynard Keynes. By the time he became Chairman in 1942, the amateur side of the work was already being absorbed by adult education bodies, a trend that he continued. Keynes had long been a supporter of the involvement of government in subsidising the arts. Just as governments ought to intervene directly in the economic system in order to maintain full employment and thus social cohesion, they should support 'the civilising arts of life' in order to replace the patronage of the rich in a more equitable society.[3] This belief in access to the arts as an aspect of democracy was one component of the growing political consensus of the war years that gave birth to the Welfare State, the 1944 Education Act and the perception that the war had swept away the old social hierarchies. In 1946, CEMA was transformed into a new organisation, the Arts Council of Great Britain, with Keynes as its first Chairman.

However, the interaction of financially powerful individuals with the arts establishment is multilayered and sometimes obscure, ranging from the direct subsidising of artists, and the self-interest of buying art works or theatre tickets, to non-financial encouragement and creation of a context that can inform the taste for a particular kind of work. In the context of the

Dartington project, one can see the spontaneous arts patronage coming from Dorothy gradually being replaced by institutions – the Arts Department, the Elmgrant Trust, the William C. Whitney Foundation. Perhaps it might appear from this that the moment of the private patron had passed. However, not only did Dorothy still make grants personally, but her taste and interests were still guiding forces for the institutionalised Dartington.[4] The late twentieth century also showed that a satisfactory funding structure for the arts needed to be achieved on many levels: national and local government subsidy and private, commercial and charitable giving.

From its outset, CEMA's definition of 'the arts' was a restricted one, clearly loaded towards the 'fine arts' and defined quite separately from popular arts, crafts and film. Music, drama and visual arts were the core areas of activity. It also supported national tours of the Sadler's Wells Ballet, Ballet Rambert and Ballets Jooss, but dance was to sit uncomfortably between drama and music departments for decades to come. In collaboration with the research institute Political and Economic Planning (PEP) and the Nuffield College Social Reconstruction Survey, the Arts Department at Dartington took on the responsibility of directing a national Arts Enquiry, intended to inform postwar planning for the arts. The results of this were variable: reports on *The Visual Arts* and *Music* were not published until 1947 and 1949 respectively, after the Arts Council was created, and the report on theatre had to be abandoned. However, it may be that the prestige of the whole undertaking and the people involved had positive benefits for Dartington, and the ideas discussed fed into post-war thinking on the subsidised arts.

By the time the Arts Council was created, any idea of subsidising the amateur arts had dropped out of view. Nevertheless, 'spreading' remained an important dimension in the sense that CEMA and the early Arts Council were aware of a moral duty to spread the fruits of the subsidised arts as widely as possible amongst the taxpayers who were the ultimate source of the subsidy. Regional offices were set up using the existing Civil Defence regions as a model; this structure was to provide for provincial needs and form a conduit for the voice of the regions. However, in the early 1950s the official policy statements of the Arts Council gradually withdrew from the commitment to accessibility in favour of the 'powerhouse' strategy, where prioritising finance for exemplary institutions such as the opera and ballet houses at Covent Garden and Sadler's Wells, drama at the Old Vic and certain orchestras was seen as fulfilling a more general function because standards in these institutions influenced standards in the whole country. Simultaneously with the outbreak of the 'Raise or Spread' debate, the Arts Council closed down all its regional offices in England between 1950 and 1956. The fact that the 'powerhouses' of culture were mainly located in the capital made this an issue with political ramifications in the regions. The 'Raise or

Spread' debate made the Arts Council politically vulnerable so that, in spite of a large proportion of its budget being spent on the London 'powerhouses' (for example, 31.8 per cent of the total grant-in-aid was spent on the Royal Opera House in the financial year 1954/55), it had to continue making small gestures of support for regional venues and local tours.

The coming of the first state subsidising of the arts mirrored at the national level some of Dartington's local dilemmas: the apparent dichotomy between amateur and professional arts; the tension between serving the creativity of the local population and offering a high level of excellent arts for them to consume; the change from personal to institutional patronage; and the problem of furthering the arts in a region far from London. Christopher Martin's idea in 1941 was to steer a course that would merge high standards in a regional setting with local provision. The financial platform on which this would be based would be teacher training. Students of music, drama, dance and painting, would also go out as artists-in-the-making to stimulate the arts locally. This plan clearly had flaws, not the least of which was the old problem of finding artists who could combine standards of excellence in execution and in teaching. Nevertheless, the proposal would ultimately lead to Dartington College of Arts.

From the quotation heading this chapter, it can be seen that, even with Dartington's impressive record, Christopher Martin saw dance as being in the rearguard of arts development. CEMA's strategy for the amateur arts was to send out Music Travellers and drama organisers, not dance teachers. The demand had not grown sufficiently yet, although he could already see the potential for dance teachers in local authority schools. In 1941 dance was still on the institutional agenda at Dartington, even though the wartime evacuation had taken Jooss and Leeder into internment and then to Cambridge, and Ullmann and Laban to evacuation in London and then to Wales. Dartington had not given up on them, although they could be said to be at arm's length. Nevertheless, there was still sporadic dance activity at Dartington. The growing interest in arts education, including dance, amongst local education authorities was the context for some early attempts to deliver courses to teachers.

In 1940 a weekend teachers' course in the arts was held for primary school teachers, with Jenny Gertz introducing movement work alongside music, drama (taught by Dorothy) and life-classes in drawing by Cecil Collins. Gertz was another Laban student who had arrived at Dartington as a refugee. In Germany she had been well known for her movement choir work with children, especially in the reform school supported by the Social Democratic Party. Her children's group was photographed in 1926, sexually mature adolescents, male and female, dancing naked together. Such exposure could only be acceptable within that body-culture with its connotations of the healthy, natural, socialised body. She clearly adjusted her practice to her new environment in Britain.[5] In Totnes she was in demand with the arrival of evacuee children from London, disorientated and even difficult as some of them would have been. In an essay, she described working with them through the school holiday period, first using exploratory movements with all parts of the body, then bringing in spatial directions and group work. At the end of the holiday, they all clamoured to do their dance, *Snowflakes*, for the last time. People found it impressive to see how much the children had improved in discipline and initiative.[6] She also gave children's classes at Dartington. Photographs show improvisation in the open-air theatre with the stimulus of 'elastics' and 'eyes closed'. A duo works on contact with different parts of the body and a girl in a tunic dances dramatically, kneeling, stretching and lying languidly on the grass.[7]

As Christopher Martin looked around for a new policy for the Arts Department in the early years of the war, CEMA's programme immediately presented Dartington with new possibilities. CEMA's Music Travellers were peripatetic musicians with the job of encouraging amateur music-making of all kinds. This fitted right in with Martin's new vision for Dartington, with amateur arts springing from the work of professionals. Imogen Holst, daughter of the composer Gustav Holst, was appointed Music Traveller in the region in 1942, cementing a close relationship with Dartington. Soon, and until her departure in 1951, she was giving Dartington all of her attention, stimulating a vibrant musical life. She also took on students to train as rural music teachers – Martin's vision of the practice of the arts alongside teacher training. For the next decade the possibility of a similar dance department hung in the air.

A later teachers' course was 'The Teacher and the Arts', hosted by Dartington for the Devon County Education Committee in 1949. Intended as a stimulus and broadening of horizons rather than outlining teaching methods, it offered participants 'dance movement', singing, play reading, and painting, with concerts and a few lectures. The staff was predominantly a Dartington one: Imogen Holst for music, Laban and Ullmann for movement, Dorothy working on play reading. There were also concerts by the Amadeus String Quartet, which had a strong link with Dartington. Visual arts were in the hands of Clifford and Rosemary Ellis from the Corsham Court teacher training section of Bath Academy of Art. This establishment became strongly influential on the development of Dartington as an educational establishment, since it had already been able to set up a recognised teacher training course but insisted upon the complete artistic development of any student who was to become a teacher. That idea resonated well with what Dartington had learned through Imogen Holst and would continue to be the ideal that would structure future development (Chapter 5).

The Arts Council's policy on dance was virtually static in its development until the late 1950s. Meanwhile, however, away from the exclusively professional concerns of the Arts Council, dance was of growing interest to the educational establishment.

The Dance as Education

The concept of dance as an educational subject, part of every child's experience at school, had twin roots. One was from European modern dance with its tradition of popular participation; the other was the British context where dance and childhood development had been an immediate concern of the pioneers of Hellenic dance, Madge Atkinson, Ruby Ginner and Margaret Morris. When the Jooss–Leeder School arrived at Dartington in 1934, there was already a European modern dance presence in London. In fact a Laban student, Anny Boalth, had given a lecture demonstration in May 1932 at Dartington, with the help of students from the School of Dance-Mime. By 1935, both she and Anny Fligg, from the Hertha Feist School in Berlin, were advertising their Laban Schools in London. Käte Eisenstädt, also a Laban student, was mentioned in the previous chapter. Besides Leslie Burrowes, there were other former Wigman students, Alice Gillette and Ernest and Lotte Berk. Vienna-trained Bodenwieser dancers were also in evidence – Jeanette Rutherston, Trudl Dubsky, Helen Elton and Lilian Harmel. Drama schools and teacher training colleges were becoming interested: Anny Fligg taught at the Royal Academy of Dramatic Art, where she deeply impressed the young (soon to be avant-garde) actor/director Joan Littlewood.[8]

There was an established interest in dance in some teacher training colleges specialising in physical education for girls. The previous standards, especially for girls and in primary schools, had been much influenced by the 'Swedish gymnastics' of Per Hendrik Ling. There were sound anatomical and physiological principles, but presentation was regimented and there was no place for spontaneous discovery. At Bedford College of Physical Education, expressive dancing in Hellenic style had been on the curriculum for some time. A member of staff, Freda Colwill, was sent to Bodenwieser's school in Vienna in 1930 and returned to introduce the subject. Jeanette Rutherston, who had previously studied with Margaret Morris, also went to Vienna after her course at Bedford College.[9] Another member of the Bedford staff, Joan Goodrich, encountered Leslie Burrowes at the Buxton Summer School in 1932. She studied with Burrowes in London and with Wigman in Dresden and continued to bring the central European influence into the curriculum at Bedford. The influence of Wigman and Bodenwieser in the early 1930s may well be related to their respective 1928 and 1929 first performances in London, Wigman's 1932 recitals and Bodenwieser's courses in London in 1933 and 1934.

In 1938 yet another Bedford, Burrowes and Wigman student, Diana Jordan, published *The Dance as Education*, probably the first book to take up this topic in Britain. Her chief concern was to identify dance in school as both creative and an art form, distinguishing it from the usual kinds of physical training. She emphasised the free use of the imagination, the mutual nurturing of mind and body and the importance of cooperative movement tasks in social training. In case anyone should think she was advocating unrestrained self-expression, she emphasised that movement choices must be guided by certain 'laws': for example, sensitivity, rhythm, the flow of energy and form. Dance was to take its place in education on the basis of its practical value for the life skills it could impart – self-control, self-knowledge and self-expression certainly, but also communication and the awareness and tolerance of others. The context in which she was writing was the increased interest in physical fitness in the 1930s, especially amongst women; the Women's League of Health and Beauty was making a big impact, and Sali Löbel successfully launched her Everywoman's Health Movement in London. Jordan's final declaration can be seen as an attempt to situate dance within the cult of exercise but offering much more – 'individual harmony', 'harmonious co-operation', 'creative and progressive forms of physical activity', 'true physical education as opposed to physical training'.[10]

This idea that education was something more than rote learning was gaining ground within the state system, with some encouragement from the experiments that had already taken place in exclusive schools such as Dartington. In 1939 even *The Dancing Times* was made aware of the significant difference between teaching syllabus work, with the emphasis on talented students, and teaching dancing as a part of a general and enlightened education. Miss Gwatkin, 'a former Chairman of the Headmistresses Association', addressed members of the Royal Academy of Dancing on the subject. As reported by The Sitter Out, she said:

in widening your field from the consideration of dancing for the stage, which presupposes an audience, and, moreover, pupils of special gifts, to dancing for all as a means of development, your aim is different and *reorientation of your ideas will be imperative.* [italics as in original][11]

The point, as she ably demonstrated in her main image, was what 'teaching Mary dancing' was to mean:

do you teach Dancing, I say, and incidentally Mary, or do you set out to teach Mary, *her whole self*, through Dancing as an important part, but only a part of her general education [?]

It has to be said, though, that when Miss Gwatkin was invited to expand on her ideas in a full article, she did not display any knowledge of developments already happening in dance at places such as Bedford, and the idea that Mary might have her own creativity to offer was totally missing.[12]

The first half of the 1940s would be a major period of expansion of interest in dance as a creative educational subject. Without diminishing the roles of any other personalities involved, it can be seen how much the partnership of Rudolf Laban and Lisa Ullmann was a catalyst. Laban had not been interned as an enemy alien but was required to leave Dartington in June 1940. By this time the alliance between Laban and Ullmann was firmly established and she accompanied him, giving up her Plymouth classes (which had restarted after she had been reclassified as a 'friendly alien') and, it may be presumed, any thought that she might be left to direct the Jooss–Leeder School while both men were interned.[13]

Some pre-history on Ullmann gives a perspective to her decision. Unlike Jooss and Leeder, she had not been a performer but had come up through the Laban schools system, firstly at Lotte Wedekind's Berlin Laban school, where she qualified to teach layman dancers. After two years' practical work and a course of higher study at Laban's Choreographisches Institut, she obtained the professional Laban Diploma. She also had some classical ballet training with Viktor Gsovsky. In 1930 she had been invited to join the staff in Essen. No doubt, as with so many other of Laban's students, she had been drawn to his charisma and was inclined to be swayed by his opinions, but there is evidence that, even before Laban had arrived at Dartington, she wanted to devote herself to a new project of her own devising. As Leslie Burrowes had found before, Dorothy was the sympathetic and encouraging listener to whom she unburdened herself.[14] She had already made links with people in education through her WEA classes in Plymouth and also through giving a course to teachers at Exeter University. She was a practical teacher, charming and humorous and an excellent networker. While Ullmann accepted Laban's leadership wholeheartedly, she expressed to Dorothy her sense that his arrival seemed an intervention of fate on her behalf that would make her own future plan possible. Her personal ability and experience must also have been appreciated by Laban: this much is apparent from the scheme he put before Leonard in March 1939. (There will be a fuller discussion later in the chapter.)

The first evacuation for the couple was to the Elmhirsts' own apartment in London. While there, Ullmann taught a course at the Dance Centre studio of Leslie Burrowes and Louise Soelberg, which brought her to the attention of the former Burrowes student Diana Jordan.[15]

We should remember that teachers with experience of the Continental modern dance schools – Jordan, Goodrich and their peers – were already making inroads into the hidebound physical education establishment before they understood that Laban himself was available to them. No doubt the presence of Laban, the renowned theorist (and a man), gave them a particularly strong hand in dealing with the established leaders of physical education. Over the next two years both Laban and Ullmann became star attractions at weekend and holiday courses, and Ullmann extended her influence by getting invitations to various teacher training colleges. 'Modern Dance Holiday Courses', headed by Diana Jordan and Ullmann, began in 1941, bringing the Laban work to teachers during school holidays. The Laban Art of Movement Guild was formed in 1946 as a professional and supportive organisation for all branches of Laban's work.

Louise Soelberg was also involved in some of these courses. Her perspective is particularly interesting because she was a professional dancer, a former member of Ballets Jooss, with a background very different from that of the physical education people who were becoming involved in educational dance. Her contribution to the literature on dance as education was a leaflet, *Modern Dance ... What is it?* (1942), which reflected the changing climate for dance brought about by the activities of Laban and Ullmann within the developing educational dance culture spearheaded by Jordan and Goodrich – a change from the context of Jordan's book. She began:

> Since so many people are wondering what the term 'modern dance' implies, and what the aims of its teaching are, it now seems a propitious moment for serious consideration of the subject, and its relation to progressive educative principles.[16]

It is likely that she meant 'progressive educative principles' to apply not just to the special environment of the progressive schools such as Dartington, but to developing thought elsewhere on child-centred education – making education meaningful on the child's own level. (Dartington, with its progressive school, could be seen as a trailblazer in the field anyway.) Like Jordan, Soelberg emphasised holistic mind/body development, creativity and the importance of social education. As a practising artist, she did not want to totally relinquish notions of skill and technique, but she considered them a primary stage. The development and expression of 'the whole personality' of the pupil should take precedence. This would be facilitated through creative involvement in making dances, alone or in collaboration with the teacher. Perhaps she developed this idea from the Leeder dance studies: like them, the dances she envisaged would be educative in the widest terms rather than dances for the stage, although perhaps she was giving more emphasis to simultaneous involvement of teacher and pupil in dance creation than Leeder had done. But in the same Leeder tradition, she wanted to go beyond

immediate technique to penetrate the deeper content. In this way, while emphasising creativity, Soelberg was bringing an artist's experience to bear
upon developments that were happening largely within the field of physical
education. Like Jordan, she emphasised dance as art but also declared that,
through the work of Laban, modern dance had invented the tools – in
Kinetography (Labanotation) and 'the harmonic laws of movement' – that
would enable the study of *movement* which, she reiterated, was 'the sub-
stance of dance'. Now dance could be 'scientifically explored and practically
applied to education'. The leaflet was illustrated with a photograph of herself
in a recital dance and a Labanesque arrangement of an icosahedron model
standing on sheets of notation – the artistic and the analytical exploration of
movement both represented. There is evidence here of Soelberg's particular
response to the space harmony aspects of Laban's work. Indeed, she helped
him refine the English text of his book *Choreutics*, written at Dartington and
elsewhere in the late 1930s and 1940s but not published until after his
death.[17]

In September 1942 Laban and Ullmann moved to Manchester, a more
convenient base for all their activities. A former Laban dancer and movement
choir leader, Sylvia Bodmer, was now an émigré herself in Manchester and
there was a great deal of interest in educational work coming from northern
counties. In particular, the West Riding of Yorkshire would become a very
supportive local authority. Alec Clegg, the Director of Education from the
mid-1940s, was a staunch believer in the arts in education, was a supporter
of the Laban/Ullmann work, and later became a Dartington trustee.

The Art of Movement Studio, directed by Ullmann, opened in January
1946. The art of movement, translated from the German *Bewegungskunst*,
encompassed not only the expressive and creative applications of movement
in dance and drama performance, in dance for education and for the layman,
but also social, ritual and functional movement (work actions and games),
where the 'art' of movement is equated with its efficiency and skill. This wide
spectrum of study was underpinned by Laban's theoretical work in
choreutics and eukinetics, movement observation and analysis (including
industrial movement) and Kinetography Laban. Students came with a variety of movement-study interests. The optimum period of study for a
thorough grounding in Laban's work was considered to be three years, but
few students could commit for this length of time, since they needed to be
self-supporting. A regular income for the Studio could be met from seconded
teachers who had their fees paid. They became the bread-and-butter work of
the Studio. A one-year course for qualified teachers was recognised by the
Ministry of Education in 1948. Year-long and short courses targeted qualified teachers, PE organisers and teacher training college lecturers who could
then take the work back into the schools, raise the profile of dance in the

local education authorities and increase the supply of dance teachers coming from general education and PE colleges.

It was probably in Manchester that the term 'modern educational dance' was first used, perhaps to solve some of the puzzle over 'modern dance' identified by Soelberg. So the educational strand of the art of movement had acquired a name, and now Laban set out to write its textbook, *Modern Educational Dance*, published in 1948. Laban of course had never taught children, but the situation demanded that he should adapt his theory to this specific area. The book introduced the sixteen basic movement themes that were to be the framework for teaching children's work in school, Themes 1–8 in primary education and Themes 9–16 in secondary education. The themes were to be a way of organising the syllabus and individual classes around creative explorations leading to understanding of basic principles of movement, rather than learning by copying the teacher or demonstrator as in traditional stage and social dance styles. Laban based the themes on his own assumptions about the normal development of the child. They built in complexity from Theme 1 (awareness of the body) to Theme 15 (with social relationships expressed as group formations) and Theme 16 (the expressive qualities or moods of movement), when the adolescent's movement creations could have more of the aspects of formed dances. Laban merely sketched out the movement themes in *Modern Educational Dance*. The work had to be later elaborated by others.[18]

In line with all the thinking on establishing a better post-war world, including through the 1944 Education Act, the concept of children's physical education gradually changed at government level. In the early 1950s new publications from the Ministry of Education made a break with the past. *Moving and Growing* (1952) and *Planning the Programme* (1953) together replaced the 1933 Syllabus of Physical Training for Schools. Now the emphasis was on the child's guided exploration of movement – an education rather than a training – with dance having a specific place as a creative arts subject within the complex of physical education. Through the Art of Movement Studio courses and Modern Dance Holiday Courses, the application of 'basic movement' (basic Laban principles) spread into the traditional physical education sphere, where it had an important influence in modernising the teaching of gymnastics.[19]

The notion that dance for children needed to be seen in relation to a fully rounded educational experience rather than to mimic the training of the professional dancer was also behind the revision of the ballet syllabus of the Royal Academy of Dancing. Its Ballet in Education syllabus was introduced in 1947 with its nods to history and geography in exercises for historical deportment and national dances. There was some hope that this would make ballet more acceptable in a school setting, although there is little evidence that this happened apart from in fee-paying girls' schools. To a certain extent, this attempt to move into schools was fuelled by a professional antagonism towards the idea that dance, finally getting some official educational recognition, was being exploited by PE teachers without any knowledge of a specific dance technique[20]. But also, at last, the current context of thought on the artistic and physical development of the child was bringing into clearer focus the question raised a decade earlier by Miss Gwatkin: what does it mean to teach Mary dancing?

Laban and Ullmann could frequently be found included in conferences organised by the Society for Education Through the Arts, which had been set up in the early 1950s by the art critic Herbert Read amongst others. Their concerns for the application of artistic frameworks for the development of individuality and creativity in school education was clearly shared by others at this time. The satisfaction that Ullmann and Laban could feel at official recognition of their work must have been tempered by the fact that dance as an art form in schools and colleges was now generally subsumed into the physical education syllabus, where it has remained as far as schools in the public sector are concerned. At the same time, dance as education still had a considerable way to go before the progress with authorities could be transformed into accepted provision throughout the country. A decade after Ministry of Education recognition, movement based on creative Laban principles, whether it was called dance or gymnastics, had become an essential part of the generalist primary school teacher's training, and all the PE colleges had staff who had been trained at the Studio.[21] This did not necessarily equate with a bold programme of dance in all schools in all areas, as comments in documents down the years about the difficulty of finding schools for teaching practice reveal.

In terms of the 'Raise or Spread' polarisation in dance, the Art of Movement Studio and its satellite courses were essentially to be involved in the 'spreading' message that dance was within the competence of every child and adult. That was a message that Dartington's Trustees would endorse while simultaneously supporting the cultivation of dance in the professional sphere.

The relationship with Dartington

Dartington remained key to Laban's and Ullman's futures. From 1940 to 1942, like other émigrés, they remained financially dependent on what the Trustees and perhaps Dorothy personally could send them. Laban and Dorothy had a close relationship: he entrusted chapters of his writing to her during the war and it appears that she was impressed by Laban's cosmic vision of dance in life, which in some ways chimed with her own vision for the arts. There were other more pragmatic connections. In 1941, Laban began a collaboration with a management consultant, Frederick Lawrence, a contact made through Leonard. The problem was to analyse movement tasks in agriculture and industry and introduce a more efficient use of the body. The result of this was Laban–Lawrence Industrial Rhythm, used of course at Dartington amongst other places, and Laban received official permission to return there for a while to work on the exercises. Another project was the Withymead Centre for Psychotherapy and Art Therapy near Exeter, run by the Jungian psychotherapist Irene Champernowne and her husband.[22] Dorothy was deeply attached to the Champernownes, especially to Irene. Laban was asked to advise on the use of movement in the therapeutic setting and this opened up yet another field for his researches, relating movement analysis to Jungian psychic functions.

But in terms of the Arts Department's own long-term plan to include a dance school when the situation allowed (a plan laid out by Christopher Martin in 1941 and never revoked by Peter Cox), Laban and Ullmann did not compare favourably with Imogen Holst, whose work was now the benchmark at Dartington both of professional standards and of promotion of a strong amateur culture. When Ullmann was in the process of setting up the Art of Movement Studio in 1945, the possibility that it could be sited at Dartington was broached. Cox was reluctant. On the one hand, there was a strong connection with Dartington, particularly with Dorothy; on the other hand, Holst was training qualified musicians to be teachers, whereas the Laban/Ullmann work, predominantly with physical education teachers, was unlikely to make dancers out of them. Furthermore, this was a potentially large enterprise, which might swamp Holst's small school.[23] The old problem of professional standards in amateur work was raised yet again.

In 1945 Cox was holding back from the dance department envisaged in 1941. It was agreed not to form a dance course as yet. There was a compromise position that could only be seen as satisfactory from a superficial standpoint: to appoint a teacher with some knowledge of Laban's work who could introduce dance on the music and drama courses that were starting up, and on the Estate.[24] Winsome Bartlett indeed had some knowledge of Laban work, since she had undertaken some of the Laban–Lawrence Industrial Rhythm training during the war, but she was not primarily a dance artist nor a teacher of the creative work. She was a skilled folk musician on the pipe and tabor and could teach traditional music and dance, which she did with great success for many years. At various times there were discussions on the subject of placements at Dartington for Art of Movement Studio students or graduates, but this did not come about for a variety of reasons.[25]

One aspect of dance was thriving at Dartington in the shape of children's ballet classes taught by Florence Burton, a much-loved secretary in the Arts Department. From 1948 and through most of the 1950s her class was fea-

tured prominently in the Barn Theatre on Foundation Day, the annual celebration welcoming visitors to the Courtyard and gardens. Photographs and
programmes from successive displays indicate that during this period these
productions developed from being typical dancing school displays of national and character dances to becoming original story ballets, often with
specially written music by Helen Glatz, a Dartington musician and composer
in Imogen Holst's department. Although recognising that children's ballet
was being produced very successfully, Peter Cox did not think that there was
a potential for ballet to become the dance art form that should be developed
as part of Arts Department policy.[26] Although he had his reservations about
the equivalence of the Laban and Ullmann work to what was happening in
music at Dartington, he had experienced the end of the Jooss–Leeder era and
joined in with their amateur classes, too.[27] Modern dance techniques would
seem far more appropriate to develop at Dartington, as his visits to colleges in
the USA would confirm.

For several years, Modern Dance Holiday Courses took place at
Dartington. Photographs show classes on the terrace of the Dance School,
brought to temporary life by a resurgence of *Ausdruckstanz*. In Ullmann's
archive there is silent film of open-air dancing at Dartington, in the open-air
theatre (in black and white) and in the courtyard of the Foxhole school building (in colour). Geraldine Stephenson, a Studio staff member, dances one of
the character solos from her recital programme. Groups share their movement and percussion compositions, surging back and forth across the lawns.
Dancers of one group play and wield their drums and blocks with large circular motions that pull them energetically forward; they are opposed by
another with instruments moved in a gentle, swinging back-and-forth motion. In another scene, more amorphous formations are in combat,
advancing and retreating, becoming a mêlée. Dancers freely improvise to a
percussion orchestra. Onlookers lounge in the sunshine on grass banks,
amongst them Dorothy and Leonard on the uppermost terrace. There is
something utopian about the scene: the environment nurturing that moment of movement.

In the grass courtyard at Foxhole there is a large group dance being performed in movement choir style by scores of people with a wide range of
dance abilities but all with maximum commitment to the movement. Small
groupings have their own movement motifs that express their characteristics
in choreutic and eukinetic terms, but there seems ultimately to be a need to
communicate and a desire to merge into wholeness. In one sub-group, members open up towards the others, who join in with them – running with arms
raising upwards, then sinking to the ground. Some of the dancers form duets. For a while they seem to dance more as individuals than as a pair, then an
impulsive movement takes each dancer into a turn, ending up with arms

flung back, totally open to each other. This is taken up by everyone else, swirling together in twos. There are other duos that are apparently defeated by a disruptive element with sharp movements led by hands held together like a beak. Forward-moving lines use threatening wide and deep body shapes with harshly accented movements. A sideways-moving group makes broad, smooth gestures, lifting, stretching and reaching out. Consolidated groups greet each other and then merge into a great mass swirling anticlockwise, drawing away into an inward-facing circle – unity achieved.

The last Holiday Course at Dartington was in1952; from then on, Dartington would be the permanent home of the prestigious Summer School of Music. However, the 1952 Holiday Course was important because it marked the start of a systematic Elmhirst patronage of the Art of Movement Studio.

The American Universities Theatre Summer School, 1950

In 1950 there was a one-off course that is indicative of the thinking and direction for Dartington. It was both problematic and stimulating in equal measures and would mark the point at which the directions of Dartington and Laban/Ullmann work clearly diverged.

As Peter Cox wrote in his Rockefeller Foundation grant application:

English interest in the part that the theatre can play in general education is growing rapidly but, as the Universities have only just begun to take an interest in the theatre as a subject for academic study, we have very few sources of leadership in this field and have a lot to learn from America.[28]

Cox had previously spent some time touring American universities and so had some background in what was going on there. The whole four-week summer school was to be under the direction of Arch Lauterer, now Director of Theatre at Mills College, but before that of Bennington and Sarah Lawrence colleges. Through involvement at Bennington summer schools, he knew the work of the American modern dancers Martha Graham, Doris Humphrey and Hanya Holm, and was known as a set designer for their dance works. At the Summer School, Lauterer would have American assistants and Hallie Flanagan was to be adviser and lecturer.

This was not to be a totally American undertaking. Dartington's own artists had to be represented, Imogen Holst for music and Laban and Ullmann in movement and dance-drama. Over the four weeks of the course, all the students would work in drama, movement and music (choral singing) and towards the final production welding together scenes from Greek and modern drama with freshly created dance-dramas. The overall theme was to be the relation of the individual to the social environment (a good one for

Dartington), the production being put on in the last weekend as *The Family of Man*, for the public and delegates at a weekend conference. An extract from *Prometheus Bound* (Aeschylus), with chorus directed by Holst, represented 'the hope of individuals in contrast to the fears and awareness of the community'. It was followed by the first dance-drama, in which Force and Violence were personified. They caused a division in the chorus. 'The dancers fight until they see their opponents for what they are: people like themselves', the programme stated, and notes indicate that this reconciliation was simply suggested by mirror movements. In the later part of this scene, Force and Violence were treated as objects of amusement for the crowd but managed to become masters of ceremonies, directing the dance. This led up to an extract from *The Lady from the Sea* (Ibsen): 'physical environment hems in the community and family'. The final dance-drama showed Prometheus as a symbol of hope and courage calling to people to connect with each other.[29]

The whole experience seems to have been full of tensions, both within the faculty and between the faculty and the predominantly British student body. Each morning began with a movement class and there was choral singing for all before lunch – both unqualified successes according to Cox. But the British students could not readily comprehend what Cox called the 'philosophical nature' of Lauterer's approach in his seminar series. It would appear from transcripts of his lectures that he was more interested in broadly based concepts of ancient, modern and 'lyric theatre' (including dance-drama) rather than the close textual analysis common in the English tradition. On his side he could have been more sensitive to the existing knowledge base of the students: in his seminar on lyric drama to which I will refer later, Lauterer made a number of references to Hanya Holm and Martha Graham that must have been quite outside the experience of the British student body.

Especial problems accrued around the dance-drama. Cox's later assessment was that it risked being dropped altogether, partly because the students generally had no experience of this kind of work. The more serious problem was that Laban and Ullmann found it difficult to work with both Lauterer and Holst, who was supposed to compose the music, although this may not have happened finally. It appears that Laban and Ullmann departed from Lauterer's stipulation that the dance-drama should suggest 'Man's quest for Light and Truth' down the centuries, filling in the historical divide between the two play extracts. For her part, Holst was shocked by their use of recorded music, a Tchaikovsky symphony with movements taken out of order.[30]

There also must have been a mismatch between Lauterer's and Laban's conception of dance-drama and the nature of movement in the theatre. Part of the study material given to students was the detailed scenario of Lauterer's own dance-drama, *Yankee Titan*, which had as its subject a mystical connection between a man of the settler era and the native American tribal rituals of Ohio.[31] Lauterer's scenario was very clearly worked out with sound and lighting effects, description of action and script of the narration. In his seminar he spoke about the images in *Yankee Titan* and the need for the images to grow through the time of the dance-drama, accruing connotations, but the images he cited were visual symbols, lighting and sound; there was no reference to specific movement images. The scenario was much more specific on the visual elements in stage properties, setting, lighting and sound than on movement. It would not be a surprise, then, if Laban had found himself at odds with this version of dance-drama, with all he believed about the specificity of movement as a language.

Although Lauterer's script for *Yankee Titan* did not make movement the prime carrier of meaning, it showed a highly theatrical sensibility and a clearly worked-out structure. In contrast, Laban and Ullmann had insisted that their dance-drama scenario would be worked out during the course. It may be that this was too problematic with a largely inexperienced body of performers. There are copious notes and drawings by Laban in Ullmann's archive. It is not possible to know which were the final ones, but they suggest a process in flux and various attempts to find a resolution.

The Summer School was significant for a number of reasons. It marks a point in Dartington's move towards the conception of the College of Arts, but it also showed how there would need to be a large degree of translation if an American-based curriculum was adopted. Dartington's move towards the college was to be a slow evolution. As far as Dartington's relationship with Laban and Ullmann was concerned, it marked the point at which Peter Cox felt their work did not match with what he wanted to achieve. It must be remembered that Laban had not created for the theatre since 1934 and Ullmann perhaps never. There was thus a clash between pre-war European and post-war American dance aesthetics. Laban and Ullmann did not fit into the academic and theatrical format that Cox had seen working in America. At times in the future when it was suggested that the Art of Movement Studio might move to Dartington, the answer would be a clear negative. Although Dartington would support their work, it was to be positioned elsewhere, in a separate realm.

The Laban Art of Movement Centre Trust

In 1954 Leonard wrote to his brother Alfred (Pom) Elmhirst:

'Labanismus' spells for me the window through which the millions of children may get their first real insight into the Arts and into their own make-up and capacities.[32]

Clearly the Elmhirsts and Dartington continued to support the notion of the spreading of dance through education and continued to believe in Laban's and Ullman's work in that area. The Elmhirsts now became once more directly concerned in the patronage of dance.

It is not clear how the original Art of Movement Studio above a printing works in Manchester was financed, although it was probably not from Dartington.[33] After a while, not only the cramped premises themselves but also the geographical location seemed restricting. Efforts were made to relocate to London but, in the end, a suburban place was found at Addlestone, near Weybridge, Surrey, in a former school with good-sized grounds where the Studio reopened in September 1953.

William Elmhirst, the youngest of Dorothy's children, became aware of Laban during the Modern Dance Holiday Course at Dartington in summer 1952. Until then he had no real notion of what Laban did or any ambition towards movement work. But at this course Laban took a men's class, and Ena Curry, former wife of Dartington Hall School's first headmaster, who was already enthusiastic about the art of movement, impressed upon William Elmhirst that he must participate. It was a life-changing experience.[34] Laban's cosmic vision intrigued him and gave him new ideas about the fusion of physical and metaphysical worlds through the Platonic crystalline forms integrated into the theory of choreutics. When it became clear in the following year that Laban and Ullmann must move south, William Elmhirst bought the Addlestone property for them and contributed further amounts when there was a necessity for a capital expenditure or to keep things afloat.[35] When it opened in 1953, with furniture and curtain material donated from Dartington's own industries,[36] he immediately embarked on a year's course at the Studio he had made possible. He became interested in the application of Laban's ideas to acting and subsequently went on to a performing career in the Royal Shakespeare Company and at the Library Theatre, Scarborough, while Alan Ayckbourn was developing his writing career.

The Studio at Addlestone was the antithesis of the grimy urban setting of the Manchester Studio. Dancing in the open air was back on the agenda as it had been at Dartington, and for some time gardening was on the curriculum, almost harking back to Laban's 'dance farm' days. This was an intimate environment entirely focused on the Laban work. Until his death in 1958, Laban continued his research work here.

The final structure for administering this gift was to be the Laban Art of Movement Centre Trust set up in October 1954. The 'Centre' was more than a building: it was partly conceptual, representing Laban's research and writing activities, 'to ensure continuance and to preserve their authenticity'.[37] It was also the teaching side of the work, most directly seen in the courses going on in the Studio but also outside it in a very big extramural undertaking. Pom Elmhirst became Chairman of the Trust. With Leonard being another Trustee and William Elmhirst, as the original donor, attending meetings (although he did not officially become a Trustee until 1959), the Trust was clearly an Elmhirst concern for furthering the place of dance and movement in post-war Britain. Joan Goodrich and Frederick Lawrence were the other two original Trustees. In 1956, Christian Schiller, from London University Institute of Education and a former Schools Inspector, became another; he was a useful adviser on the workings of educational bureaucracies. Vested in the Trust were the freehold of the property, the 'assets, liabilities and goodwill' of the Studio and the books and papers that were the outcome of Laban's research. Laban and Ullmann (who was Director of the Centre and Principal of the Studio) were to become employees, but there is evidence of their own disquiet about their lack of control.[38] Was this another case, as with Jooss, of Dartington patronage seeming to mean a loss of independence? Like Jooss, they found it disturbing that the price of Trustee sponsorship was a level of decision-making above them, but it is clear that the undertaking would have foundered without the continued support of the Trust. Nothing like financial viability was achieved until the mid-1960s. The financial support of William Elmhirst and of the Elmhirst trusts, Elmgrant and Applegreen (William Elmhirst's own charitable trust), were essential to the Centre's continued existence.

Apart from any affection that everyone concerned in the Trust had towards both Laban and Ullmann, the main concern, and certainly the motivation behind William Elmhirst's financial support, was to preserve and facilitate the work of Laban himself, in all its manifestations both theoretical and practical. Ensuring the Laban intellectual legacy became one of the major concerns of the Trustees. 'The Movement Research Foundation', announced by the Centre's leaflet of 1954, for which 'Laban's collection of movement records is available for further investigation', did not materialise in any significant manner.[39] After Laban's death in 1958, the Trust became very critical at the lack of progress there, partly because Ullmann was possessive about the materials (which had been willed to her by Laban, probably against the terms of the Trust Deed) and partly because the Trustees doubted her ability to communicate and further Laban's ideas.

It should have been the Studio, the money-earning part of the enterprise, that kept the Centre solvent; but throughout the 1950s it was financially shaky, with a considerable financial crisis late in the decade. The problem of getting enough students was similar to the ones encountered at the School of Dance-Mime and the Jooss–Leeder School. What sort of expenditure was justified to achieve this? For a while the answer seemed to be to build a hostel, with Elmgrant finance. For whatever reason, this did not come about. The

Trustees debated the problems at length in 1957. There were not enough students being supported by public funds. Unlike the case in the West Riding of Yorkshire, the London education authorities were resistant to introducing dance in schools, and there was some concern that Ullmann was not articulate or sensitive enough to press the case in the best way.[40] She was also completely overworked, with a busy Extramural Department as well as regular courses. There were evening classes at Addlestone (used by students for teaching practice[41]) and sometimes in London too, as well as weekend and holiday courses.

The financial crisis and the death of Laban forced the Trust to face some difficult issues, one of which was whether the Centre and Studio had a future at all. There exists a document, a 'Diagnosis of the Centre's Ailments', resulting apparently from a discussion between Pom Elmhirst and Diana Jordan. One can imagine that the Chairman of the Trust would wish to seek the opinion of an educationalist from outside the institution. At this point it looked impossible to improve on student numbers. What is more surprising is the extent to which Jordan was unhappy about the quality of teaching at the Studio and the standard of the teachers it produced. 'Students become very enthusiastic as performers but seem *not* to become inspired to teach – are not creative teachers.' The 'Suggested Programme for Developing Laban's Work' involved closing the Studio, setting up Ullmann in a property where she could house the archives and research could happen, and making her available for consultancy and short courses.[42]

At about this time a change of Government policy on teacher training offered new opportunities. The Ministry of Education increased the length of all teacher training courses from two to three years, making it possible in 1960 to start a course for intending teachers of dance as a specialist subject in secondary schools – a two-year course at the Studio, to be completed by one year in a general teacher training college, in this case Trent Park College in north London. This so called '2 plus 1' format was to provide a solution for specialist arts-teacher training in other small colleges such as Dartington. This was one of the factors enabling a financial stabilisation in the mid-1960s. Now alongside qualified teachers or lecturers on one-year courses who generally had a physical education background there were students mainly coming straight from A-levels, attracted first to dance as a creative subject and already with some dance training, either in a neighbourhood dancing school or in secondary schools where dance was embedded.

I remember clearly the moment in 1964 when I started to talk about dance teaching in secondary schools as a career choice for myself, as opposed to the ballet teaching career I had wanted previously. 'Creativity' was the word I used a lot. Somehow or other I had come across the idea that I could bring together my own spontaneous desire to create dances (never brought to fruition up to that point in conventional ballet school and grammar school environments) with the need to earn a living. I also had an idealistic belief, perhaps nurtured by my time as an active Young Socialist, that I had to break down elite notions of dance as performance and aim for something more democratic. In terms of creativity the Studio did not disappoint. From the first moment of the year, 'Creation Day', the baptism of fire when every student had to show something original (mine was *Poem with Hollow Percussion*), every class required us to translate something learned into something created individually or in collaboration. But this was no Monte Verità of personal freedom, in spite of the onset of the sixties student revolt. As a group we were physically drilled, obedient and totally committed to each other – 'a Roman army', as I remember an older student remarking. The transition to the bigger college at Trent Park was painful, as was that to the world of work. The price of getting a place for modern educational dance in secondary schools was its association with physical education and disassociation from arts education. No matter how much the Studio promoted dance as a creative art, students who left the course as qualified teachers of dance as a specialist subject would typically find themselves working in physical education departments and, no matter whether they had any knowledge or not, were expected to 'help with sports and games'.

How ironic is it that the Studio started to look a more viable institution at the moment in the 1960s when 'modern dance' began to mean 'American modern dance', or 'contemporary dance' as the more commonly used term in Britain? In the latter half of the 1960s the context of dance in Britain changed markedly, as will be more thoroughly mapped out in the next chapter, since Dartington had a major part to play in that narrative. With a swelling interest in technical modern dance training, the new generation of Laban-trained teachers were operating in a changed dance environment. This was acknowledged at the Laban Art of Movement Guild Conference in 1968 when a 'Brains Trust' on dance in education included on the panel, alongside Ullmann, the ballerina Beryl Grey and Robin Howard, who had brought into being the London School of Contemporary Dance based on training in Graham technique. They answered such questions as:

Does the panel consider that there is such a thing as 'Educational Dance' as distinct from the Art of Dance, and if so what are its distinguishing features?

Unfortunately there is no record of their answers. These issues were already causing controversy at Dartington, as will be seen in the next chapter. Other questions addressed the vexed issue of dance technique. How much was necessary in general education? Could a dancer master more than one technique?[43] Even the possibility of an academic place for dance as a degree subject was mooted. This was not a direction that could be taken by the Art of Movement Studio under Ullmann: the syllabi reveal how much this was a monoculture, the reference of all knowledge being Laban's own books, *The Mastery of Movement*, *Modern Educational Dance* and *Choreutics* (when it had been substantially edited by Ullmann and published posthumously), without other critical content.[44] In the 1950s, an attempt to widen the technical base had been resisted. Gert (Yat) Malmgren, a Swedish dancer who joined the staff for the 1954/55 academic year, taught a technique class in 'American Dance', but it would appear that this was not acceptable to Ullmann and he moved on to develop Laban's work in actor training.[45] New modern dance techniques and the demands of academia might have been seen as twin threats. As Ullmann wrote in some lecture notes in 1969, 'Dance is now in danger to be killed as a creative experience by academic and technical approach' [sic].[46] By the time she wrote this, the technical approach, if not yet the academic approach, was well-bedded-down at Dartington. The Laban Art of Movement Centre Trust set up by the Elmhirsts, whose members understood how academic and artistic affairs were moving, would soon begin the process of translating the Studio from being a predominantly teacher training establishment in Surrey into an academic and technical dance institution in London, known from 1975 as the Laban Centre for Movement and Dance.[47]

Spreading the Art of Movement: Lay dancing in Britain

It is somewhat surprising, considering what subsequent years brought, that the new field of her own that Ullmann was looking to develop in the late 1930s was not education, but the community dance work with non-professionals, as in her Plymouth classes. Perhaps here she saw a real opening for her own talents in something that the Jooss–Leeder School was not doing. One might have thought that her greatest satisfaction would be in the standard of attainment of the Jooss–Leeder students destined for the profession; but, much later, Ullmann spoke more of the frustration when the professional's life would be so short and worn down by touring. (The example of Ballets Jooss must have been in her mind.) In contrast with this sad erosion of promise, the non-professional dancer would always be accruing the benefits of dance.[48]

The previous chapter mentioned the Laban/Ullmann submission to Leonard in March 1939. The plan, or 'Practical Outlook', showed two parallel institutions side by side under the heading of Dartington Hall: the 'Education centre for professional dancers and stage-dance teachers', which was the current Jooss–Leeder School but without its Diploma for teaching amateurs or its obligation to conduct amateur classes for the estate, and the 'Education centre for layman dance, for teachers and leaders of movement choruses and community dance groups'. The studies necessary in each case were different. In the education centre for the layman dance, there would have to be complementary studies 'in anatomy, psycho-physiology, therapeutic knowledge, sociology, etc.' The teachers of the centre, assisted by their students, would be involved in the community dance work at Dartington, in the countryside and in nearby cities. The target populations would be adults, adolescents and children, and special groups, the elderly and sick. Particular occupational groups could be catered for, but the mixing of social classes should be seen as the most valuable form of organisation, the most revealing of the social value. Performing in public was not advised, at least in the first few years. ('Vanity is the greatest enemy of layman's dance culture.') Groups should meet together for festivals, perhaps at Dartington; 'the climax should be the common awareness of the value of fitness, and the ethic, social feeling in the community-dance'.[49] The commitment to community dance was absolutely implicit in Laban's thought as an aspect of an often mystic vision linking the movement of the individual to movement in the cosmos. One of the documents he sent to Leonard along with his letter was an extract from the address he gave to the meeting of sixty movement choirs that preceded the 1936 Berlin Olympics. On this occasion he spoke about the integration of mind and body (psycho-physiological synthesis) leading to unity in the body as a microcosm of the unity of the community and even unity with Nature itself.[50]

Was the 'Practical Outlook' Laban's plan or Ullmann's? There is a paper in her archive, apparently in her own hand, showing in diagrammatic form the concept of the new school more or less as it appears in the letter to Leonard. Although it has been suggested that, at least in the early years of their partnership, Ullmann was dependent on Laban's guidance, it would seem more likely here, especially with what we know of the way Ullmann's work had been developing before he arrived, that this was a cooperative effort both in the emerging concept and in crafting the language that Laban was still trying to master.[51]

The dance form introduced into Britain under the title of movement choir, movement chorus or choral dancing originated in the movement choirs of pre-war Germany. Movement choir production and leadership was part of Ullmann's Laban school training in Berlin. Movement choirs were popular and widespread, often associated with professional dance schools or opera houses. Jooss had worked with a movement choir attached to the opera house at Münster. Evidence and current scholarship on the German movement choirs is quite problematic because those things that made the genre distinctive – the possibility of enormous performing groups, the nature of the themes, the close relationship with a leader – are intertwined with the subsequent history of the Third Reich and Germany's post-World War II negotiation of its past. The propaganda exercise of the movement choir spectacles at the 1936 Berlin Olympic Games has been seen as the paradigm of the genre; however, we have to remember that movement choirs were groups who met regularly to experience dancing and moving together. Productions large or small were not a necessary outcome.

In general practice, groups were small enough in membership to be able to work easily together. They often exercised with group improvisation, mirroring, opposing or following the leader or another group; but they could also be taking part in a choreographed spectacle alongside other movement choirs.[52] Laban referred to choral dancing as 'the most highly developed form' of community dancing, emphasising that it developed the capacity to empathise with others and that this was transferable to other areas of life.[53] The theme of a movement choir piece might be its abstract patterning or there might be a narrative or metaphysical theme (*Prometheus*, *Dance of the Colours*, *Machine Rhythms*, *Work and Leisure* were some that Ullmann remembered[54]). The absolute essence of the movement choir was the lay status of the members, the simple but effective vocabulary and its forms derived from amateur choral singing. Laban's movement observation research had led him towards the theory that people had differentiated movement characteristics that tended them towards different movement levels. 'High dancers' drew away from the ground, more easily conveying lightness and resistance to gravity. They could be especially effective in elevation and movement with an upright carriage. 'Deep' or low dancers enjoyed playing with the effects of gravity, including rolling, bending, pounding into the ground. Medium dancers were obviously between the two, emphasising the skimming, turning and travelling potential of the medium level. There were intermediaries between these types (the 'medium-high' or 'medium-deep' dancers). These divisions appeared to Laban to be analogous to vocal divisions in a choir. Groupings of these movement types formed the basis for the different 'voices' of the movement choir working in counterpoint. Implicit in this conception was the notion of groups characterised by their differences but striving towards unity. As Ullmann remembered of her introduction to a movement choir in Germany:

> There were groups of men with strong and vigorous rhythmical movements countering the women creating smoothly flowing patterns, there were dramatic moments when one group seemed to imprison and subdue another one and when finally at first a few and then more and more dancers emerged from a maze-like entanglement in a pulsating rhythm of joy and harmony.[55]

Shifting images of separation and wholeness can be seen in photographs of movement choirs from the pre-war period in Germany and in their later manifestation in Britain, as also in the film I described earlier (see page 144-145). The play of abstract patterning and group structure can be seen in working diagrams used in production.

It will be remembered that Ullmann had made a start on movement choir work in Plymouth. By the summer of 1939 she considered that her group had made enough progress to form the core of a large movement choir. She made preparations to enlarge the scope of her work to Exeter, Newton Abbot or Torquay. The onset of war put a stop to this, but her reclassification as a 'friendly alien' in October 1939 made it possible once more to arrange classes. Meanwhile she appears to have begun working with the Dartington amateur class along movement choir lines. When her Plymouth class re-started in May 1940, she wrote to members encouraging them to bring friends along. Members of the class had agreed to admit men to the group. There were plans in place for 'a large-scale choral dancing together' of all her groups at a Midsummer Festival at Dartington Hall in June.[56] This could not take place because of restrictions that came into place in June and Laban's and Ullmann's move to London.

The move to Manchester and the Modern Dance Holiday Courses provided further opportunities to develop movement choirs. Sylvia Bodmer, resident in Manchester, had been a movement choir leader in Frankfurt. Movement choir work was one of her specialities, which she taught on various courses both in Manchester and nationally.

Now in the context of Britain, not everybody appreciated the kinds of group experience that the movement choir offered. Jane Winearls found it distasteful that, 'we found ourselves in enormous, amorphous groups in which we became some unidentifiable particle which was being pressured by the size and vital power of the group'.[57] The other extreme is expressed by Geraldine Stephenson, remembering a movement choir session led by Sylvia Bodmer in 1946:

> How wonderful to be part of a group that could shrink or expand; heave up and down, all of us breathing as one creature; to be in the centre, then on the periphery, to break away, find a space and proceed to interweave and meet everyone – no doubt in one of Sylvia's right or lefthand chains![58]

Movement choirs in pre-war Germany had flourished in a specific context of philosophical and artistic life, within a pervasive modern dance culture, fed by notions of the healthy body as metaphor and conduit of the German social community (*Gemeinschaft*). The British context was quite different and there were sometimes barriers of 'traditional' British reserve, as well as a fundamental distrust of people in a mass (as in Winearls's account). Britain also lacked an indigenous terminology. How could a dance for 'the people' be described? It was not folk dance, although Laban believed it could become the folk dance for the twentieth century. The terms 'movement choir' and 'lay dance', both direct translations from the German, had no history here. In the 1940s and 1950s various terms arose. The label 'movement choir' retained some currency, mostly to describe a massed choreographed dance. 'Saltata' (derived from cantata) was also briefly used as a term in the 1950s. According to a note by Laban, this term implied a development of the movement choir idea towards a longer dance clearly structured around musical form.[59]

For the Festival of Movement and Dance organised by the Central Council for Physical Recreation (CCPR) at Wembley in 1955, Laban and Ullmann worked on a large movement choir or saltata of eighty female dancers, performed to Bizet's *L'Arlesienne Suite*. The dancers were grouped according to their predominant movement characteristics, dressed in calf-length skirts that strengthened the visual impact of the blocks, lines and circles of dancers in that huge space. High dancers were in pale grey, medium dancers in red, and low dancers in black. A photograph shows asymmetrical groupings of dancers, each one stating the theme of the three levels in simple body posture and arm position. Another shows perhaps the climax of the dance, the whole cast massed together in a three-dimensional group from the low outer edge to the high centre, and an expression of exultation. Ullmann reported that 'the audience spontaneously applauded the climax of the last dance just before the end'.[60] One of the participants, Janet Goodridge, recalls Laban and Ullmann poring over their drawings of floor patterns and groups.[61] They must have seen this as an important moment in bringing the art of the movement choir to public notice: in a leaflet for their London movement choir work it was referred to as Britain's 'first large scale public presentation'.[62]

It would be surprising if lay dancing did not change, both in style and terminology, once established in Britain. Fascinating accounts of the dancing at various courses occur in the Laban Guild Magazine during the 1960s. Some of the dances have the group-orientated characteristics of movement choirs, but there is also a strong tendency to make dances in a format starting with the individual, leading on to duo, trio and larger-group relationships. This emphasis on the individual within a gradually socialising process rather than immediately having to identify with a group or subgroup seems to be a development of lay dancing that fitted more easily into the social context of Britain. Lay dancing as an activity that would not necessarily lead to public productions acquired the title 'recreational' or 'recreative' dance, terms being used by Ullmann from the early 1940s. The former was a useful term to indicate a healthy, leisure-time activity, which must have facilitated the incorporation of dance within the bodies such as the CCPR promoting amateur sports, gymnastics and 'keep-fit'. 'Recreative dance' was an even more compelling term.

> When people come together to take part in recreative dancing it is meant to be, as is implicit in the word, a creative activity. Personal participation and enjoyment are the first essentials. Secondly, the experience of physical exertion together with the awakening of movement awareness is important. Thirdly the feeling of relationship and belonging to a group is awakened. Fourthly, as dancing is an art form, it involves the full integration of one's personality and lifts the participant out of everyday life.[63]

Opportunities for recreative dancing continued in the Modern Dance Holiday Courses and the Laban Guild courses; and, once established in the better facilities at Addlestone, the Art of Movement Studio held holiday courses and evening classes. Even before becoming established at Addlestone, Laban and Ullmann had begun regular classes in London, advertised as 'contemporary movement patterns', 'choral dance plays' or movement choirs, the work sometimes under the auspices of the London Movement Choir. These courses continued well into the 1960s. Many amateur dance groups were affiliated to the Laban Guild. Amongst the most prominent were the Manchester Dance Circle, founded by Bodmer and Ullmann, and the West Riding Movement Study Group, both of which indicate the healthy amount of interest in Laban's work in the north of England. Also still operating was the Birmingham Contemporary Dance Club, originally founded in 1941 with the encouragement of Louise Soelberg, who became its first artistic director. My own first exposure to recreative dance was in this club in the year 1964–65, long before I had heard of Louise Soelberg.

To what extent, though, was the notion of a dance experience for everyman and everywoman framed in terms of a concept of 'community', however that might be defined? A course in 1955, *Dance: Its Contribution to the Life of Communities* (organised by the National Association of Organisers and Lecturers of Physical Education), would seem by its title to promise a developing theory, but it is difficult to be sure. Lecturers included Ninette de Valois and Beryl de Zoete. Ullmann's class on modern educational dance took place alongside classes in folk dance and social dancing of various styles.[64] There is nothing here to indicate that communities were conceptualised, as they would later be by the community dance movement, in terms of a specific neighbourhood or the needs and contributions of differing age groups, ethnicities and abilities. The 1955 event does, however, point to the plurality of approaches to dance for the amateur and the acceptance that amateurs should actively participate in dance activities. With their special concern for individual creativity, leaders trained in the art of movement strengthened the place of dance as a recreational and communal activity, and this would later feed into the widespread development of community dance projects from the 1970s.

The evaluation of Dartington's promotion of Laban and Ullmann is mixed and rather paradoxical. The Art of Movement Centre Trust concerned itself mostly with the educational side of the Studio work, probably because this was where its finances were concentrated and where it was most vulnerable. Laban's 'Practical Outlook' of 1939 for the 'Education centre for layman dance, for teachers and leaders of movement choruses and community dance groups' might have served Dartington's desire to develop dance in its local community, unfulfilled since Barr's time, but it was impractical in 1939 and priorities changed in the post-war period. A lot was now happening at Dartington in provision for music, drama and visual arts, but there was no one at hand permanently to press the 'Practical Outlook' for dance.

Although I made it clear in my Introduction that I am concerned in this book to explore the history of the art of dance at Dartington, it would seem perverse at this point to disregard the fact that traditional dancing at Dartington was a developing field for non-professional participation. The Dartington Institute for Traditional Arts was set up in 1969, headed by Peter Kennedy, son of Douglas Kennedy of the English Folk Dance and Song Society, and providing a nucleus from which research and participation flowed. A separate initiative was the founding of the Dartington Morris Men in 1968 (still active now). Winsome Bartlett played for them and they had Leonard's direct support. He named them, recalling his own past when he danced the Morris, and he allowed the dancers to wear as insignia Dartington Hall's own crest of the White Hart on a red rose. The 'pillar studio' in the Courtyard was their first home.[65]

Dartington Hall: A regional dance venue

The parallel narrative to that of the art of movement, spreading nationally for children and lay dancers with Dartington's support, is that of professional dance performance at Dartington. That narrative brings to the surface the debate about the viability of the regional arts, the metropolitan concentration of Arts Council funding and the smaller but persistent voice demanding a more adventurous grant-giving that would favour the emerging small ballet companies and choreographers or even dance outside of the dominant classical genre.

The south-west region, far from London, characteristically had small centres of population with few or small arts venues. Clubs and small arts centres were the dynamic behind artistic life outside the major cities such as Bristol and Plymouth. However, in 1952 the Arts Council withdrew its policy of association with these small venues in an attempt to get local authorities to take more responsibility for arts in their own areas as they were allowed to do under the Local Government Act of 1948 and as was implicit in the 1944 Education Act. Arts Council Annual Reports repeatedly complained about the poor response.

By 1954, the Arts Department at Dartington had demonstrated that it was serving both the immediate locality and the arts in general. It had a good post-war history of public performances and exhibitions, a vigorous amateur dramatic Playgoers Society headed by professional directors and a resident course for musicians; it hosted courses for various arts and education organisations and now it had the Summer School of Music. On the strength of this it was renamed the Dartington Hall Arts Centre and Peter Cox became its Warden. The Arts Centre was unique in the facilities it had at its disposal. Four spaces were available. There was the Barn Theatre (seating 208) with its intimate proscenium stage, the large and flexible space of the Dance School, the Great Hall, much used for concerts, and outdoor areas including the Courtyard itself.

Peter Cox was one of the chief influences in bringing venues and organisations together in the South Western Arts Association in 1954. The firm opposition of SWAA to regional Arts Council closure resulted in a new kind of financial relationship with the Arts Council, whereby SWAA became the distributor of small local grants to members and an organisation capable of setting up tours of local venues. In effect SWAA would become the first of the regional arts associations, serving a large and mainly rural population stretching from Cornwall and Devon in the south to Bristol in the north and Dorset to the east. Peter Cox remained closely involved in the management of SWAA (later South West Arts), becoming Chairman in 1983 when he retired from Dartington.

The funding context for dance in the 1950s was very restricted. The Arts Council did not have a development strategy for dance other than for its main clients. This is not surprising, since its internal structure did not recognise dance as an independent art form, dance issues being handled by the Music Department, with reference to the Drama Department on occasions. This structure rendered dance invisible and doubly so, because not only was there no separate Dance Panel or Dance Director, but the Arts Council was fixated on dance as one half of the 'opera and ballet' duo – Siamese twins, conjoined in the opera houses, their powerhouse institutions. The demands of regional audiences and financial crises within dance companies were given consideration as they arose; but without internal structures to put dance development on the agenda, there was resistance to expanding the number of clients. After the closure of Ballets Jooss in 1947, and apart from the period in 1948–50 when the Arts Council directly managed a company, St James's Ballet, to visit 'theatreless' towns (this was before the 'Raise' side of the debate got the upper hand), the regular client list did not change for a decade: Sadler's Wells Ballet and Sadler's Wells Theatre Ballet (together becoming the Royal Ballet in1956), and Ballet Rambert. There were occasional contracts for small groups to undertake regional tours to the smallest venues. These might include other genres of dance as well as ballet, Spanish dance or the occasional performer in the European modern dance tradition.

The Arts Council's quinquennial revue of 1950 expressed the need for permanent opera and ballet companies to be set up away from London in the Midlands or northern England, but this was not acted upon. The notion of a creative, energetic company independent of the powerhouse structure did not enter into institutional thinking, neither did the development of modern dance (remembering that Martha Graham's first London season of 1954 was a critical and financial failure for want of knowledgeable audiences and critics). British ballet was on a 'high' of international acclaim, particularly in the USA. The contemporary appeal of ballet choreographers from France, Roland Petit and Janine Charrat, highly popular with London audiences, was nevertheless rather exotic and foreign. This perception was going to be challenged by a new generation of British ballet choreographers in the 1950s who showed they could turn the balletic vocabulary into something as relevant as the contemporary film they so admired. This is part, but perhaps not the main part, of the changing climate of opinion in which a new Arts Council dance client company materialised in 1957. This was Western Theatre Ballet (WTB), a company that benefited from a close relationship with Dartington.

This company grew out of the Bristol School of Dancing. As early as 1952 the principals, Muriel Carpenter and Mary Hoskyn, had attempted to set up a small regional company, the West of England Ballet. They had been introduced to Peter Cox, who then watched a try-out for Western Theatre Ballet in Bristol in 1956 and felt that 'this was a company we could support and make use of in building up an audience for the Barn Theatre'.[66] Direction of the company was by Elizabeth West and Peter Darrell, both of them choreographers but with different talents: West the indomitable guiding force, Darrell with a sophisticated aptitude for choreographing complex human relationships.[67] Their plan was twofold: to tour the small and medium venues of the west and south-west of England and to make the programmes theatrical in the broadest sense, with predominantly new choreography on contemporary themes. Not for them the cut-down classics with a *corps de ballet* of four, although they would often include classical *pas de deux*. A problem that emerged very soon, however, was that there was a tension between these two objectives: performing new and often challenging work could prove unpopular in some quite conservative communities.

The first tour in 1957 was given a guarantee against loss of £500 by the

Arts Council; it had to be paid in full. In 1958 there was an outright grant for production costs. By 1961 the grant had risen to £4000. Equally important was the week's accommodation for rehearsal and scenery painting before the opening performances in the Barn Theatre. This became a feature of the relationship with Dartington – in-kind support of rehearsal and backstage costs and the best possible terms the budget would allow, sometimes contracting the company on a guaranteed-income basis rather than the percentage of box-office, which was the arrangement they had to accept in many other places.

Why did the Arts Council give funding to Western Theatre Ballet in 1957 on its first application? Another company performing in small venues, including in the south-west, Ballets Minerva (admittedly a much more ramshackle affair), had been applying without success since 1953. No clear answer has emerged but a number of factors must have aided the company's first bid and persuaded the Arts Council to continue looking favourably on it. The cause of dance in the smaller regional venues all over the country had been coming up as an unresolved issue since the time of St James's Ballet. Before regional offices were closed, some Regional Directors, including Cyril Wood, Director of the South West Region and subsequently of SWAA, favoured funding for a small company that could give the experience of ballet to smaller towns never visited by the larger companies.[68] The other side of the coin was that small-scale ballet was associated with poor quality; therefore the answer frequently given in refusals of subsidy was that there had been a policy decision not to subsidise companies of this sort. If only the demands of 'Raising' and 'Spreading' could be meshed – high-quality performance alongside the greatest possible access.

Western Theatre Ballet had advantages in its strong support from SWAA, not just because of its regional conception but also because its professional standards in production and performance were high. Added to artistic merit, the company's administration proved vigorous in following up alternative funding providers, including the ones the Arts Council was constantly urging and shaming through its annual reports to take more of the funding load. To a small degree they were able to raise funds through local businesses (such as the Bristol sherry company of John Harvey) and to build up a support base of shareholders and well-wishers who were able to supplement their finances. They also explored other grant-giving such as local authorities (they drew a blank here in 1958), television companies (the Arts Council believed that these companies had a duty to support the arts, since they were responsible for a downturn in attendances – 'reafforestation', as it was called[69]) and the Gulbenkian Foundation (newly coming into arts funding), which supported the 1960 tour of the south-west and subsequently gave them a three-year funding package.[70] When all else failed, they sold their services to the commercial theatre for pantomime and musical productions. This is not to say that the money rolled in for them – indeed, it did not – but they were doing all the things the Arts Council approved of.

There were also some astute moves in getting advisors and board members whose credentials were highly influential and strongly 'establishment': the board of Governors included Arnold Haskell (critic, Principal of the Sadler's Wells Ballet School and well known to the Arts Council) and A.H. Franks (dance writer and editor of *The Dancing Times*). Western Theatre Ballet's success with the Arts Council was one step towards a change; it now became impossible to ignore other companies on the grounds of policy. In November 1960 the Music Panel agreed to give 'modest support' to Ballets Minerva and Harlequin Ballet (a small company based on the School of Russian Ballet in London). Indeed, the thinking that emerged from the Music Department at this time was that supporting small-scale touring had priority over funding another large-scale company.[71] So a combination of circumstances enabled Western Theatre Ballet to break the mould at the Arts Council, although it would be further decades before dance would be placed on an equal footing with the other arts.

The inaugural tour of Western Theatre Ballet opened in the Barn Theatre on 24 June 1957, with a programme including the premiere of *The Prisoners*, with choreography by Peter Darrell. This work came to represent for WTB what *The Green Table* was to Ballets Jooss: it was the ballet that absolutely stood the test of time in the repertoire and represented in most concentrated form the company's commitment to contemporary themes. Two men, Baudin and Christophe, escape from prison and hide out at the home of Madeleine, Christophe's wife. She is resentful of his return but is attracted to Baudin. They become lovers and Madeleine induces Baudin to murder Christophe, stabbing him in the back. From this moment of high drama, Madeleine's feelings for Baudin change. She returns to enjoying her social contacts, dancing with the neighbourhood men, but Baudin is confined to the house. He has become a prisoner once again; in his final gesture he stretches out from the window as he previously stretched out between the bars of his prison cell.

Danced to Bartok's *Music for Strings, Percussion and Celesta*, which magnified the edgy tension of the choreography, *The Prisoners* was a taut narrative of character and psychology, with Darrell using the classical vocabulary in unexpected ways: Madeleine's stabbing *pointe* work characterised her vicious individualism and when she used the men for support, she bore down on them rather than being lightly elevated. There were no balletic fairies and swans here, and Barry Kay's original costume designs referred to mundane contemporary clothing: a leather jacket for Christophe, a pullover for Baudin and Madeleine wore a cardigan over her dress, taking it off in order to seduce Baudin.

The themes of sexual intrigue, betrayal, confinement and contemporary culture were ones to which the repertoire would return. Examples include *A Wedding Present* (Darrell, 1962), about a bride's discovery of her husband's homosexual past; *Sonate à trois* (Maurice Béjart, WTB production 1960), based on Sartre's *Huit clos*; and *The Web* (Laverne Meyer, 1962), in which a prevented suicide becomes so dependent on her saviour that he murders her in order to be free. There were light and up-to-the-minute pieces too: *Non Stop* (Darrell), a jazzy trio set in a coffee bar, made during the 1957 rehearsals at Dartington,[72] and *Mods and Rockers* (Darrell, 1963) to the music of The Beatles.

Finding the right repertoire for the south-west tours was a problem, even though programming leavened the serious works with light ones. The early summer tour of 1958 had to be abandoned because of poor houses, and the company took up an offer of a free studio in south London and a last-minute booking in Dublin. The company manager Mary Hoskyn wrote to Peter Cox asking for advice. How could they bring in the public they so wanted to impress? Was the work too experimental or contemporary? Cox was forthright. Some of the new works he believed to be just bad, leaving him 'embarrassed and exhausted' and the audience 'completely nonplussed'.[73] His disapproval mainly fell on two recent acquisitions: *Girl in a Mask* (Wolfgang Brunner), based on Brecht's play *The Good Woman of Setzuan*, and Darrell's new work, *Impasse*, to a *musique concrète* score, about a group of people trapped in a labyrinth. The company was in a double bind however, with finances unable to allow the discarding of ballets that did not work. Restructuring of the repertory was a slow process that was begun in 1959.

The relationship with SWAA and its arts centres was useful to WTB, although there were not enough suitable venues. The company was also important as a resource for SWAA; it regularly came up on the agenda for conferences and meetings, many of which were hosted by Dartington in the Great Hall or the large spaces of the Dance School. However, in the end and for a variety of reasons, the 'Long Term Project for Western Theatre Ballet'[74] to be resident in the West Country for at least six months of the year, to work with designers, composers and dancers from the region, and to become proactively involved in developing audiences and educational work in partnership with local authorities, proved impractical. It was also to a degree in tension with their other desire to be adventurous and experimental, 'to try out new ideas on a shoe-string, and to be at ease in the smaller theatres' and 'to take up ... the challenge of French experiment'. The relationship with local authorities did not develop and the regional situation was also a disadvantage in putting them at a distance from London and hence not able to lobby effectively.[75] For critical support, they needed to perform in London venues. It also became clear that their aesthetics enabled them to make good foreign contacts, particularly with Maurice Béjart and the Théâtre de la Monnaie in Brussels. Regional touring abroad contrasted with the situation in the south-west; even small towns in Holland of the size of Taunton or Bridgewater had an excellent theatre, Elizabeth West reported.[76]

Although the notion of becoming a regionally based company in the south-west gradually perished, Western Theatre Ballet retained its connection with SWAA and with Dartington well into the 1960s. Its dissolution in 1968 provided the core for two regional and still existing ballet companies, Northern Ballet Theatre (based in the north of England) and Scottish Ballet, the first attempts to bring into reality the devolution perceived as a necessity by the Arts Council back in 1950. The case study of Western Theatre Ballet shows some of the problems faced by dance and ballet in particular, trying to do the small-venue circuit: recouping the high cost of productions, selling an unknown repertoire and finding suitable stages and auditoria. The material and financial infrastructure was not in place at that time.

It is as well to be realistic about the extent to which Dartington Arts Centre was able or wished to programme dance. There is no doubt that music was Dartington's first love, with drama coming a close second. Having Imogen Holst in residence enabled connections with major musicians: visits from Benjamin Britten and Peter Pears, residencies by the Amadeus String Quartet, performances of the Opera Studio in the Barn Theatre and the formation of the Dartington String Quartet were some of the important musical events at Dartington over the post-war decades. In terms of the themes running through this book, of dance in its various functions in society as they are exemplified at Dartington, it is an important point that music and drama developed well-established audiences for professional work in parallel with well-established amateur performance-making, both based on the presence of resident professionals. This has something in common with Christopher Martin's plan of 1941 – small professional schools training artists and teachers who would also go out to the community. From 1940 to 1965 there was no comparable dance course at Dartington itself and no amateur dance work. The real development of public dance performance at Dartington would not happen until there were dance artists permanently resident there again.

Early on, much of the dance programming at Dartington came about through personal contacts. As a schedule, it looks sparse but also eclectic. In 1949, four dancers from Ballet Rambert, Walter Gore, Paula Hinton, Cecil Bates and Annette Chappell, performed as part of a summer festival. This was just when Rambert's company had returned from their Australian tour with their finances wrecked and with no work. Remembering how Dorothy had helped Rambert in the past, it is most likely that this performance was a way of sponsoring them. There was a general welcome for dancers with a Dartington connection, including recitalists such as the former Jooss–Leeder student Yoma Sasburgh and the Art of Movement Studio staff member Geraldine Stephenson. Cox was blunt when asked to programme the British Dance Theatre, a small group of performers who had all been students at the Art of Movement Studio in Manchester. Invited to see them perform at Altrincham in 1950, he reported that he could not recommend them technically or artistically. They were not invited to perform at Dartington.[77] The former student and Ballets Jooss member Lucas Hoving with two other dancers from the José Limon company came in 1964. Performances by former students and present and former dance faculty members would become a feature of the lively dance environment in the College in the 1970s and 1980s, to be explored in Chapters 5 and 6.

The cultural interchange of music and dance between India and Dartington that went back to the 1930s continued in the post-war years. In 1951 Imogen Holst spent a term at Santiniketan, and a sitarist from there made a return visit to Dartington. There continued to be comings and goings between Dartington and Santiniketan, the two utopias. Beryl de Zoete was essential in introducing to Dartington some of the Asian performers of the early post-war years. Three Javanese dancers with a Balinese repertoire, Liong, Edo and Tamar Sie, came in 1948; and a kathakali dancer, Shivaram, performed in the Barn Theatre for the Modern Dance Holiday Course. These four dancers performed together in London.[78] The dancer Shanta Rao, trained in bharata natyam, mohini attam and kathakali styles, was introduced through Beryl de Zoete in 1955. Even though remote from London and other metropolitan centres, Dartington became a stop on the network of venues for Indian dance. The national context of performance and audiences was quite different from that of the pre-war years when dancers such as Uday Shankar were trading both on their charismatic stage presence and on orientalist perceptions of the exotic East. By the 1950s, the struggle to authenticate the Indian dance forms as properly 'classical' (although there had been reconstruction and revision) was largely won. Now they were carriers of both the heritage and contemporary identity of the newly independent and democratic state of India, whose dancers and musicians were taking on the world in greater numbers. There was also an increased and knowledgeable audience from the Indian diaspora, and increasingly there were British-based artists. The Asian Music Circle in London, founded in 1953, became a central platform and promoting body for dancers and musicians. It presented a programme of films at Dartington in 1958 and a performance of 'Indian and Kandyan Music and Dance' in 1960 and facilitated the booking of other artists.

Between them, the dancers who visited Dartington covered most of the classical dance styles of India: bharata natyam, kathak, kathakali, kuchipudi, manipuri, mohini attam and odissi. Artists such as Ritha Devi (related to the Tagore family) and Raja and Radha Reddy were well established and receiving appreciative reviews in London. Balasaraswati, representing the hereditary line of bharata natyam dancers going back for generations, visited Dartington in 1965 after appearing in the Edinburgh International Festival. Other notable dancers who performed and gave workshops were Durga Lal, a celebrated kathak dancer of the Jaipur School, Anjali (the Canadian Anne-Marie Gaston) and the young bharata natyam dancer Shobana Jeyasingh, who would later become a trailblazer in using her classical dance vocabulary in contemporary dance choreography. For a regional and rural dance venue, Dartington's performance platforms encompassed a wide horizon. It would be naive to assume the audience was always appreciative. Peter Cox found that it was not until the 1960s had popularised the sounds of Indian music and the notion of 'the hippy trail' that the size of the audiences reflected the stature of the performers.[79]

Cox decided to take a risk by engaging the Merce Cunningham company for the Barn Theatre at short notice in 1964 before their London engagement on their world tour. The company had a free week, and Dorothy had apparently met Cunningham when he was at the Cornish School, which he attended during 1936–39.[80] The normal ticket prices were significantly raised in order to cover the cost and the performances were all sold out, but this would be a very different experience compared with other recent dance visitors to the Barn Theatre, Western Theatre Ballet or even Lucas Hoving from the José Limón Company. Cunningham and his music and design collaborators, John Cage and Robert Rauschenberg, represented a source of the avant-garde that would radically mould dance at Dartington in the next decade but that at this moment could only be a shock to the system. Cunningham was reacting against the dominant dramatic and literary themes and urgent emotional communication of the first generation of modern dance artists such as Martha Graham, with whom he had danced. Movement, sound and visual effects were themselves the subject of his dance works. He had abandoned the accepted norm that dance, music and design were bound together to produce cohesive meanings. Instead, they were to coexist on the stage as autonomous channels. Music and dance were created independently, related by the durations of sections and of the whole dance, but not consciously being made in each other's image. They might never have been performed together until the first night.

Cunningham had been experimenting with chance procedures such as flipping a coin or rolling dice, in order to find unexpected, non-habitual ways of ordering material and giving new challenges to dancers and to himself to fit movements together in unfamiliar ways. His dances did not pretend anything about fantasy worlds or characters, but incorporated images of everyday life. Any movement could be dance material even if it was awkward or mundane, but these movements were woven into the choreography, which nevertheless remained technically demanding. In the same way, Cage and Rauschenberg often used 'found' sound and materials out of everyday life – the sound of tin cans or packing cases on stage. The ultimate challenge was for the audience, which might find itself floundering, searching for meaning in what might seem a chaotic amalgam of sensations.

There were two performances and an open rehearsal at Dartington, in all giving eight of Cunningham's works, including *Winterbranch*, *Antic Meet* and *Story*.[81] The printed programme for the Dartington performances included explanatory notes for most dances. It was not really Cunningham's way to offer apparent meanings to dances that were essentially ambiguous, but the tour had issued a brochure to presenters to offer some background to the work and many, including Dartington, had printed those notes.[82] In *Antic Meet*, Cunningham danced with a chair strapped to his back as a satire on the support given to a ballerina partner, the programme note indicated. He also wrestled to put on a jumper with four arms but no hole for the head. In the paradoxically named *Story*, which was anything but a linear narrative, dancers chose their own costumes from a pile in the wings. Cunningham made a choice by chance procedure before each performance about the order of the dance sections and the overall duration. Dancers also had a limited amount of choice during the performance itself. At each venue Rauschenberg made a design environment out of what was to hand. At Dartington, he and his assistant Alex Hay made an appearance on stage, quietly ironing shirts at the back, unconcerned at the dance going on around them, although the dancers apparently felt upstaged.[83] In *Winterbranch* (for which no programme note was given), in semi-darkness and with a screeching electronic score, Rauschenberg controlled shafts of bright light that randomly illuminated the dancers. Cunningham's intention was to make a dance about the action of falling, but it has often been interpreted by audiences as a representation of nuclear catastrophe. Dorothy wrote some notes on her programme about the appearance of trying to break free from something.[84]

Cage, Cunningham and Rauschenberg appeared in public to explain their methods. The audience was

> dumbfounded to experience John Cage walking down the aisle of the auditorium rattling the pipe of a vacuum cleaner on the radiator grills and when reaching the orchestra pit slamming down the lid of the grand piano ... [85]

No doubt Cage was provocatively drawing attention to his credo that any sound could constitute music, and Rauschenberg in *Story* was making every-day movement into art.

Although they had to perform their repertory on a much smaller stage than they were used to, the week at Dartington gave them some respite in a gruelling tour. John Cage, who was also an expert in edible fungi, went out on a hunt in the gardens, coming back with a variety of specimens that he cooked for the group, much to the horror of the kitchen staff. In spite of his later reflection that the Cunningham performances had alienated some of his audience from anything unfamiliar for several years, Cox tried unsuc-cessfully to arrange further visits in 1966 and in 1972. Although this did not happen, one of the dancers, Steve Paxton, would become a significant visit-ing and resident artist.

The national and regional infrastructure for arts and dance funding began to change in the mid-1960s. In 1965 a Ballet Sub-Committee of the Arts Council Music Panel was set up, later renamed the Dance Theatre Sub-Com-mittee but for some time dominated by a ballet outlook (Ninette de Valois was chairman until 1972). At about the same time, the Arts Council committed itself to working through the regional arts associations, which had prolifer-ated after the example of the South West region. So the imperative of 'spreading' arts provision to the regions was reaffirmed and the regional arts associations were able to establish funding partnerships with local authori-ties, incorporating the kind of local commitment the Arts Council had long wished for.

In 1967, professional arts programming at Dartington was taken over by Dartington Arts Society, a body of subscribers with an executive guided in its programming policy by advisory panels for the different art forms. There was a Dance and Drama Advisory Panel. By this time, as will be seen in the fol-lowing chapter, dance had been established alongside drama as a college subject and there were resident dance professionals. An arts officer was ap-pointed in 1972, enabling the programme to expand in collaboration with South West Arts. To this period belongs a series of residencies by music and dance ensembles following their appearances at the International Festival of Youth Orchestras in the summer. The first of these was the Dance Theatre of Fiji in 1974. This was clearly a large and important undertaking for Dartington Arts Society, which organised the Fijians' tour of the south-west and a journey to London to dance before the Queen at the centenary celebra-tions of the ceding of Fiji to the Crown. The company spent a week based at Dartington and was given a full programme of entertainment, facilities for rehearsal and media promotion. The farewell performance in the Barn Thea-tre was attended by the High Commissioner, Sir Joshua Rabakawaqa, whose son was a student at the Summer School of Music and was staying on for a further term. In following years the Courtyard, Barn Theatre and Great Hall rang out to the rhythms of the Nigerian Dance Mime Company of Ahmadu Bello University, choreographed by Peter Badejo, the Phe Zulu Troupe and Maori Dancers from a high school in New Zealand. Badejo would later become resident in Britain and be key in the development of contemporary African dance and performance.

In the next chapter I will be exploring the change in the national professional dance culture of the 1960s and 1970s. We could call this an 'explosion' of interest in modern dance performance, coming about through a first generation of dance students from both Dartington and the London School of Contemporary Dance who were pushing the boundaries, trying to find work and trying to raise the profile of the art form while the institutions were struggling to keep up with them. While regional associations were showing interest in setting up regional small companies, Jane Nicholas from the Arts Council of Great Britain (the officer responsible for dance to the Dance Theatre Sub-Committee of the Music Panel, but without a department of her own) was urging caution on financial grounds.[86] The regions were still poorly served at advisory and officer level, but there was agitation to remedy this.[87] At least dance became a topic of special interest, with meetings of regional arts association officers devoted to it.[88] One of the outcomes of these was a regional tour of the Paul Taylor Dance Company from America, performing in Paignton in the south-west.

It is within this atmosphere that, in 1974, South West Arts (formerly SWAA) brought into its Theatre Advisory Panel a dance professional living locally. This was Peter Curtis, a former dancer with Ballet Rambert, now with a dance school in Dawlish and also formerly a teacher at Dartington College of the Arts. He wrote a report on dance in the region. He was most keen to develop a 'dance presence' on multiple levels, especially the small and medium scales. Of course many venues were unsuitable, but companies could learn to adapt repertoires to different ways of relating to audiences.[89] This resulted in South West Arts setting up its own Dance Advisory Panel in 1975 with Curtis as chairman. Although it had a small budget, the panel worked on a number of levels, offering guarantees to encourage the booking of large ballet companies in places such as Paignton, offering choreographic commissioning fees for dance company premieres in the region, arranging highly successful tours of dance films to small venues, and working through the Arts Council's Small Scale Dance Touring Scheme to part-fund regional tours. Under this scheme, small dance companies – EMMA Dance Company (the regional company set up by East Midlands Arts), Extemporary Dance Company and Basic Space – were able to perform at Dartington, as well as elsewhere in the south-west. Dartington Arts Society extended its reach, promoting performances in a larger space at Totnes and organising coach parties to attend performances in Exeter of London Contemporary Dance Theatre and Ballet Rambert.

Other schemes coming from South West Arts' dance panel aimed for a more grass-roots approach to dance – encouraging the slow development of dance centres for public participation in Bristol and Exeter, and funding a peripatetic dance teacher post and even a regional dance company. Dance Tales was founded by Tim Rubidge in 1978 and based at Rolle College, Exmouth, undertaking performance and educational work in the South West region.[90] In a way, the re-emergence of regional arts brought together both sides of the 'Raise or Spread' debate. It was not a matter now of amateur arts versus professional arts or metropolitan venues versus local ones, but a matter of linking all those together: metropolitan companies in regional residencies, locally based professionals working in education and with amateurs. This is not to say that any of this suddenly became easy or financially viable, but at least there was a developing notion of integration.

At the Arts Council of Great Britain, it was not until 1980 that the Dance Advisory Committee within the Music Department was upgraded to a full panel and a separate Dance Department was formed with its own Director. This change at the centre of arts funding in Britain was in part a result of the intense activity and proliferation of dance, with vociferous dancers aiming to take their own routes into dance creation and making their case for more radical and generous funding – they were active in Dartington as well as in London. It will be seen in the next chapter that the most consistent support for dance performance at Dartington would come with the presence of resident dance artists/educators within an academic framework.

The Dance School

This chapter has been a bridge between two periods of dance activity intrinsic to Dartington, the first in 1927–40 and the second from 1965 onwards. Nationally, the development of Laban's work in education and in amateur dance formed a parallel stream to the development of subsidised theatre dance. In the latter area I have carried the narrative forward to the late 1970s in relation to the regional situation around Dartington. This forms a background to the story of dance at Dartington itself in the next chapter, when the two streams of educational and professional dance flowed together as the development of dance in higher education increasingly came to mean a more profound study of dance as art and as performance. Along with that, questions about the social significance of the arts came to be seen once more as fundamental at Dartington.

Within this bridging period we have seen that dance did not disappear from Dartington, coming back sporadically to its performance spaces, including the Dance School. Although at times Barr's large studio might have seemed an overlarge 'white elephant' (and in 1965 it was significantly reduced in length), its usefulness continued and perhaps the promise remained that it would once more come into use for its intended purposes. From 1951 to 1964 it was the site of the annual Children's Christmas Festival. The Festivals point up several things about Dartington's direction in this period when there was no permanent dance course. They show the way that Christopher Martin's 1941 concept of small professional schools could nurture local arts and the arts in education. Local schoolchildren were brought together with the students on Dartington's courses in music, art and drama and with the professional staff at Dartington. For a week, they came up to the Hall for a day of activity and, as concepts of child-centred, creative education spread over the decade, they were involved more directly in making the performance themselves. Throughout the Autumn term there would be extensive contact between Dartington and the schools, choosing and rehearsing carols, learning dances and creating the decorations. One year, Yoma Sasburgh performed and made dances for the children.[91] The Christmas Festival 1959 was televised in a programme for BBC TV, introduced by Huw Wheldon. Inside, the Dance School had been transformed into an environment of castles, mountains and trees (every school contributed a tree and every child made a star) for *Christmas Journey*, the telling of the Christmas story, centring on the story of the Three Kings. Dorothy spoke the introduction and the children were involved in processions and country dances accompanied by Winsome Bartlett on pipe and tabor. Afterwards they all processed to the Great Hall for carols.[92]

'This was once the home of an adult ballet company, an unsuccessful experiment', Wheldon commented. The Jooss era of professional performance seemed to be very far behind. But was it? Even though the Dartington policy towards dance was focused on education at that moment, the search for dance professionals to be permanently based there had not been abandoned.

Chapter 5

Artists and Educators

It suddenly dawned on me that this was the most potent educational form of decision-making that I had ever witnessed, involving simultaneously both mind and body, building up in this group of boys an incredible resource. Nothing could have done more to persuade me that dance should become once again an integral part of our work at Dartington.
Peter Cox, 2005[1]

Here was Peter Cox observing a movement class in the West Riding of Yorkshire: a group of boys collaborating to make a dance on the Biblical story of Ezekiel and the dry bones. He had been taken by Ruth Foster, a Schools Inspector and colleague of Christian Schiller in London with a special interest in dance education. She had been Dartington's trusted adviser for many years. Her inside knowledge of the Inspectorate and the Ministry of Education were invaluable both to Dartington and to the Laban Art of Movement Centre Trust. A movement-education insider with close ties to Laban associates such as Diana Jordan, she also had a broader perspective. Like Cox, she had seen at first hand how dance was integrated into higher education in America.

Dance officially returned to the heart of the Dartington project in 1965, four years after Dartington Hall Arts Centre had become Dartington College of Arts. The development of the College and its courses reveals a slow and often difficult evolution in the general direction of Christopher Martin's initial idea of 1941 – teacher training and a local creative culture going hand in hand. From the 1940s, courses developed in a pragmatic manner from the activities of the artists based at Dartington: Imogen Holst's small trainee programme was the prototype, becoming the Preparatory Course in Music. In 1948, the lower studios of the Dance School were converted to music practice rooms. The training was intense and artistically fruitful, creating within Dartington a focus and resource for amateur music-making and appreciation in the district. After leaving, students could then proceed to further vocational study or teacher training. Dartington also provided for the amateur arts in the Playgoers Society (an amateur dramatic group working with professional directors) and the Adult Education Centre. These led in a seemingly natural way to similar preparatory courses in drama and art. But Dartington's status as a private institution put it outside the national framework of higher education, making it difficult for prospective students to obtain local authority grants and calling into question its financial viability. In 1961, there was official recognition of new courses for music teachers, with one or two years at Dartington followed by a teacher training college in Exeter to obtain qualified teacher status – the '2 plus 1' format that had been entered into at the Art of Movement Studio one year earlier. The price for this recognition was the need to work closely with another institution, a college of education that was part of the teacher education system, conferring a nationally recognised qualification. At this point the Centre was renamed Dartington College of Arts.

Institutionally at this time the College was in a rather strange position, one that its first Principal, Peter Cox, has called 'a pretty odd and risky set-up'.[2] It had its own governing body, made up of representatives from Dartington's Trustees, Devon County Education Committee and the universities of Exeter and Bristol. Local education authority involvement was enormously helpful in the development of the College, but its constitutional position remained unclear for many years. The College was an integral part of the Trust, and the Trust was an independent body nurturing it financially. However, the College had no constitution of its own, with its position made problematic by incorporating the Devon Centre for Further Education, a County Council body, as one of its departments, set up in the East Wing of the Courtyard. It was thus rather less under the total control of the Trust than the Trustees would have liked. It was not until 1975 that the College entered the public sector, with 'assisted status', receiving public funds as part of the County Plan for Further Education. This relieved the Trust of a large part (but not all) of its expenditure on the College, although again causing concern at an apparent distancing from the Trust's direct control. There is no doubt, though, that the College as it was set up had at its heart the core values of the Trust, specifically to serve the Elmhirst vision of the arts in everyday life. The Arts Department became the Arts Centre, then became the College, in a sequence that reflected new needs and possibilities to fulfil those aims. In the 1960s the Trust was still dominated by the founders (Dorothy was to die in 1968 and Leonard resigned as chairman of the Trust in 1972, himself dying in 1974), but a considerable source of continuity of aim across the years was provided by Peter Cox, Director of the Arts Department, Warden of the Arts Centre and Principal of the College until 1983.

In 1965, Ruth Foster became Vice-Principal of the College and Head of the Dance and Drama Department, expanding on its preparatory course in drama with a new course for specialist teachers of dance and drama in secondary schools. This '2 plus 1' course combined two years of immersion in the arts at Dartington to obtain the Diploma in Dance and Drama Education with a year in Rolle College, Exmouth, intensively working on educational theory and practice in order to obtain qualified-teacher status. Dance and drama were again bedmates in the Dartington plan, as they had been in the 1930s. Students took both along with subsidiary arts subjects in the first year, specialising in dance or drama in the second year. Why dance and drama together? There seem to have been pragmatic issues alongside educational and artistic ones. Ruth Foster had strong connections in both areas of education and perhaps it seemed the safest way of building on what was already in place. In any case, this combination was to characterise the field at the College for decades.

Bringing dance back to Dartington

Before moving on to a more detailed assessment of the course from a dancer's perspective, we need to examine the Dartington of the 1960s within a context of developments in dance as education and dance as art. Peter Cox suggests in his memoirs, in the passage partly quoted at the opening of this chapter, that the practice of dance teaching in school education had provided the impetus to get the course started. However, to a certain extent he was being influenced by other circumstances, including the availability of somebody who would fit into the overall artistic environment. Geraldine Stephenson, a student and colleague of Laban and Ullmann, did some work with the preparatory drama course in autumn 1959 but, although she was wanted back, remoteness from London caused a conflict with other work.[3] In 1962 there was some correspondence between Cox and Kurt Jooss about the possibility of Jooss's daughter Anna or another *Folkwangschule* student becoming the dance teacher, but there was clearly at this stage no sense of developing a full-time post.[4] About one thing Cox was determined: this was not a position for Lisa Ullmann. The artistic environment of the College was to be one of practising artists who were also teachers – they must be artist/educators like Imogen Holst. Creating and performing at a professional level and collaborating across disciplines were the touchstones; these were not the areas where Ullmann had demonstrated her greatest ability.[5]

From their knowledge of the teaching of dance in American universities, both Foster and Cox leant towards importing a teacher from there. At this point, Dartington College of Arts did not have degree-level courses and nationally there were no degree-level courses in dance, so why look towards the US for the training of dance teachers as a creative subject in state secondary schools? Some light on this is shed by Cox's draft proposal to the Trustees in 1964. He wished to differentiate markedly the Dartington course in its dance aspect from that of the Art of Movement Studio. Dartington was to provide 'a new creative tradition'. He had in mind that it should be a source of college lecturers and that there should also be a preparatory course in dance, just as in drama and music, suitable for young aspiring professionals.[6] This did not happen, and the preparatory courses for art and drama were to close down in a few years; but the clear implication is that the model of dance teacher education at Dartington was to be of a new sort, breaking out of the Laban/ Ullmann mould.

If Cox was leaning towards an American model of dance as a discipline area in higher education, what did that mean in the 1960s? The first American dance major had been offered at the University of Wisconsin as early as 1927. In the 1930s, the development of the 'big four' modern dancers – Martha Graham, Doris Humphrey, Charles Weidmann and Hanya Holm – had been encouraged by the regular summer schools at Bennington College, Vermont, where they not only taught but also had the facilities to create and premiere new work. Bennington seeded the development of dance in higher education in other colleges as the summer students went back to teach. So this symbiosis between the professional practice of modern dance and the institutions of higher education was set in place early, while American modern dance was, as it were, still finding its feet as a cultural force. The spread of college modern dance departments also offered the professionals residencies and performance opportunities – the so called 'gymnasium circuit'. It is no surprise, therefore, that dance in higher education in America leant towards these codified techniques of modern dance. Alongside this went notions of teaching dance composition in a systematic way, much influenced by Graham's musical director, Louis Horst, who conducted classes in dance composition, initially based upon musical form.[7] Learning the craft of 'well-made' dances was integral to dance in the higher education curriculum, although the prescriptiveness of this approach was increasingly challenged from the 1960s onwards with the influence of Merce Cunningham and others. In this chapter we will see this succession of approaches to dance-making as they arrived at Dartington.

In Britain, the wider context is what may appear to be an explosive interest in American modern dance in the 1960s. However, the nature of that explosion needs to be moderated by a sense of a more slowly changing aesthetic response. It is notorious that Martha Graham and her company had an unsuccessful season in London in 1954. Critical acclaim was split and audiences were small. It took nearly a decade for the time to be ripe for a Graham triumph in London in 1963. The visit of the José Limón Dance Company to London in 1957 (including the ex-Jooss dancer Lucas Hoving) was perhaps a perceptible staging point when British audiences saw a different technique and choreographic approach from that of Graham and started to appreciate the diversity of American modern dance. There was also undoubtedly a change in the general cultural outlook from the defensive, inward-looking post-war world-view to the acceptance that America now stood for political leadership in the West. What is more, they had an awesome cultural vitality, epitomised by Jerome Robbins's jazzy ballets for his company

'Ballets: USA' (visiting in 1959) and in the musical *West Side Story*. In 1959 a film on Graham and her work, *A Dancer's World*, was shown in London and transmitted on BBC television. By the early 1960s there was a strong lobby in some areas of the dance press to raise awareness of American modern dance and to promote it as the coming thing:

> now that the Central European tradition of expressionist dance has virtu-
> ally dried up, practically everything that is of interest in non-classical,
> non-ethnic theatrical dancing has its roots in America.[8]

This foreclosure on European modern dance as a theatrical genre was typical of critics of the period, although of course the European dance had not gone away but was represented by its educational and recreative strands (Chapter 4) and a persistent though struggling recital culture. Already by 1963 there were American dancers teaching modern dance in London, and some British dancers had gone in the opposite direction, experiencing the Graham School in New York – Elizabeth West of Western Theatre Ballet being one. This was the background to the successful Graham season in London in 1963, which had been brought about by the intervention of a wealthy hotel owner, Robin Howard.

Howard was a patron in the Elmhirst mould, albeit with less money behind him, supporting British students at the Graham School in New York personally and then through a trust. From May to July 1965 there were London classes given by principals of the Graham Company and continued by some of the British dancers who had already trained in New York. This was the embryonic London School of Contemporary Dance, but it had no premises and no settled existence until a studio was found in 1966. Thus, while Dartington was settling its new course into its existing Dance School, the London School was struggling to be born. Ruth Foster knew Robin Howard well and was abreast of all these developments.

The educational establishment, represented by dance teachers and college lecturers trained in Laban work, was already being introduced to American modern dance technique. Ruth Foster had been instrumental in this. During a visit to America she had been very impressed by Dorothy Madden from the University of Maryland. Foster had the influence at college and inspectorate level to make the connection between dance as it appeared in the US college system and its very different UK counterpart. Madden was brought over for a term to work at I.M. Marsh PE College in 1963. In 1964 Lucas Hoving toured PE colleges and the West Riding of Yorkshire, where dance in schools was well established, and he performed with his group at Dartington too.[9] Dartington began to host Madden's summer courses for training college lecturers and teachers in 1965, when she also brought a group of her

Maryland students for a tour of twenty-five venues, including the Barn Theatre, and to lead classes and demonstrations. Also on this occasion, some of the first contacts of the incipient London–Dartington dance connection took place. Ethel Winter of the Martha Graham Dance Company, currently teaching the classes mentioned above, gave a lecture demonstration at Dartington with some London students and Robin Howard shared his vision of the future for British dance.[10] There were courses again in 1966, 1967 and 1968. Madden was first choice for the post at Dartington but could not be released from her university work in America until 1969. In spite of a warm relationship with Peter Cox and many references in correspondence to Dartington as her spiritual home, she spent only one full academic year there and did not become a permanent member of staff.[11]

Madden's courses at Dartington, with funding from the Department of Education and Science, did much to subvert the ascendancy of European modern dance in education. This to some extent resulted from her own qualities as a teacher. Her technique classes were a rich mixture of her influences, with some exercises from Graham technique but overall having the rebounding quality of Humphrey–Weidman technique – suspension, fall, recovery. She also had some of the German modern dance influence from two sources: through her first dance teacher, who had studied with Wigman, and from Wigman's student Hanya Holm, who had set up her New York school in 1931. Technique, though, was only a means to an end – creativity, choreography – although the approach to creativity differed markedly from the Laban approach. She worked on the skills and craft of choreography, and her criticisms of choreographic tasks were incisive. 'She knew what you could do ... she somehow sensed what you were capable of within the limitations of that task.' 'She gave you the technique and you could use as much of it or as little of it as you liked because she was very creative; she wasn't restrictive ... her dance technique, that was a beginning and not an end.'[12]

Her method of teaching choreography was developed from Doris Humphrey's treatise *The Art of Making Dances* (1959) and her studies with Graham's musical director, Louis Horst, who taught choreographic form both through pre-classic dance/music forms and twentieth-century modern art and music. Madden used music and visual arts as stimuli. Students remember a pavane study when Keith Yon (the department's musician) tailored a musical pavane to each student's composition.[13] Contemporary art was a stimulus for what Horst called 'strange space design'.[14] Unlike the Laban work, with its emphasis on authenticity of feeling and inner participation, Madden's approach emphasised a theatrical context. Every dance had to be created with reference to the indoor or outdoor space it was to be seen in: Dartington's spaces were used in all their splendour and diversity. It was essential that the choreographic task communicate to an external eye.[15]

The ways in which academics involved in teacher training, mostly from a PE background, accepted this new approach varied. Obviously some remained sceptical. It had been normal practice for student teachers to be given their movement training in the same mode that they would be expected to teach in schools, drawing the movement out of each individual: this was child-centred education as applied to dance. Copying movement was anathema, a denial of the child's own creativity; and this was also the approach in teaching the prospective teacher. That Madden was coming in with a new idea and with Ministry of Education support caused some confusion. For some who had originally been trained in gymnastic and games skills, however, it was refreshing to find in this work some sense of a more developed system of physical body training than they had encountered in Laban work. A number of lecturers became highly enthused by Madden's approach and introduced some aspects of it back into their colleges. Even at the Art of Movement Studio, a lecturer, Sam Thornton, introduced some of the exercises he learnt from Madden into his body-training classes – with Ullmann's agreement, he says. Another, Janet Goodridge, invited a teacher from the London School of Contemporary Dance for a session.[16]

The changes in the national structure of higher education during the 1960s and 1970s, from a two- to a three-year teacher training and then subsequently to three- and four-year degrees conferring qualified-teacher status, made it imperative to deepen and broaden the content of dance courses. The focus turned towards the study of dance as a performing art, with all that that implied about clarity of form. Some would deprecate those aspects that were antithetical to Laban work – copying movement from the teacher rather than originating it oneself, prioritising the appearance of movement on the body rather than the experience within the dancer. But even Lorn Primrose, a member of the 'old guard' of Laban's work in the 1940s, while remaining philosophically opposed to Madden's approach, accepted that there could be a move towards more rigour in training the performance aspects of the Laban dance that she taught.[17] For those who had an arts background, Madden's courses were a confirmation of their perception that dance as art, crafted and perfected, had a place in higher education.[18] There was also a challenge here in the technical clarity that Madden's American students could achieve. Should it not be possible to achieve that with British students in higher education too?

Dance and drama education

Dartington's full-time '2 plus 1' course began in 1965 with seventeen students and without a teacher of American modern dance. Instead, for one term Diana Jordan came to teach Laban work. The first dance teacher to take up a post at the College was an American, Flora Cushman. Her appointment at Dartington in 1966 came about through the friendship between Foster and Robin Howard. Cushman was suggested by Robert Cohan, co-director of the Graham company, who later came to direct the London School of Contemporary Dance and London Contemporary Dance Theatre. She had a talent for enthusing people to dance. Under her, the main focus of the work in dance was the formal teaching in Graham technique, rather than choreography as it had been in Madden's courses. She was training the students as dancers. Specialisation in dance or drama did not happen until the second year, and so dance technique in the first year could start only from a low base because some students would not have any previous training. However, there was 'special dance', an invitation-only technique class that the best dancers of any year aspired to. There was indeed a marked contrast between the formality of the dance training and what was going on in drama, where there was experiment and improvisation. This might be seen as an exciting balance or an awkward mismatch but, although apparently there were complaints, the only student from the first intake to specialise in dance, Rosemary Butcher (then Rosemary Martin), found the contrast stimulating.[19] Whatever the problems of making the course coherent, it is clear that within the first few years Dartington had developed a reputation as a place that was training dance performers who would have the additional benefit of a recognised teaching qualification (although some students elected not to go on to Rolle College). The flow from Dartington into professional dance performance is impressive for what was supposed to be a teaching course. Even more so, the creative talent developed at Dartington was significant; for example, in the late 1960s Rosemary Butcher, Sue MacLennan and Janet Smith were students, all three to go on to significant and still thriving choreographic careers.

There was a substantial area of concern around their curriculum: was it appropriate for students who were expected to become teachers of dance or drama in state schools? In 1967, Foster sent a paper to Leonard that she had prepared apparently in response to the criticism that Graham technique in dance was being included for students who eventually wished to specialise in drama. Leonard sent it to William Elmhirst for comment. Did he know of any drama colleges where Graham technique was being taught? As a former Laban student, an actor with the Royal Shakespeare Theatre and now a college governor, William Elmhirst had relevant experience to draw on and did not appear too impressed with Foster's defence. He did not think she had adequately distinguished the movement training every actor needs from the dance training they were currently getting in their first year. He felt that her criticism of Laban work ('A Laban dancer is, too often, embarrassing to watch') missed the point that Laban's dance was about inclusivity – dance for everybody. Now that Dartington's preparatory courses for intending professional performers in drama had been abandoned, he questioned whether the '2 plus 1' was properly focused. They had to remember they were training teachers, not performers.[20] Clearly there is truth in this in terms of the coherence of course content. But at the same time, the issue is not cut and dried. The Dartington model at that moment was of the artist/educator, a model originally broached by Christopher Martin and generally considered to have been given full form by Imogen Holst. If Dartington students were to be seen as artist/educators in the making, how else to do this but to bring to Dartington the ideas currently in the forefront of the art of dance in Britain? However, the connection between the technical base in the art of dance and the project of an accessible and relevant dance education in schools appears to have been quite tenuous at that time.

Ruth Foster taught a class of her own devising called 'Resources', which had a basis in Laban work, although this does not appear to have been made explicit. The body was taken as the ultimate resource for dance and theatre work – using the senses, understanding breath and energy, relating to space, relating to other bodies, and often within a format of directed improvisation.[21] The lack of explicit reference to Laban is interesting in its own right. Perhaps Foster's reservations about aspects of Laban work had something to do with this, or perhaps she was focused on a new beginning for dance education. It is informative to refer to her book on the nature of expression in dance and drama, *Knowing in My Bones* (1976), written after her retirement from Dartington and financed by the Elmgrant Trust. The term 'resources' is used here to refer to the child's technical understanding of movement, for example in dynamics and use of space; but, apart from a mention of Laban on her Acknowledgement page, there is no direct reference to Laban-derived theory or practice and much of the discussion derives from interviews with artists, including Cunningham and Jooss. This is indeed a new vision, the perceptions of professional artists having much to say of relevance to the school context.

Despite concerns broached by some, for others the breadth of the whole dance and drama course seems to have been a great strength, including as it did aspects of performance that a dance student would not normally expect to have available. Fionna McPhee, a student who began at Dartington in 1969, remembers singing and voice production with Keith Yon, who made apparent the link between music and the body. There were projects with music and visual arts departments. The atmosphere was enlivened by the presence of Indian musicians of the stature of Ravi Shankar and Imrat Khan, who taught their students in the open air when weather allowed. A well-known jazz musician living locally, Mike Westbrook, occasionally came to play for dance classes, sometimes with other members of his trio. 'They would take off improvising and we would just keep going.'[22] There was always a sense of horizons opening up. Rosemary Butcher remembers that it was 'incredibly focused on creativity. It didn't set so many rules for people.' Students were offered the independence to find their own direction in creative work.[23]

Students were also encouraged to see themselves as part of the larger project of Dartington, its history, its major artists and its values. 'Dartington People and Places' was a series of afternoon seminars in which students were shown other areas of Dartington's work, introduced by Leonard (in 1969) in the Private House, then continuing with visits to Dartington's industries – tweed mill, pottery, glass factory and farm.[24]

After the intensity and excitement of the Dartington experience, the move to Rolle College was bound to be difficult, particularly for those of the dance students who were by now interested in becoming artists rather than teachers. They had, after all, been trained for performance for two years and now faced the problem of converting their body of dance knowledge into something suitable for school-based work. To ease frustrations, they could return to Dartington for 'special dance' once a week. They were, of course, getting no technique there but Laban work suitable for teaching. Ann Cottis taught them from the Laban perspective and, though she might have found them sometimes difficult as student teachers, was impressed with their creative ability.[25] Some students took the opportunity to start technique classes and make pieces with the wider student body at Rolle.[26] The teaching qualification was useful, though perhaps only a safety net, but there was also the dilemma of then wanting more training. Under the influence of Flora Cushman there was a tendency to go on to the London School of Contemporary Dance – Sue McLennan did this, as did Karen Burgin and Kate Harrison (who would become a dancer in London Contemporary Dance Theatre).

Of the eight dance specialists leaving Rolle College in 1972, three went straight on to further training and to subsequent performing careers: Janet Smith went to America, and Ruth Foster suggested that Fionna McPhee and Linda Colston go to Rotterdam, where Lucas Hoving had been invited back in 1971 to found the Rotterdam Dance Academy.

But some of that artistic dance perspective also filtered back into schools: we can take as examples Rosemary Butcher and Sue McLennan, who taught in London schools after their time in New York. It was an advantage for them to have steady work in London at a time when the Arts Council support for small-scale and experimental dance was negligible; but they are also early examples of qualified teachers with a strong technical and creative training who were active in state school education. Another is provided by Janet Smith who, on returning from study in the US, taught at a teacher training college, Trinity and All Saints College in Leeds. Working with male PE students, she made dances on sporting themes for them. One was *Square Leg* (a cricketing reference) with music by a Dartington musician, Gordon Jones, who also toured as her accompanist in her first solo shows around this time. This piece was also performed by the demonstration group from the London School of Contemporary Dance, directed by Flora Cushman after she left Dartington – again the London–Dartington connection at work. This interface between the state education system and the professional dance world would become more interesting and mutually beneficial as time went on.

Flora Cushman, with her rigorous interpretation of Graham technique, remained at Dartington for three years. Other dancers brought different interests and emphases. Cushman's sister Georgia followed her, bringing a more lyrical approach to contemporary dance and a training in Indian classical dance, which resonated with Dartington's developing expertise and interest in Indian music. A Dartington student went on to Kalakshetra, the renowned school in Madras where Cushman had trained in bharata natyam. Stuart Hopps (a British dancer and choreographer with a background in Laban-based work who had also studied in America) taught Cunningham-based technique. After her final year at Rolle, Rosemary Butcher spent a year training in America, with Dorothy Madden in Maryland and at the Graham and Cunningham studios in New York with funding from Elmgrant. She came back to teach at Dartington in 1969, which was also the year that Dorothy Madden spent there. In the early 1970s, another former Dartington student, Janette Brookes, came back to teach, bringing a varied experience in American modern dance techniques. Peter Curtis, formerly with Ballet Rambert, joined the staff, bringing a body of knowledge that was steeped in balletic training but had absorbed the Graham technique that had been taught to the company since 1966 and the varied styles of the contemporary choreographers he had worked with.[27]

So it appears that dance training at Dartington swiftly took on a more eclectic flavour that reflected the varied and competing aspects of what was now known as 'contemporary dance', with the assumption that it was contemporary because it was coming from America. Of course, it was not new at all to label modern dance as contemporary dance. In the 1940s, Ballets Jooss had been advertised as 'the contemporary dance theatre' and in the 1950s critics had used the term 'contemporary dance' to mean those recital dancers and groups with a basis in the European tradition of Laban and Wigman. This had been conveniently forgotten while the new enthusiasms were sweeping in.

The London–Dartington connection was at work in bringing a miniature dance from Dartington to the first concert given by a group from the London School of Contemporary Dance performing with their new artistic director, Robert Cohan, and guests from the Graham company, Noemi Lapzeson and Robert Powell. This was in autumn 1967 at a small theatre outside London, attended by a curious dance press and including Rosemary Butcher from Dartington as one of the performers. *Piece for Metronome and Three Dancers*, choreographed by Patrick Steede, had been created at Dartington earlier in the year. The piece illustrates clearly the minimalism that would become one of the trends of 1970s dance in Britain. Perhaps the most significant issue about this occasion from a historical perspective is that, despite any concerns about the formality and rigours of Graham technique for the students at Dartington, the whole ethos of exploration in movement, sound, speech, text and situation was already, after only two years, capable of nurturing a creative output that could stand up to full public scrutiny.

As its title implies, the piece was performed to the ticking of a metronome placed centre stage. The three dancers, in black, grey and white, hardly moved from their places, one rocking mesmerically, the others gesturing occasionally towards each other but not communicating. There were isolated arm and head movements, 'balances, slow kneeling, rolls with occasional suggestions of Egyptian reliefs'.[28] Time and spatial patterns emerged as movements were performed in unison or sequentially. One rolling body was impeded by the legs of another – end of dance.

Cultural transitions

The years in which the College course in Dance and Drama Education was running (from 1965 to the last intake in 1975) are roughly equivalent to the period of cultural and political radicalism in Britain commonly known as 'the Sixties'.[29] The period encompasses the youthful hedonism and stylishness of 'Swinging London' along with underground and fringe movements seeking to undermine the political and cultural hierarchy. It saw the beginnings of the women's movement and gay liberation. It was the time of 'Pop Art', redolent of popular culture and mass media; of anti-art and conceptual art; and of the 'Theatre of Cruelty' stemming from Antonin Artaud with, amongst other things, a belief in the power of movement as ritual. Multiple challenges to conventions of performance and presentation suggested that free-form and mixed-media 'events' and 'happenings' could set up an alternative to the convention that theatrical productions must be 'well-made' pieces for a conventional theatre space and a conventional theatre audience. The pan-European experience of 'student power' exploded in 1968 with riots and sit-ins.

Not that this was the universal experience for the people of Britain, although events such as anti-Vietnam War demonstrations and the Hornsey College of Art student occupation were major and destabilising. People involved in the arts, though, at the very least had to be aware of the disturbance of perceptions either in the centre or at the margins of their fields. Even though radical Britain was quite buoyant, the transatlantic avant-garde was welcomed – the beat poet Allen Ginsburg, William Burroughs, iconoclastic author of *The Naked Lunch*, as well as the composer-designer-choreographer combination of John Cage, Robert Rauschenberg and Merce Cunningham. The Cunningham company had been in London in 1964 (also at Dartington) and 1966 and Rauschenberg had also been exhibited. Certainly by 1967 they had inspired experiments in various places on chance procedures and 'found' material. For example, the composer Michael Finnissy, who was closely associated with the London School of Contemporary Dance, was giving lectures and concerts influenced by Cage. There were experiments in choreography-by-chance – for instance, by Henrietta Lyons, a British student at the Graham Studio in New York who had come back to teach at the London School; and even at the Art of Movement Studio Geoffrey Sutherland was trying it out, as I experienced myself in 1967.[30]

'The Sixties' was a period of cultural transition in dance as in other areas of British life, but the dance culture that came about through that was quite a complex thing. The wind of change blowing in from America brought the Graham technique and approach to performance, seized on as 'new' in the British context but by then well bedded down as a decades-old establishment over there. Simultaneously it seems, the post-Graham ideas such as those of Cunningham were arriving, and in short succession there were post-Cunningham developments. In the 1970s, the British radicalism that resulted from some of those cross-Atlantic currents defined itself in opposition to both the long-established theatre dance tradition of ballet and the newly recognised contemporary dance coming from the London School of Contemporary Dance. All those strands of the art of dance existed simultaneously – naturally with some mutual influence and even antagonism. While Dartington would tend towards the leading edge of dance experiment in the 1970s, in the country as a whole many of us (myself and others: non-professional dancers and audiences, professionals and aspiring professionals) were happy to pursue the idealised physical form of ballet or the emotional inner landscapes of the Graham technique, rejecting the radicals as overly intellectual followers of fashion. This is the reality of history – simultaneity rather than linearity.

Butcher went to New York for the second time in 1970 and it was then that she became fully aware of the extraordinary range of experimental choreographers and multi-art collaborations, involving people such as Merce Cunningham, Yvonne Rainer, Steve Paxton and Meredith Monk. When she came back, she was ready to experiment. Amongst her first group in London were three former Dartington students – Fionna McPhee, Judy McCartney and Sue Maclennan. She returned to Dartington on teaching and performing assignments from the mid-1970s, now as a radical choreographer with an individual voice.

Children from Jenny Gertz's classes in the open air theatre at Dartington Hall, early 1940s.
[© Lisa Ullmann Archive, National Resource Centre for Dance, LU/F/1/49, 55, 70]

Improvisation on 'elastics'.

Rudolf Laban with William Elmhirst at the Art of Movement Centre, Addlestone.
[© Rudolf Laban Archive, National Resource Centre for Dance, L/F/3/55]

Movement choir rehearsals in the grounds of the Art of Movement Centre, Addlestone, early 1950s.
[© Lisa Ullmann Archive, National Resource Centre for Dance, LU/F/5]

A choreographic study from Dorothy Madden's summer school at Dartington, 1967, based on animal imagery from the Bayeux Tapestry. Left to right, Sheila Lee, Janet Goodridge and Elizabeth Murdoch, choreography by Peggy Wooderson; graphics by Catherine Turner.
[© Dartington Hall Trust Archive]

Rosemary Butcher (left) and Liz Webber perform *Piece for Metronome and Three Dancers*, choreography Patrick Steede, Dartington College of Arts, 1967.
[Dartington Hall Trust Archive]

Class in the Dance School, 1970/71, pianist Gordon Jones. Photo: Humphrey Sutton. [© by permission of Nancy Grimes; Dartington Hall Trust Archive]

Mary Fulkerson's Release class in the Dance School, c.1977. Photo: Brian Haslem. [Dartington Hall Trust Archive]

The Dance Theatre of Fiji performing in the Courtyard, 1974. Photo: Nicholas Horne
[© Dartington Hall Trust Archive]

Sitarist Imrat Khan talks to students during the Tagore Festival at Dartington, 1976, Mary Fulkerson kneeling on the left of the picture. Photo: Humphrey Sutton. [© by permission of Nancy Grimes; Dartington Hall Trust Archive]

Dance class taught by Durga Lal, Tagore Festival, 1976. Photo: Humphrey Sutton.
[© by permission of Nancy Grimes; Dartington Hall Trust Archive]

Mary Fulkerson outside the Dance School.
Photo: © Chris Crickmay.

Mary Fulkerson in *I Saw Myself Standing*,
1978. Photo: © Chris Crickmay.

Mary Fulkerson in *Remember Hearing*, installation by Graham Snow.
Photo: © Chris Crickmay.

Mary Fulkerson in *Field*, 1982, devised and performed by Mary Fulkerson and Chris Crickmay.
Photo: © Graham Green.

Steve Paxton teaching in the Great Hall at Dartington. Photos: Chris Harris. [© V&A Images/ Victoria and Albert Museum, London]

Lisa Nelson and Steve Paxton performing *PA RT*, 1980. Photos: Chris Harris.
[© V&A Images/ Victoria and Albert Museum, London]

Contributors
1987

Ariana Economu	Jo Bresslin
Ingunn Rimestad	Kate Dalton
Lise Nelson	Rosemary Lee
Steve Paxton	The Cholmondeleys
Ria Higler	Liz Aggiss
Pauline de Groot	Nic Nuttgens
Allessandro Certini	Helen Crocker
Jaap Klevering and	Kedzie Penfield
Jaana Turunen	Danielle Hogan
Mary Fulkerson	Jane Hansford
Christine Juffs	New Midlands Dance
Mary Prestidge	Jacky Lansley
Tony Thatcher	Fergus Early
Susie Ater	Tim Rubridge
Miranda Tufnell	Bonnie Meekums
Emilyn Claid	Valerie Briginshaw
Judy Sharpe	Ramsay Burt
Jointwork	Anthony Peppiatt
Helen Roberts	Michael Huxley
Matt Hauxwell	Christy Adair
Gary Rowe	Kay Hunter
Research and Navigate	Stephanie Jordan

Flyer for the last Dance at Dartington festival, 1987. Photos: © Graham Green.

The monster 'Gar' approaches along the Harbourne River at Harbertonford, May 1978. Production of *Raindough* devised by Peter Kiddle. Photo: © Cathy Kiddle.

The Chromosols dance in celebration of the defeat of Gar, *Raindough*, 1978.

Springwake, 1979. A Guardian of Winter attempts to repel the procession of townsfolk and the Queen of Spring from the grounds of Totnes Castle. Photo: © Graham Green.

Cotton Duck, student choreography by Yolande Snaith, danced by Helen Kent and Claire Bush, Dartington College of Arts, 1983. Photo: © Graham Green.

Students performing at the Leechwell, in *Dreams and Images on Totnes Streets*, Theatre Department project led by Mary Fulkerson and Graham Green, 1983. Photos: © Graham Green.

Totnes market place at night, from *Dreams and Images on Totnes Streets*.

Dance at the petrol pumps from *Dreams and Images on Totnes Streets*.

Michael Hulls and Jane Hansford in a Rotherhithe Theatre Workshop performance on the River Thames near Wapping.

Dancing in the RTW studio/theatre space in Rotherhithe.

Katy Duck improvising in the small studio at Warren House, originally built for Kurt Jooss.
Photos: © Hugo Glendinning.

Even before that, in the early part of that decade, a Dutch dancer, Pauline de Groot, had been making regular teaching visits. She had received a broad modern dance training in the US during the early 1960s, encountering a range of techniques, including Graham, the Humphrey-influenced technique of José Limón and the technique of Erick Hawkins, who was breaking away from the dramatic, tension-filled modern dance movement epitomised by Graham. More importantly, de Groot had encountered the ideas of André Bernard, who was influenced by Mabel Elsworth Todd's 1937 book, *The Thinking Body: A Study of the Balancing Forces of Dynamic Man.*

Todd was a faculty member of Teachers College, Columbia University. She wrote of the body as beautifully constructed in function and form to fulfil its work and also as a holistic entity in which psychology and biomechanics were entwined. To understand the working of the body was to achieve an economic balance between all its functions and in everyday living. Todd's book was to set off many dancers working in a completely new way, sensing from the inside of the body as opposed to imposing an outer 'look'. That line of influence from Todd would become crucially important at Dartington in the future, bringing in new concepts of the body. Dancers began to look to the body therapies for new ways of conceptualising an integrated thinking, feeling, moving unity. At Dartington, de Groot was searching for her own way of teaching, with a free use of the technical vocabularies she had learnt but certainly also aiming for students to understand principles of good alignment and tension-free movement.[31]

Dartington's connection with the London School of Contemporary Dance was consolidated in February 1968, when it was the first port of call on the tour of the Contemporary Dance Group that grew soon into the London Contemporary Dance Theatre.[32] The Dartington–London axis brought Richard Alston to the College as a guest teacher. He was a student in the early years of the London School of Contemporary Dance but one who had early on become a radical offshoot, influenced by Cunningham and the other avant-garde media and cultural manifestations of the Sixties, although he had not so far studied in America. Furthermore, from his reading, he had become intrigued by the experiments of post-Cunningham radicalism in New York and was already exploring these ideas in his choreography – chance procedures, choreographic alternatives to codified dance techniques, perhaps ordinary movement and functional movement tasks. He came to Dartington with the dance group Strider (formed 1972), an extremely influential vehicle for the new developments in British choreography of the early 1970s.[33] Thus students at Dartington were already getting some reflection at a distance of what radical American choreographers had been doing from the early 1960s and what radical British choreographers were now beginning to attempt.

But things were also changing in the world of teacher education, and the last intake on Dartington's dance and drama education course was in 1975. It is informative at this point to look back to the idea embodied in Christopher Martin's proposal of 1941 for teacher training courses that would simultaneously invigorate the arts locally. The verdict about the success of that idea must be rather mixed, with more to show in the areas of music, drama and art than in dance. This should not be surprising, since, at least in part, the preparatory courses in music, drama and art that developed into the teachers' courses had arisen from the encouragement of amateur arts by resident professionals. This was not the case in dance: the dance artists who came to Dartington to teach the teachers of the future were coming from the direction of their own professional practice and not building on their own or Dartington's notions of dance for the community. However, the College and Dartington Arts Society provided the focus for limited but diverse dance performance programming (Chapter 4). As the degree courses developed, there would be a much stronger impulse towards the community aspects of Dartington's core values.

As for the success of the course as a training for specialist dance teachers in state schools, it is useful to consider the Gulbenkian Foundation report *Dance Education and Training in Britain* (1980), which resulted from a national survey undertaken from 1974 and thus overlapping with the period of Dartington's dance and drama education course. Several issues from its consideration of the training of dance teachers for the state sector cast light on Dartington as a case study within the changing conception of what such training should imply. By 1980 there was 'a wider notion of dance' beyond purely Laban work, and 'the dance taught is more clearly identifiable as an art form'.[34] Dartington's course and Foster's convictions could be seen as examples of this. However, nationally there were factors inhibiting the study of dance academically as an art form. The lack of scholarly texts and visual material was one, positioning dance awkwardly in comparison with other arts subjects. A further issue was the one of technical standards, with varying amounts of time being allocated to practical study in different courses. As the report stated:

> future dance teachers [for secondary schools], being specialists, need to be seen to have mastered their instrument (the body) just as the teacher of music is expected to have mastered the piano or the violin. ... Complementing this requirement is a need to master theory and history, to acquire a wide dance culture as performers and spectators and to become expert as teachers able to educate young people to dance.

Teachers needed to be 'reasonably expert' in at least one dance form, and the report suggested that one way of achieving this was to bring dance professionals, dancers and choreographers into the college curriculum.[35] Although there might be concerns at times about the appropriateness of its curriculum for the needs of intending teachers, it is apparent that Dartington was leading in this aspect of the development of dance as a valid discipline in higher education – the integration of dance professionals who would become artists and educators. Other organisations came later to the same conclusion – for example, in 1976 London Contemporary Dance Theatre began residencies in colleges and universities, including work with local schools; and in 1980 the Arts Council supported a pilot scheme, 'Dance Artists in Education', in which dancers spent a block of time working in secondary schools.

Creating a degree subject

At Ruth Foster's retirement in 1971, Colette King became Head of what was now named the Theatre Department. She had previously been a drama lecturer at Dartington for two years from 1967 and had a great deal of experience in drama departments at teacher training colleges and at the Central School of Speech and Drama (where she had also been a student before taking a degree at Oxford University). It is apparent from the memories of her colleagues that she was the one who fostered the whole environment of what would eventually become the degree course, laying down some central tenets that were to make the course unique. She valued unusual people and looked for students with interesting personalities rather than already developed talents. Her approach to reconceptualising the course was to aim for coherence, with all components supporting each other. As far as she was concerned, the dance input had not been consistent and not always appropriate to the basic needs of students exploring the expressivity of their own movement in a body that was not necessarily trained. A dance post was advertised in 1973 and a dancer from Strider, Nanette Hassall, suggested that Mary Fulkerson, whom she had known at the Cunningham Studio, should apply for it. However, it took some persistence to get her to the interview day.[36]

Fulkerson was experienced in dance in an academic setting in America, having been on the staff of the University of Rochester, New York. Currently she was finding it difficult to sustain her own creative work in Europe while her husband, the musician Jim Fulkerson, was engaged on a Fellowship programme in Berlin. The manner of her arrival showed how completely different her approach would be. On the interview day, when all applicants gave a demonstration class, she followed another job applicant's very formal Graham floor-exercise class by simply getting the students to run around the studio for what seemed like ages. Having shed their expectations and their inhibitions, she set about getting them to experience the physical presence of their individual bodies. She literally came as a breath of fresh air. Fulkerson was appointed as Head of Dance on the course that was, up until 1976, still the '2 plus 1' in Dance and Drama Education.

The first professional dancers on whom Fulkerson had an impact in Britain were Richard Alston and other members of Strider. In 1973 Strider was at Dartington in April and October, meeting and working with Fulkerson on the latter occasion. Returning in March 1974, their repertoire included pieces choreographed by her and they stayed for an extended period of work in the summer. Her company from America, the Tropical Fruit Company, was also in residence. After this, Hassall remained to teach at Dartington for a while. Fulkerson brought into their movement vocabularies her anatomical alignment work, coming from sources similar to those that de Groot had encountered, with a softening of their Cunningham-influenced technical base. In terms of choreography, she introduced them to her own practices of imagery and improvisation. Alston has spoken of the 'liberation' of working with Fulkerson, and she has said of him at that time, 'his own movements changed' and 'you could see him playing in different territories of mind-body'.[37]

It was now imperative for the team that King had assembled to put together a degree programme proposal to replace the teacher training course. There are a number of reasons why change was inevitable. Most compellingly, government policy had moved towards a graduate teaching profession and many colleges had set up Batchelor of Education (BEd) degree courses. Dartington College of Arts had to devise degree-level courses or cease to exist. However, the oversupply of teachers for the falling school population forced a contraction in this area of higher education. Although the visual arts at Dartington elected to go towards a Diploma in Higher Education, which could be topped up to a BEd at Exeter University (a route that proved in the end to be riven with problems), music and theatre departments aimed for degrees that could be delivered wholly at Dartington and these were to be arts degrees, not degrees in education.

Dartington's first honours degree validated by the Council for National Academic Awards (CNAA) was the Degree in Music, commencing in 1974. Negotiations then started with the CNAA for an Honours Degree in Theatre. This was an interesting juncture in the history of dance in higher education. Hitherto, dance had only held a foothold in British institutions of higher education through specialist teacher training courses leading to a Certificate in Education, similar to the ones at Dartington and the Art of Movement Studio, or through courses at non-specialist training colleges or colleges of physical education. The new BEd programmes offered the opportunity to expand and develop the study of dance as a discipline and an art form, a change in context observed by the Gulbenkian Report quoted above. In higher education outside teacher training, dance had a difficult time getting established. At first, it entered into BA degrees only as part of a combination with other arts subjects, as Combined Studies or Creative or Performing Arts, or with physical education as part of Human Movement Studies. This was the situation until 1976, when the first BA (Hons) in Dance opened at the Laban Centre for Movement and Dance, successor to the Art of Movement Studio. However, it was not until 1984 that the first university-based, single-honours dance studies BA (Hons) course opened, at the University of Surrey (having been preceded there by postgraduate-level dance studies). Developing the curriculum and rationale for the study of dance at this level was fairly new in the country as a whole, and Dartington's proposal would be quite different from any model so far generated.

Colette King was the driving force in producing a scheme that fully integrated all areas of theatre study arising from the current practice of all the artists working there. In its overall content, the guiding concepts were ones already established in the Dartington tradition. Dance and drama would continue to go hand in hand along with writing for performance at the core of a course that had even wider interdisciplinary aspects. Theory and principles would arise from practice; the educators would themselves be practising artists; theatre was to be seen as an effective force in society. King is remembered as having been especially articulate and radical about the social relevance of the arts. This was inscribed in the preamble to the first prospectuses:

> The course as a whole is designed primarily for students of theatre who seek to put themselves and their resources at the service of those communities which the established theatre does not serve.

Arising from her perception of some of the isolation and self-importance that could be engendered at Dartington, King devised a four-year course, the whole third year being spent on placement in an urban community. 'Theatre language' was the overall name for communicating skills that interlocked on the course. There were three Central Studies – acting, moving and writing – which all students must take. They could later choose to specialise in one of the three Extended Studies: Acting and Directing, Writing for Performance, and Moving for Performance (which was the specialist dance course). The fourth core study was a course conceptualised by Colette King from her own interest in Stanislavky's theory of psychological truth in acting and issues of communication through theatre. This course, Individual and Social Processes, provided a theoretical foundation on how theatre communicates, staffed by specialists in psychology and social studies, speaking *from* their own disciplines but not teaching their disciplines per se: so perception, learning, emotion, group dynamics, and urban and rural life were examined. Alongside these were the Related Studies, which included music, design, folk studies (Dartington now had its Institute for Traditional Arts), and non-Western performing arts focusing on India, Indonesia and Japan, very often resulting in interdisciplinary projects. (The heritage from Tagore remained potent, and Richard Odlin had long ago established a collection of Javanese puppets from the journeys that Dorothy funded.) Back at College after a baptism of fire (sometimes literally) in the inner city, the fourth year was to be project-based, building on growth and perceptions garnered in the 'third year out'.

By the time she arrived at Dartington, Fulkerson was practising and teaching the method broadly known as Release, informed by the ideas in Mabel Elsworth Todd's *The Thinking Body*. She set out the movement content of the degree course along the lines of this work, which she was already using with the students on the teachers' course. Although the degree was agreed in principle in 1975, and its first intake was in September 1976, this was without Moving for Performance as an Extended Study; in other words, specialisation in dance had not been validated, although it had been accepted as a Central Study for all students. The CNAA Panel, which included some of those academics at the forefront of trying to make dance a respectable and respected discipline in higher education, had serious reservations about the syllabus as described. Release was an unknown area to them, as was the concept of 'pedestrian choreography' (that is, to include the mundane movement of the human body), perhaps a contradiction in terms when the crafting approaches of Humphrey and Horst were now widely accepted. They required a much more fleshed-out and scholarly exposition of the method and its progression over the period of the course. For it to be a specialised subject at honours degree level, they believed it needed to be taught within a wider critical and historical framework that included the American modern dance techniques becoming recognised in higher education.[38] After a revised syllabus and a further Panel visit to observe the teaching of Release, Moving for Performance was accepted for the beginning of the 1977 academic year. It appeared to Peter Cox that the most potent factor in the CNAA panel's change of heart on that visit was the clear manner in which students could articulate from their own bodily experience the value of Fulkerson's work.[39] However, there was still the condition that there should be a consistent technical training alongside Release work. Cunningham-based technique was approved – although there may be some doubt that this was the outcome in practice, as the frequent guest lecturers brought their own notions of how to train the body within the creative focus of the course.

What exactly was the position of movement within the degree course? How did it interact with the other areas of study? Mary Fulkerson wrote:

it was never seen as a dance course within the theatre department, but as a component joined to other components important in the making of the theatre image, theatre being defined as performance, and/or interaction in a broad and experimental context. [40]

So composition was the focus of the whole course, and Fulkerson was 'responsible for setting up a programme to train the body and the mind for performance and interaction, allowing for a diverse manifestation of work arising.'[41]

The Language of the Axis

Fulkerson had been personally influenced by Mabel Elsworth Todd's student Barbara Clark and by Joan Skinner, whom she had encountered while a student at the University of Illinois in the 1960s. Skinner had devised a method still known as Skinner Releasing Technique (SRT). In applying the perceptions of good body use from Alexander Technique to teaching dance students, she had discovered that imagery and imagined movement, presented initially to students in a resting position, proved highly effective in conveying kinaesthetic information in order to re-educate the body without setting up harmful counter-tensions. The technique enabled dancers to move with better anatomical alignment, with less tension and more economy. This knowledge could then be taken into performance in a traditional technique. Skinner wrote of the appearance of dancers trained in her method:

> The muscles appear to be lengthened and wrapped around the bones rather than contracted or gripped. The joints give the appearance of having space in them and the limbs of being unbound though belonging to the torso. There is a suspended relationship to gravity which can be likened to the suspension of a dust particle in a shaft of light.[42]

The importance of these ideas to the emerging theatre work at Dartington can be gauged by their visibility in the Theatre Department's regular publication series, *Theatre Papers*. In the first series of twelve (1977) there were two papers by Barbara Clark on imagery and anatomical alignment and a very lengthy one from Fulkerson, *The Language of the Axis*, that could be described as a primer on her method as she was developing it in the early part of her time at Dartington. There were other dance papers also, an interview with Steve Paxton on contact improvisation (a practice discussed later in this chapter) and a paper on the San Francisco Dancers' Workshop by Anna Halprin (Fulkerson had studied with her in 1965).

The Language of the Axis takes up and expands in a dancer-oriented way on Barbara Clark's paper *How to Live in Your Axis*. The axis here is the spine ('All parts of the body speak to one another through the axis.'[43]) and the 'language' is one of imagery and physical sensation that integrates thought and action and promotes a holistic sense of self rather than the Cartesian dualism of mind and body. Images are presented initially in stillness in the 'Anatomical Rest Position' with an initial concentration on the breath. Through practice, the image is fused with action: 'To forget the image is to become it.'[44] Fulkerson's initial images are simple forms to enable thinking about the internal structures of the body's anatomy, their relation to movement and thus to the world: the axis through the spine and limbs, the bridge that carries information side to side and front to back, bowls at shoulder girdle and pelvis which fill with water and empty as the body moves in and out of the upright.

In her own practice, Fulkerson noticed how the images moved around the body in predetermined ways that promoted anatomical alignment and easy action; she named these Action Flows.[45] She gave students simple sequences of movement to experience the images in easy action – lying, rolling, crawling, curving, walking, running – the unforced body coming to terms with principles of leverage and momentum from the interior. Then they took those principles into working together in contact. This was not a dance technique to be imposed on the body from outside, but guidance for a discovery that the students made for themselves. Accompanying photographs of Fulkerson's classes show the main studio of the Dance School in use as an experimental environment, with students as individuals exploring their everyday bodies rather than formally chasing an ideal of perfection. There was no performing to the mirror, no performing the same movement lined up in unison.

The imaging work in Release importantly became a process of exploration and investigation to allow choreographic material to emerge from the body. In *The Language of the Axis,* more complex images were suggested as bases for dances – images fusing an aspect of the physical body with an aspect of the physical world, for example. Fulkerson wrote about her own process in poetic language, a process that often appears mystical or hallucinatory. Out of stillness and listening to the body in space, images arise and offer possibilities.

The image falls through the body, deeper and deeper, and then it gets light and spacious. It is present without effort. The image suggests movement.

Once the image becomes 'a body state', it can be discarded as a separate entity.[46] Mind and body are one.

She explored the concept of stillness as an active state, part of the creative process and an essential one for her, in another Theatre Paper, *The Move to Stillness.*[47] To be a 'moving stillness' there must be a protracted time devoted to it in order that one can become properly receptive. She describes deepening layers of attention to thoughts and images as the stillness proceeds, up to the point where the thoughts are dreamlike, difficult to tie down in words, but presenting possibilities unknown to the mind and body working with a prosaic awareness.

Mary Fulkerson: Time, identity, text

Fulkerson's choreographic output over her time based in Britain was astonishingly prolific, especially so when we remember her responsibilities within the College – apparently she made some thirty-five solo and small-group pieces. Nevertheless, at the point when she was about to leave after fourteen years, Stephanie Jordan called her 'one of the most elusive and enigmatic figures on the British new dance scene'.[48] A colleague at Dartington, Chris Crickmay, noted that her work often referenced the contemporary world of 'women's problems, the inner city, ecological waste, disaster, love...'[49]; but it is also apparent from much of the work that Fulkerson made at Dartington, specifically her solo work, that there is a constant thread of an exploration of personal identity. Her imaging process as a resource for her choreography took her deep into her interior life. Alongside this she discovered and used a Jungian framework of collective unconscious and female archetypes. Recurrent themes address a sense of the self as layered both temporally and in a gendered way, and there is often a 'dark side', a Jungian shadow.

In *Late Nite Soup*, her first piece created in Britain, she actually cooked soup, served it up after the performance and made a paper dress. Less complex than some of her later solos, it nevertheless demonstrates another of her fascinations – with time. In this case the temporal scheme is 'real time' – the dance lasts as long as it takes to cook the soup. (This was some years before Tim Miller surprised a Dance Umbrella audience in London in 1982 by cooking a hamburger on stage in his piece *Post-war*.) A critic, Kathy Duncan, wrote of a New York performance of *Late Nite Soup*:

> She had three processes going on at once: soup, music and dance. What a wonderful idea, that soup! It was visually interesting, for one thing. The colors of lush vegetables, the wooden chopping board, the chrome pot ... It had a beginning, when Fulkerson was chopping vegetables; a middle, when she does a collection of dances and from time to time returns to stir the soup; and an end in the audience members' stomachs.[50]

The linear notion of time is much simpler here than in some later works, and the soup was a generous acknowledgement of the audience but not necessarily typical of Fulkerson's notion of the way performer and audience should interact. Duncan stated that this kind of theatre required the audience to make the first step towards engagement with the material, not to expect the attention to be held the whole time, but to be there and open to and active in witnessing the event. Fulkerson herself has written:

> Release performers strive to exist in the real time of the performance, and to allow the audience space to enter as full participants of mind/body exploration. The audience must be asked to work in an investigative way rather than to be entertained.[51]

She also recognises that the performer must create moments to help the audience into the process, moments such as a repetition that might give the onlookers a hook for understanding and experiencing.

Real time in performance remains important for her, especially within works that have an improvisatory form, but at Dartington she also plunged into the exploration of time as a condition of life. At about the same time as *Late Night Soup*, Fulkerson was making a trio that explored a woman's selfhood through the ages of her life, *Making Light Work*. The title puns on the word 'light' as both the quality of work carried out with assurance and aptitude and as the phenomenon of light in the physical world: as Fulkerson saw it, the source and connecting force of life, attending the ageing process and assuring continuance.[52] Three dancers portrayed the woman at the ages of 27, 37 and 77, their actual ages. Fulkerson herself was the youngest, while the eldest was Paula Morel, dancer with Margaret Barr and Louise Soelberg in the 1930s, still fully involved in the Dartington arts. It was shown in a Strider programme at the ICA, London, in January 1974, although it did not go into the repertory. In a further link with the past, it was then seen by Kai Tai Chan, one of Margaret Barr's dancers in Australia, who was currently involved in the dance scene in London and becoming a choreographer himself.[53] Fulkerson had made a highly physical role for herself, running, falling and full of kinetic energy. Morel's role was built around pedestrian gestures and functional movement, something she found very difficult, tending to elaborate movements according to the aesthetics of her 1930s dance training. Her climactic gesture, highly significant in terms of the theme, was to set a young plant in a pot.

Alongside the preoccupation with self and time, an enduring characteristic of Fulkerson's work has been the use of spoken and/or taped text in her dance works, which often dealt with narrative in what she has described as almost a minimalist exploration of plot.[54] In 1977 at Dartington she embarked on a series of eight solos exploring a woman's life – a woman who was simultaneously herself and the collective experience of women. She has written that this was the first time that she 'significantly and directly' connected her experience of life with her choreography.[55] The overall sense of the eight solos is that each represents a moment on a journey from one place to another that becomes a journey towards understanding; each solo represents a moment on that journey. The solos were produced over three years, performed as completed. Then in March 1979 Fulkerson performed the complete cycle at Dartington, two a night, taking four nights spread over a week; this was partly because she wanted to experience the growth of understanding in herself but also because she recognised that the pieces were almost indecipherable when presented separately.

The cycle begins with *The World is Round*, with title and text from Gertrude Stein's children's story of 1939 in which the young Rose (this is one of Stein's own reiterations of her famous 'Rose is a rose is a rose' quotation) ascends a mountain in order to comprehend her own place in the world.[56] As in the other dances, a chair takes on an important role as something domestic that encapsulates a history but is also a viewing position; this also is from Stein's story. But in Fulkerson's solo the woman begins her journey as an adult, separating herself from all that she knows. As with Stein's story, it has the sense of the beginning of independence.

Robin Fly South finds her a long way into the journey, struggling to find a direction. She has a slide projection of small pebbles that indicated for Fulkerson something primal and enduring like memories of home. Half-remembered snatches of Schubert songs come into her mind. 'How does the robin know to fly south?', her taped text asks. She dons a feathered costume and makes bird-like movements with a feathered glove. She reaches a moment of disillusionment, ending with the words, 'There where you are not, all joy is there.'

I Saw Myself Standing begins with the question, 'We survive because we use words; is this true?' She is pulled between different solutions and different attitudes to her journey. She has her first moment of insight, 'a faint image of her harmonious place in the world, but that image is not positive enough to allow her journey to finish.' Strapped to her belly is a soft modelled cat, which she seems in photographs to hold protectively and for comfort. It has connotations of female fertility and wild nature. The last words, 'dark coming', lead on to the fourth solo, titled *Dark Coming*, in which she loses direction, endures dark moments, becomes untamed and unmanageable, and discovers the power of magic and the temptation of the abuse of power. She drops the stuffed cat on its head. In contrast, by the time of the fifth dance, *I See the Edge*, she is 'clear, poised and lucid', performing a pure dance piece to Schumann's *Five Pieces in Folk Style*, but also wielding her chair like a weapon in moments of purposeful violence.

The journey is resumed in *Remember Hearing*. The chairs are now a set of miniature deckchairs, toys that evoke memories of childhood, and the taped text is of remembered stories. But this is another kind of rejection: the rejection of living in the present. 'Trying to avoid the truth of this moment seems to be this woman's occupation', the programme states. This leads on to *Waiting and Waiting*, and another moment of insight. The 'Game of Mouse', which is one of her creative processes, a serial association of words and movements according to rules that can only be made up in the playing, helps her to make choices 'rooted in the present'. Out of formlessly piled-up black cloth she constructs an installation using extension poles. The final solo, *She Said*, incorporates and accumulates memories and material of all that has gone before. The costumes of all the dances lie on the chairs and she throws them wildly into the air at a run so that they stick to her by force of her speed. She finally understands the times of her life as all being present in the same moment, a 'now' that is 'a beautiful time to be alive'. She is old and young at the same time and decides to write her last book first.[57] There is a notion here that life is a kind of inscription, a narrative that we ultimately may control.

Real Life Adventures or *The Woman Writer Speaks*

Jennifer Dunning, writing about a performance in New York in 1984, noted the shock when Fulkerson tells the audience at the outset that there had been a deception: the dance advertised as *Real Life Adventures* is in fact *The Woman Writer Speaks*.[58] She proceeds to read to the audience about two characters she is developing, both female archetypes and acknowledged as part of herself: a young and an old woman, each with a different understanding of time. There are in addition male characters in the woman writer's mind, also part of herself, including the violinist Paganini. Fulkerson now makes a historical journey to discover women from previous eras who are still connected to herself as a woman. This is effected by an amazing costume, a seemingly endless tube of blue silk (designed by Maria Liljefors, a frequent collaborator from Dartington) that can be manipulated into multiple forms to suggest the fashion of various moments from the nineteenth and twentieth centuries. The costume and the theme of the dance came out of a dream of a river connecting her with women's history.

After her 1920s costume, she escapes into freedom dressed in a boiler suit, a simulated flight with a silk parachute. Finally, though, she is drawn back to the table that has been a permanent part of the set, and now, her body hung with kitchen utensils, discourses angrily on the demands of domesticity.

Fulkerson sees those years at Dartington, especially the ones from the late 1970s to the early 1980s, as ones when her sense of self, the set of places she was able to reach with her Release process, was expanding. The characters that emerge through her dances and writing of this period are both fractions of herself and of everywoman. They cross centuries. There are male aspects of herself alongside the female. Paganini emerged from *The Woman Writer*

Speaks (quite literally he became part of her consciousness, she says) and was developed in a later company piece called *Paganini*. His female counterpart, and a pun on his name, is Pagan Annie in the companion piece, *Feminine Psyche in Trouble*.[59] That work was a complex of variables opened up by process in performance. Created to be performed by three to fourteen performers, its sections could happen in any order. Pagan Annie is feminine consciousness fragmented into the Jungian archetypes of Witch, Seductress, Innocent and Amazon as well as The Shadow, the dark side of her ego. Performers, including musicians, were assigned at least two identities, male and female, which they had to shift between during the performance, beginning in their opposite gender, so that it became a psychological exploration of themselves in relationship to the feminine. They are all Pagan Annie.[60] In her own role, Fulkerson began as a Victorian gentleman, reintegrating her feminine self as a female sex symbol.

Fulkerson's writing is both prolific and challenging, whether in performance or in writing about performance. Alongside information on her works, her process and her aesthetic and ethical position, the latter includes poetic streams of consciousness, messages from her interior image world that the reader must encounter in the same open interaction that she expects of her audiences. It seems that 'the woman writer' is an important aspect of Fulkerson's sense of herself and one that acquired greater importance at Dartington. It is already apparent in *The Language of the Axis*, which could be seen as a poetics of her mind–body model. Writing not only was part of her image formation in performance and supported the research for her dance pieces but also had an independent life, although bound up with her dances in exploring the same themes and the same process into consciousness. Thus *The Same Story* was not only an independent solo but also an interactive text that she wrote in association with *The Woman Writer Speaks*. It was not intended for publication but was 'a method for seeing my history as a dancer and writer'.[61] Voices of The Woman Writer, the old woman, the young girl and the voices of men, animals and birds were scripted in column format for deconstruction of linear narrative – the exploration in text of multiple personas and of the layering or fragmentation of linear time. She thinks of moments in time and aspects of character as being simultaneously present as well as consecutive – split images as in a prism or a bee's eye.[62] Why does she refer to herself so often as 'the Woman Writer'? She admits that she believes in the power of the written word, but also perhaps the 'Woman Writer' is a label that strongly suggests the struggle of a woman in the arts – arts practice as always qualified by gender.

It also highlights contextually a whole area of significance to British dance of the 1970s and 1980s – the influence of feminism upon dance practice and choreography. Although Fulkerson's response to that was to

question the nature of male and female as demarcated genders, other dancers and choreographers in Britain would confront head-on the stereotypes of
female and male that dance traditionally represented, revealing their sources
in gender politics and unequal power.[63]

Fulkerson's predilection for words is also indicative of the trend of the
1970s and 1980s towards mixed-media dance works in which movement
was just one of the materials, which could include installations, film and
slide projections, costumes like art works on the body, recorded and live text,
dance movement and pedestrian movement, music and found sounds. If
dance works approached closely and crossed the boundary into other art
forms, much was also flowing in the other direction. Many theatre makers
were freeing themselves from the authority of the text as a political gesture
and turning towards notions of a more democratic theatre. So physical performance practices with roots in popular culture, such as *commedia dell'arte*
and clowning, became more significant as ways of training the performer
and making theatre works. Added to this, interest in non-Western dramatic
forms, such as noh and kabuki from Japan and kathakali from southern
India, raised awareness of physicality in a performance, bringing together
text, music and movement. Some visual artists attempted to free themselves
from the economics of the gallery, to embrace the notion of art as being as
ephemeral as a performance, rather than a material and marketable commodity. There was a sense that dance, theatre and visual arts were
approaching each other, creating a richly mixed genre of performance with a
variety of names: physical theatre, visual theatre, physical performance, live
art. Fulkerson was clearly positioned in the latter area in her collaborative
project begun in 1980 under the name of Little Theatre, working with improvisation and installation in gallery settings with other dancers and Chris
Crickmay from Dartington's Art Department.[64]

Fulkerson's time directing dance at Dartington (1973–87) corresponds to
a period of intense development in British contemporary dance. The London
School of Contemporary Dance, London Contemporary Dance Theatre
and Ballet Rambert (which had switched to being a contemporary dance
company in 1966) soon came to be seen by the more radical British choreographers as representing a conservative mainstream both in training
practices and in choreography. Direct and indirect connections with America
and the influence of the cutting-edge creativity in performance art and film
in Britain set off some trends brought together under the title 'British new
dance'. The event that focused new dance most clearly was the founding of
the X6 Collective (1976–80)[65] in a warehouse space in Bermondsey, East
London, and its magazine, *New Dance* (1977–88). As a label, 'new dance' is
difficult to define and generally went out of use after the magazine ceased
publication, unsurprisingly considering how quickly labels like 'new' or

'modern' can become dated.[66] New dance is useful as a label to indicate that this was a generation (not all of whom were connected with X6) interested in pushing the boundaries of dance into radical directions: for example, alternative dance-making processes; challenges to the dominant hierarchies of the dance world; different interactions with audiences; women asserting their identity; reclaiming the dancer's body from ravaging techniques. Quite apart from challenges to the artistic consensus, the 1980s Britain in which new dance matured provided plentiful political targets. It was, after all, the decade dominated by Conservative Party politics under Margaret Thatcher, whose government was seen by many as authoritarian and centralising and, in limiting public spending, no friend of the arts. It was also a period of social divisiveness, with high inflation and unemployment, rioting and hotly contested industrial strikes. This was the background against which the radical arts, including new dance, attempted to perform a better version of social relations.

The X6 Collective, new dance and Dartington developed a strong mutual influence, initially through contacts with Mary Fulkerson and Steve Paxton.

Steve Paxton: Everyday Dancing

Photographs from the late1970s show the Great Hall at Dartington in use for a different kind of movement activity. Barefoot and dressed in a variety of dance and non-dance clothing, people are spread out, mostly in twos, some on mats, others lying or standing on the polished wood floor and some right up by the massive stone fireplace. Something is going on that involves one person giving their body weight to a partner who, lying down, supports and manipulates it with their feet. Steve Paxton sits on the steps in front of the fireplace watching the exercise.

While Fulkerson set the agenda for dance development, Paxton became the other most influential artist/educator in Dartington in the 1970s and 1980s. A former member of the Merce Cunningham company who had appeared at Dartington with Cunningham in 1964, Paxton came with a ready-made reputation as a fine performer, but had also been at the heart of the alternative dance-making world of the New York group known as Judson Dance Theater in the early 1960s. This group had included Trisha Brown, Lucinda Childs, David Gordon and Yvonne Rainer. To a great extent, these dancers had been liberated by the example of Cunningham and Cage to consider that the previous boundaries within which dance-works were to be judged had been breached or even demolished. The subject of dance was movement itself, but any movement could be part of that vocabulary. The sacred twinning of dance and music was no longer applicable. Music and design could be 'found' and dance could be 'found' by applying arbitrary rules or chance procedures to making choreography. Yet, for the most part,

Cunningham's choreography retained theatrical and dancerly values of performance and virtuosity. He 'opened many doors, but chose not to go through all of them'.[67] The 1960s Judson group raced through the doors and often literally right out onto the streets or roofs to dance there. If any movement could be dancing, then a dance could be totally composed of pedestrian (functional) movement. Dance could be performed in everyday situations. Therefore, could anybody be a dancer? Could the process of dance-making become part of the performance, for example by chance procedures used during the performance or by improvising during the performance (which had happened rarely in Cunningham's work)? The whole context fuelling this avant-garde also included groupings in visual arts where boundaries between art and theatre, art and audience, and notions of the permanence of the art object were being obliterated – such as the work of the dadaist Fluxus group and the makers of Happenings. There was already by the early 1960s in America an increasing confidence in youth that developed into political action against materialism, authoritarianism and nuclear weapons and for the Civil Rights Movement and greater democracy.

Paxton's interest at Judson and for some time later, also shared by others of the group, was in 'pedestrian movement': that is, everyday movement. Walking, standing, running and other functional movements became the movement material of many of their dances. Paxton went further into minimalism by making dances about walking and being still – movements in the vocabulary of any person. Several of these were later restaged at Dartington. In *Satisfyin' Lover*, a large group of people had to follow precise written instructions on walking across the space, sometimes standing or sitting, including how many steps to take and what spatial relationship to maintain to others. In *State*, shown as the complement to *Satisfyin' Lover* at Dartington and elsewhere, the dancers walked in and stood still for three minutes, moving at will each time there was a blackout, to be found perhaps in a different configuration when the lights went up again. In *Flat*, Paxton walked around the space, occasionally pausing in mid-movement, took off his clothes and hung them on hooks taped to his body.[68] These walking dances, especially when performed by non-dancers, are instructive of the sheer diversity of bodies, postures and walking styles. At Judson, this was part of the current exploration of what makes 'dance' material, but for Paxton it was also about breaking down the self-consciousness of the trained dancer that seemed to inhibit the smooth interactions achieved by people performing functional tasks.[69] It also seems that his experience with Cunningham's repertory left him some concerns. In choreography disassociated from the emotional and literary excesses of the 'moderns' such as Graham, there was some danger of the dancers expressing an emotional neutrality, devoid of 'human stuff'.[70]

Paxton also joined some other ex-Judson people in the 1970s in a work by Yvonne Rainer called *Continuous Project – Altered Daily*, made up of pre-cast chunks of material that could be rearranged in a variety of ways. It was when *Continuous Project – Altered Daily* was on tour that Mary Fulkerson met Paxton.

He first came to Dartington as a guest teacher in 1974, from then becoming a regular visitor and a full-time member of staff from 1978 to 1980, returning many times after that. The first visits to Dartington were situated at an interesting moment in his artistic development, just a couple of years after the earliest experiments in contact improvisation in 1972 at Oberlin and Bennington Colleges, also including Fulkerson and some of her students from the University of Rochester, New York State.[71] Contact improvisation evolved out of the 'human stuff' of two bodies moving together in contact: a movement dialogue, taking and giving weight on all body surfaces, sensing and intuiting the possibilities for making an instant dance.[72]

In his first visits to Dartington, Paxton responded to the varied physical abilities of the students, giving introductory levels of his own varied background: simple ballet, Cunningham technique, yoga and aikido exercises and the initial exercises from contact improvisation that relate to sensing what he called 'the small dance'.[73] '*In the midst of standing still something else is occurring and the name for that is the small dance*' is the title of an interview, published as a Theatre Paper. Paxton's stillness is a period of standing on the spot, relaxing all the muscles, losing the tension in the body until the skeleton is felt in alignment as the support of the body. In 'the small dance', all the tiny, involuntary adjustments made internally to balance the body come into play. 'You become aware that very small falls are constantly being forestalled by slight pulls or stretches in the body.'[74] But this was not an easy exercise: relaxing in this way, going against the normal life experience and very much against conventional dance training, is hard to achieve. Standing still and the 'small dance' were always used as a training exercise for contact improvisation, but standing still could also constitute a complete class. The exercise opened up the body to the sensing of its own reflexes that would become so much part of the contact duet, taking weight, rolling, sliding, jumping, swinging with another person in constant movement invention.

The Japanese martial arts form aikido fed into the development of contact improvisation, offering its perpetual alertness, dual interplay of energy and skills to reduce the danger of impact on the floor. Paxton said, 'I think the body is designed by nature, or has evolved in nature, to throw itself around the landscape with great efficiency.'[75] Bodies work together, using gravity, momentum, support from each other's physical surfaces that evolves from moment to moment as the contact changes. The movement can be sinewy and flowing or high-energy, thrilling to watch, when, according to Paxton's experience, there is a sense of being wide awake, adrenalin-flooded, length-ening the moment as in a car crash, instinctively grasping safe possibilities.[76]

At Dartington, Paxton and Fulkerson reinforced each other's teaching. Both Release and contact improvisation stem from the understanding of the body from the inside, from sensing rather than conforming to an external 'look'. Paxton contrasted the full sensing of sound, sight, movement, smell, taste, which all come into play in contact improvisation, against a hegemonic Western concentration on the focused gaze, which admits of less knowledge of diverse and peripheral viewpoints; against, too, the Western social taboos on touching.[77]

It is an interesting connection with Dartington's past that Paxton had read and been impressed by Laban's book *Modern Education Dance* at about the same time that contact improvisation was developing. It was the first theoretical text on dance he had come across and he found it relevant to his interest in the practice of improvisation, as well as offering a blueprint for dance as socially beneficial. (In his introduction Laban discussed the benefits of dance and movement against the constraints of mechanical work on the industrial labour force.) Paxton found that the text could be used as a 'score' to structure and develop movement work. 'Scores' were used by dance mak-ers of the Judson grouping as one procedure, alongside others such as 'chance', to develop material. Scores in this context are analogous to music or dance notation scores but are verbal or graphic. Sometimes, as with Paxton's written score for *Satisfyin' Lover*, they describe in detail what is to be done. In other cases they provide a starting place for the dancer's explora-tion. It appears to be in this way that Paxton used the text of *Modern Educational Dance* for an improvisation on Laban's eukinetics, filmed in 1972.[78]

The notion of improvisation has been a quiet presence through this chap-ter and previous ones. On one level, it needs no definition. The ideal of spontaneous movement, erupting as it were, fresh-minted from the dancer/choreographer in response to a stimulus or in exploration of a task, was deeply embedded in the twentieth-century modern movement in dance. It was essential to creative dance as an educational experience. It also moved outside the classroom and the rehearsal studio into the performance itself. To many of the 1960s generation of American modern dancers, the prescrip-tive notions of structuring dances, epitomised in the treatises of Louis Horst and Doris Humphrey, seemed just to lead to the same old clichés in perform-ance. Chance procedures and improvisation could break that mould.

In the early 1970s in the US, partly during the period of the initial experi-ments that would become contact improvisation, Paxton was one of the dancers in the Grand Union, performing unscripted and unset evening-length improvisations, theatrical in the widest sense, not exclusively dance-based.[79] Daniel Nagrin was making dance improvisations with the

Workgroup, based upon game-like tasks that stimulated deep involvement and movement invention at the point of performance.[80] While the Grand Union performances were unrehearsed and unset (although they might in fact fall into 'routines' they had done previously), the Workgroup programmed and practised their performance structures, though their interpretation would be freshly made at each showing. Approaches to improvisation in performance range on a spectrum between and beyond these two examples, from free-form to improvisation within fixed structures, including the alternation between improvisation and set material. Improvisation can also be seen as choreography crafted in the moment of performance, the demonstration of all the dancer's skills in structuring, observation and communication. The rigorous practice of improvisation can be taken as a paradigm for the integrated mind-body that challenges Cartesian dualism. 'For it is while improvising that the body's intelligence manifests itself most ineluctably, and that the fast moving, agile mind becomes a necessity. The body thinks. The mind dances.'[81]

PA RT

Paxton's improvised performances include dancer/musician collaborations with the on-stage percussionist David Moss and solo dances to recorded scores, notably Bach's *Goldberg Variations* and *Some English Suites*.[82] In 1978 at Dartington he worked in the Dance School with a regular partner, Lisa Nelson (she had also been part of Nagrin's Workgroup), on a new dance to the electronic score of *Private Parts* by the American composer Robert Ashley, with keyboard, percussion and Ashley's voice intoning a text in a quiet, flat voice. *PA RT* became a repertory piece for them over many years, so it is an interesting phenomenon that this frequently repeated duet was also an improvised dance within the fixed structures of the recorded score and the dance structure of solo (Nelson), duet, solo (Paxton) and a final duet.

Paxton has spoken of his shifts of attention as the improvisation proceeds, aware of all the parallel lines of media through the dance, but making choices to engage most fully with one strand at a particular moment (percussion, keyboards and text of the score; the partner's movements; the physical space and its lighting) and reflecting on that strand through movement.[83] This flexibility of attention allows the dance to speak differently at each performance and remain an improvisation.

A duet is the most fundamental social interaction, never without associations of relationships, be they explicit or inferred. My own reading of the dance is formed by one viewing of a video recording when I felt myself drawn into a relationship that seemed both tender and ambiguous. The external physical appearances they adopted suggested that they came into the dance as characters. Paxton wore a sleeveless vest and trousers, informal in dress as usual, but in *PA RT* he also wore dark glasses. Nelson was in baggy knicker-bocker-like trousers coming to the knee and a floral, Hawaiian shirt. She had a thin moustache painted onto her face.

Just as there are different lines within the dance for the dancers to follow, there are different lines for the observer. There is certainly contradiction here. The text, spoken by a man, is about a woman's state of mind, and this gender mixing might also be seen in Nelson's shirt and moustache, which add a male touch to a distinctively female body. Does it refer to the real moustache that Paxton wears? Some commentators have focused on the Eastern references in the music and have seen in Nelson's costume and moustache a reference to the East too. By implication, then, Paxton would be her Western opposite.

I sensed uncertainty about individual identity. Their facial appendages, Nelson's moustache and Paxton's 'shades', introduced an element of disguising that I also found in the movement quality, as if the relationship to be expressed was one of tentative feelings, half-unsure. I noted that, on Paxton's entry during Nelson's opening solo, the space between them slowly lessened as if it were an enormous gulf. In Paxton's solo after their duet, he appeared to be absorbed in his own thoughts as the text spoke of numbers and calculations. They had tender moments, though not face to face, playing with notions of not seeing; in their final duet, they held on to each other's extremities, as though unable to commit any further. I interpret *PA RT* in terms of the separation implied in the title. At another performance in 1979, a reviewer saw the dancers achieve unity in the end. East/West, unity/disunity – the dance is rich in lines to follow.[84]

Paxton offered me the following commentary on the imagery they worked with. I print it here with thanks to him. It adds yet again to the richness of the work.

The vest and white painter's trousers were a deliberate costume, dark glasses added in homage to Ashley, who wore them at the time. They became the 'motive' for a slow deliberate entrance, as though blind. This was interesting if Lisa were seen in her north African trousers and Hawaiian shirt as a traveler – a person in perpetual dark and a person who gets around the world. The moustache is a reference to several things, including the Mona Lisa of Duchamp, references which need not be seen by the audience to make sense of the relationship, but which gave shadings within the relationship. The text refers to a traveling salesman in the section Lisa danced. Her costume and moustache were my vision of such a man, if the traveling were to stick to her as she traveled. Also in the text he has a vision of "two men on a park bench" that may be Ashley's retelling of a Buddhist parable. The second solo, mine, is a strange internal monologue. It is a woman whose memories and feelings involve numbers ... whether they are ages of her father, the year of the memory or other obscure references is interpretable. ... *PA RT* ends with an extended sunset. The end of the relationship? The mere end of a day? The coming of a night, the dark, or the revelation of the heavens? We ended differently each time. The word '*PA RT*' contains a separation but also still unites to form a word. A word which means something which contains a gap. The gap in the title is a portrayal of the meaning.[85]

Consolidating connections

Connections between Dartington and the new dance generation based in London grew rapidly. The connection with X6 was a starting point that continued after the members spread out to other projects after 1980. Soon that 200-mile distance between London and Dartington did not seem so far. Dartington became three things for the London-based dancers: a place to teach, a place to learn and a place to perform. An interchange had been established when Alston came to Dartington to teach, perform to students and learn from Fulkerson, and it continued with Paxton's charismatic presentation of the new contact improvisation. Artists visiting Dartington included students from the earlier courses who were now connected with new dance in London (for example, Butcher and MacLennan). In the other direction, Paxton and Fulkerson taught in London, introducing other American associates, so that Release, alignment and contact improvisation became embedded in the vocabulary of new dance.

From 1978 to 1987 Dartington became the home of an annual festival – Dance at Dartington. Encouraged by Peter Cox, the first festival was partly a celebration of the finally safe validation of Moving for Performance as an Extended Study. Seeing how the London-based dancers felt misunderstood by mainstream dance journalism, Fulkerson was also very intent on providing a supportive, non-competitive environment, 'predicated more toward development than achievement'.[86] The festivals became part of an emerging network, sustaining new dance practitioners. Dartington's dance faculty, visitors from America, dancers on the London scene and current and former students mixed and cross-fertilised. At the first festival, Fulkerson had programmed the dancers from the US whom she had currently working as visiting lecturers – Nancy Topf, Marsha Paludan and Nancy Udow – with other American visitors (Susan Motycka and Katherine Litz) and Steve Paxton, about to become a full-time tutor. Amongst the British performers were Alston, Butcher, Janet Smith and Miranda Tufnell (not a Dartington student, but a frequent performer with Butcher who would forge her own relationship with Dartington). To add to the local colour, there was a fête in the courtyard, 'with vigorous folk dancing, cream teas and free samples of local wine'.[87]

The festival, which normally occupied a five-day slot in spring, had a tightly packed schedule of classes and performances daily and well into the night. For ten years Dartington became a recognised centre of the national dance scene, one end of the Dartington–London axis. The festival exploited Dartington's utopian aspect, in Devon, in spring, with some participants camping by the river. It was above all a celebration of radical dance in a supportive atmosphere. Costs were kept low; there was a small subsidy from South West Arts and festival performers were not paid. Performers and non-performers joined together in the workshops and classes, and the habitual warmth of reception for performances was, although sometimes too easily expected, a relief from what was often overcritical and uninformed press coverage in London.

Dartington's reputation was promoted through the festival, mainly within the international network of independent artists. In a different way, the annual Dance Umbrella, which commenced in the same year, an international dance festival of several weeks' duration in London venues and elsewhere around the country, exposed Dartington in a more critical frame. Paxton appeared in 1980 and 1982 (performing *PA RT* as well as other pieces on both occasions). Fulkerson's work was included from 1981 to 1984, showing both solo and group work.[88] But the most telling sign of Dartington's significance was the inclusion of Dartington-trained dancer/choreographers on a regular basis: Rosemary Butcher, Janet Smith, Laurie Booth, Sue MacLennan, Libby Dempster, Yolande Snaith, Matthew Hauxwell, Jonathan and Barnaby Stone (performing as Ralf Ralf). Val Bourne, Dance Umbrella's director, credited Dartington, and particularly Fulkerson, with creating a generation of dancer/choreographers marked by individuality: 'all the people who have come from there have gone in very different directions. ... They can't be pigeonholed, but they have a very different approach which sets them apart from the Rambert/London Contemporary group.'[89]

Katie Duck: A European theatrical model

Fulkerson's fourteen years at Dartington offered a period of growth and stability to movement and choreography there, stretching from 1973, when the new dance scene was only just beginning, to 1987 when it was well established. Fulkerson's and Paxton's contribution to this, not least through the festival, is clear. Just to consider another pattern of the period, Fulkerson's time at Dartington also took her from the relatively easy financial circumstances of the early 1970s into the late 1980s when things for Dartington would become very difficult indeed. In her last year at the College she became acting Head of the whole Theatre Department, perhaps a fact contributing to her conviction that she needed to move on in order to keep her own work advancing. Her position was taken by Katie Duck.

Duck's career illustrates a valuable corrective to those narratives of British modern dance during and after the 1960s that focus exclusively on the American connection. Of course, Atlantic-crossing was central to the development of artists such as Butcher, Smith and Alston; and Americans in Britain such as Paxton, Fulkerson and Duck were dynamos for development here, but mainland Europe also provided specific contexts where British and American artists would find stimuli. Amsterdam was an especially vibrant centre of radical performance and experiment where artists from America and Europe intersected.

In the early 1980s, European dancers were invited to the Dartington festival and Dance Umbrella. Among them was Pauline de Groot, based in Amsterdam, a founder of the studio that would later become the School for New Dance Development. She had taught at Dartington and choreographed for the London Contemporary Dance Theatre in the early 1970s. Katie Duck's first appearance at Dartington was in the festival in 1983, invited by Fulkerson, who had seen her work in Amsterdam. She had been a student at the University of Utah with a background in ballet and modern dance techniques (Graham and Cunningham), but her introduction to the French school of mime and to clowning was decisive in moving her towards work with narrative and character. In 1975 she was one of the founders of the Great Salt Lake Mime Troupe with other dancers and jazz musicians, touring in America and then Europe, where she settled.[90]

In Amsterdam she discovered the free improvisation practised in jazz and avant-garde contemporary music and met musicians in the network, including from Britain and Germany. Although difficult to define, free improvisation is unlike the traditional jazz improvisation based upon a known repertoire of themes and improvisational structures. Some musicians associate it with an anti-hierarchical social network and a political statement denying the commodity value of music, while others find it immerses them in the authentic process of music-making. Duck was fascinated by this way of working, where 'forms were built and busted'.[91] She became one of the dancers to develop successful collaborations with free-improvisation musicians. (Steve Paxton working with David Moss is another instance, mentioned previously.)

Leaving the Mime Troupe in 1976, Duck went on to perform solo shows and street theatre, also developing her own approach to improvisation, choreography and working with musicians. A key musical collaborator was the American cellist/composer (also based in Europe) Tristan Honsinger. She was also absorbing some of the European modern dance tradition, from the Dutch dancer Jaap Flier (a founding member of Netherlands Dans Theater, influenced by Jooss) and Traut Faggioni in Italy, who had been a student of Wigman. In 1979 she formed Gruppo in Florence, to work intensively with dancers and musicians, using improvisation to discover material (which might be set) and also as a way of exploiting choice and chance in perform- ance. Before coming to teach at Dartington, Duck had been based in Europe for ten years, chiefly in Florence and Amsterdam and really belonging in her approach to that artistic environment – a European artist, then. At Dartington she reconnected the 1980s to the 1930s, bringing back some of those old Jooss students to give seminars – Simone Michelle, Dai Ailian and Ann Hutchinson Guest.

At the Dartington festival in 1983 Duck performed a duet with Honsinger, *Talk to Me.* A review remarked on the novelty of this kind of work, and indeed on the novelty of discovering what dancers might be doing currently in Flor- ence. Their theatricality was broadly based.

> It is hard to package these two who invade each other's media, improvis- ing around their relationship, in structured scenes, singing daft out-of-key songs to cello, engaging in a repartee of non sequiturs about domestic life, free movement (mime to a story, veiled and transformed into an Italian woman and Honsinger, her ageing maid), in procession with squeaky duck and whistle accompaniment.[92]

In 1984 Gruppo toured with a major production, *Rutles*, bringing it to the Dartington festival and later to Dance Umbrella in London. Performed with (and sometimes against) a selection of Beatles songs, it was a collage-like or episodic series of incidents that had been developed through the process of research and improvisation that Duck had developed with Gruppo. Research and free association of ideas in workshop situations released diverse images to work with. This was an interior process, but differing from Fulkerson's Release imaging. Duck terms this a 'fantasy', allowed to develop through associations, growing into movement, text and use of props.[93] Starting points for *Rutles* were the history of the Beatles, 'saying goodbye at the air- port', the film *The Deerhunter*, and the astronaut Neil Armstrong. Not that any of this was finally apparent in the work, since these were only the start- ing points for journeys into fantasy, character creation and encounters in non-communication that had some disjointed logic because they had flowed from a coherent process. This work had been rigorously set, although it re- tained the verve and spontaneity of improvised performance, having, according to one observer, 'the same fascination as observing a patch of sea and the movements of driftwood within it. ... Arrivals, exits, pockets of dance, drama, and concentrated posing combine in a continuous kinetic conversation.'[94]

Next year, Duck and Gruppo were resident artists at Dance Umbrella, per- forming *The Orange Man* and giving workshops. They also showed an improvised piece, *Reckless*. Alongside the improvising dancers and musicians from Gruppo, it included dancers who were significant on the British new dance scene and visitors to the Dartington festival – Gaby Agis, Kirstie Simson, Julyen Hamilton and Lloyd Newson.[95] Duck was teaching full-time at Dartington from 1986.

Duck's artistic process was in flux while at Dartington. She had been working with Gruppo for eight years, in a very special style dealing with objects, vocals, music, narrative, movement and light. She was used to the process of developing a piece, including research and developing material by association, taking a whole year. Most of this work was set into rigorous forms overlaid with other forms, complicated choreographic structures that appeared to be the outcome of spontaneous choices in performance. The contradictions of this situation were beginning to impress themselves on her.[96] She began to break open the structures by introducing guest improvisers into formed and structured works, for example Steve Paxton during a performance of *The Orange Man* at the Dartington Festival in 1985. *Wild Card* was a duet piece made specifically to have a different guest at each performance – literally a 'wild card' – and *Mind the Gap* referred, as the title suggests, to the gaps or points of entry where the performer had choices to make. In the video *Katie Duck: Small Scale Dances*, Charlotte Zerbey performs a dance of set material (literally 'small scale' because the dance is framed in a constricted space in which she cannot stand). Steve Paxton comes into the dance only with the information that he should stay behind her. His attempts to relate to her only seem to emphasise Zerbey's self-contained movement patterns. This became part of *Brown Eye, Green Eye* (1988), a piece for four musicians and four dancers, using both set material and improvisation, which was the final piece made under the Gruppo name, although Duck would continue to work with some of the members.[97] She was moving towards the full exploration of free improvisation of dancers working with musicians. This was what she would go back to Amsterdam to work on in 1991, founding Magpie Music Dance Company.

Duck's background in mime, clowning and character gave her a broad performance background that had much in common with colleagues in other branches of theatre. I have already outlined some of the ways in which dance and non-dance theatre moved towards each other in the 1970s and 1980s, towards a genre of performance that highlighted experimental and collaborative theatre-making, working with images in an allusive way, images that were generated in the process of devising theatre. Duck worked with a colleague in the Theatre Department, the writer and director Ric Allsopp, using a company name, NoVeMBer. *Ante-Chamber* and *Thought Sonata* were performance pieces of music, text, sound, dance and movement. They now think of *Thought Sonata* as being the most successful of their collaborations, partly because, during its time in their repertory, it moved into a much more sophisticated use of sound technology, with the live sampling of sound generated from the live text, sound tape and environmental sounds. Its declared theme was the 'contradictions between actions of thought and actions of impulse', but this only seems to be one of many starting places.[98] The text by Allsopp speaks of a garden, a man who visits it (sometimes called 'the gardener') and a woman who seems to be in a timeless state there (in some versions she is identified as 'the statue'). Adam and Eve in the Garden of Eden and Samuel Becket's play *Waiting for Godot* also provided some of the images they layered together in making the piece. While they talked of the danger outside the garden – of conflict and burning cities – and of the nature of time and thought, Allsopp moved sixteen rocks around into patterns and piles. Duck's initial movement material developed into a final dance to music from one of Bach's Brandenburg Concertos.

To take a contrasting form, I now want to describe a session in free improvisation as caught on an in-house video camera at Dartington in 1987 or 1988.[99] I find this intriguing not only because it shows the interaction of musicians and dancers in a free improvisation, and is a moment to observe and compare the personal movement styles of Mary Fulkerson and Katie Duck. Here is the Dance School as a performance space, again displaying its flexibility, with yet another form of dance-making decades after Margaret Barr first occupied it.

The three musicians, Tristan Honsinger (cello), Alex Maguire (piano) and Steve Noble (percussion of drums and gongs with additional wind instruments), are set up towards the back of the performing space. The four female and three male dancers, including Fulkerson and Duck, are dressed in practice gear of trousers and tops and the audience is seated on the floor – an informal gathering. What immediately becomes apparent is the way in which the whole improvisation of some forty minutes resolves into vignettes of relationship, sometimes humorous, sometimes tender, sometimes virtuoso interaction. Never a free-for-all, the performers all notice and give space to the small engagements of solo, duet and trio, dancers and musicians taking time out sitting on the widow sills, or moving away from the central space. There are moments of stillness as well as frantic movement, frequent transitions to, from and on the floor, and an overall resilient, unforced movement quality.

The set begins with Fulkerson making a long sideways stretch to the reverberations of the percussion's first notes, softly resolving her weight into the floor, rolling, scooting along and gesturing, then smoothly rising to embrace the floor again and again. Her movements melt into each other even when she and the percussionist have together increased the pace and dynamic contrasts. Three other dancers arrive, including Duck. She is mercurial, with bursts of energy coming between pedestrian transitions. These three move around separately, establishing their own movement identities, before they start to interact. To clusters of notes from the piano, they get into spiralling off-balance descents to the ground and up again. When the final three dancers take to the area, the cello is in too, and the piano sometimes gets an unconventional treatment, wires rubbed directly along their length.

Through what follows, the boundaries between sound-making and movement-making blur. Honsinger leaves his cello to sit and converse with Duck or brings it into the dancing area to play. Maguire mimes piano-playing, puts on a yellow plastic mac to chat about the weather, and dances the twist to a jolly harmonica tune. The dancers make noises and speak, often for sound rather than sense. They pick up on each others' movements and on musical rhythms and textures. Duck gets involved in a duet with another dancer: continuously passing close to each other they adopt an overarm throwing gesture giving impetus to the movements. A persistent rhythm in the piano gets overlaid with a romantic melody on cello and develops into a dance while Fulkerson gyrates by herself, like the only one listening to the music at a party. There are bursts of contact improvisation, and an absurd incident with Fulkerson and Duck both balancing on another dancer's back in an ungainly and tangled heap. They converse about how to get out of it and there is some business trying to grab a hat. But Honsinger calls an end to the set!

Artist/educators in practice

The idea that Dartington's artists, including dancers, should also function as educators went back to Christopher Martin's plan of 1941 and had been kept alive by the Arts Centre and College ethos fostered by Peter Cox. Speaking in 1978, Fulkerson saw her job at Dartington as that of a choreographer who also had teaching commitments. 'I knew I would be teaching dance and I would be able to do it in my own way, which I had done at Rochester as well: to be in charge of the situation. And it has been incredibly supportive.'[100] However, it is clear that the post was not without its tensions for the artist having to negotiate between the demands of the job and the need to create and perform. Both Duck and Fulkerson speak now of careful planning to make their own time for studio work alone: Duck in the small studio of Warren House (built for Jooss) where she lived on the ground floor, revelling in the historical connection, Fulkerson in college studio space at lunch times. Fulkerson managed long performing tours, including Europe and South and North America, by negotiating some free time to be taken abutting College vacations. Duck saw Dartington as giving her a settled base and a space for reflection, 'five years to conduct research and teach'.[101] For these two and Paxton as well as for many of their guest lecturers, the teaching was the outcome of personal artistic practice. They taught what they had discovered for themselves, and in some cases teaching was part of the discovery.

Up to the late 1980s, when finances at the College became much more constrained, the range and artistic standard of visiting lecturers was remarkable. Fulkerson brought in guest teachers from America who were friends or associates, many with the same release and contact-improvisation background as herself, or, like Albert Reid and Valda Setterfield, having a Cunningham background (both had danced in his company). Some stayed for weeks or a term, others, such as Nancy Udow and Steve Paxton, for several years. Udow's contribution to Dartington included the presence of her husband Michael, a percussionist, and their performances together. Fulkerson's own trombonist/composer husband taught and played at Dartington as well. He composed for some of her dances and also worked with other British choreographers. Nancy Topf, Marsha Paludan and Udow were exploring the influence from Skinner Releasing in their own ways. Simone Forti, a former performer with Halprin on the West Coast and in Happenings and Fluxus in New York, brought her own perspective on improvisation. In the same way, when Duck was heading the subject area, she was able to bring in her own European associates, Jaap Flier and various members of Gruppo.

Former Dartington students such as Rosemary Butcher, Sue MacLennan, Laurie Booth and Yolande Snaith and other representatives of the new dance scene in Britain and Europe were frequent guest teachers, as well as the Americans – festival performance and teaching contracts were often interlinked. The students were exposed to an array of approaches and ideas. For example, Jenna Agate (a student in 1983–7) can reel off a whole string of names: as well as Fulkerson, Paxton and Duck ('wild and challenging improvisation sessions'), she had Simone Forti, Nancy Topf and Stephanie Woodard, and she also remembers vividly classes with some of the performers from London's new dance – Jacky Lansley, Fergus Early and Mary Prestidge, and the contact improvisation duo of Kirstie Simson and Julyen Hamilton.[102]

With so many teachers, with many different approaches, was this a recipe for confusion or a rich and varied diet? For the most part, in spite of their own researches taking them in different directions, they shared and communicated a common basis in alignment work and/or contact improvisation. By the mid-1980s it appeared possible to define some characteristics of Dartington's dance. Whether this was a 'Dartington style' or a generally conceived British new dance style influenced by American and European trends is open to debate. In movement style, the consistent training in unforced movement in all areas of space including the floor gave them what the critic Sophie Constanti believed she could distinguish in Dartington students, something she called 'that relaxed, tumbly movement style'.[103] Pedestrian movement and minimalism were apparent as they were elsewhere in Britain and, although mixed-media performances were not specific to Dartington alone, mixing of media had a broad base within the Dartington ethos of cross-disciplinary work. The varied approaches across writing, acting and moving were all in their different ways involved with the creation of theatrical images – it was possible to see them as 'different streams of the same river', and choreographers coming out of Dartington in the 1970s and 1980s (for example, Laurie Booth, Kevin Finnan and Yolande Snaith[104]) have a strong sense of visual and theatrical impact in their work.[105] All three of those choreographers experienced an attraction towards the drama work while at Dartington, and Booth in particular came away from Dartington to work in physical theatre, only towards the end of the 1970s gravitating to movement work in more of a dance context (sometimes a fuzzy boundary anyway, as already discussed). At Dartington, the influences he was taking from Fulkerson and particularly from Paxton (with whom he shared a background in aikido and meditation) were given further depth through acting studies, incorporating thinking from Jerzy Grotowski and Antonin Artaud – the body of the actor/dancer trained as a complete instrument to speak in movement to the audience, drawing on both personal and shared emotional landscapes. As a frequent and influential tutor at Dartington in the 1980s, he fed back to students a movement philosophy that he had begun to form there as a student himself.

The Theatre Department as a whole emphasised project work, tutor-led with resident tutors or visiting professionals who were able to work with students in sometimes small groups on a daily basis for days or weeks. This immersion in the studio was a virtual apprenticeship in the artistic process with an established artist, working out ideas with which he or she was intimately involved and perhaps only beginning to explore experimentally. Here was the principle of the artist/educator in practice. Students were often involved in the personal theatre projects of tutors. Mary Fulkerson toured with a group she named Dance Alliance in 1983, including some current and former Dartington students. While students coming out of the course in the 1960s had felt they were being trained as dancers (although they were supposed to be teachers), the ethos after Fulkerson arrived in 1973 was to challenge conventional notions of training a dancer's body as an interpretative instrument of the choreographer's work. Now in dance-based work (as it had been all along in drama-based work) students were being trained as creators.

Project work with professional artists schooled students in professional production values. In 1982 a piece made for students at Dartington appeared in Dance Umbrella in London (not a usual arena for non-professional work). *Constant Trouble* (the title apparently a tongue-in-cheek reference to the student condition) was the result of eight students, not all of whom were primarily interested in dance, working daily with Laurie Booth for six weeks, and was presented on Booth's own solo programme. Alastair Macaulay reported it as:

> The most entertaining work I've ever seen for students. Movement was very simple, but quickly established as a common bond between them. You saw them as a community, as a community of dancers, and you saw them as soloists, each one after another giving a party-trick.[106]

Stephanie Woodard wrote an account of a project she led at Dartington in spring 1984. This was a first-year group, and it is indicative of the depth of project work that she had a daily programme for five solid weeks with just twelve students. In the weekly schedule they had three technique classes (which was an unusual experience for these students), two anatomy and release classes, four rehearsals of her choreographed material and two workshops for the students' own choreography. The final performance was *Sweetheart, You're Late* – even by the standards of the department a strange concept, since the performers had no clear view when it would start, beyond that they needed to acquire a critical mass of performers on Totnes streets, or in College. After being scheduled for some time after two in the afternoon, it got under way at about six o'clock and the finale was a devised piece involving dismantling a car behind the Barn Theatre.[107]

'A Day in the Life of a Theatre Student' was prone to such hazards, stimulating in their own way but possible to lampoon, as one student did in a perhaps affectionate satire in the estate newspaper. When he eventually retired to bed, he was 'shivering slightly after four hours of moving stillness in the car park', where the Car Park Event (one of the Theatre Department's many site-specific projects) was being rehearsed, and 'trying to get to grips with the physicality' of a particular model and registration of Ford car.[108] This account, satire though it is, at least depicts the actuality of a day's work that was full to overflowing and might be extended well into the evening by the enthusiasm of students or staff, or both together, to try out something new.

Part of the richness on offer to students at the College from the 1960s onwards was the expanding study of Asian music, with what that meant in terms of encountering visiting artists of world stature and widening notions of musical form. By this time the climate of East/West interchange in music and dance had altered considerably. There was a general world view seeping into popular culture encouraging a growing fascination with India. There was the notion of a more open, intuitive, divergent way of thought and a fascination with meditation and non-Western religious experience, while the sound of the sitar penetrated popular music. Dartington made some impressive alliances in music that attracted students from across the departments. In 1967 Ravi Shankar, who had been at Dartington with his older brother Uday in the 1930s, visited as a sitar virtuoso in his own right. In 1968 there was a College festival of the Indian arts, including activities for local schools. There were residences by sitarists, the brothers Vilayat and Imrat Khan, the latter developing a strong relationship with Dartington, particularly in the years 1968–70.[109] The Centre for Asian Music was set up in 1970, its courses becoming absorbed into the College music department in the 1970s. Indian, Indonesian (especially gamelan) and Japanese instruments were studied. Dartington's Tagore Festival of 1976 was an occasion that brought many brilliant artists together, including Imrat Khan, and dancers Anjali, and Durga Lal.

In Chapter 4 I mentioned many of the performers who appeared at Dartington as it became a regional venue for all forms of dance at the time when the notion of what dance encompassed was also expanding. Here I ask whether visiting dance artists who performed mainly in the classical styles of the Indian sub-continent were dancer/educators in quite the same way as the dancers from American and European traditions who have occupied this chapter or indeed as were their musician counterparts. To what extent did Dartington as an institution support their performance and creative work and to what extent were they able to use Dartington to disseminate knowledge of their art forms? One dancer who developed a special relationship with Dartington was Anne-Marie Gaston, a Canadian who performs under the name of Anjali. She recalls visiting Dartington from her then base in Oxford to perform and teach once or twice a year from 1971 to 1978. She remembers it as a supportive and inspiring environment that also fostered an artistic partnership with the sitarist Alistair Dick who headed the Asian music subject area, a programme that they took to the Edinburgh Festival. Working with students, she used the bharata natyam and odissi techniques, teaching the step units separately and forming them into a short dance by the end of a week of study. Students across theatre and music subject areas were interested in the work, but she was disappointed that no particular place could be made for this within the dance curriculum of what had become the theatre-degree course with dance as an extended study by 1977.[110]

There were common areas between the dancers and musicians from the current Eastern and Western traditions. Improvisation was one of them, although the conventions were different. There were times when Dartington's resident dancers, staff and students, interacted with musicians and dancers from the Eastern traditions. We have seen earlier in this chapter that there are abiding memories from a student of the 1960s. Peter Cox also mentions a time during the Tagore Festival (1976) when Durga Lal (kathak dancer) and Imrat Khan (sitar) worked with students and resident dance and theatre lecturers.[111] It is also clear that musicians of the stature of Ravi Shankar, Imrat Khan and others were absolutely embedded in a global culture in which their traditions were admired and taught, but also in which they participated in the kinds of East/West collaboration sometimes known under the musical category of 'fusion'. But did dance fare in quite the same way? It appears not, since there never was a consistent Indian classical dance presence that could stand alongside the music. Perhaps the closest that Dartington's dance came to that was in the time of Georgia Cushman's lectureship.

The celebrated tabla player of the Benares tradition, Sharda Sahai, became a senior lecturer and artist in residence in 1985. His wife, Munni Sahai, had an amateur kathak class and daughter Padma Sahai taught a children's class, but these were outside the institutional College setting, although absolutely in tune with Dartington's ethos of opening arts to the community. By now, the Asian music subject area was led by Frances Shepherd, who had been a student there herself in the 1960s and later had been a dedicated student of Sahai. She brought to Dartington the best dancers of the now considerable diaspora. One was Nahid Siddiqui, an acclaimed kathak exponent who, memorably, after an all-night recital of music in the Great Hall in June 1987, danced the audience into wakefulness along with Sahai's tabla playing.[112] These dance artists performed and gave workshops but none was on the staff. The alliance with the dance of South Asia was never seriously pursued at the College. The dynamic between the polarities of East/West, contemporary/traditional, which we now see in twenty-first-century Britain exemplified by such dancer/choreographers as Akram Khan and Shobana Jeyasingh, did not develop at Dartington.

The distance between London and Dartington, which had seemed to Christopher Martin in the early 1940s to be such a barrier to developing work with professional artists, proved from the 1960s onwards to be rather less so. Dartington became a staging post in an interchange of ideas between London, America and Europe. In fact, looking closely at the dancers who came to Dartington from the 1930s onwards, we can see how entwined were notions of European and American modern dance. We can see also how the arts of the Indian sub-continent were becoming embedded in British culture.

That defining idea that Peter Cox pursued – the artist as educator – and that was implicit in the development of the College came to flourish for dance especially with the rich input of guest teachers under Mary Fulkerson and the institution of the Dance at Dartington festival. Up until the contraction in funds of the late 1980s, the College had a confident dynamic as an environment for artists making their own work, in a way carrying on that tradition of arts patronage begun by the Elmhirsts. Students from the College of Arts were educated as artists in a fostering environment of experiment and collaboration across disciplines. Emilyn Claid, of the X6 collective, recognises Dartington and X6 'running on parallel trajectories' in the period of new dance radicalism of the 1970s and 1980s, Dartington inevitably focusing on developing student artists, while at X6 professional artists were questioning their already formed bodies of knowledge, 're-thinking dance ... stripping away dance and life patterns in order to go forward.'[113] But the two were mutually influential on each other and the development of dance at the end of the twentieth century.

The late 1980s were less happy years at Dartington. The progressive Dartington Hall School, historically the definition of all that signified Dartington's approach, closed in 1987 amidst scandals that possibly could have been surmounted if the Trust had been more supportive.[114] This was also the last year of the Dance at Dartington festival and the year of Fulkerson's departure to the School for New Dance Development in Amsterdam. Following this, Katie Duck, now in charge of dance, was wresting with the revalidation of the degree on the lines of a modular system, with much less flexibility and spontaneity than previously in sending students off onto multifarious projects. The workload and costs involved were perhaps reason enough not to revisit the festival idea. After ten years, Duck saw that it needed to move in new directions, to raise the standard by being more selective and paying fees. This was just not possible in the current financial climate.[115]

The Trust and the College were both being shaken by financial problems. The inflation of the 1970s caused by the oil crisis following the Arab/Israeli War of 1973 had badly affected the Trust's assets. The election in 1979 of a government (Margaret Thatcher's) dedicated to cutting public expenditure, including in higher education and the arts, put further pressure on the College. By the late 1980s there were serious problems of finance affecting everything at Dartington, and dissension within the Trust about the way ahead. Assets and industries were sold off. Dartington went through a period of traumatic change. Then the provisions of the Education Reform Act 1988 required the separation of the College from the Trust, with its own governing body and constitution with charitable status – another defining moment. The College of Arts that had been Dartington Arts Centre, that had been the Arts Department, that had been originally the personal beliefs and preferences of the Elmhirsts, in particular Dorothy, was set adrift from its anchor, as it were. By the time the new governing body took control of the College, it was very clear that it was on the edge of bankruptcy.[116] It just managed to survive, but not without some difficult decisions, including condensing the theatre course from four to three years.

Dance went through another period of Dartington reinventing itself. I do not follow this history further in any detail, although I will later give a sketch. In the following chapter I return to the 1970s and 1980s to look at the aspects of Dartington's theatre that burst out of its rarefied and artistic ambience, making connections to other people and places.

Chapter 6

Dancing with People and Places

The theatre of the neighbourhood is made by the people of the neighbour-hood; it is made by those that seek association with those of the neighbourhood. It evolves slowly. Intuition and spontaneity chart the work. Time is measured in years rather than weeks and months.
David Slater, 1986[1]

In previous chapters, Dartington has emerged as a location for cutting-edge artistic and educational ideas – not an isolated place, certainly, given the many connections that built up with contemporary and new dance in Britain and abroad and with the arts of India, but a location immersed in its own identity. Now in this final chapter I will examine the years of the 1970s and 1980s from another perspective, that of Dartington's outreach to people and places in everyday life. The old imperative made explicit by the Elmhirst founders, to explore the relevance of the arts to life, continued after the deaths of Dorothy in 1968 and Leonard in 1974. It remained implicit in the work of the Trust and therefore in the College to which it had, as it were, given birth.

Any tendency for Dartington to be isolated from its own rural community was partly redressed by the Adult Education Centre set up by the Trust at Shinners Bridge in 1947, mostly giving popular courses in art work and crafts of various kinds but also music and drama. There were also major events sponsored by the Trust that encouraged community participation. The Children's Christmas Festivals have already been mentioned. On an even bigger scale were the Coronation Pageant in 1953 and the Tournament of Ancient Sports on Foundation Day 1957, for both of which the local villages made splendidly attired individual team presentations. In later years, events from the College theatre department were occasional, focusing on celebratory or festive events. This is at least partly explained by the contemporary notion that acknowledged a more complex relationship between the theatre artist and the community than Barr would have imagined. For now, in the 1970s, after all the revolutionary hippiedom of the late 1960s and beyond, it did not seem that the artist could teach the community anything. It was rather that the community, the amalgam of people and place, held a latent theatricality to which the artist could give an outer form but which the people themselves must inhabit. The community also had the right to define its own needs as an active rather than a passive participant in the arts.

A vernacular theatre

In late May 1978, a 'strange object from outer space' was found floating in the Harbourne river at Harbertonford, a village close to Dartington. It stimulated curiosity and signalled that something would happen, but there was no pre-knowledge in the village of what that would be except that it might be associated with the approaching Country Fair. A trapezoidal tower of scaffolding poles had been erected in the school yard, also with no apparent explanation. The arrival of various costumed characters on Saturday afternoon persuaded curious inhabitants to gather on the river bridge alongside a character said to be 'the Village Fool'. Upstream the river was overhung by trees and, out of this shade, the sound and light of a flame-thrower signalled that something was approaching, splashing through the water. This was a low, black monstrous thing, gushing flame and accompanied by wet-suited minders with goggle eyes! The effect was potent and even more scary when the creature began to climb the bank of the river and advance along the village street. Its name was Gar and its intention, according to the dialogue of the actors, was to steal the Rainbow Lady's secret recipe for Rainbow Bread. The people retreated up the main street of the village, lined with stone cottages. They encountered the 'Mayor' and his pet mouse at tea and were persuaded that Gar's threat was real. They must take the Rainbow Bread from its hiding place under the bridge up to the school for safety. Meanwhile, spontaneously it seemed, children attacked the monster with missiles from the windows of their houses.

Everyone gathered in the safety of the school grounds. Up on her trapezoidal tower, the Rainbow Lady was wakened. She signalled with her yellow flag for the 'Chromosols' from the spaceship in the river to come to their aid. Fireworks and kites went up from surrounding hills to answer her call. The Chromosols were students, of course, encased in bouncy muslin coverings held out in shape by hoops, with only their feet free. Up on a raised grassy area they danced a sacred circle to keep the bread safe. (This segment had been choreographed by Nancy Udow, then a dance tutor in Mary Fulkerson's dance programme.) But the monster was now amongst them. The dance in the field turned into a combat, a tug-of-war in which Gar was defeated and led back, subdued, to the river. The Village Fool and the Chromosols performed a celebratory dance and the Rainbow Bread was handed out to everyone, participants and onlookers – a fitting finale to this unique performance of *Raindough*. Colette King remembers it as a unique experience of feeling again the wonder and fright of a small child.[2]

Peter Kiddle, a tutor in the Theatre Department, devised *Raindough* and other similar events. He had worked for some time with the theatre group Welfare State, a fluctuating group of practitioners around the director John

Fox, making 'celebratory theatre designed for specific environments, seasons and social occasions', using a host of skills in music, performance, writing and construction.[3] This kind of theatre is far from the tamed and safe theatre of the conventional performance. It utilises the power of myth and ritual along with pre-theatre forms of pageant and procession to bring a community together – a community action that has some local meaning.[4] The roots of this vernacular theatre are very deep, drawing both on old and surviving traditions such as the Mummers' Plays and the Padstow May Day hobby-horse ritual and on a contemporary notion of everyday life as being theatrical of itself, staged on the everyday streets or fields of a community's own geography, a 'language of the people' or a 'common tongue' rather than a theatre of literature.[5] Based at Dartington, Kiddle arranged a number of events like this in Plymouth, Totnes, Rotherhithe in London, and the rural area around Dartington, under the collective name of The Department of Public Works (later changed to Theatre of Public Works to avoid the governmental connotations). *Raindough* illustrates again the richness of Dartington's cross-disciplinary staff/student project work. Design was by students of the newly established course in Art and Design in Social Contexts, led by lecturer Karen Watts. Even a music student might be involved in the theatrical role of one of Gar's attendants.[6] Students invented a verb, 'kiddling', for this kind of activity – making large outdoor performance pieces accompanied by plenty of time in the local pubs![7]

Some of the regular features of the vernacular theatre events are encapsulated in this narrative – the mixture of ancient, good-versus-evil symbolism with more modern character types (visitors from outer space and a hint of the Mad Hatter's tea party); the archetypal theme of a threat to a community with its resolution in cooperative action; the spontaneous gathering of a crowd to be led by music and action in a peripatetic way through the story, making it both an actual and a metaphorical journey; and the sharing of food as a symbolic act of communality.[8] The American feminist art critic Lucy Lippard, who had coincidentally come to spend a year at a nearby farm to think and write, included it in her book *Overlay* (1983). Living in South Devon had revealed to her the potency of the surviving archaeological monuments. She noticed a trend in contemporary visual and performance artists to turn to images and symbols from prehistoric and ancient cultures, to rediscover an art that was central to everyday life rather than separated from it. The relationship of these contemporary art works to the deep past was an 'overlay' analogous to the multiple layering of nature and culture on the landscape over time, but achieving an organic wholeness.[9]

To what degree, though, does it show us where the longstanding Dartington ethos of opening to the community stood within the radical theatre of the College in the 1970s? In one sense, because it was a

Dartington-made event with only College people involved in the making, the villagers were distanced from it; but in another, their participation in the processional and celebratory aspects made them essential to the whole theatrical expression. It brought theatre into the everyday and opened up a channel of communication. It appears that Harbertonford at this time was quite cautious about Dartington. On the whole, the families living there had no direct contact with Dartington's industries or with the College. The dance that had been arranged in the village hall on the evening after *Raindough* was poorly attended by local people but remembered for the College dance student who got everyone up to do a tango in formation.[10] However, all the efforts did result, as was hoped, in initiatives coming from the village: suggestions that Peter Kiddle could support the work in the school, youth club and dramatic society. This is very much the way that Kiddle sees vernacular theatre developing into something truly *of* the community, but also he makes the point now that vernacular theatre is enriching for a lifetime because it leaves behind potent visual images and memories.[11] I endorse this from my own experience: a taxi driver at Totnes recounted to me his own memories of being a child 'jouster' representing his hamlet in the Tournament of Ancient Sports celebrating Foundation Day 'up at the Hall' in 1957.

Another vernacular theatre event was *Springwake* in Totnes, celebrating the Spring Solstice in 1979, with all the College departments involved and scores of local schoolchildren who had been working with students. The Bird of Spring is greeted in the forecourt of the Civic Hall by the real Mayor of Totnes. He asks her to help rid the town of the Winter King who has taken up residence in the castle. A large procession sets out through the streets accompanied by the Town Band and the Ragged Drum Band of College students (Winter has impoverished them), looking for the house of a young woman who will make a suitable Queen of Spring. When she is found, the procession sets off again, and after various halts for magical events they arrive at the castle that overlooks the town. Meanwhile, the Bird of Spring has been captured and put in a cage in the court of the Winter King, where 'strange dances' are performed by the Winter King's retinue. At last the Bird of Spring is rescued and the Queen of Spring crowned. The procession takes the Winter King down to Borough Park, where there is a celebration of music, dancing, food and drink. Finally, to expel the Winter King for good (or at least until next year), he is brought with great jubilation to Totnes Station and sent away on the evening milk train![12]

While theatre artists like Kiddle were developing ways of merging a place and its people into participatory events, site-specific theatre works were happening in and around Dartington as part of the normal project work for staff and students. Fulkerson employed the latent theatricality of Totnes in *Dreams and Images on Totnes Streets*. Inspired by the Italo Calvino novel *The*

Castle of Crossed Destinies, in which the images of tarot cards were used to tell travellers' stories, this dance and photographic project, led by Fulkerson and Graham Green, started with cards made from photographs and sketches of people of the town. From these stimuli, the rich experiences of the people and the imagery that accrued around them, the students made moments of dance and movement for sites all over Totnes – on the River Dart embankment, in an old people's home, on the Lepers' Walk and at the Leechwell. There were night-time masked street processions, and a solo bag lady performed in the marketplace. Pausing at a nearly deserted petrol station to fill the van that was shuttling performers around, it seemed too good to resist making a dance there: a couple got out and danced in full evening dress under the neon lights, with passing cars honking their approval![13]

Performing communities

Inevitably, this chapter will raise comparisons between what Margaret Barr and the School of Dance-Mime were doing for the community in the early 1930s and the very different context of Dartington's work in the community more than forty years later. I also ask how the Laban work for lay dancers fits into the history of community arts happening at Dartington and elsewhere. However, there must be some initial caution about those comparisons. The institutional differences are striking. Before 1934 the Arts Department did not exist and the arts policy was guided predominantly by the beliefs and tastes of the Elmhirsts themselves. By the 1970s the Arts Department had metamorphosed into Dartington College of Arts: artist/educators and their students in music, visual arts and theatre, working within the national structure of higher education. There are a few threads joining together these different historical contexts. One of them is the long leadership of Peter Cox stretching back to the Arts Department under Christopher Martin. Another is that the Dartington Hall Trust still remained the parent body of the College of Arts. Both these continuities transmitted those core values of the original Dartington ethos, including notions of the role of the arts in everyday life. But, as the growing community arts movement would ask, whose everyday life do we mean? Is this a 'top-down' distribution of arts to the masses, or do the masses have anything worthwhile of their own to contribute? Is the intervention of the artist constructive or is it patronising?

Institutionally, the College nurtured various pedagogic manifestations of those core notions of the value of arts in society. It was in fact far better placed in terms of structures and personnel to develop community work than Barr had been, and as an institute of higher education it was capable of developing theory as well as practice. In 1971/72 there were inter-departmental seminars on The Artist and the Community, including in non-Western cultures. Music in Society was an option on the CNAA-

validated Music degree commencing in 1974, and later there were two diploma courses (Dip HE), in Music in the Community and Art and Design in
Social Contexts, which developed community placement schemes. The
groundbreaking aspect of the BA (Hons) degree in Theatre, from its first
intake in 1976, was its structure as a four-year course with the entire third
year out on community placement in an urban environment.

While this was happening at Dartington, a self-conscious community arts
movement was gathering pace in the country, though mainly in urban areas.
It was to a large extent the offspring of the political, social and cultural transformation of the 1960s, with objectives of bringing about change from the
grass roots and of democratising culture, while it also drew from the avant-
garde questioning of the hegemony of the favoured institutions and
conventional norms of 'high' art. The political and often combative stance of
the movement was bound to put it into contention with the Arts Council's
establishment views of what constituted art worth subsidising. In 1974 the
report from the Arts Council's Community Arts Working Party (the Baldry
Report) endorsed the concept of community arts and artists, though rather
in terms of democratising culture through greater access to the arts on a
local level. This was not the way that the more politically active community
arts workers saw their role, which was much more about supporting individual and group creativity for personal and community empowerment.[14] In
1978, Su Braden's book *Artists and People* emphasised the divide between the
community arts projects that were literally in the control of the arts workers
and those that arose from the creativity of the grass-roots community. This
was an influential book in the national community arts debate, and was
reviewed in *Dartington Hall News*.[15] Historically, notions of democratic access
to already accepted art forms had dominated the thinking of the Elmhirsts.
In later years, while regular arts programming through Dartington Arts Society and the College continued to offer democratic access through a
diversity of artistic participation and appreciation to anyone who cared to
come, the 1970s also saw the attempt to reconnect with communities in a
proactive way.

There was also the significant notion that 'arts for everybody' must include those with disabilities. At Dartington, music and visual arts subject
areas had developed projects with handicapped children. In 1978,
Dartington College of Arts was host to a seminar, 'Arts for the Benefit and
Care of Disability'. The report of the seminar indicates how firmly dance and
movement had taken on the challenges of this field of work. Presenters included the Laban-trained dancer Veronica Sherborne, working in dance and
movement with children with severe learning difficulties. Another section of
the report describes work on theatre, movement and dance with sight- and

hearing-impaired adults. In fact, a comment on the topics covered was that there was too much of an emphasis on theatre and movement work.[16]

On the basis that there would be an input from scientists from the disciplines of psychology, sociology and anthropology (recognised areas whereas theatre practice was still regarded with academic suspicion), the Division for Higher Education of the Council of Europe funded a Theatre and Communities Workshop at Dartington in 1983.[17] This large undertaking brought together delegates from across Europe, such as John Fox of Welfare State, representing theatre projects that had been working in specific communities for ten years or more. But dance as a distinct community art form was invisible in this undertaking. One can wonder why this was so, when the Theatre Department was so committed to its dance artists. Perhaps one reason was that the radicalism of dancer/educators such as Mary Fulkerson was about rigorously reshaping the art form from their own practice. It was quite different from the kinds of radicalism that put the artist at the service of the community, as Colette King had written into the theatre degree she headed. Both stances are political because they assert the individual against the pressures of conformity, but the latter questions the right of the artist to a special and distinct voice in society. It elevates the primacy of communication and attempts to reconsider what is 'high' and 'low' in terms of culture. On the whole, Dartington's resident dance artists did not follow this route, so one may imagine that there was no one speaking up for community dance practitioners. Dance in the community as a consciously articulated movement arrived later than in other forms of community arts, but had done so by the time of the Council of Europe Workshop. The first community dance animateurs had been appointed in 1976. A South West Arts conference was held at Rolle College in 1980 to consider 'The Scope of Community Theatre and Dance'. Perhaps the late arrival of community dance projects in relation to other community arts meant that they did not qualify under the definition of the long-term projects examined in the Council of Europe Workshop. Colette King remembers having visited some community dance projects in Europe, but she did not find anything comparable to the theatre projects attending the workshop or to the movement and dance currently in evidence at Dartington.[18]

The two main locations for the third-year Theatre Department projects were Plymouth Action Community Theatre (PACT), based in the Stonehouse area of Plymouth, and Rotherhithe Theatre Workshop (RTW) in the East End of London. These were both inner-city, working-class areas with levels of financial deprivation and certainly could be seen as deprived in terms of arts access.[19] The College also took on a building in Totnes, the Mansion, in order to work with the local community and give students some experience of this earlier in their course.

Before these projects were set up, there were attempts to put some of the ideas into practice with the last cohorts of the Dance and Drama Education course. By now it had been recognised that many of the students wanted professional experience, before or after going to Rolle College or even instead of going there. Three dancers, Laurie Booth, Arianna Economou and Sarah Willis, were set up at the Frederick Street Community Centre in Plymouth in 1978 as a small company, The Dancemakers. This was to be a group that would make and show its own dance pieces as well as work with the community. They performed in London[20] as well as at the Dance at Dartington festival. However, the community placement aspect of the work does not seem to have taken root and they were brought back to Dartington after a term. In a similar way, a small drama company of ex-students, The Red Earth, had failed for want of experienced direction.

There are some tensions within this insistence on an urban community placement, as if somehow the needs of these areas were more real than those of Dartington's rural population: as if somehow it was only in inner cities that the challenge of life in the raw could be met. But the original degree-proposal to the CNAA in 1975 made a specific point about 'the current trend, particularly in urban locations, towards the alienation of one person from another' – something theatre could ameliorate.[21] Students were placed in the thick of a difficult situation. Rotherhithe was a particularly challenging environment of run-down estates where the remnants of a tight-knit, East End community felt embattled while the up-market redevelopment of London's Docklands went on around them. Southwark Council had provided six 'hard to let' apartments so that the students were living right in the community, which was nevertheless suspicious of them. RTW was set up in the empty Hope (Sufferance)[22] grain warehouse on the river; it had already been converted as a dance studio but the intended company had not moved in. On the floor above were crafts people's workshops. This was a serendipitous discovery by Peter Kiddle through entering into conversations in local public houses.

Likewise, PACT managed to develop its own warehouse working space in the Stonehouse area of Plymouth, where there were many social problems. In these environments the students often felt they were unwanted and separated from the host community by class, education and expectations. The ultimate 'put-down' was when PACT was burnt down by some locals after a couple of partial arson attacks.

The rationale for taking up the full year on placement was that the students needed to negotiate an understanding of the environment and a relationship with their host community, and from that to devise a programme fitting in with what the locality wanted rather than one imposed because of some pre-existing notion of art. Students needed to be taught how to draw upon the specifics of the community where they worked. This was quite a daunting prospect, involving having to build contacts with community members, schools, homes for the elderly and other institutions. It often involved engagement with local people on an everyday domestic or social level before being able to engage with them using the Dartington theatre skills. Workshops and clubs were set up at the project bases, and students also went out to institutions in the community. The paradox surrounding this notion of a long placement for students that they had to negotiate for themselves was that, in terms of their host communities, the presence of any group of students was short-term and there was no guarantee of continuity in anything that had been set up.

There were also matters of geography that had a bearing upon whether or not the urban project was successful. David Slater believes that part of RTW's success was the way in which the studio opened straight onto the pavement, so students might be working with doors open in full view, drawing people into their world. 'It was literally a theatre at the end of the street.'[23] Out of this opening-up to the neighbourhood also came an opening of expectations for some individuals who, only because of those workshops they had experienced, became students themselves at Dartington.[24]

As we look for the way in which dance figured in these schemes, we must notice again how the niche occupied by dance at Dartington had been subsumed into more multi-stranded notions of theatre. The core theatre subjects that everyone experienced in the first year – acting, movement and writing – contributed to a convergence in the concept of performance that was often difficult to pigeonhole as 'dance' or 'drama'. It is also apparent that this paralleled an area of convergence in professional theatre: in Chapter 5, I discussed the work of specific dance artists, showing how this wide concept of performance facilitated collaboration with their colleagues from other disciplines. It follows from this that looking for dance in Dartington's community projects requires a broad view of what dance encompasses.

Alan Read, the resident tutor at Rotherhithe, found that it was often the students who had been most immersed in dance who found greatest difficulty. They had the relevant skills, but it sometimes seemed that the language in which dance was taught and discussed at Dartington – a language of images, sensations and arcane processes – was alien to this community with its mundane concerns. However, that initial translation from one world to another could be overcome and they did discover young people and older people in that neighbourhood to work with, many of whom found 'great strength in doing things about stillness, about neutrality... particularly pedestrian movement'.[25]

Nevertheless, one can sense that any student dedicated to dance performance might find the work in the neighbourhood hard or dull, even while their

understanding of the social situation was growing. The following story is
from a student on the Plymouth project.

> Apart from some classes which I took with *[another dance student]* in the
> summer, to which friends and a few prancey girls from the Arts Centre
> came, my only excitement in the dance area occurred when four of the
> boys from the Probation Home were encouraged along to our Release ses-
> sion. ... I started going roller skating with them and to their local *[pub]* ...
> During the preparation of the cabaret *[they]* would often come and watch
> us in rehearsal and took a real interest in what we were doing. They would
> sit and watch fascinated. ... I realised that their attendance at the session
> they came to each week at the Warehouse was motivated more by the
> desire to have contact with us than to learn to dance. Despite this they
> gave themselves to the rolling and imaging and relaxing we put them
> through (although often the rest position got the better of them and sent
> them to sleep). *[Notes added.]*[26]

These students managed to put into effect some regular classes drawing
directly from their own training. Others did the same, whether setting up a
contact improvisation group or trying to reformulate everything they knew
as something they could call, for programming purposes, 'basic movement'.
But, inevitably, people in the community itself, whose ideas were key to this
concept of community arts, had their own notions of dance filtered through
personal experience of television or film. So cabaret, revue and musical-
theatre formats were very useful for packaging a dance experience, both in
the students' own productions and in the performances they facilitated in the
community. For example, it was a moment of 'absolute magic' when two
senior citizens who had recently learned some tap dancing from one of the
students were able to perform a 'Fred and Ginger' routine in a community
cabaret.[27]

Although the notions of dance performance they had absorbed at
Dartington were not always useful for work in the community, in one other
respect they had learned something central to the needs of this kind of work.
In their own training in release and contact work, they had been given the
opportunity to explore movement starting from the place of their own individual physicalities and movement potential. It was possible to use that
embodied knowledge of personal change to find the point of entry in movement work for the disparate groups they encountered, including people with
disabilities, institutionalised elderly people, children in care and young people being treated for addiction. The individualised learning for students in
this year made it possible to set up training to support specialised applications – for example, movement and disability.[28]

Dartington's theatre department was, of course, thoroughly immersed in notions of performance, but in what terms could community performance be conceptualised? Read was beginning to theorise an artistic area he called 'lay theatre'.[29] Lay theatre arises from the place itself, from its history and geography and from the everyday theatricality of its architectural and public spaces. Often the theatre that arose from the Rotherhithe and Stonehouse projects used the place quite literally in the street theatre and processions, carnivals, rituals and ceremonies of vernacular theatre. Read and his colleague David Slater, who had also been his predecessor as resident tutor at Rotherhithe, went further in initiating a dialogue with people in the community who surely had something to say and often a latent talent for expression in singing, dancing or story-telling that was in the truest sense theatrical, but 'lay-theatrical', not making the economic distinction between producer and consumer, not valuing the theatrical talents any higher than the other talents of everyday life.[30] Rotherhithe Theatre Workshop's management committee was made up of strong-minded people from the community itself: they were the permanent community, while the theatre folk were transient. So the position of the artist was to make theatre *with* the local community, not *for* it. 'Lay theatre' as a term resonates with Laban's notion of the lay dancer: both terms avoid the diminishing label of 'amateur', with its implications of low quality. Lay theatre, which I will expand from Read's term to include a lay dance theatre, can use the most sophisticated production techniques when supported by professionals, but its quality lies in the full engagement of its participants. They must have a desire to communicate something central to their lives. So there were youth theatre productions such as *Rotherhithe Kids 'Live'* (it was also shown in a display by London dancing schools), *The Back Streets of Bermondsey*, a children's musical, and *Southside Story*, in a similar genre. Oral history played a part in productions such as *Down Hopping*, based on elders' memories of the traditional summer move of whole families down to Kent for hop-picking. Young at Heart was one of the older people's performance companies that grew out of RTW. One of their shows was *Century*, in which they recalled the work patterns of packing biscuits at the Peak Freen factory as the basis for a dance performance piece.

In 1984 there was a massive performance project built around the story of Lee Boo, a chief's son from the Palau Islands in the North Pacific, who had come to Rotherhithe in 1784. The story had many dimensions. Firstly, it was a piece of Rotherhithe history that spoke of its significant seafaring past, something made concrete in its architectural landscape and monuments. Then, in a more exploratory way, it could be treated as a metaphor for immigration (not an easy subject in a predominantly white, working-class community) and an exploration of the ethics of East/West contact within a fairly safe story setting. It was a story that could bring together street theatre and events along the river embankment with sketches and dances inside the Workshop and in the local church. The East India Company packet ship *Antelope* had been shipwrecked on the Palau Islands, but the crew had received every help there to build a boat to get them off the island. The chief was impressed and asked for his son to be brought back to England, to be educated in its marine technology. Lee Boo lived with the ship's captain and his family in Rotherhithe, was apparently treated with courtesy aligned with curiosity in London, but died of smallpox after only a few months – the sad and deadly outcome of the unequal encounter. His tomb and memorial were in the churchyard adjacent to the RTW base.

This project was an attempt at integrating the various community sections that were often understood as fragmented within community arts ventures – children, youth, adults, elderly people. The story brought together many contexts for exploration – the exotic other places of imperialism, the local community that had interacted with Lee Boo, the church that had buried him (although there is some doubt whether he became a Christian). For six months, students worked in schools and with groups of adults. In the course of a day, the people of Rotherhithe celebrated Lee Boo's life and death. Processions through the streets enacted the sea journeys of the story – to Palau, back to Rotherhithe and then (the outcome that the organisers most wanted) the virtual repatriation of Lee Boo. Cars and drivers had been recruited to present carnival floats, one of them an enormous whale. Children danced behind as Palau islanders. They arrived at the RTW studio, which had been decorated to represent the Pacific islands. Sketches and dances depicted the life of the islands. In the church, they commemorated the life and funeral of Lee Boo in Rotherhithe and then symbolically his 'coffin' was sent off in a rowing boat, returning him to his home across the sea. There was a community party with fruit donated by Fyffes, a local business and a famous importer of bananas (ironically, considering the anti-colonial subtext of the event).

Meanwhile, of course, there were tensions over the ethics of RTW and PACT, expressing the community's ownership of their own creativity and the fact that here were students (and indeed artist/educators) who needed to carry on their own creative practice and technical training in these environments where they were sometimes resented. The studios at Plymouth and Rotherhithe were also bases for showing Dartington work more generally, as well as making work with local people. If we look at just one programme from Rotherhithe in summer 1980, there were plays and dance programmes by students, including an improvisational dance performance by second-year students and dance pieces choreographed by third-year students. Music students and staff also came to give concerts and children's workshops.[31]

Students were not isolated from the teaching staff of Dartington and its roster of visiting lecturers: tutors from across the disciplines visited regularly, working with students and sometimes also with the local community. Members of X6 gave open classes for the neighbourhood.[32] Dance students at Rotherhithe were also in a good position to get to London classes and mix with the new dance people who were regulars at the Dance at Dartington festival. The X6 Collective's warehouse base was a bit further west along the Thames, and its successor, Chisenhale Dance Space, north of the Thames in Bow.

Also at Rotherhithe, Read developed a strand of work that was very much about students developing their own practice while being embedded in the experience of working in this neighbourhood. In 1988 there was a site-specific work involving all the students at Rotherhithe to mark the closure of the Peak Freen factory that turned out biscuits, cakes and puddings – a major local employer for decades and a distinctive olfactory presence in the locality. *Multiple Angel* was written as a verse drama, following workers on the night shift as they prepared for the wedding of two of them the next day. The piece grew out of research carried out over the year in the factory itself, where the Dartington people were able to create a research office as a base for investigating the work, lives and stories of the workers and the factory at the height of its production before World War II. At that time, the bride would have left the factory at her wedding, taking with her a tier of cake for every year she had worked there.[33] *Multiple Angel* had a new score by Graham Fitkin (who has since become an important composer for dance) and a vocabulary of stylised movement. *The Cone-Gatherers* was another student production, an adaptation of a novel (1955, Robin Jenkins) set on a Scottish estate during World War II. The set constructed in the RTW studio was a scaffolding structure representing the treetops; performers spent the whole production up in the air. Productions such as these made full use of all the skills of the theatre students, including skills in movement and dance, and belonged in that genre of performance where theatre and dance converged. So visitors like Mary Fulkerson or Yolande Snaith could perceive them as forms not far removed from the dance theatre they practised themselves.[34]

The 'third year out' gave students a freedom to experiment and to reflect on their processes as well as challenging them to understand theatre skills in a community context. The outcomes were not assessed: what mattered was the insights they had gained, illustrated through the dissertations they wrote on their return to Dartington. For some students it was hard, bordering on impossible. For others, the experience was formative for later careers.

Yolande Snaith made her fourth-year final choreographic piece using images and experiences that she had been synthesising throughout her time at Dartington and particularly during her third year at RTW, when she had

worked with a young man with learning disabilities, whose only communication was in drawings – balloon-like heads with limbs dangling from them.
Cotton Duck was her attempt to portray visually and atmospherically his inner world. A male actor portrayed the isolated figure, fixing his attention on
a yellow plastic duck, standing in a corner made by a brick wall, below a
menacing hanging construction filled with bricks. There was a score of
slowed-down sounds of bricks clashing together. The female dancers wore
black dresses and white muslin headdresses ending in a dangling rope that
could be swung around or wrapped around their heads like a turban. They
'did a lot of strange, haunting wild and gestural dancing throughout the
space while the actor remained locked in his own little world with his yellow
plastic duck'.[35]

Urban/rural, amateur/professional, college/community – although they
seem opposite poles, they were encompassed within the College ethos. Mara
de Wit and Cathy Josefowitz left Dartington in 1983 to form a company
named Research and Navigation that they managed to establish in a barn in
rural mid-Wales. This choice arose through a combination of many things,
including the prospect of limited funding but also certainly the sense that
they could take the Dartington spirit with them. Research and Navigation
was both an expression of the College ideal of a life centred on daily artistic
practice and a reflection of the confidence that could come from the third-
year experience. Neither of the founders of Research and Navigation was
rural or from Wales, but the third year had given them the tools for coming to
a new locality and perceiving how it worked, the nodes and linkages from
which they could begin to build a more active cultural landscape including
performing, teaching and working with local agencies.[36]

Yet the third-year placements and their inner-city bases were expensive to
maintain, growing more expensive as the property increased in value. They
fell victim to the financial crises of the late 1980s. The Stonehouse base in
Plymouth was closed down in 1988, replaced by a more fluid arrangement
of individual placements in the South West or further afield, sometimes in
Eire or Europe, under the title of Network Project. Rotherhithe closed in
1991 as the Theatre degree was reformulated on a more conventional three-
year pattern.

Sharing movement

One of the notions that supported Dartington's students in their interactions
with diverse groups with varying physical abilities was the basic premise of
contact improvisation: everyone has a body, knowing the world through sensory perceptions; everyone knows the movement of their own breath and
everyone has a fundamental relationship with gravity. In the 1980s, as the
British community arts movement began to identify special groups within

the community as priorities, including those with specific impairments, contact improvisation offered a route for bringing movement and dance into people's lives. The approach to the body through the sensations and the equitable give and take of weight embodied a democratic and non-judgmental notion of the capacity of each body. Contact improvisation has become one of the techniques, although certainly not the only one, embedded in the practice of community dance as it has developed.

To take one example, Kevin Finnan left Dartington College of Arts in 1985 to work in the New Midlands Dance Company, one of the regional companies working in performance and residencies in a community setting. Finnan was, and is, absolutely clear that dance can develop even with people whose physical movements are limited. Speaking of a workshop with adults having severely impaired physical abilities, he wrote:

> We taught about weight and momentum and they learned that their seemingly immobile weight could affect change in someone else ... using counterbalance and shared balances back to back or side to side, people could support themselves on unfamiliar levels.[37]

For Finnan, working with New Midlands Dance and still now with the company he started in 1988 with Louise Richards (Motionhouse, based in Leamington Spa), the approach to any other body in the community – able, disabled or incarcerated – is a matter of development from his own experience of the physical transformation from inside his body that started for him at Dartington.[38]

In 1986, Steve Paxton began a systematic exploration of the way that contact improvisation could give blind and partially sighted people an experience of movement and dance. His colleague in this was Anne Kilcoyne, a trained psychotherapist and theatre director on the staff of the Theatre Department. This project began with financial support from the Elmgrant Trust and in cooperation with the Royal National Institute for the Blind's Rehabilitation Centre in Torquay. Dartington students were given training in the physical and psychological effects of impaired sight and came in as partners in the workshops.

Why did this prove to be such an appropriate experience for men and women with a visual impairment? One of the side effects of these conditions is that movement often also becomes restricted through difficulties in negotiating space and fear of falling. The body can become tense and over-projective. Contact improvisation works with a reduced emphasis on the focused gaze, and an absolute emphasis on the sense of touch through all the body surfaces.

But it is not easy to enter the contact world with a rigid body and a fearful attitude to space. In a video made in 1993, by which time the name of Touchdown Dance had been adopted, we can see just how the slow and steady progress over a five-day workshop could have a transformative effect on movement rigidity and protective stance. Together with sighted dancers, the visually impaired participants progressed through simple relaxation exercises, understanding what is rigid and what is relaxed; lying down, they came to understand breath and gravity and progressed through hand, arm, back of torso and head contact to surfing over each others' bodies. This was of course only the observable and physical effect. Kilcoyne saw the body as a metaphor for the whole person, including the psyche. She said, 'Once you begin to get a sense of the possibilities of your body, other possibilities open up.... Flexibility of the body engenders flexibility of the mind.'

The creativity in contact improvisation was always opening further possibilities. As the video shows, contacts were always 'evolving into a dance'. But for a few of the visually impaired participants their own skills took them into the full, high-energy contact work, in which they could hold their own in performance with sighted partners. In 1989 there was a performance at Dartington by a small group under the title of Blind Faith – Paxton, Julyen Hamilton (a frequent performer and teacher at Dartington) and Gerry Overington, who had come from the Touchdown workshop. In the 1993 video, Bill McKinlay (with little useful sight) creates a high-energy dance with Karen Nelson (a sighted and experienced contacter). They move over all of each other's surfaces, are in constant counter-movement using all levels from floor to standing; they up-end each other dangerously and support each other when a steady balance is found. Her faith in him is beyond doubt. She leaps, is caught, is dangled loosely and moves from there to shoulder supports that dissolve into both bodies softly sinking away into other movements. She also supports his body, then allows him to roll away from close proximity. Occasionally she cues him to the space of the room by hand-touch or by clapping her own hands. Their dance is a beautiful exhibition of the sensory body – mostly they hear, smell and touch each other, sight much lower in their hierarchy of communication.[39]

From lay dance to community dance

In the 1970s and 1980s, the work in the four-year Theatre Degree at Dartington again brought into focus one of the core values of the Elmhirsts, in continuous transmission down the years: that the arts at Dartington should be made available to all. I have suggested in previous chapters that there were areas of uncertainty in the Elmhirst approach to dance for amateurs that prevented the work from flourishing in the 1930s. Clearly there was a value in the practice of dancing for everybody, but when it came to performance, how could that be judged? Leslie Burrowes worked with children and adult amateurs to demonstrate the Dartington project through the dances in *Comus* (Chapter 1). Margaret Barr took on the agenda of the WEA to produce dance-mime in villages and she put large groups of non-professional dancers on stage in her own choreography (Chapter 2). Barr (page 57) and Leonard Elmhirst (page 91) had some intuition that all individuals had a need for expression through movement, validating dance for the amateur. But should this include public performance?

I suggest that there were three issues that complicated dance as amateur performance. Firstly, without a theorised practice such as existed for the movement choirs of central Europe, by what standards was amateur dance to be judged? Secondly, unlike the amateur actor interpreting Shakespeare or the amateur musician playing Purcell, both of these being unquestionably an approach to appreciation of elevated art works of the canon of 'greats', the amateur dancer was always interpreting something newly made; its merit could be debatable and its modernity could be unsettling. Finally, through all this, the amateur dancer had broken the lingering taboos about physical exposure to public view in a still rather repressed society.

The Jooss–Leeder School did not seriously follow through on the implications of the lay dance movement that had been so strongly embedded in the modern dance work of 1920s Europe. It was left to Lisa Ullmann to start this up in Plymouth, and later Laban and Ullman together devised the plan for an 'Education centre for layman dance, for teachers and leaders of movement choruses and community dance groups' at Dartington, a plan that remained unfulfilled. In the decades after World War II, college-trained teachers and members of the Laban Guild evolved Laban's lay dancing into multiple forms – recreative dance circles, youth dance, performing adult dance groups and dance with disabilities. All this emerged from and transformed the principles that Laban and Ullmann had disseminated concerning the benefits of dance in everyday life and the expressive qualities of the everyday body, and was one of the streams feeding into the community dance movement as we know it today.[40]

The national movement of the 1970s towards a concept of community arts rather than 'amateur' arts brought pressure on the Arts Council, resulting in its Working Party on Community Arts. This remained in existence as a Community Arts Committee or Sub-Committee until the responsibility for community arts had been absorbed by the Regional Arts Associations in the early 1980s. By this time, posts for community dance workers or animateurs had proliferated after the first were set up in 1976. Funding was coming into the community dance arena from a mixture of Regional Arts Associations, local authorities and charitable funders such as the Gulbenkian Foundation. At the Laban Centre for Movement and Dance, the Professional Diploma in Community Dance was established in 1982. The National Association of

Dance and Mime Animateurs was set up in the late 1970s (later becoming the Foundation for Community Dance), so that there was now a body speaking specifically for community dance in the field. According to Peter Brinson, the development of community dance as a later, discrete area meant that it was less politically radical than the earlier community arts movement and was more inclined to be institutionalised within national structures.[41] However, it can be countered, as in a recent article in *Animated*, the journal of the Foundation for Community Dance, that 'Community dance is a conspicuous British success ... and it also reflects the process of institutionalisation that takes place when a new development is seen to be effective.'[42] Although it may seem from this that the success story of community dance has been founded upon an ability to meld with established authorities and funding bodies, there is no doubt that it developed much of its vibrancy from the dance radicalism and counterculture of the 1970s. The dancers that clustered around X6 and the Dance at Dartington festivals challenged the established norms of ballet and contemporary dance – hierarchies, elitism, chauvinism, a punishing physical regime. It was a short distance from there to spanning the divide that was supposed to separate the active performer from the passive audience, or the skilled professional from the unskilled amateur. That political radicalism, standing for the demystification of the art form, collaborative working and engagement with the everyday body and its movements, came into community dance as a second and revivifying stream alongside the well-established Laban one. When X6 had to leave their original space, they founded another. Chisenhale Dance Space opened in 1983, becoming a base for inner-city community dance development alongside the experimental development of the art of dance.

But what is the 'community' in the community arts? Does the community equate with a neighbourhood, the identity of its people and their sense of place, as in Liverton, Harbertonford, Rotherhithe or Stonehouse? Or is the community the special and often underprivileged groups within it? Community dance has been seen to offer a range of physical interventions that can be socially empowering, countering social exclusion. Sometimes it seems that a social-service concept of arts provision has made it easier to validate dance as useful and worthy of subsidy.

Is there really a concept of community dance that is separate from the art of dance? Mara de Wit remembers how surprised she was in the 1980s when the work of Research and Navigation in Wales was referred to as 'community dance'. After all, their aim was good art, although the method of working offered multiple entry points for people of varying abilities and experience.[43] Now, in the early twenty-first century, the debate around the artistic and social nature of community dance serves to highlight the fact that the practice of dance in the community is widespread and diverse, involving many choreographers who work across professional performance and community dance culture. Excellence in participatory performance by non-professionals remains as difficult to define now as it was in the 1930s. It seems to be one of those ephemeral qualities that can only be known when seen, but is most often recognised as a total involvement by the performers in the need to communicate through movement something that has been deeply understood. Participation on this level glows and sizzles with life. Back in 1934 Leonard had recognised, but hardly been able to articulate, this 'something to say' of the amateur dancer.[44]

Revisiting Utopia

If Dartington has ever been a utopia, it has been able to stay in existence longer than most. Why is that? In the Elmhirst period, money and patronage underpinned it and ownership gave rise to unquestioned leadership. The gradual professionalisation of institutions brought forth another kind of patronage in which the artist was, like the dancer/educators of the College, given a supportive base. In spite of reversals of fortune that have brought conflict and near bankruptcy, the core values remaining from the earliest foundation have persisted, bound together with the environment into something that inspires affection.

Utopias have traditionally attempted a separation from the world that has been both impossible and the cause of downfall. A combination of good administration, good taste, good luck and the magnetism of the place has kept Dartington open to trends in the national and international arts through a succession of exceptional artists. Dartington sits in a special place in relation to the whole development of dance in twentieth-century Britain. This is not to exaggerate its influence but to note how this history challenges the metropolitan focus of most histories.

In its quest for the good place (*eutopia*), Dartington allowed a place for dance, and that place became entwined with great themes – education, the mind/body question, community, communication, patronage, art. Aiming for utopia, it has seemed that the question was not just: What makes good art (dance)? The further question had to be: What is it for? I maintain that this has been a thread of underlying discourse throughout the century, and not just at Dartington.

It is January 1984. A film camera takes us up into the branches of trees, to an overcast sky above. Then there is an elevated view over the Courtyard towards the Great Hall. A voice announces that this dance is inspired by the constantly changing weather of the Devon countryside. January, February, March, April ... the run-down of the months is in the vocal score and 'Today there will be weather, whether you like it or not', but the weather outside hardly impinges on the dance, which is filmed totally inside the Great Hall.

'Like some giant time-capsule, Dartington Hall passes from hail to sunshine.' The calendar and the weather, twin ideas that come through the text, are translated into dance as dynamics of human relationships – volatile, aggressive, tender, detached, hot to cold. At times, with the muted tones of the costumes, the groups of dancers move like clouds.

In many ways this dance, *January*, is an enigma, speaking about Dartington but not *of* it. Back in 1964, Viola Farber had been a dancer with the Cunningham company that had visited Dartington. Now she had come back, not as an invited teacher but as the partner of Curtis Roosevelt, who took over from Peter Cox as Principal of the College in 1983. Their relationship was on rocky grounds when in 1984 she obtained American funding to choreograph and film a dance at Dartington. This turned out to be the last performance of her own company.[45] Perhaps all of this accounts for a sadness that suffuses what could have been an exuberant evocation of landscape and architecture. Transmitted by the local independent television franchise, Television South West (TSW), it seems to have been totally ignored by reviewers.

I have often seen Dartington as a dancer's landscape, in part because the nature of surviving visual sources projects me in that direction. The photographic records of *Comus* and the School of Dance-Mime showed Dartington as an archaeological space, matching dancers to steps, walls and arches. Ballets Jooss and the Jooss–Leeder School put dancers into the gardens and open-air theatre, with the backdrop of ancient yew trees and the Hall. Through the decades, dancing in all the open spaces has been captured in a way that celebrated place and people in harmony: this is part of the utopian myth of Dartington. Interior spaces have been given the same treatment less regularly, the Barn Theatre hardly at all. An exception is the Dance School. Those tall windows, on one side only of the large studio, define and organise the light into shafts that correspond to the volume of the room. Dancing expands into this space in photographs and films. As for the Great Hall, I like to think of it at points when its fourteenth-century feudalism was subverted by twentieth-century democracy, when it was simply recorded as a workshop space for all the people who came to perform and participate in Dance at Dartington, but never without acknowledgement of its architectural features. *January* challenges this idealism. Whatever may have been intended, it is simply a dance performed in a non-specific space. Occasionally a window comes into view, but the Great Hall is mostly represented by a great expanse of floor.

So *January* as filmed just seems to make its initial, clichéd, visual and verbal reference to Dartington as a rural paradise, as other films have done, with no attempt to truly represent the place itself. And yet perhaps it is a reminder of utopia as *outopia* (no place), especially when the people within its boundaries are at odds with the setting. On another level, *January* as a dance work represents a typical Dartington collaboration. The music score of electronically manipulated vocal tracks was by Gordon Jones, who worked across music and theatre departments. It is a chanted, rhythmic, multi-tracking of high voices (all of them Jones). The costume design of simple tops and trousers in shades of beige (blue-grey for Farber) relieved by interesting textures, were designed by Maria Liljefors, who also had worked with Fulkerson.

Myths about Dartington as a utopian community can only ever be a partial truth. A former Dartington student, now a choreographer and teacher in the region, recently reflected on his feelings of community and even exclusiveness:

> We rolled and slept, lay and fell, improvised and contacted, opened and closed, composed and created ... in the depths of Devon's fat green world, defined by shared artistic variation, an 'open field' of experimental possibilities, and occasional bouts of small kingdom syndrome.[46]

He enlarged on 'small kingdom syndrome' as the effect of a great number of complex interactions going on in a small place: 'imagine a cupboard with 10,000 lit light bulbs!!'. Dartington could be 'an environmental pressure cooker' with results both good and bad for students and artists.[47]

So, in a similar vein, let me suggest that *January* can be seen as a dance that attempts to exploit the Dartington myth but brings a note of realism to what may sometimes have seemed too rosy a picture of a history that must encompass people and events at their worst as well as at their best.

'Disputes cloud future of Utopian legacy', clamoured a headline about Dartington in *The Independent* newspaper in 1991.[48] There is no doubt that Dartington was going through a painful and possibly disastrous time, which had been simmering through the late 1980s, a period of financial problems for the Trust and the College. This had gathered pace as a new framework for higher education was coming into place. The assisted status by which the College was funded by Devon County Council, an arrangement that had also been useful in terms of helpful local connections, was to be no more. Now, after the Education Reform Act 1988, this responsibility would pass to a central body, the Polytechnics and Colleges Funding Council. Furthermore, the new arrangements demanded a College governance that was wholly independent from the Trust.

So in April 1989 the College was separated from the Trust in all but the leases on its properties. However, it was a number of months before the new body could take effective control, by which time the College's deficit rendered it 'virtually bankrupt'. The disputes went deeper than whose fault this was. There had been tensions for some time between Trustees and College.[49] A large part of this revolved around the issue of how the original Elmhirst vision was to be interpreted. Were the Dartington values and objectives to be interpreted with the underlying pragmatic approach that had characterised the Elmhirsts, and which suited the needs of the College, having to meet many external criteria within its national education framework? Or should those values be reconceptualised in altogether a more undiluted form, as a unified Dartington, advocating the kind of holistic life balance and unity across the estate that had been inherent in the Dartington of 1925?

For a while in 1990, it did seem that the College would close, but it was eventually saved by a financial package from the Trust and elsewhere. The rumblings of controversy around the role of the Trust in all of this continued for some time, as the article in *The Independent* shows. For the College, financial stringency dictated some painful moves, including closing down the Department of Art and Design and redesigning the Theatre Degree as a three-year course, no longer with its urban outposts, and with community placements reduced to weeks or days. The College became associated for degree validation with the Polytechnic of the South West (later named Plymouth University) from 1991. The separation of the College from the Trust was made physically explicit by its removal from the Courtyard buildings, the heart of Dartington since the beginning, to make way for the Dartington Conference Centre.

Utopia has never been without its arguments, changes of direction, differing interpretations of its founding myths and sometimes crashing dissolutions. But utopia is a journey, not an arrival: it exists conceptually. So Dartington – Trust and College – set about reinventing themselves, plotting a course towards the same goals but along new routes. I do not follow those routes further in any detail – the historical traces are not available – but the end of the narrative is not the end of the history. Dance did not disappear from Dartington. In the 1990s there was no specified dance route through the Theatre Degree, but the department's physical approach to performance and the interests of the resident artists continued to encompass those areas of theatre where dance and movement entwined with text and other media. Diana Theodores came onto the staff, a dance critic, choreographer and theatre director, and there continued to be visiting artists such as Laurie Booth and Nigel Charnock, whose work merged dance and physical theatre. Perhaps those close practices of dance and drama at Dartington, evident since the 1930s, had never been so close in practice as they were in the 1990s.

The most recent years have seen an important change. Now dance at Dartington has re-emerged as a distinct, profession-led discipline. While those traditional Dartington values of cross-discipline and inter-departmental collaboration are still in place, the specifics and core techniques of dance are embedded in the BA degree in Choreography, first recruiting in 2003. The emphasis on choreography, the creation of dance work, is in line with the longstanding focus of the College on devised theatre. The subject area is directed by Emilyn Claid, who as a member of the X6 collective had established a link with the Dartington of Mary Fulkerson and the dance festivals of the 1970s and 1980s. Along with Chris Best, Claid also directs the annual Music and Dance Exchange (MADE at Dartington), a residential week when selected choreographers, composers and other theatre and visual artists come together to explore collaborative work. The special environment of Dartington remains potent in that mix; 'the sense of peace, tranquillity and beauty are conducive to an attitude of experiment, creative reconnection and escape'.[50] This is part-funded by Dartington Plus, an arm of Dartington Arts and the Trust, which promotes regional arts within a national and international framework. Dance South West, a National Dance Agency, works successfully in the region to promote a range of popular participation in dance as well as regional professional development, and Dartington collaborates with it in these roles.

It is spring, March 2006 to be exact, and rain is falling. Clumps of snowdrops rise up from carpets of pink and white heathers and there are crocuses in every shade of purple. Amazingly, there is no one else here: the rain has made Dartington Hall, or at least its gardens, all mine. Climbing up the steps that lead above the open-air theatre, I have everything at my feet – the carefully composed vistas, the grey stone, tall windows and White Hart flag of the Great Hall, the Twelve Apostles (yew trees on the edge of the Sunny Border). Buds are bursting from twigs that coexist with their lichens (pure air and a soggy climate). Down on the lawns, oblivious to me, blackbirds are hunting worms and the robins are more lazily tolerant of people than elsewhere (I am reminded that it was here that David Lack did his initial research for *The Life of the Robin* in 1941). I am bewitched by tamed nature that simultaneously embraces and ignores me.

I visit the statue of Flora in the upper garden, where the ashes of the Elmhirst founders were scattered, and am satisfied that, as always, she has been given anonymous offerings – seasonal flowers and leaves from the garden. In her stone hand she holds up rhododendron leaves and camellia flowers; there is real flora on top of the stone basket she carries. This unbroken link going back through time, acknowledging the past in the present, is wonderfully evocative of living history. Since no one can see me, I believe I might dance!

Postscript

In November 2006 it was announced that negotiations were under way for Dartington College of Arts to leave its Dartington campus in a few years' time, destined for a location where it could expand its student numbers and accommodation and where there could be a relationship with another higher education establishment specialising in the arts. The Trust remains committed to developing its own arts policy. Dartington is yet again reinventing itself.

Notes

The following codes are used for archival material. Quotation from archival sources is with permission.

DHTA: Dartington Hall Trust Archive:
    DAS: Dartington Arts Society
    DCA: Dartington College of Arts
    DWE: Dorothy Whitney Elmhirst
    LKE: Leonard Knight Elmhirst
    MC: Michael Chekhov Theatre Studio, Deirdre Hurst du Prey Archive
    NOD: *News of the Day*
    PM: Paula Morel collection
    T: Dartington Hall Trust documentation
LAB: Laban Oral Archive, held in the archive at Laban, Creekside, London
NRCD: National Resource Centre for Dance, University of Surrey, Guildford:
    L: Laban collection
    LU: Lisa Ullmann collection
NYPL: New York Public Library for the Performing Arts, Jerome Robbins Dance Division
SLNSW: Margaret Barr Collection, Mitchell Library, State Library of New South Wales, Sydney
V&A: Victoria and Albert Museum, Archive of Art and Design and Theatre Museum Collection
    ACGB: Arts Council of Great Britain archive

Introduction: Making Dance History

1. NRCD: Fernau Hall (1950) 'Summer School at Dartington Hall', manuscript in Fernau Hall Archive, File: 'Dartington Hall Summer School'. See Chapter 4 for a discussion of this event, the American Universities Theatre Summer School. Archive material held by the National Resource Centre for Dance is used with permission.

2. For a general introduction to the subject, see Krishan Kumar (1991) *Utopianism*.

3. When the Arts Council made a video combining a docudrama on Morris with narrative from *News from Nowhere*, the assembly at the harvest festival did indeed dance as 'folk'. See Alister Hallum, dir. (1978) *News From Nowhere*, Arts Council of Great Britain.

4. See W.G.A. Armytage (1961) *Heavens Below: Utopian Experiments in England 1560–1960*, which situates Dartington in the history of practical utopias.

5. Copy of a letter, recipient unknown, probably February/March 1927, quoted in Michael Young (1996) *The Elmhirsts of Dartington*, p.150.

6. This is not to deny that ballet was greatly indebted to other forms of dance, including national dance styles and to the character-based mime and movement of the *commedia dell'arte*.

7. See Ivor Guest (1972) *The Romantic Ballet in England*.

8. Jim Davis and Victor Emeljanow (2004) 'Victorian and Edwardian Audiences', in Kerry Powell, ed. *The Cambridge Companion to Victorian and Edwardian Theatre*, p.104. For the most comprehensive source on ballet in the music halls, see Alexandra Carter (2005) *Dance and Dancers in the Victorian and Edwardian Music Hall Ballet*.

9. Mrs Lilly Grove was a French author and translator. In 1896, a widow at the time, she married the classicist Sir James Frazer, author of *The Golden Bough*, the compendious study of mythology and religion first published in 1890. *Dancing* was published in the series entitled *The Badminton Library of Sports and Pastimes*, edited by the Duke of Beaufort. Grove's book attempted a survey of dancing from antiquity, taking in various nations, ritual dancing, stage dancing and the ballrooms of her own time.

10. ibid., pp. 5 and 380.

11. Lillian Loewenthal (1993) *The Search for Isadora: The Legend and Legacy of Isadora Duncan*, p.196.

12. The Isadorables, her favoured pupils, stayed at Oldway Mansion more than once. They were at Paignton for a holiday, with some of the young pupils from Duncan's Paris School, in 1914 when war broke out. They were sent directly to America (Loewenthal, p.67).

13. See Felix Cherniavsky (1991) *The Salome Dancer: The Life and Times of Maud Allan*.

14. Nina Auerbach (2004) 'Before the Curtain', in Kerry Powell, ed. *The Cambridge Companion to Victorian and Edwardian Theatre*, p.6.

15. This is described in Lydia Goehr (1992) *The Imaginary Museum of Musical Works*.

16. See John Cottingham (1992) 'Cartesian Dualism: Theology, Metaphysics, and Science', in John Cottingham, ed. *The Cambridge Companion to Descartes*, 236–57.

17. Alan Munslow (1997) *Deconstructing History*, p.22.

18. See, for example, Joyce Appleby, Lynn Hunt and Margaret Jacob (1995) *Telling the Truth about History*, first published 1994; Peter Burke, ed. (1991) *New Perspectives on Historical Writing*; Keith Jenkins (1991) *Re-thinking History*; Alan Munslow (1997) *Deconstructing History*; John Tosh (2000) *The Pursuit of History*, 3rd edition.

19. Hayden White (1973) *Metahistory*.

20. Alexandra Carter (2004) 'Cara Tranders's Reveries: The Autobiography of Cara Tranders, Ballet Girl at the Empire Palace of Varieties, 1892–99', in *Rethinking Dance History*, pp.69–79.

21. John Tosh (2000) *The Pursuit of History*, p.93.

22. David Carr (1991) *Time, Narrative and History*, first published 1986.

23. ibid., p.64.

24. The term 'historicity' (*Geschichtlichkeit*) he takes from Edmund Husserl and Martin Heidegger, writing in the 1920s and 1930s.

25. ibid., p.113.

26. For example, one can find charts, either graphic or implied, in histories of American modern dance that group dancers/choreographers into 'families' and generations. So we have the

Denishawn descendants – Martha Graham, Doris Humphrey, Charles Weidmann – and then their descendants, dancers who worked with them. These models assume a very restricted concept of artistic influence.

27. I am not suggesting here that broadly chronological narrative is the only way of writing a history of dance at Dartington. Michael Young's indispensable history, *The Elmhirsts of Dartington*, follows a part-chronological and part-thematic model.

28. Peter Burke (1991) 'History of Events and the Revival of Narrative' in Peter Burke, ed. *New Perspectives on Historical Writing*, p.239.

29. Victor Bonham-Carter (1958) *Dartington Hall: The History of an Experiment*, p.11.

30. For example, he writes of Kurt Jooss's famous anti-war work, *The Green Table*, that the Gentlemen in Black of the first and last scenes 'were meant to be puppets on strings pulled by Death' (p.225). There is nothing in their movement to suggest this, but he may have been remembering the scene in 'The Aftermath' when the procession of the dead (not including the Gentlemen in Black) is led away by Death. There is a movement motif in which their movements are puppet-like, as if dangling from strings. Although Young's statement is misleading of the work as a whole, it is also suggestive of the strength of that particular image.

31. (1999) *My Time at Dartington, 1940–83: A Personal Record of Involvement in Administering the Arts at Dartington Hall and Creating Dartington College of Arts*.

32. See also Lena Hammergren (2004) 'Many Sources, Many Voices', in Alexandra Carter, ed. *Rethinking Dance History*, pp. 20–31.

33. Daniel Schechter (1996) *Searching for Memory*, pp. 66, 89–97.

34. It is still possible to find specialist companies that can perform transfers from outdated video formats to DVD. In connection with this book, I have been able to resurrect and view some video in the old U-matic format, but disappointingly little. It is a disturbing point that moving images recorded only twenty years ago have, in some cases, been as ephemeral as the dance itself.

35. Claude Lévi-Strauss used this first in *The Savage Mind* (1966), first published in French in 1962.

36. Susan Manning (1993) *Ecstasy and the Demon: Feminism and Nationalism in the Dances of Mary Wigman*, p.12.

37. In this text I have followed the policy of naming each individual by full name or surname only. I found this almost impossible to do for the Elmhirst founders, however, because their names appear in frequent proximity. In order to allow the text to run along in a tidy manner, I indicate these two by first names only. No disrespect or familiarity is intended.

38. Simon Schama (2006) *Rough Crossings: Britain, The Slaves and the American Revolution*, first published 2005, p.459.

Chapter 1: Why Dartington? Why Dance?

1. DHTA: DWE Arts 14, Drama 5, Folder A, letter from Dorothy Elmhirst to Ellen Van Volkenburg, 20 July 1928. Archive material held by the Dartington Hall Trust Archive is used with permission.

2. Michael Young (1996) *The Elmhirsts of Dartington*, pp.105–107

3. For biographical details of the Elmhirsts prior to their marriage, see Michael Young (1996) *The Elmhirsts of Dartington* and William Swanberg (1980) *Whitney Father, Whitney Heiress*.

4. This was the first Metropolitan Opera House, on Broadway between 39th and 40th Streets. The auditorium was gutted by fire in 1892 but subsequently rebuilt. The second Metropolitan Opera House was opened at Lincoln Center for the Performing Arts in 1966.

5. Swanberg (1980) p.187.

6. Swanberg (1980) p.343.

7. Swanberg (1980) p.384.

8. Lectures delivered at the New School formed the basis of John Martin's influential book, *The Modern Dance* (1933).

9. Rabindranath Tagore (1961) 'The Religion of an Artist', in Amiya Chakravarty, ed. *A Tagore Reader*, pp.230–40. Quotation from p.240.

10. Leonard Elmhirst (1992) 'Personal Memories of Tagore', in Kissoonsingh Hazareesingh, ed. *A*

Rich Harvest: The Complete Tagore/Elmhirst Correspondence and Other Writings, p.8.

11. For the history of the Shakers and descriptions of their rituals, see Edward Deming Andrews (1962) *The Gift to be Simple: Songs, Dances and Rituals of the American Shakers*, and (1963) *The People Called Shakers: A Search for the Perfect Society*.

12. Andrews (1962), p.136.

13. ibid., p.152.

14. Andrews (1963), p.136.

15. Andrews (1962), p.144.

16. In *Natural Symbols: Explorations in Cosmology* (1973), the anthropologist Mary Douglas equates ritual to a 'restricted code' (a concept she derives from the linguistic analysis of Basil Bernstein), a manner of communication that is formed in and expresses social structure rather than individual needs. She writes that 'bodily control is an expression of social control' (p.99).

17. Robert Dale Owen (1824) *An Outline of the System of Education at New Lanark*, reprinted in Harrison (1968) *Utopianism and Education: Robert Owen and the Owenites*, pp.129–72. See p.146.

18. ibid., p.167.

19. ibid., p.168.

20. Robert Owen (1816) *Address to the Inhabitants of New Lanark*, reprinted as 'The Institution for the Formation of Character', in Harrison (1968), pp.80–117.

21. Judith Lynne Hanna (1987) *To Dance is Human*, second edition.

22. Martin Green (1986) *Mountain of Truth: The Counterculture Begins: Ascona, 1900–1920*, p.169. See also: Harald Szeemann (2003) 'Monte Verità' in Claire Roussier, ed. *Être ensemble: Figures de la communauté en danse depuis le XXe siècle*, pp.17–40.

23. For a biography of Laban, see Valerie Preston-Dunlop (1998) *Rudolf Laban: An Extraordinary Life*. For a wider survey of German dance and body culture, including Laban, see Karl Toepfer (1997) *Empire of Ecstasy: Nudity and Movement in German Body Culture, 1910–1935*.

24. Walter Sorrell (1973) *The Mary Wigman Book*, p.33.

25. Rudolf Laban (1975) *A Life for Dance*, translated and annotated by Lisa Ullmann, pp.85–6, first published in German in 1935 as *Ein Leben für den Tanz*.

26. For further analysis of the concept of *Festkultur*, see Carole Kew (1999) 'The Rise and Fall of Rudolf Laban's *Festkultur*', *Dance Research*, 17, no. 2, Winter, pp.73–96.

27. Dalcroze eurhythmics is not to be confused with the eurythmy of Rudolf Steiner. Steiner (1861–1925), the spiritual thinker who was the originator of anthroposophy, developed eurythmy from 1912. It uses forms of speech and music as a basis for movement, and aims for an integration of the spiritual and physical through movement forms.

28. For a consideration of Dalcroze from a dance studies viewpoint, see Selma Landen Odom (1986) 'Wigman at Hellerau', *Ballet Review*, 14, no.2, Summer, pp.41–53; (1991) *Dalcroze Eurhythmics in England: History of an Innovation in Music and Movement Education*; (1992) 'What is Dalcrozian?', *Dance Research*, 10, no. 2, Autumn, pp.121–31.

29. Odom (1992), p.129.

30. Dalcroze writing in an undated letter to Adolphe Appia, quoted in Richard Beacham (1987) *Adolphe Appia: Theatre Artist*, p.55.

31. Architect, Heinrich Tessenow; lighting system by Alexander von Saltzmann, a Russian painter. Sometimes referred to as the *Festspielhaus*. See Odom (1986) for a thorough account of Dalcroze and Hellerau.

32. Quoted in Beacham (1987), p.61.

33. Directed by Dalcroze, set and lighting designs by Appia. Choreography by Annie Beck.

34. The line occurs in Upton Sinclair's novel *World's End* (1940), quoted in Irwin Spector (1990) *Rhythm and Life: The Work of Emile Jaques-Dalcroze*, p.169. There was a reconstruction of this production at Warwick University in 1991 and it is currently (2007) the subject of a digital reconstruction project based at Warwick University in cooperation with Selma Odom of York University, Toronto.

35. DHTA: DWE Arts 4, Folder F, Dorothy Elmhirst, *The Arts at Dartington*.

36. For a discussion on the Elmhirsts and building, see Michael Young (1996), pp.253–69.

37. For perspectives on Tagore and dance, see Mandakranta Bose (2001) 'The Dance Re-Invented: Rabindranath Tagore's Vision', in *Speaking of Dance: The Indian Critique*, pp.99–115; Santidev Ghose

(1978) *Music and Dance in Rabindranath Tagore's Educational Philosophy*.

38. DHTA: LKE Tagore 3, Folder B, Typescript 'Personal Reminiscences' dated 19 January 1960, pp.16–17.

39. Reviews in English in Rudraprasad Chakraborty (1995) *Rangamancha O Rabindranath [The Stage and Rabindranath]*, pp.182–85, quotation p.183. I am indebted to my colleague Prarthana Purkayastha for finding this source and identifying the occasion.

40. Tagore, 'A Poet's School', in Leonard Elmhirst, ed. (1961) *Rabindranath Tagore: Pioneer in Education*, p.50.

41. ibid., p.58.

42. Originally published in the *Visva Bharati Quarterly*, Spring 1956 and later in Britain in the *Art of Movement Guild Magazine*, October 1956, pp.24–9. It was republished in *Rabindranath Tagore: Pioneer in Education* (1961) as 'The Art of Movement in Education' pp.101–11, that title confirming the current influence of Rudolf Laban's and Lisa Ullmann's work (see Chapter 4). Quotation from the 1961 publication, p.102.

43. Kissoonsingh Hazareesingh, ed. (1992) *A Rich Harvest: the complete Tagore/Elmhirst Correspondence and Other Writings*, p.159.

44. Nancy Lee Chalfa Ruyter (1979) 'The Genteel Transition: American Delsartism', in *Reformers and Visionaries: The Americanization of the Art of Dance*, pp.17–30.

45. Ruyter (1979), p.25.

46. Linda Tomko (1999) *Dancing Class: Gender, Ethnicity, and Social Divides in American Dance, 1890–1920*.

47. On the other hand, Eric Rauchway (1999) strongly argues that although Dorothy originated and strongly pressed forward the projects she devised, supported and underwrote, she did not substantially challenge the boundaries of the woman's sphere but worked in conjunction with the men who occupied the male sphere. See 'A Gentlemen's Club in a Woman's Sphere: How Dorothy Whitney Straight Created the New Republic', *Journal of Women's History*, 11.2, pp.60–85. This is an interesting case, which might, with further research, be compared to Dorothy's methods when developing the arts at Dartington.

48. Michael Straight (1983) *After Long Silence*, p.20.

49. Linda Tomko (1999), pp.79–103.

50. For strands of dance teaching in teacher training colleges in the US, see Tomko (1999), pp.191–95 and Nancy Lee Chalfa Ruyter (1998) 'United States of America: Social, Folk, and Modern Dance Education', in Selma Jean Cohen, ed. *The International Encyclopedia of Dance*, vol. 6, pp.293–96.

51. Staff of the Elementary Division of the Lincoln School (1927) *Curriculum Making in an Elementary School*. See in particular pp. 54,155, 235, 306.

52. Michael Straight (1983), p.27. The William C. Whitney Foundation (a later name for the Committee set up under Anna Bogue) funded Fonaroff to attend the Cornish School and the Bennington College Summer School. She became a dancer with Martha Graham in the 1930s and 1940s and had an important place in the development of contemporary dance in Britain when she began teaching choreography at the London School of Contemporary Dance in 1972.

53. NYPL: Angna Enters, Correspondence, Box 2, Folder 80, Letter 24 December 1926, Anna Bogue to Angna Enters. Her arrival at Dartington was recorded in *News of the Day*.

54. DHTA: DWE Arts 8, Folder E, Letter from Martha Graham to DWE, 17 August 1931; DWE US Office 10, Folder B, Letter Anna Bogue to DWE, 17 November 1938.

55. Michael Straight (1983), pp.42–3.

56. DHTA: DWE US Office 2, Folder F, Letter 7 October 1930, DWE to Anna Bogue.

57. See Marcia Siegel (1987) *Days on Earth: The Dance of Doris Humphrey*, p.183; Sali Ann Kriegsman (1981) *Modern Dance in America: The Bennington years*, p.48.

58. NOD, 2 November 1928.

59. Maurice Browne (1955) *Too Late to Lament*, p.159.

60. Nellie Cornish (1964) *Miss Aunt Nellie: The Autobiography of Nellie C. Cornish*, p.111.

61. ibid. p.93. For Mary Hinman, see Tomko (1999), pp.145–60.

62. Bonnie Bird, a former member of Martha Graham's company, was on the faculty at this time. She had a later, profound influence on the development of dance education in Britain. In 1974 she

became Director of Dance Theatre at the Art of Movement Studio, soon to be renamed the Laban Centre for Movement and Dance (see Chapter 4), developing degree-level courses and dance as a performing art within higher education. She had also been a student of the Cornish School, taught by Louise Soelberg. See Karen Bell-Kanner (1998) *Frontiers: The Life and Times of Bonnie Bird*.

63. NRCD: Laban Guild Oral Archive Project, Leslie Burrowes interviewed by Margaret Dunn, 23 June 1983.

64. DHTA: DWE, Arts 14, Drama 5, Folders A and I. Thanks to the Ingham family, eurhythmics was well established in Britain, and Dalcroze himself taught there nearly every year. See Odom (1991), p.24.

65. NRCD: Laban Guild Oral Archive Project, Burrowes interviewed by Margaret Dunn, 23 June 1983.

66. NOD, 24 September 1929.

67. Margaret Morris (1972) *Creation in Dance and Life*, pp.38–58.

68. Documents are in DHTA: T Arts Dance 2, Folder C.

69. NOD, Monday 24 June 1929.

70. The quotation is a note in the Trinity College MS, as indicated in an editor's note in the Milton Tercentenary edition, London: Novello and Company Ltd., 1908.

71. In the original production, the Lady and her brothers were played by the young children of the Earl and Countess of Bridgewater: Lady Alice Egerton, Lord Brackley and Thomas Egerton. Henry Lawes, the children's music master and composer of the songs, took the role of the Attendant Spirit.

72. The text was based on the Milton Tercentenary (1908) text, published by Novello and Company Ltd, London.

73. DHTA: DWE, US Office 2, Folder E, Letter 24 June 1929, DWE to Anna Bogue.

74. DHTA: T Dartington Hall School, A, 1, Folder C, 'Miss Leslie Burrowes' Report of the Senior Juniors' Dancing Class: Autumn Term 1928.

75. NRCD: Laban Guild Oral Archive Project, Burrowes interviewed by Margaret Dunn, 23 June 1983.

76. Letters are preserved in DHTA: DWE Arts 7, Dance 1, Folder A.

77. Leonard Elmhirst (1992) 'Personal Memories of Tagore', in Hazareesingh, ed. *A Rich Harvest: the complete Tagore/Elmhirst Correspondence and Other Writings*, p.7.

78. ibid., p.14.

Chapter 2: Dance Mime for the People

1. DHTA: T Arts Dance 2, Folder B, 'Dance-Mime Work'.

2. *News of the Day*, 6 January 1929, reporting on Maurice Browne taking the Savoy Theatre to produce *Journey's End*, noted that *The Times* and *The Observer* had carried this story.

3. Nellie Cornish (1964) *Miss Aunt Nellie: The Autobiography of Nellie C. Cornish*, p.203.

4. DHTA: T Arts Dance 2, Folder A. Information on scholarships appears in Barr's 'Report for the Year Ending 29 July 1933 and Plan for Next Year'. Bethene Miller, Deirdre Hurst and Edward Harrington were former Cornish students.

5. Michael Young (1996) *The Elmhirsts of Dartington*, p.221.

6. DHTA: DWE Arts 7, Folder B, Margaret Barr, Letter 9 July 1930, suggests she had recently been in the Cambridge Festival, a fact not so far confirmed.

7. Caryll von Sturmer (1993) *Margaret Barr: Epic Individual*. The Margaret Barr Collection is held at the State Library of New South Wales, Sydney.

8. Letters are collected in DHTA: DWE Arts 7, Folder C1, C2 and PM 1, Folder D.

9. W. Adolphe Roberts (1928) 'The Fervid Art of Martha Graham', *Dance Magazine*, August, p.13.

10. See Jane Sherman (1979) *The Drama of Denishawn Dance*, pp.4–16. She describes the classes at the New York Denishawn school of the early 1920s as being based in ballet but freer in application and with the technical adjustments brought about by dancing barefoot. 'Ethnic' styles were taught through classroom dances.

11. Documents in the Margaret Barr Collection, State Library of New South Wales, Sydney, Box 9.

12. Garry Lester (1997) 'Margaret Barr: Epic Individual and Fringe Dweller', *Proceedings: Society of Dance History Scholars*, p.10.

13. ibid.

14. A receipt for audition fees at the Civic Repertory Theatre, found in the Margaret Barr Collection, suggests the date of Barr's arrival in New York. Von Sturmer states that the Barr sisters intended to study drama in New York alongside Margaret's dance classes. She dropped out of drama in order to concentrate on dance. Graham advertised her studio at Carnegie Hall in *Dance Magazine* in December 1926 and January 1927. Her tenure there was certainly longer than that, but sources generally agree that she could not afford to advertise.

15. Caryll von Sturmer (1993) *Margaret Barr: Epic Individual*, p.14.

16. See particularly the evidence of Martha Hill and Gertrude Shurr. Hill was able to observe the change in Graham's technique over the couple of years she was away from New York, 1927–29. For Hill, see Robert Tracy, ed. (1997) *Goddess: Martha Graham's Dancers Remember*, pp.12–14. Shurr first studied with Graham in about 1926. See Schurr in Marian Horosko, ed. (2002) *Martha Graham: The Evolution of Her Dance Theory and Training*, pp.33–43. Also, NYPL: *MGZMT 5-697, Interview with Gertrude Shurr, transcript, pp. 42–5. The development of Graham's movement vocabulary over time is analysed in Henrietta Bannerman (1999) 'An Overview of the Development of Martha Graham's Movement System (1926–1991)' *Dance Research*, 17 no. 2, Winter, pp.9–46.

17. It is not clear why this pseudonym was chosen or why Barr did not want to perform under her own name. There is an unidentified press-cutting image in her papers showing the 'Rhys Meredith Dancers', but she is not one of them. However, the long, medieval-style gowns do bear a strong resemblance to costumes for one of her pieces choreographed at Dartington.

18. Von Sturmer (1993) p.12.

19. Nellie Cornish (1964) *Miss Aunt Nellie: The Autobiography of Nellie C. Cornish*, pp.172, 201.

20. Duncan herself did not appear in America between her last, politically controversial tour of 1922–23 and her death in 1927. For an account of the work of her immediate successors, see Lillian Loewenthal (1993) *The Search for Isadora*.

21. Lillian Karina and Marion Kant (2003) *Hitler's Dancers: German Modern Dance and the Third Reich*, pp.33–4.

22. For Ito, see Helen Caldwell (1998) 'Michio Ito', in Selma Jean Cohen, ed. *The International Encyclopedia of Dance*, v.3, pp.558–60.

23. Cornish (1964) p.201.

24. DHTA: DWE US Office 3, Folder D, Memo 10 May 1932, itemising classes and costs.

25. Janet Soares (1992) *Louis Horst: Musician in a Dancer's World*, p.73.

26. Cornish (1964) p.207.

27. DHTA: T Arts Dance 2, Folder A, Letter 9 October 1930.

28. 'A School Song' from *Today and Tomorrow*, a Dartington Hall School Magazine, reproduced in *A Dartington Anthology 1925–1975*, p.26.

29. DHTA: T Arts Dance 2, Folder A1, Margaret Barr, Programmes/ Prospectuses.

30. Dating is based on the content of the film, which documents the building of Foxhole, fitting it out with equipment and furniture, and activities when the children had occupied it. South West Film and Television Archive, Dartington Hall Collection, Box 11, Dart 35.

31. DHTA: T Arts Dance 2, Folder B. Both terms are used in 'Suggested Estate Programme for 1931–1932'.

32. In 1934 she reported that, of 122 children from nursery to senior, 94 took eurhythmics: (1934) 'Dartington Hall, Devonshire', *Journal of the Dalcroze Society*, May, p.37. See also Winifred Edwards (1935) 'Eurhythmics at Dartington Hall', *Journal of the Dalcroze Society*, May, pp.23–4.

33. DHTA: T Arts Dance 2, Folder B, Report 16 Jan–28 March 1931.

34. Thomas was author of (1939) *The Changing Village: An Essay in Rural Reconstruction*. He mentioned Liverton as an 'outstanding village drama group', p.123. Mary Kelly wrote (1939) *Village Theatre*. See: Mick Wallis (2000) 'Unlocking the Secret Soul: Mary Kelly, Pioneer of Village Theatre', *New Theatre Quarterly*, 16, no. 4, pp.347–58.

35. See Linda Tomko (1999) *Dancing Class: Gender, Ethnicity, and Social Divides in American Dance, 1890–1920*.

36. DHTA: T Arts Dance 2, Folder B1, Spring Term Report 1931–1932.

37. For the former, see DHTA: T Arts Dance 2, Folder B, 'Manifesto': 'The group will give its support to any idea which it accepts from anyone of its members, thus by pooling ideas create a life within it independent of any one individual.' For the latter, see her letter of September 1933 to DWE (DWE Arts 7, Folder B) in which she explains how the group in the professional School is essential to developing her creative ideas.

38. DHTA: T Arts Dance 2, Folder B, Letters from Barr to Trustees and to DWE and LKE, July 1934.

39. DHTA: DWE Arts 7, Folder B, Letter 18 June 1932, F.G. Thomas to DWE. He also wrote about this production in (1932) *The New learning: An Experiment with Educational Films in the County of Devon*.

40. DHTA: T Arts Dance, 2, Folder B, General Outline for 'The Spring Festival'.

41. ibid. Suggested Estate Programme for 1931–1932, Reasons for Spring Festival.

42. Supplement to NOD, 17 January 1933.

43. The roof of the Great Hall was completed in 1933, with interior renovations taking several more years.

44. Young (1996) p.157.

45. Maurice Browne, (1931) 'Between Curtains', *Theatre Arts Monthly*, October, pp.862–67.

46. Maurice Browne (1955) *Too Late to Lament*, p.158.

47. John Martin, 'The Dance: In England: The Dance Mime Project at Dartington Hall is a Model of United Effort', *New York Times*, 14 August 1932, p.X5.

48. DHTA: T Arts Dance 2, Folder A1, Note on School of Dance-Mime programme, 2 April 1932. This musicality was also commented upon by Basil Langton (her second husband and a School of Dance-Mime student). 'She was a fine musician herself, which made her dance compositions rich in counterpoint between movement and sound.' DHTA: MC S4/27, Folder G, Confessions of Basil Langton, p.12.

49. anon.(1932) 'Dance-Mime at Dartington', *The Dancing Times*, May, p.118.

50. F.G Thomas (1932) 'The People', *The Dancing Times*, October, p.20.

51. DHTA: DWE Arts 7, Folder B, Cuttings. J.J.J. (1932) 'Dance-Mime', *Western Independent*, 31 July.

52. Thomas (1932), p.19.

53. ibid.

54. SLNSW: Margaret Barr Collection, video recording VB6158. *Margaret Barr*, interviewed by James Murdoch, December 1986.

55. ibid.

56. Young (1996) p.125.

57. See Michael Straight's autobiography (1983) *After Long Silence*, p.43. He writes of a passionate but unconsummated relationship with Barr at this time, when he was still only fifteen years old.

58. Young (1996), p.224.

59. See 'Morris On' (1932) 'An International Summer School', *The Dancing Times*, no. 257, February, pp.573, 576–77; and anon. 'First International Summer School' (1932) *The Dancing Times*, no. 264, September, pp.267, 269.

60. See Claudia Gitelman, ed. (2003) *Liebe Hanya: Mary Wigman's Letters to Hanya Holm*, p.28.

61. Martin, 'The Dance: British Style', *New York Times*, 21 August 1932, p. X5.

62. Martin, 'The Dance: Three Artists', *New York Times*, 28 August 1932, p. X5. The Camargo Society was formed in 1930 in order to support the development of ballet in Britain through mounting occasional seasons in London theatres. *Façade* was premiered by the Camargo Society in April 1931 and *The Origin of Design* in June 1932. Both were taken into the repertories of the existing fledgling ballet companies: *Façade* into that of the Ballet Club (directed by Marie Rambert) and the Vic-Wells Ballet (directed by Ninette de Valois), and *The Origin of Design* into the Vic-Wells Ballet.

63. John Martin, 'The Dance: Art of India', *New York Times*, 4 September 1932, p.X7.

64. John Martin, 'The Dance: Paris Events', *New York Times*, 11 September 1932, p. X7.

65. John Martin, 'The Dance: at Salzburg', *New York Times*, 18 September 1932, p.X6; 'The Dance: in Austria', *New York Times*, 25 September 1932, p.X6; 'The Dance: War Satire', *New York Times*, 2 October 1932, p.X8.

66. For an analysis, see Suzanne K. Walther (1994) *The Dance of Death: Kurt Jooss and the Weimar Years*, pp.58–73. Joffrey Ballet recorded the work in 2000, but probably the preferred recording,

despite its being in black and white, must still be that made in 1967 for the BBC, produced by Peter Wright, a former Jooss student, that featured the Folkwang Ballett of Essen directed by Jooss. See also Claudia Jeschke (2003) 'Jooss' Wise Covenant with Death', in Kurt Jooss and Anna Markard, *The Green Table: a Dance of Death in Eight Scenes*, Part 2, pp.19–25.

67. John Martin, 'The Dance: German Issues', *New York Times*, 9 October 1932, p.X8.

68. DHTA: T Arts Dance 2, Folder A, Report for year end 29 July 1933 and plans for next year, 2 September 1933.

69. DHTA: T Arts Dance 2, Folder A, Estimated Budget year end 31 August 1933.

70. DHTA: T Arts Dance 2, Folder B, Letter 29 August 1933, Bill Curry to DWE.

71. DHTA: T Arts Dance 2, Folder A, Letter 31 July 1933, Mark Tobey to LKE.

72. Langton, Basil (1996) 'Alan Rawsthorne', *The Creel*, [Journal of the Alan Rawsthorne Society and Alan Rawsthorne Trust], v.3, no. 3, issue 10, Spring, pp.33–4.

73. DHTA: T Arts Admin. 1, Folder A, Report to the Trustees, July 1934.

74. Michael Young (1996, p.227) states that the first scene of *Subject to Alteration*, set in a board-room, was a satire on the first scene (The Gentlemen in Black) of *The Green Table*. I have not found any evidence to suggest this to be the case.

75. The Elmhirsts were also directors of a company owning two London theatres, the Globe and the Queens (G & Q Ltd). The Globe was leased back to M & B Ltd. Browne stated in his autobiography that these were bought with proceeds from *Journey's End*, but it is clear from Dartington's records that the money for these was raised independently by the Elmhirsts. See DHTA: LKE General S15, Folder E (Maurice Browne, Transcript 2), recorded 7 October 1957.

76. See Young (1996), p.206. Dorothy Elmhirst paid for the publication of Waley's book *The Way and Its Power – A Study of the Tao-te Ching and its Place in Chinese Thought* (1934).

77. In the 1930s she wrote articles and reviews on dance and published, with Walter Spies, *Dance and Drama in Bali* (1938).

78. Originally choreographed to Alexandre Tansman's *Sonatine Transatlantique*; in 1935 Tansman wrote a new score adapted to the original choreography.

79. John Gruen interview with Kurt Jooss and Anna Markard, 1976. NYPL: *MGZTC 3-638, audio cassette Side A.

80. This was a particular speciality of Jooss, as remembered by Peter Wright (1994) 'Wright on Jooss', in Adamson, Andy and Clare Lidbury, eds. *Kurt Jooss: 60 Years of the Green Table*, pp.56–7.

81. I am grateful to the Joffrey Ballet of Chicago for permission to view videos of their Jooss reper-toire held in the Jerome Robbins Dance Division of the New York Public Library for the Performing Arts. For an extended analysis of the whole programme, see Suzanne K. Walther (1994) *The Dance of Death: Kurt Jooss and the Weimar Years*.

82. DHTA: DWE Arts 9, Folder E, Jooss interviewed by Ruth Foster, 1973.

83. DHTA: DWE Arts 9, Folder A, Letter Beryl de Zoete to DWE, 25 September 1933.

84. Patricia Stöckemann (2001) *Etwas ganz Neues muss nun entstehen: Kurt Jooss und das Tanztheater*, pp.197–8.

85. NRCD: Laban Guild Oral History Archive, Lisa Ullmann interviewed by Hilary Corlett and Athalie Knowles, 24 June 1984.

86. DHTA: T Arts Dance 1, Folder A, Letter from Kurt Jooss to DWE and LKE, undated, received 8 December 1933.

87. DHTA: T Arts Visual, Folder D. The mural of grieving figures over an internal door reflects the group design made up of unison gestures and interlinked arms that was part of Barr's style in choreography. Tobey designed the costumes of long jersey dresses and head coverings used in *The Three Marys*. Paula Morel, Louise Soelberg and Eddie Harrington modelled for the figures. Some effects in the mural are not unlike those in Martha Graham's *Lamentation*. The mural was painted over in the 1940s because it was water-damaged, according to Peter Cox. DHTA: T Arts Visual 1, Folder D, Mark Tobey 1, Correspondence re mural.

88. DHTA: T Arts Dance 2, Folder B. The document, written on the headed notepaper of Camp Deerlands, Raquette Lake (the Whitney estate in the Adirondacks, New York State), is unsigned but the identification as Leonard's is based on characteristic capital letters, typical of him at this period.

89. DHTA: T Arts Dance 2, Folder B, 'Manifesto'; Letters to the Trustees and to the Elmhirsts, July

1934; F.G. Thomas, Notes on the School of Dance-Mime, 4 August 1934.

90. Bridget d'Oyly Carte became director of the opera company in 1948 and subsequently employed Peter Goffin, who devised a modular staging system that could be used to make the large touring repertoire more economic by deploying a fixed number of modules in multiple configurations. There may be an interesting link here via the School of Dance-Mime back to Hellerau.

91. DHTA: DWE Arts 7, Folder B, Letter August 31 1934, Christopher Martin to DWE.

92. anon. 'Plays and Pictures: Dance-Mime', *New Statesman and Nation*, 4 August 1934, pp.152–3.

93. 'Get up and Do It', *Dartington Voice*, July 1982, p.4.

94. DHTA: T Arts Admin. 1, Folder A, Report to the Dartington Hall Trustees, July 1934.

95. See, for example, (1926) 'Health and Physical Exercise' in *Margaret Morris Dancing*, pp.11–33.

96. See especially 'Ballet: Some Practical Considerations', in Harold Downs, ed. *Theatre and Stage*, vol.1, pp.431–4.

97. Rudolf Laban (1975) *A Life for Dance*, p.156. Original German edition published 1935.

98. For an exposition of the use and abandonment of the movement choir by the Nazi regime, see Carole Kew (1999) 'The Rise and Fall of Rudolf Laban's *Festkultur*', *Dance Research*, 17, no. 2, Winter, pp.73–96. For an account of the technical workings and meaning of movement choirs, see Yvonne Hardt (2003) 'Relational Movement Patterns: The Diversity of Movement Choirs and their Social Potential in the Weimar Republic', *Proceedings: Society of Dance History Scholars*, pp.45–50.

Chapter 3: Dancing on the World's Stage

1. Hallie Flanagan (1934), 'Kurt Jooss at Dartington Hall', *Theatre Arts Monthly*, May, p.338.

2. The term 'Hindu' was widely assumed, in the West, to refer to anybody from the sub-continent, although some of this company were Muslim. For Shankar, see writing by Joan Erdman, particularly. (1987) 'Performance as Translation: Uday Shankar in the West', *The Drama Review (TDR)*, 31, no. 1, T113, Spring, 64–88.

3. Kissoonsingh Hazareesingh, ed. (1992) *A Rich Harvest: the complete Tagore/Elmhirst Correspondence and Other Writings*, p.155, Letter 28 January 1934, Tagore to LKE.

4. Protima Devi (1949) *Nritya*, Kolkata: Visva Bharati University Press, p.22. The date is recorded in the Dartington Visitors' Book. Reference is also in Manjusri Chaki Sircar 'Tagore and Modernization of Dance', in *Rasa: The Indian Performing Arts in the Last Twenty-Five Years*, v.1, p.246.

5. Ravi Shankar writes of this residency in his autobiography (1997) *Raga Mala*, pp.73–7.

6. This term is not equivalent to 'expressionism', although some of the artists working within the genre displayed traits in common with artists of the expressionist theatre, film and visual arts.

7. For the development of Laban's theories through his German and English publications, see Vera Maletic (1987) *Body – Space – Expression*.

8. Kinetography has divided into two versions, the European-based Kinetography Laban and Labanotation, which, although originally based on American refinements to the system, is now also widely used in Europe.

9. John Hodgson and Valerie Preston-Dunlop (1990) *Rudolf Laban: An Introduction to His Work and Influence*, pp.126–7.

10. Kurt Jooss, 'Mein bisheriger Lebenslauf', MS. Essen, November 1927, quoted in Anna Markard and Hermann Markard, eds. (1985) *Jooss*, p.31.

11. For expressionism and New Objectivity in relation to Jooss, see Hedwig Müller (1985) 'Jooss and Expressionism', in Anna Markard and Hermann Markard, eds. *Jooss*, pp.13–17. For the influence of modern dance on drama staging, see David Kuhns (1997) *German Expressionist Theatre: The Actor and the Stage*.

12. In 1935 Flanagan was made director of the Federal Theatre Project, one of the schemes under the US Government-funded Works Progress Administration to put unemployed Americans back to work. Controversy arising from allegations of communist leanings in some productions led to her being called to testify in front of the House (of Representatives) Committee on Un-American Activities, and the FTP was closed down in 1939.

13. Shankar (1997) pp.74–5.

14. DHTA: Victor Bonham-Carter (1956) 'The Arts', in *Dartington Hall, 1925–56: A Report*, unpublished report prepared for the Trustees, p.15. He includes Hein Heckroth and headmaster W.B. Curry in this grouping. Dartington also had a relationship with the left-wing Fabian Society.

15. DHTA: Interview with Bernard Leach in video (1993) *From the Archive*, Dartington Hall Trust.

16. NOD, 15 March and 22 March 1935.

17. Young (1996) *The Elmhirsts of Dartington*, pp.305–7.

18. NRCD: Lisa Ullmann Collection.

19. DHTA: Minutes of Trustees Meeting, 9 July 1937. Christopher Martin also reported that there were five dancers in the company who had come from Essen and two with no previous connection. The company was completed by a stage manager, a wardrobe mistress, two pianists, a General Manager, and Kurt and Aino Siimola (his wife, also acting as his assistant).

20. See Jane Winearls (1958) *Modern Dance: The Jooss–Leeder Method*; and Anna Markard (1993) 'Jooss the teacher: His pedagogical aims and the development of the choreographic principles of harmony', *Choreography and Dance*, vol. 3, Part 2, pp.45–51.

21. Ann Hutchinson Guest (2006) 'The Jooss–Leeder School at Dartington Hall', *Dance Chronicle*, 29, pp.161–94. See page 177.

22. See Ann Hutchinson Guest (1985) 'Sigurd Leeder: Images for the Dancer', *Ballett International*, October, pp.14–20.

23. Beryl de Zoete, 'The 1,000,000 Mile Journey: VI', *Ballet*, Nov/Dec 1950, v10, no. 3, p.37. He later moved to New York, working with the School of American Ballet as well as choreographers Doris Humphrey and Hanya Holm.

24. Ron Riley (1980) 'Sensory Awareness', *New Dance*, no. 36, Spring, pp.20–21.

25. (1992) *Speaking of Dance: Lucas Hoving*, [Videorecording] produced and directed by Douglas Rosenberg, Durham, N.C.: American Dance Festival

26. For a review of a school production including *Danse Macabre*, see Beryl de Zoete (1939) 'The Jooss–Leeder School of Dance at Dartington Hall', *The Dancing Times*, no. 348, September, pp.626–8. See also Ann Hutchinson Guest (2006), pp.189–91. The work has been notated and reconstructed, for which see Grete Müller (2001) *Sigurd Leeder, Tänzer, Pädagoge und Choreograf, Leben und Werk*, pp.52–4.

27. DHTA: T Arts Dance 1A, Folder G, programme of farewell performance of Birgit Cullberg and Barbro Thiel.

28. Ann Hutchinson Guest (2006), p.171.

29. DHTA: T Arts Dance 1A, Folder G, Register for amateur class; Folder D, letter re David Walker. He danced under the name David Kerval with International Ballet and Ballets Jooss and finished his career with the National Ballet of Canada.

30. NRCD: Lisa Ullmann Archive, Box LU/007, Folder 1. It is probable that Ullmann took over a class slot originally earmarked for Margaret Barr, since there is a class proposal in Ullmann's archive that appears strongly to suggest Barr's work (but is undated and unsigned).

31. DHTA: T Arts Dance 1, Jooss–Leeder School of Dance Aliens Register.

32. DHTA: T Arts Dance, 1A, Folder G2, Jooss–Leeder School of Dance Register 1934–39.

33. DHTA: Minutes of Trustees Meeting, 22 May 1936.

34. Letters in DHTA: DWE Arts 9, Folder A.

35. Statistics of tour from NOD, 13 July 1937.

36. See, for example, DHTA: T Arts Admin.1, Folder C, Administrator's Report, 22 May 1936; Folder D, Administrator's Report, 27 February 1937.

37. DHTA: DWE Arts 9, Folder B, Letter 17 January 1938, Fritz Cohen to LKE and DWE.

38. NYPL: *MGZHB 4-1668 Jooss Ballet (Motion picture), Ann Barzel Collection. I believe that there are a few frames of a male trio from *Chronica*, not included on the catalogue summary or captioned on the film, following the *Spring Tale* material.

39. The main sources for a notional reconstruction of *A Spring Tale* and *Chronica* were cuttings files in the V&A Theatre Museum collection, London; A.V. Coton's (1946) *The New Ballet* and Cyril Beaumont's (1942) *Supplement to Complete Book of Ballets* and programme notes.

40. H.F., 'New Jooss Ballet', *Sunday Times*, 28 May 1939, p.5.

41. Gender studies would provide a productive area for future analysis of the Jooss repertoire.

Audrey Williamson, a dance writer who admired the Jooss works, pointed out during the 1940s that his female characters tended to be victims, or passive, or evil. This had been apparent to a group of servicewomen to whom she lectured during World War II. See: Williamson (1946) *Contemporary Ballet*, p.148.

42. David Mellor draws parallels between the image of the Prince in *A Spring Tale* and the recurrent image of the innocent fool in Collins's work in the 1940s. See (1987) *A Paradise Lost: The Neo-Romantic Imagination in Britain 1935–1955*. Hein Heckroth, Jooss's design collaborator, had later connections to the neo-romantic cinema through work on the Michael Powell and Emeric Pressburger films *A Matter of Life and Death* (1946), *The Red Shoes* (1948) and *Tales of Hoffmann* (1951).

43. Rachel Harrison has examined Dorothy's art patronage and preferences. See (2002) *Dorothy Elmhirst and the Visual Arts at Dartington Hall, 1925–45*, p.78. Collins appears to have had a particular attachment to the notion of a revival in art brought about through rediscovering folk arts.

44. There was some praise for it: Alfredo Corvino, a dancer recruited in Uruguay, admired *Chronica*, but thought the times were not right for it. (Interview in NYPL: *MGZMT 5-560, Transcript)

45. For example in G.P., '"Chronica": New Ballets Jooss Production', *Manchester Guardian*, 26 April 1939, p.13; 'Old Vic: Ballets Jooss', in *The Times*, 23 May 1939, p.14, considered the plot an allegory of current politics.

46. Lillian Karina and Marion Kant (2003) *Hitler's Dancers: German Modern Dance and the Third Reich*, pp.170–3, 217–8, 241–2.

47. For different interpretations of Laban's interaction with the Third Reich, see Lillian Karina and Marion Kant (2003) *Hitler's Dancers: German Modern Dance and the Third Reich*; and Valerie Preston-Dunlop (1998) *Rudolf Laban: An Extraordinary Life*.

48. Menon, or 'Menen' as it was sometimes spelled, was of Indian and Irish parentage.

49 André van Gyseghem (1979) 'British Theatre in the Thirties: an autobiographical record', in Clark, Heinemann *et al.*, eds. *Culture and Crisis in Britain in the Thirties*, p.211.

50. 'The Experimental Theatre: Production that is "Different", By Our Dramatic Critic', *The Morning Post*, 10 November 1934, p.12.

51. For accounts of the left-wing theatre movement in Britain, see Colin Chambers (1989) *The Story of Unity Theatre*; Raphael Samuel *et al.* (1985) *Theatres of the Left 1880–1935: Workers' Theatre Movements in Britain and America*.

52. Quotation from an unpublished manuscript autobiography by Fernau Hall in the Fernau Hall Collection at NRCD. Hall was active in mass recitations at Unity Theatre and went on to become an established post-war dance critic.

53. For the historical context and analysis of such pageants, see articles by Mick Wallis: (1994) 'Pageantry and the Popular Front: Ideological Production in the Thirties', *New Theatre Quarterly*, 10 (38), May, pp.132–56; and (1995) 'The Popular Front Pageant: Its Emergence and Decline', *New Theatre Quarterly*, 11 (41), February, pp.17–32.

54. The Souvenir Programme contains full scenario and text of the pageant, and photographs include some of the dance groups. The film, *Towards Tomorrow*, was produced by Frank H.W. Cox for the CWS National Film Service. The National Co-operative Archive, Manchester, holds copies. Barr's photograph as 'The Spirit of Co-operation' appeared across pages 2 and 3 of a Supplement to the *Co-operative News*, 9 July 1938. The incident is described in Caryll von Sturmer (1993) *Margaret Barr: Epic Individual*, pp.31–2.

55. See, for example, Kaye Russell (1938) 'Dancing for Progress: New Dance Technique with Social Purpose', *The Millgate*, April, 407–9 and articles in *Ourselves: A Journal for C.W.S. Employees* in August and November 1938 and February 1939.

56. Documentation of Alan Bush's involvement with the Workers' Propaganda Dance Group can be found in the Alan Bush Collection, MS MUS 453, vol.128, British Library. See also: Nancy Bush (2000) *Alan Bush: Music, Politics and Life*, p.36.

57. Fernau Hall, the well-known post-war dance writer who included an account of Barr's work in *Modern English Ballet* (1950), was also involved in Unity Theatre. In 1938 he wrote about her Britannia Street performances in *The Dancing Times* ('Modern Dancing at King's Cross: the Dance-Drama Group', January, pp.526–8.) At both times he confined himself to the aesthetics of the work

without revealing any political sympathies. The British scene did receive some contemporary attention in America: Leslie Daikin (1936) 'English Letter', *New Theater*, June, p.30.

58. For the workers' dance movement in America, see Lynn Garafola, ed. (1994) *Of, By, and For the People: Dancing on the Left in the 1930s*. A forthcoming book by Stacey Prickett, *Embodied Politics: Dancing Protest and Identities in the US and Britain* will constitute a profound enquiry into selected historical contexts, including that of 1930s London.

59. Undated programme and invitation in Margaret Barr Collection, State Library of New South Wales, Sydney.

60. von Sturmer (1993), pp.32–3.

61. NRCD: Fernau Hall, 'The Modern Scene in Ballet', manuscript, Fernau Hall Collection.

62. DHTA: T Arts Dance 2, Folder A, Letter 15 March 1936, Peter Goffin to Margaret Barr.

63. Hall (1950), p.142.

64. For Barr's later career, see Caryll von Sturmer (1993) *Margaret Barr: Epic Individual*; Lynn Fisher (1994) 'Considering Margaret Barr', *Brolga*, no. 1, December, pp.8–61; Garry Lester (1997) 'Margaret Barr: Epic Individual and Fringe Dweller', *Proceedings: Society of Dance History Scholars*, pp.9–19.

65. NYPL: *MGZMT 3-565, Jooss Interview Transcript, p.31.

66. DHTA: T Arts Dance 1A, Folder C: 'At one time engaged as Ballet Director in the Folk Theatre Berlin, but dismissed by the Nazis in the summer of 1936.'

67. DHTA: T Arts Admin.1, Folder J. 'Reason for leaving Germany: Dismissed from post as ballet director by Nazis summer 1936, refused permission to work owing to his philosophical and artistic outlook.' This version of events has been challenged by Lilian Karina and Marion Kant (2003) following extensive archival research in the contemporary German sources. The essence of their accusation is that Laban and other major figures of German modern dance cooperated willingly and not under duress. They removed all Jewish students from their schools (Laban was at that time ballet director of the Berlin opera) voluntarily in 1933 and before being compelled by law to do so. (ibid. Karina, p.16; Kant, p.92, p.152, note 39). Karina and Kant allege that, even after his mass dance for the arts festival preceding the Olympic Games had been banned and he was too ill to carry out his work, he retained a position as a consultant until October 1937, earnestly applied to be reinstated, leaving Germany finally in November 1937 when it became clear that would not happen (ibid, Karina, p.60).

68. DHTA: T Arts Admin 1, Folder F, Report to the Trustees, 9 February 1940.

69. DHTA: T Arts Admin 1, Folder F, Report to the Trustees, 27 July 1940.

70. See Julie Kavanagh (1996) *Secret Muses: The Life of Frederick Ashton*, pp.270–1; Roger Berthoud (1982) *Graham Sutherland: A Biography*, p.101. In addition I am grateful to my colleague Geraldine Morris for sharing her research on *The Wanderer* with me.

71. DHTA: T Arts Admin 1, Folder G, Report to the Trustees, 7 February 1941; programme of Sadler's Wells Ballet in DWE Arts 12, Folder C.

72. Stöckemann (2001), pp.280–1; also DHTA: T Arts Dance 1, Folder C2 Legal, Letter 8 May 1940 from F.A.S. Gwatkin to Fritz Cohen; and T Arts Dance 1A, Folder D, Letter 10 May 1940 from Jooss to Hans [?] Züllig.

73. DHTA: Minutes of Trustees Meeting, 30 November 1940.

74. DHTA: DWE Arts 9, Folder C 1941–46, Letter Elsa Kahl Cohen to DWE, begun 20 Feb 1941 in Bogota, completed 15 May in Caracas.

75. Quotation from *Growing Up in Public* (monologue show), extract in *Speaking of Dance: Lucas Hoving*, [Videorecording].

76. Joy Skinner (1999) *Over the Hill with a Magic Carpet*, p.39.

77. DHTA: DWE Arts 9, Folder C,1941–46, letters from Yoma Sasburgh, Inka Sloth-Blaauboer, Bill Charnley, Kurt Jooss, Clifton Parker (pianist). Note that Bill (later Michael) Charnley went on to become one of the emergent generation of young British choreographers in the 1950s, although the trajectory of his career in prominent ballet companies did not proceed as expected. For an early assessment of his potential, see Frank Jackson (1953) *They Make Tomorrow's Ballet*.

78. DHTA: DWE Arts 9, Folder C, Letter 13 March 1941, Kurt Jooss to DWE, and reply 28 March 1941.

79. DHTA: T Arts Dance 1, Folder B, Letter 25 February 1942, Fritz and Elsa Cohen to DWE and LKE. Fritz Cohen went on to a distinguished teaching career in America, including as Director of the Juilliard Opera Theater, 1946–63. When Fritz Cohen died in 1967, Elsa wrote to Dorothy asking to return to Dartington for a while to contribute something to the community. Clearly, the memory of Dartington days still meant something very special.

80. In order to get a perspective on the monetary value of the time, this can be compared with the example of some of the salaries paid. Jooss was the highest earner at £1000 per annum, while Leeder received £750 and other teachers of the School about a third of that. Board and lodging had to be paid out of this.

81. DHTA: T Arts Dance 1, Folder C2, undated paper on the financial position of the Arts Department [probably c.1942]. I have tried to reflect Christopher Martin's meaning in this report. On the other hand, in *Dartington Hall, 1925–56: A Report*, Victor Bonham-Carter states ('The Arts', p.11) that net expenditure by the Trust on Ballets Jooss, 1935–40, was £21,000. I am not currently aware where these figures come from.

82. DHTA: T Arts Admin.1, Folder D, Report to the Trustees, 1 July 1937. This sum may also include the costs of restaging *The Prodigal Son* with new costumes.

83. DHTA: T Arts Dance 1, Folder C, Letter 6 December 1939, Fred Gwatkin to LKE.

84. DHTA: T Arts Admin.1, Folder E, Report to the Trustees, 4 May 1938.

85. DHTA: T Arts Admin. 1, Folder G, Report to the Trustees, 7 February 1941.

86. Karina (2003) in Karina and Kant, p.8.

87. Other Swedish modern dance choreographers employed by Skeaping were Ivo Cramér and Birgit Åkesson.

88. Ai Lien Tai in Dartington records. Dai is the family name.

89. Hutchinson Guest (2006), p.191.

90. Susan Jeffs (2003) 'A revolutionary art form: Ballet in China 1930–1960', *Dance Gazette*, Issue 2, 17–19. A visit to Dartington is recounted in 'Second Blossom of the Lotus Dancer', *Dartington Hall News and South Devon Scene*, 8 May 1981, p.3. There is a television interview with her in *Dance on: With Billie Mahoney*, August 17, 1983, NYPL *MGZIC 9-647.

91. Ann Murphy (1998) 'Lucas Hoving', in Taryn Benbow-Pfalzgraf, ed. *International Dictionary of Modern Dance*, pp.366–9.

92. I am grateful to my colleague Prarthana Purkayastha for sharing her knowledge of *Kalpana* with me.

93. For a view at mid-decade, see.: Jeanette Rutherston (1935) 'The German Influence', *The Dancing Times*, October, pp.42–4.

94. NRCD: Fernau Hall, '*The "Star" Ballet*', manuscript article in Fernau Hall Collection.

95. See Larraine Nicholas (2004) 'Dancing in the Margins? British Modern Dance in the 1940s and 50s', in Alexandra Carter, ed. *Rethinking Dance History*, pp.119–31.

96. DHTA: DWE Arts 8, Folder F, Letter 22 June 1947, Marie Rambert to DWE; reply 26 June 1947. Dorothy did not give Rambert all she asked for, but encouraged her to find a matching sum from another source.

97. DHTA: DWE Arts 9, Folder E, Jooss interviewed by Ruth Foster, 1973.

98. Cox (2005), pp.133–4.

99. DHTA: T Arts Admin. 1, Administrator's Report to the Dartington Hall Trustees, 18 May 1939, p.5.

100. In spite of the internment of Heckroth and Soukop, the Art Studios lasted until 1943, under Cecil Collins. The opera studio did not become a reality.

101. Harrison (2002), p.156.

102. DHTA: T Arts Dance 3, Folder A, Letter 10 March 1939, Laban to LKE.

103. See Cox (2005), p.139; Young (1996), pp.271–2.

Chapter 4: Spreading the Art of Movement, Raising the Art of Dance

1. DHTA: T Arts Admin. 1, Folder H, Plan for the Arts Department, Christopher Martin, 1941.

2. For the history of the Arts Council of Great Britain, see Eric Walter White (1975) *The Arts Council of Great Britain*; Andrew Sinclair (1995) *Arts and Cultures: The History of the 50 Years of the Arts Council of Great Britain*.

3. Arts Council of Great Britain (1946) *1st Annual Report*, p.21.

4. See Peter Cox (2005) *The Arts at Dartington 1940–1983: A Personal Account*, pp.150–4; also Rachel Harrison (2002) *Dorothy Elmhirst and the visual arts at Dartington Hall 1925–1945*, unpublished Ph.D thesis, Plymouth University.

5. For her German children's movement choir, see the photograph at Figure 8 in Valerie Preston-Dunlop and Susanne Lahusen, eds. (1990) *Schrifttanz: A View of German Dance in the Weimar Republic*. For the context of nudity (*Nacktkultur*), see Karl Toepfer (1997) *Empire of Ecstasy: Nudity and Movement in German Body Culture, 1910–1935*, especially pp.303–04 on Gertz's method. Fernau Hall (1950) *Modern English Ballet: an Interpretation*, pp.253–5, describes her later work. According to Hall, her escape from Czechoslovakia before the war was financed by donations from Jooss, his dancers and students.

6. DHTA: T Arts Dance 2, Folder D, 'Recreation Through Play', in manuscript *Children and Movement*, p.5. See also DHTA: T Arts Admin.1, Folder L, Letter 19 April 1940, Christopher Martin to LKE.

7. NRCD: Photographs in the Lisa Ullmann Collection, LU/F/1/73.

8. Joan Littlewood (1994) *Joan's Book*, p.120.

9. According to Rutherston (1935) 'The German Influence', *The Dancing Times*, October, p.42, 'three English girls and a teacher' went to Bodenwieser from Bedford College.

10. Diana Jordan (1938) *The Dance as Education*, p.84.

11. The Sitter Out, *The Dancing Times*, February 1939, p.600.

12. Gwatkin (1939) 'Teaching Mary Through the Dance', *The Dancing Times*, April, pp.8–9.

13. In October 1939 she had been reclassified as a 'friendly alien': NRCD: LU/E/11/6, Letter from Christopher Martin to Ullmann. Classes restarted in May 1940. Various references in letters suggest that Dartington's Arts Department would have preferred to place the remnants of the Jooss–Leeder School under an Ullmann/Laban directorship rather than leaving it at Dartington.

14. NRCD: Ullmann Archive, LU/E/16/1, Draft Letter, undated, Ullmann to DWE.

15. Mary Skeaping also attended this course. NRCD: Laban Guild Oral Archive Project, Lisa Ullmann interviewed by Hilary Corlett and Athalie Knowles, 24 June 1984.

16. DHTA: DWE Arts 7, Folder C, leaflet, *Modern Dance ... What is it?* (1942).

17. This is acknowledged in Ullmann's Preface to Rudolf Laban (1966) *Choreutics*, p.ix.

18. See, for example, Valerie Preston (1963) *A Handbook for Modern Educational Dance*.

19. This was, however, a development largely led by women and was not popular with most male physical educationists. For a discussion of the introduction of basic movement into physical education and the disparate reactions of male and female teachers and lecturers, see Sheila Fletcher (1984) *Women First: The Female Tradition in English Physical Education 1880–1980*, pp.132–9. For a historical overview of the influence of Laban upon gymnastic teaching and theory, see Elizabeth Mauldon and June Layson (1979) *Teaching Gymnastics*, 2nd edition, pp.1–11.

20. See Arnold Haskell (1951) *In His True Centre: An Interim Autobiography*, pp.243–4.

21. NRCD: LU/E/13/10, 'Art of Movement Studio: Memorandum on Movement Education in Training Colleges', 15 December 1958.

22. See Michael Young (1996) *The Elmhirsts of Dartington*, pp.210–14.

23. DHTA: T Arts Admin. 2, Folder A, Report on Arts Department for Trustees Meeting, 23 February 1945.

24. DHTA: T Arts Admin. 2, Folder A, A Report on the Economics of the Arts Department, 1945.

25. For example, DHTA: Peter Cox Papers: Letter 26 January 1949, Ullmann to Cox.

26. Cox, Peter (1999) *My Time at Dartington, 1940–83: A Personal Record of Involvement in Administering the Arts at Dartington Hall and Creating Dartington College of Arts*, unpublished MS, Dartington College of Arts, p.82.

27. ibid., p.14.

28. DHTA: T Arts Drama 3A, Folder A, grant application 24 August 1949.

29. DHTA: T Arts Drama 3A, Folder B, Outline of Programme; Folder E, *The Family of Man* Programme. Notes on the dance drama are to be found in NRCD: UL/E/11/13.

30. Peter Cox (2005) *The Arts at Dartington 1940–1983: A Personal Account*, p.57.

31. DHTA: T Arts Drama 3A, Folder E.

32. DHTA: T Arts Dance 3, Folder B, Letter 12 March 1954, LKE to AOE.

33. Compare F.M.G. Willson (1997) *In Just Order Move: the progress of the Laban Centre for Movement and Dance, 1946–1996*, pp.33–4; Preston-Dunlop (1998) *Rudolf Laban: An Extraordinary Life*, p.231.

34. Interview with William Elmhirst, 28 July 2005. Also Laban Oral Archive, LAB 2005/37/23.

35. Willson (1997), p.81.

36. Preston-Dunlop (1998), p.261.

37. Memo by F.C. Lawrence for initial Trustees Meeting, 27 October 1954, quoted from Willson (1997) p.65.

38. Willson (1997) pp.61–2.

39. NRCD: LU/E/9/15.

40. DHTA: T Arts Dance 3, Folder C, Notes of Management Committee and Trustees Meeting, 1 December 1957.

41. NRCD: LU/E/6/14. Art of Movement Studio, Notes for a Report, 1958/59.

42. DHTA: T Arts Dance 3, Folder C, 'Notes on Discussion between A.O. Elmhirst and Diana Jordan', September 1959.

43. NRCD: LU/E/12/ Folder 12.

44. See syllabi in NRCD: LU/E/8, Folders 16 and 18.

45. Preston-Dunlop (1998), p.264. See timetable in NRCD: LU/E/8.

46. NRCD: LU/E/12/12, Lecture: ATCDE (Association of Teachers in Colleges and Departments of Education)/Dance Section, April 1969.

47. See Willson (1997). Marion North succeeded Lisa Ullmann in 1973. The original Trust was replaced by the University of London Goldsmiths' College Delegacy in 1974 and the Centre became independent in 1989. Since 2002 it has been known simply as Laban.

48. NRCD: Laban Guild Oral Archive Project, Lisa Ullmann interviewed by Hilary Corlett and Athalie Knowles, 24 June 1984.

49. DHTA: T Arts Dance 3, Folder A, 'Practical Outlook'.

50. DHTA: T Arts Dance 3, Folder A. 'Extract from an address held by Mr. Laban on a meeting for community-dance in 1936', was also published in *Laban Art of Movement Guild Magazine*, no. 52, May 1974, pp.6–11.

51. For the relationship between Laban and Ullmann, see Preston-Dunlop (1998), pp.214–15. The document referred to is in NRCD: LU/E/11/6, Lectures/WEA, Plymouth.

52. Compare the following: Colin Counsell, (2004) 'Dancing to Utopia: Modernity, Community and the Movement Choir', *Dance Research*, XXII, no. 2, Winter, 154–67; Yvonne Hardt, (2003) 'Relational Movement Patterns: The Diversity of Movement Choirs and their Social Potential in the Weimar Republic', *Proceedings: Society of Dance History Scholars, Twenty-Sixth Annual Conference, Stoughton, Wisconsin: Society of Dance History Scholars*, 45–50; Karl Toepfer (1997) *Empire of Ecstasy*, pp.300–06.

53. 'Notes on Choral Dancing', *Laban Art of Movement Guild Magazine*, no. 43, November 1969, pp.5–7. This was introduced as a hitherto unpublished article by him, but there is no indication when it was written.

54. Lisa Ullmann (1956) 'Recreative Dancing in the Movement Choir', *Laban Art of Movement Guild Magazine*, March, p.25.

55. ibid., p.24.

56. NRCD: LU/E/11/6, various documents.

57. NRCD: Laban Guild Oral Archive Project, Jane Winearls interviewed by Athalie Knowles, June 1968. Winearls founded a dance group in the 1930s, Demeter Company, influenced by varying styles, including Hellenic dance. She joined the Leeder School of Dance in London in 1947 and introduced the Jooss–Leeder Method in the PE course at Birmingham University in 1965.

58. Geraldine Stephenson (1998) 'The Long Story in a Brief Series of Happenings', *Movement and Dance: Quarterly Magazine of the Laban Guild*, 17, no. 4, Winter, 6–7, quotation from p.6.

59. NRCD: L/E/32/75, Notes on Saltata.

60. Ullmann (1956) 'Recreative Dancing in the Movement Choir', *Laban Art of Movement Guild Magazine*, March. Photographs are on pages 26 and 21 respectively and the quotation is from page 27.

61. Personal communication from Janet Goodridge, 5 October 2006.

62. Flyer for The London Movement Choir, 1955/56.

63. Sylvia Bodmer (1966) 'Recreational Dance', *Laban Art of Movement Guild Magazine*, no. 37, November, p.30.

64. NRCD: LU/E/12/1, flyer.

65. Information supplied by Iain Davison, Bagman of Dartington Morris Men.

66. Peter Cox (2005) *The Arts at Dartington 1940–1983: A Personal Account*, p.102.

67. On Peter Darrell, see The Peter Darrell Trust (1998) *Man of Tomorrow: Peter Darrell CBE (1929–1987)*. On Western Theatre Ballet, see Annette Massie (1988) 'Elizabeth West and Western Theatre Ballet', *Dance Research*, VI, no. 1, Spring, pp.45–58; Kathrine Sorley Walker (2002) 'Westward, Ho', *Dance Now*, 11, no. 2, Summer, pp.55–71 and 11, no. 3, Autumn, pp.75–88.

68. See, for example, V&A: ACGB/125/40, Ballets Minerva, Extract from minute paper, 11 November 1953, Cyril Wood to Donald Mather.

69. Arts Council of Great Britain (1958) *A New pattern of Patronage: 13th Annual Report*, p.10.

70. The Calouste Gulbenkian Foundation published its report in 1959: Lord Bridges et al. *Help for the Arts*, identifying support for experiment and the needs of the provinces as key areas of need. Lord Bridges and the Countess of Albermarle, members of the report committee, had been guests at Dartington around this time (Cox, 2005, p.150).

71. V&A: ACGB/125/40, Ballets Minerva, Extract from Minutes of Music Panel Meeting, 17 November 1960; ACGB/125/21, Ballet General 1960, note from John Denison, Director of Music, 11 November 1960, reference to an application from Festival Ballet, 'I feel that the claims of smaller scale work are stronger than those of another full scale company.'

72. Massie (1988), p.47.

73. DHTA: Peter Cox Papers, Letter 11 June 1958, Peter Cox to Mary Hoskyn.

74. V&A: ACGB/125/93, Western Theatre Ballet, File 288.

75. V&A: ACGB/125/93. Points raised in letter, 17 October 1958 from Charity James (WTB Chairman) to William Emrys Williams (Arts Council Secretary General).

76. V&A: ACGB/125/93, Western Theatre Ballet, File 295, letter, Elizabeth West to Eric White (received 1 November 1960).

77. DHTA: Peter Cox Papers, Dance Miscellaneous.

78. Beryl de Zoete (1948) 'Notes on Sivaram and the Kathakali Style', *Ballet*, 6, no. 2. November, pp.19–21.

79. Cox (2005), p.382.

80. David Vaughan (1997) *Merce Cunningham: Fifty Years*, p.140.

81. The full programme was: on July 23, *Suite for Five* (1953–58), *Crises* (1960), *Untitled Solo* (1953), *Story* (1963); on July 24, *Septet* (1953), *Winterbranch* (1964), *Paired* (1964), *Antic Meet* (1958).

82. Email communication from David Vaughan, Cunningham Dance Foundation, 21 November 2006.

83. Vaughan (1997), p.131.

84. DHTA: DWE Arts 8, Folder D.

85. Cox (2005), p.157.

86. V&A: ACGB/125/117, Dance within the Regional Arts Associations, 1972–74, Letter 22 August 1972 from Jane Nicholas to regional arts associations.

87. V&A: ACGB/125/117, Dance within the Regional Arts Associations, memo 16 April 1974 from Neil Duncan to Jane Nicholas; it was also discussed at the meeting of regional arts associations on 13 May 1974.

88. But the poor attendance of some of those officers, who might be responsible for two or three art forms, was noted. The Greater London Arts Association was the first RAA to appoint a dance officer in 1977. See V&A: ACGB/125/119, Dance within the Regional Arts Associations, 1978–81, Minutes of CORAA (Council of Regional Arts Associations).

89. V&A: ACGB/125/117, Dance within the Regional Arts Associations, Peter Curtis (February 1974) Dance in the South West: a report prepared for the Theatre Advisory Panel of South Western Arts Association.

90. Tim Rubidge had been a student of Sigurd Leeder, later becoming involved in new dance; Merry Dufton (1986) 'Dance in the South West', *New Dance*, no. 38, Autumn, pp.10–11.

91. For the history of the Christmas Festivals, see Cox (2005), pp.112–40.

92. South West Film and Television Archive, Box 9, E4, Dart 5. *Dartington Christmas Festival*, directed by John Irving, 1960, BBC TV West Region Production.

Chapter 5: Artists and Educators

1. Peter Cox (2005) *The Arts at Dartington 1940–1983: A Personal Account*, p.153.

2. ibid., p.162.

3. DHTA: Peter Cox Papers, Folder: Dance Miscellaneous .

4. DHTA: Peter Cox Papers, Folder: Kurt Jooss.

5. Cox (2005), pp.153–4.

6. DHTA: T DCA Theatre 1, Folder F, Draft Scheme for Training at Dartington Teachers of Dance and Drama.

7. Louis Horst (1937) *Pre-classic Dance Forms*.

8. Part of a review of the American modern dancer Christyne Lawson's dance, *Vignettes*. The dance was shown at the Sunday Ballet Club, an occasional platform for aspiring choreographers. Clive Barnes (1961) 'It Always Reigns on Sundays', *Dance and Dancers*, 12, no. 6, June, pp.28–9.

9. DHTA: Peter Cox Papers, Folder: Lucas Hoving.

10. T. Fisher and J. Holbrook (1965) 'Some Impressions of the Course in Modern American Dance for Training College Lecturers', *Laban Art of Movement Guild Magazine*, no. 35, November, pp.7–9.

11. For further background on Madden's courses at Dartington, see Valerie Preston-Dunlop and Luis Espana (2005) *The American Invasion 1962–72*, DVD.

12. Interview with Sam Thornton, 27 September 2005.

13. Interview with Karen Morgan, 12 September 2005.

14. Laban Oral Archive, Janet Goodridge, LAB: 2005/37/1. For 'strange space design', see Louis Horst and Carroll Russell (1987) *Modern Dance Forms in Relation to the other Modern Arts*, p.34 (first published 1961).

15. Interview with David Henshaw, 20 September 2005.

16. Interview with Sam Thornton, 27 September 2005; Laban Oral Archive, Janet Goodridge, LAB: 2005/37/1.

17. Laban Oral Archive, Lorn Primrose, LAB: 2005/27/5. Primrose was a lecturer at IM Marsh College of Physical Education during Madden's teaching assignment there in 1963.

18. Laban Oral Archive, Janet Goodridge, LAB: 2005/37/1; Interview with David Henshaw, 20 September 2005.

19. Butcher in Valerie Preston-Dunlop and Luis Espana (2005) *The American Invasion 1962–72*, DVD.

20. DHTA: T DCA Theatre1, Folder F, Letter 21 April 1967 from Ruth Foster to LKE; Letter 30 April 1967, William Elmhirst to LKE.

21. Laban Oral Archive, Sue McLennan, LAB 2005/37/10; Valerie Preston-Dunlop and Luis Espana (2005) *The American Invasion 1962–72*, DVD.

22. Interview with Fionna MacPhee, 17 June 2005.

23. Laban Oral Archive, Rosemary Butcher, LAB 2005/37/13.

24. Interview with Fionna MacPhee, 17 June 2005.

25. Interview with Nic Cottis, 8 March 2006.

26. Laban Oral Archive, Sue McLennan, LAB 2005/37/10.

27. Curtis taught part-time at Dartington from 1972 to 1975 while running a ballet school in Dawlish. Interview with Peter Curtis, 5 July 2006.

28. Peter Williams and John Percival (1967) 'Contemporary Break-out', *Dance and Dancers*, Decem-

ber, pp.20–23, 44–5, quotation p.22. See also the *Dartington Hall News*, 16 February 1968, with photograph and summary of the broadsheet newspapers' response to the dance.

29. The cultural historian Robert Hewison argues that the cultural phenomena associated with the Sixties begin in about 1963 and faded away in the mid-1970s. See Robert Hewison (1986) *Too Much: Art and Society in the Sixties 1960–75*.

30. Memory of author and conversation with Henrietta Lyons (Bannerman), 14 January 2006.

31. Email communication, Pauline de Groot, 19 January 2006.

32. Interview with Janet Eager, 12 April 2006.

33. For discussion of Richard Alston and Strider along with other aspects of British dance radicalism of the 1970s, see Stephanie Jordan (1992) *Striding Out: Aspects of Contemporary and New Dance in Britain*.

34. Calouste Gulbenkian Foundation (1980) *Dance Education and Training in Britain*, p.79.

35. ibid., pp.80–1.

36. Interview with Colette King, 18 January 2006; Mary Fulkerson (1978) 'Mary Fulkerson: an interview', *New Dance*, no. 7, Summer, p.12.

37. Mark Kidel, dir. (1996) *Just Dancing Around? Richard Alston*, Euphoria Films for Channel 4.

38. DHTA: T DCA, Theatre 1, Folder A, Report on a visit to Dartington College of Arts, 9 July 1975; T DCA, AC 1, Folder D, Letter 18 December 1975 from CNAA to Peter Cox; also interview with David Henshaw, 20 September 2005.

39. Cox (2005), p.314.

40. Mary Fulkerson (1985) 'Moving for Performance', *New Dance*, no. 32, Spring, p.12.

41. ibid.

42. Quoted in Joan Skinner, Bridget Davis, Sally Metcalf and Kris Wheeler (1979) 'Notes on the Skinner Releasing Technique', *Contact Quarterly*, 5, no. 1, Fall, 8–13. Quotation on p.11. Skinner had been a member of the Martha Graham and Merce Cunningham companies.

43. Mary Fulkerson (1977) 'The Language of the Axis', *Theatre Papers*, p.75. *Theatre Papers* are available from the Arts Documentation Unit, director Peter Hulton, Exeter University.

44. ibid., p.14.

45. Later she associated these with Chinese Meridians.

46. Fulkerson (1977), pp.93–4.

47. Fourth Series, no. 10 (1983–4).

48. Stephanie Jordan (1987) 'Mary Fulkerson', *Dance Theatre Journal*, v.5, no. 3b, p.4.

49. Chris Crickmay (1988) 'Fragments of Daily Life: Mary Fulkerson's World of Images and Compositional Ideas ', *Contact Quarterly*, Spring/Summer, 13, no. 2, p.10.

50. Kathy Duncan, *Soho Weekly News*, 1 February 1974.

51. Mary O'Donnell Fulkerson, *Release*, ebook available from www.releasedance.com, p.70.

52. Interview with Mary O'Donnell (Fulkerson), 12 February 2006.

53. DHTA: T Arts Dance 2, A, Letter from Kai Tai Chan to Paula Morel, 20 January 1974.

54. Fulkerson (1978), p.13. She defines narrative to include 'any line that connects, such as the continuity of knowing' (*Release*, p.303).

55. Mary O'Donnell Fulkerson, *Release*, p.161.

56. Along the way she carved on a tree 'Rose is a Rose is a Rose is a Rose is a Rose until it went all the way around.'

57. My notional reconstruction of these dances is based on reviews, press releases, photographs, references in Fulkerson's (1982) *The Move to Stillness* and interview, 12 February 2006. See two contrasting reviews of *Robin Fly South* and *I Saw Myself Standing*, performed in New York in 1978: Ken Peake and Diane Torr,'"Leap" says the World and I Fly', *The Soho Weekly News*, 16 March 1978, p.51; Amanda Smith 'Fairly Frozen', unidentified press cutting in 'Mary Fulkerson, Cuttings', Dance Division, NYPL.

58. Jennifer Dunning, 'Dance: 'Real Adventures,' A Solo by Mary Fulkerson', *The New York Times*, 15 April 1984, reproduced in *Release*, p.177.

59. The exploration of male and female in companion pieces happened also in two solos, *Tony Charger* and *Charger's Woman*, in which she took on male and female characters and their perceptions of each other.

60. Mary Fulkerson, Postmodern Paper IV, *Release*, pp.423–31, quotation from p.423.

61. Fulkerson, *Release*, p.181.

62. ibid., p.165.

63. See Emilyn Claid (2006) *Yes? No! Maybe ... Seductive Ambiguity in Dance*, pp.53–70, for atmospheric descriptions of such work coming from the X6 collective.

64. Dancers with Fulkerson and Crickmay included Miranda Tufnell, Dennis Greenwood and Libby Dempster. The group set up improvisational events, collaborations in open form where often the audience could come and go. The collaboration between Tufnell and Crickmay has been an influential one, producing two books on improvisation and performance, *Body, Space, Image* (1993) 2nd edition and (2004) *A Widening Field: Journeys in Body and Imagination*. See *Body, Space, Image*, p.125 and p.133 for a description of the working process of Little Theatre and *Field*, a duet collaboration between Fulkerson and Crickmay.

65. The collective consisted of five professional dancers: Emilyn Claid, Maedée Duprès, Fergus Early, Jacky Lansley and Mary Prestidge.

66. See Stephanie Jordan (1992). Issues of definition are especially pursued in the Introduction and Chapter 3.

67. Steve Paxton and Aat Hougée (1994) 'Chaos and Order: Improvisation taken to the limit', *Ballett International/Tanz Aktuell*, November, pp.21–6. Paxton attributes these words to Carolyn Brown, p.24.

68. All three dances originated in the 1960s. *Satisfyin' Lover* (1967) and *State* (1968) were shown in Dance at Dartington in 1983; *Flat* (1964) was performed there in 1980. For the written score of *Satisfyin' Lover*, see Sally Banes (1987) *Terpsichore in Sneakers*, pp.71–4. For *Flat*, see Sally Banes (1987) 'Vital Signs: Steve Paxton's *Flat* in Perspective', in *A Spectrum of World Dance: Dance Research Annual XVI* (Congress on Research in Dance), pp.120–34.

69. Steve Paxton (1982) 'Contact Improvisation', *Theatre Papers, Fourth Series*, no. 5, p.3.

70. (1996) *Speaking of Dance: Steve Paxton* [videorecording].

71. For Paxton's description of the processes that evolved then, see (2003) 'Drafting Interior Techniques', in Ann Cooper Albright and David Gere, eds. *Taken by Surprise: A Dance Improvisation Reader*, pp.175–83.

72. For a socio-cultural analysis of the development of contact improvisation, see Cynthia J. Novack (1990) *Sharing the Dance: Contact Improvisation and American Culture*.

73. Email communication from Steve Paxton, 4 November 2005.

74. 'In the midst of standing still something else is occurring and the name for that is the small dance', Paxton interviewed by Peter Hulton, Summer 1975, published in *Theatre Papers* 1977, p.4.

75. Steve Paxton (1982) 'Contact Improvisation', *Theatre Papers, Fourth Series*, no. 5, Theatre Department, Dartington College of Arts, p.13.

76. 'In the midst of standing still something else is occurring and the name for that is the small dance', interviewed by Peter Hulton, Summer 1975, published in *Theatre Papers* 1977, pp.1–2.

77. Steve Paxton (1982) 'Contact Improvisation', *Theatre Papers, Fourth Series*, no. 5, p.17.

78. This was for Lynne Blom, co-author with L. Tarin Chaplin of books on choreography and improvisation: *The Intimate Act of Choreography* and *The Moment of Movement*. Email communication from Paxton, 7 November 2005.

79. For the Grand Union, see Banes (1987) and Elizabeth Kendall (1975–6) 'The Grand Union: Our Gang', *Ballet Review*, 5, no. 4, pp.44–55.

80. See Daniel Nagrin (1994) *Dance and the Specific Image: Improvisation*. He coined the term 'EGAS' (exercises, games and structures) for the structures used in practising and performing improvisation.

81. David Gere (2003) 'Introduction', in Ann Cooper Albright, and David Gere, eds. *Taken by Surprise: A Dance Improvisation Reader*, p.xiv.

82. See Yvonne Rainer (1979) 'Backwater: Twosome/Paxton and Moss', *Dance Scope*, 13, nos. 2/3, pp.8–10; Ramsay Burt (2002) 'Steve Paxton's Goldberg Variations and the Angel of History', *TDR*, Winter, vol.46, no. 4, pp.46–64.

83. Interview in Ana Maria Rebouças and Renata Ferreira Xavier (2001) 'Lisa Nelson and Steve Paxton', *Revista D'Art*, no. 8, Dezembra [online].

84. My analysis is based on the performance in *Contact at 10ᵗʰ and 2ⁿᵈ: Program 4*, recorded 16 June 1983, Jerome Robbins Dance Division, NYPL, *MGZIA 4–169. Reviews are: Silvy Panet-Raymond (1979) 'Tuesday 27 March ...', *New Dance*, no. 9, pp.12–13; Claire Hayes (1983) 'Dance Umbrella', *New Dance*, no. 24, Winter/Spring, pp.18–19; Stephanie Jordan and Howard Friend (1982) 'Dance Umbrella 1982', *The Dancing Times*, December, pp.190–2; Katie Doitch (1983) 'Paxton and Nelson: Libby Dempster', *Dance and Dancers*, January, 30. Paxton and Nelson performed *PA RT* from 1978 to 2005.

85. Email communication from Steve Paxton, 15 February and 25 February 2007. Quoted with permission.

86. Fulkerson (1985) 'Moving for Performance', *New Dance*, p.13.

87. Jan Murray (1978) 'Dance at Dartington: at Dartington College, Devon', *Dance and Dancers*, August, pp. 34–5, quotation p.34.

88. 1981: solos *Testament to One Thought*, and *Swedish Dances* (choreographed by Alston); *The Raft is not the Shore*, choreographed for Michael Clark and Beverly Sandwith; *Field*, improvisation with Chris Crickmay. 1982: *Put Your Foot Down Charlie* and *The Same Story*, and group work *Undergrowth*. 1983: *Track Follows* (collaboration with Eva Lundquist and Wind Witches) and *Fine Romance* with her group Dance Alliance. 1984: solo *Real Life Adventures*.

89. Val Bourne and Donna McDonald (1992) 'The Tapestry of British Contemporary Dance', *Choreography and Dance*, 3, no. 1, pp.27–39, quotation from p.29.

90. Original name Katie Appenzeller. 'Duck' was a psuedonym adopted for the tour of a solo piece, *The Duck Play* (1976).

91. Ric Allsopp and Jane Fitzgerald (1987) *Katie Duck: Small Scale Dances*, Dartington Video Paper.

92. Stephanie Jordan (1983) 'Dartington International Dance Festival', *The Dancing Times*, July, pp.791–2, quotation p.791.

93. Jhamal (1984) 'Katie Duck Talks to Jhamal', *New Dance*, no. 28, Spring, pp.28–9.

94. For reviews, see Sophie Constanti (1985) 'Passion in Parts', *Dance Theatre Journal*, 3, no. 1, Spring, pp.14–17; Judith Mackrell (1984) 'Katie Duck', *Dance Theatre Journal*, 2, no. 3, Autumn, pp.39–40; Alys Daines (1984) 'Katie Duck/Group O in *Rutles*', *New Dance*, no. 31, Winter, pp.25–6. Quotation from Daines, p.26.

95. One of the musicians was the guitarist Derek Bailey. She joined him and seven other musicians in a week of improvisation at the Arts Theatre, London, in 1987. See Richard Cook (1987) 'Don't Fence Them In', *The Sunday Times*, 10 May, available online from LexisNexis.

96. 'Interview' (n.d.), *Tangent*, Montreal, Canada, available from www.katieduck.com/interviews/.

97. Andy Solway (1988) 'Blue Eye, Brown Eye'[sic], *New Dance*, no. 44, June, p.22.

98. *Thought Sonata* flyer, 1990. I also have drawn on conversations with Katie Duck and Ric Allsopp (2006) and various versions of text and cue sheets in Allsopp's possession.

99. In the library at Dartington College of Arts, the video is catalogued under 799PAX and the label notes the date as 'Jan 21ˢᵗ ?1988'. There is another set of improvisations on the same video, evidently performed on the same night and including Steve Paxton.

100. Mary Fulkerson (1978) 'Mary Fulkerson: an interview', *New Dance*, no. 7, Summer, p.12.

101. 'Interview' (n.d.), *Tangent*, Montreal Canada. For Duck's more recent development of improvisation, see David Corbet (1999) 'Katie Duck: An Interview', *Proximity* [contact improvisation newsletter, Melbourne], 2, no. 4, December, available online from http://proximity.slightly.net/.

102. Email communication from Jenna Agate, 6 February 2006.

103. Sophie Constanti (1985) 'Passion in Parts', *Theatre Arts Journal*, 3, no. 1, Spring, p.14–17, quotation from p.15. The critic Alastair Macaulay saw that in terms of 'a new lyricism' coming from Dartington, from which I infer that he was noticing a softening of bodily movement rather than a relationship to melody. See (1983) 'One at a Time', *Dance Theatre Journal*, 1, no. 1, Spring, pp.15–21. See page 16.

104. Students at Dartington over these years: Booth, 1975–8; Snaith, 1979–83; Finnan, 1981–5.

105. Interviews with Kevin Finnan, 29 November 2005, and Laurie Booth, 2 December 2005. Quotation from Kevin Finnan.

106. Alastair Macaulay (1983) 'One at a Time', *Dance Theatre Journal*, 1, no. 1, Spring, pp.15–21. Quotation from p.16.

107. Stephanie Woodard (1985) 'Teaching Dance at Dartington', *New Dance*, no. 32, Spring, p.21. Jenna Agate remembers that these first-year students were not used to formal dance-technique classes. Email communication 6 February 2006.

108. Julian Webber, 'A Day in the Life of a Student', *Dartington Voice*, no. 25, December 1978, p.12. The reference recalls Fulkerson's 'moving stillness' (see page 192).

109. anon. (1968) 'The sitar family Khan', *Dartington Hall News*, 26 April, pp.6–7.

110. Email communication from Anne-Marie Gaston, 16 September 2006.

111. Cox (2005), p.290.

112. anon. (1987) 'Just a Touch of God', *Dartington Hall News and South Devon Scene*, July/August, pp.4–5.

113. Emilyn Claid (2006) *Yes? No! Maybe ... Seductive Ambiguity in Dance*, p.86.

114. See Maurice Ash, 'A Personal View: Reports of the School's death are greatly exaggerated', *Dartington Voice*, May 1986, pp.3–5; also letters in June edition, p.9.

115. Interview with Katie Duck, 11 February 2006.

116. Cox (2005), p.369.

Chapter 6: Dancing with People and Places

1. Notes on the Management of Rotherhithe Theatre Workshop as at 23 September 1986; document in possession of David Slater.

2. Interview with Colette King, 18 January 2006.

3. John Fox and Sue Gill (1984) 'Welfare State International (England)' in Peter Hulton, ed. *Theatre and Communities: A Council of Europe Workshop*, Theatre Papers, Fifth Series, no. 16, 27–42.

4. Richard Allsopp, ed. *Vernacular Theatre*, Theatre Papers Series 4 (1981–2), no. 8.

5. Interview with Peter Kiddle, 9 March 2006.

6. *Dartington Hall News and South Devon Scene*, 30 June 1978, pp. 1, 3.

7. Email communication from Angus Balbernie, 11 January 2007.

8. This is a gesture influenced by the radical, American *Bread and Puppet Theatre*.

9. Lucy Lippard (1983) *Overlay: Contemporary Art and the Art of Prehistory*.

10. Interview with Nic Cottis, 8 March 2006.

11. Interview with Peter Kiddle, 9 March 2006.

12. Scenario as described in 'Spring', *Dartington Hall News*, 16 March 1970, p.2.

13. Email communication from Mary O'Donnell (Fulkerson), 26 February 2007.

14. Peter Brinson argues this in (1991) *Dance as Education: Towards a National Dance Culture*, p.126.

15. Nic Cottis, 'Culchah', *Dartington Hall News and South Devon Scene*, no. 3018, 15 December 1978, p.3.

16. Arts for the Benefit and Care of Disability (ABCD), *Report of a Seminar Sponsored by the Carnegie UK Trust in association with the Royal Association for Disability and Rehabilitation and Dartington College of Arts, 7–9 July 1978*.

17. The Council of Europe, founded in 1949, is distinct and separate from the European Union and involves more states. Its most important activities are in the areas of human rights (it set up the European Court of Human Rights in 1959) and cultural cooperation.

18. The transcripts of most presentations are in Peter Hulton, ed. (1985) *Theatre and Communities: A Council of Europe Workshop*, Theatre Papers, Fifth Series, no. 16. I also draw on interview with Colette King, 23 March 2007.

19. These projects were described in Dartington's Theatre Papers. Roger Sell and William Fitzgerald wrote *Third Year Plymouth* (Series 1, no. 7), based on student reports; and Graham Green (1985) *An Educational Theatre Project* (Series 5, no. 12). The Plymouth project began in 1975 and settled into its own premises in 1978/79 after being hosted by Plymouth Arts Centre and the Frederick Street Community Centre. RTW was opened in 1978 after one year based in nearby Greenwich.

20. Jacky Lansley (1978) '"Dance-Makers". Lauri Booth [sic] Arianna Economou, Sarah Willis', *New Dance*, no. 5, New Year, p.9.

21. Quoted in Mara De Wit (2000) *New Dance Development at Dartington College of Arts UK, 1971–*

1987, unpublished PhD thesis, Middlesex University, p.118.

22. 'Sufferance' refers back to the period of the working port, indicating the terms for landing cargo.

23. Email communication from David Slater, 23 February 2007.

24. Email communication from Peter Kiddle, 21 February 2007.

25. Interview with Alan Read, 15 June 2005.

26. Graham Green and Alan Read (1985) *An Educational Theatre Project*, Dartington Theatre Papers (Series 5, no. 12), p.17.

27. 'Students talking about their work', Prospectus 1985.

28. Email communication from Jenna Agate, 13 March 2007.

29. Alan Read (1993) *Theatre and Everyday Life: An Ethics of Performance*.

30. ibid, pp.34–5.

31. Flyer, *An Invitation to RTW* , 1980.

32. Flyer, *An Invitation to RTW* (1980), mentions ballet and gymnastics. The latter would have been led by Mary Prestidge, dancer, member of the X6 collective, and former Olympic gymnast.

33. Read (1993), p.47.

34. Interview with Alan Read, 22 November 2006.

35. Email communication from Yolande Snaith, 30 March 2007.

36. See Caroline Pegg (1986) 'Research and Navigation', *New Dance*, no. 31, Summer, pp.10–12; personal communication from Mara de Wit, 9 May 2007.

37. Louise Richards and Kevin Finnan (1988) 'Still Moving: Contact with Special Needs', *Contact Quarterly*, Winter, 41–3. Quotation from p.42.

38. Interview with Kevin Finnan, 29 November 2005.

39. The following sources document this work: Anne Kilcoyne (1989) 'Trusting to Touch', *Dartington Voice*, February; Steve Paxton and Anne Kilcoyne (1993) 'On the Braille in the Body: An Account of the Touchdown Dance Integrated Workshops with the Visually Impaired', *Dance Research*, XI, no. 1, Spring, pp.3–51; Steve Paxton and Anne Kilcoyne (1993) *Touchdown Dance* [video], Arts Archives no. 3, Arts Documentation Unit, Exeter. Since 1994, Touchdown has been directed by Katy Dymoke, with a base in Manchester and a programme that includes performance projects as well as workshops.

40. This has often been embedded in the more long-established, better-funded, physical recreation establishment, while perhaps subverting its purely physical goals with artistic ones. See Renee Waterman (1998) 'The Influence of Rudolf Laban on the Teaching of Keep-Fit in Birmingham 1945–1998', *Laban Guild*, 18, no. 2, Summer, pp.7, 10.

41. See Brinson (1991), p.133. He was a key figure in the development of community dance and also a friend of Dartington on the CNAA dance panel that validated its degree. He was chairman of the Gulbenkian Foundation reports *Dance Education and Training in Britain* (1980) and *The Arts in Schools* (1982).

42. Christopher Thomson (2006) 'We are a Dancing Nation', *Animated*, Spring, pp.5–8.

43. Personal communication from Mara de Wit, 9 May 2007.

44. See, for example, Brinson, 1991, pp.111–13; Gordon Curl (2006) 'Aesthetic Qualities in Community Dance: "Deal" or "No Deal"?', *Animated*, Summer, pp.7–9.

45. For Farber's career, see Jeff Slayton (2006) *The Prickly Rose: A Biography of Viola Farber*. The personally desperate conditions surrounding the choreography and filming of *January* are documented, pp.218–23.

46. Angus Balbernie (2004) 'The Skin of Our Nature/The Nature of Our Skin', *Animated*, Autumn, pp.12–15, quotation p.13.

47. Email communication from Angus Balbernie, 26 January 2007.

48. Mary Braid (1991) 'Disputes cloud future of Utopian legacy; Controversy is growing over some activities of the Dartington Hall Trust', *The Independent*, 1 February, p.7.

49. Cox (2005) indicates some areas of disagreement. See particularly Chapters 30 and 31.

50. Dartington Plus 2004/5 Pilot Year Projects Report, p.15. Available from: http://dartingtonplus.org.uk/documents/D_Plus_Pilot_Year_Report%20.pdf.

Selected Bibliography

Adamson, Andy and Clare Lidbury, eds. (1994) *Kurt Jooss: 60 Years of the Green Table*, Birmingham: The University of Birmingham

Albright, Ann Cooper and David Gere, eds. (2003) *Taken by Surprise: A Dance Improvisation Reader*, Middletown, CT: Wesleyan University Press

Andrews, Edward Deming (1962) *The Gift to be Simple: Songs, Dances and Rituals of the American Shakers*, New York: Dover Publications; first published 1940

Andrews, Edward Deming (1963) *The People Called Shakers: A Search for the Perfect Society*, New York: Dover Publications; revised edition; first published 1953

Armytage, W.G.A. (1961) *Heavens Below: Utopian Experiments in England 1560–1960*, London: Routledge and Keegan Paul

Appleby, Joyce, Lynn Hunt and Margaret Jacob (1995) *Telling the Truth about History*, New York: W.W Norton & Company

Auerbach, Nina (2004) 'Before the Curtain', in Kerry Powell, ed. *The Cambridge Companion to Victorian and Edwardian Theatre*, Cambridge: Cambridge University Press, 3–14

Banes, Sally (1987) *Terpsichore in Sneakers*, Hanover, NH: Wesleyan University Press

Beacham, Richard (1987) *Adolphe Appia: Theatre Artist*, Cambridge: Cambridge University Press

Beaumont, Cyril (1942) *Supplement to Complete Book of Ballets*, London: Cyril W. Beaumont

Bodmer, Sylvia (1966) 'Recreational Dance', *Laban Art of Movement Guild Magazine*, no. 37, November, 30–32

Bonham-Carter, Victor (1958) *Dartington Hall: The History of an Experiment*, London: Phoenix House

Bose, Mandakranta (2001) 'The Dance Re-Invented: Rabindranath Tagore's Vision', in *Speaking of Dance: The Indian Critique*, New Vistas in Indian Performing Arts, no. 3, New Delhi: D.K. Printworld (P) Ltd., 99–115

Braden, Su (1978) *Artists and People*, London: Routledge and Keegan Paul

Brinson, Peter (1991) *Dance as Education: Towards a National Dance Culture*, Basingstoke, Hants: The Falmer Press

Browne, Maurice (1955) *Too Late to Lament*, London: Victor Gollancz

Burke, Peter, ed. (1991) *New Perspectives on Historical Writing*, Cambridge: Polity Press

Bush, Nancy (2000) *Alan Bush: Music, Politics and Life*, London: Thames Publishing

Calouste Gulbenkian Foundation (1980) *Dance Education and Training in Britain*, London: Calouste Gulbenkian Foundation

Carr, David (1991) *Time, Narrative and History*, Bloomington and Indianapolis: Indiana University Press; first published 1986

Carter, Alexandra, ed. (2004) *Rethinking Dance History*, London: Routledge

Carter, Alexandra (2005) *Dance and Dancers in the Victorian and Edwardian Music Hall Ballet*, Aldershot, UK: Ashgate

Chakraborty, Rudraprasad (1995) *Rangamancha O Rabindranath [The Stage and Rabindranath]*, Kolkata: Ananda Publishers

Chakravarty, Amiya, ed. (1961) *A Tagore Reader*, London: Macmillan

Chambers, Colin (1989) *The Story of Unity Theatre*, London: Lawrence and Wishart

Claid, Emilyn (2006) *Yes? No! Maybe ... Seductive Ambiguity in Dance*, London: Routledge

Cornish, Nellie (1964) *Miss Aunt Nellie: The Autobiography of Nellie C. Cornish*, Seattle: University of Washington Press, edited by Ellen Van Volkenburg Browne and Edward Nordhoff Beck

Coton, A.V. (1946) *The New Ballet: Kurt Jooss and His Work*, London: Dennis Dobson

Cottingham, John, ed. (1992) *The Cambridge Companion to Descartes*, Cambridge: Cambridge University Press

Counsell, Colin (2004) 'Dancing to Utopia: Modernity, Community and the Movement Choir', *Dance Research*, XXII, no. 2, Winter, 154–67

Cox, Peter (1999) *My Time at Dartington, 1940–83: A Personal Record of Involvement in Administering the Arts at Dartington Hall and Creating Dartington College of Arts*, unpublished MS, Dartington College of Arts

Cox, Peter (2005) *The Arts at Dartington 1940–1983: A Personal Account*, Totnes, Devon: The Dartington Hall Trust

Crickmay, Chris (1988) 'Fragments of Daily Life: Mary Fulkerson's World of Images and Compositional Ideas', *Contact Quarterly*, 13, no. 2, Spring/Summer, 9–18

Dartington Hall Trust (1975) *A Dartington Anthology, 1925–75*, Dartington: Dartington Press

Derra de Moroda, Friderica (1935) 'A Day with Kurt Jooss', *The Dancing Times*, no. 296, May, 140–2

Downs, Harold, ed..(1934) *Theatre and Stage: a Modern Guide to the Performance of all Classes of Amateur Dramatic, Operatic, and Theatrical Work*, London: Sir Isaac Pitman and Sons

Dufton, Merry (1986) 'Dance in the South West', *New Dance*, no. 38, Autumn, 10–11

Edwards, Winifred (1935) 'Eurhythmics at Dartington Hall', *Journal of the Dalcroze Society*, May, 23–4

Elmhirst, Leonard (1975) *Poet and Plowman*, Calcutta: Visva-Bharati

Erdman, Joan (1987) 'Performance as Translation: Uday Shankar in the West', *The Drama Review (TDR)*, 31, no. 1, T113, Spring, 64–88

Fisher, Lynn (1994) 'Considering Margaret Barr', *Brolga*, no. 1, December, 58–61

Flanagan, Hallie (1934) 'Kurt Jooss at Dartington Hall', *Theatre Arts Monthly*, May, 337–9

Fletcher, Sheila (1984) *Women First: The Female Tradition in English Physical Education 1880–1980*, London and Dover, New Hampshire: The Athlone Press

Foster, Ruth (1976) *Knowing in My Bones*, London: Adam and Charles Black

Fulkerson, Mary (1977–78) 'The Language of the Axis', *Theatre Papers*, First Series, no. 12, Theatre Department, Dartington College of Arts

Fulkerson, Mary (1978) 'Mary Fulkerson: An Interview', *New Dance*, no. 7, Summer, 12–14

Fulkerson, Mary (1983–84) 'The Move to Stillness', *Theatre Papers*, Fourth Series, no. 10, Theatre Department, Dartington College of Arts

Fulkerson, Mary (1985) 'Moving for Performance', *New Dance*, no. 32, Spring, 12–13

Ghose, Santidev (1978) *Music and Dance in Rabindranath Tagore's Educational Philosophy*, New Delhi: Sangeet Natak Akademi

Green, Martin (1986) *Mountain of Truth: The Counterculture Begins: Ascona, 1900–1920*, Hanover, New Hampshire: University Press of New England

Guest, Ann Hutchinson (1985) 'Sigurd Leeder: Images for the Dancer', *Ballett International*, 8, no. 10, October, 14–20

Guest, Ann Hutchinson (2006) 'The Jooss–Leeder School at Dartington Hall', *Dance Chronicle*, 29, 161–94.

Gyseghem, André van (1979) 'British Theatre in the Thirties: an autobiographical record', in Jon Clark, Margot Heinemann, David Margolis and Carole Snee, eds. *Culture and Crisis in Britain in the Thirties*, London: Lawrence and Wishart, 209–18

Hall, Fernau (1938) 'Modern Dancing at King's Cross: the Dance-Drama Group', *The Dancing Times*, no. 328, January, 526–8

Hall, Fernau (1950) *Modern English Ballet: An Interpretation*, London: Andrew Melrose

Hanna, Judith Lynne (1987) *To Dance is Human*, 2nd edition, Chicago and London: University of Chicago Press

Hardt, Yvonne (2003) 'Relational Movement Patterns: The Diversity of Movement Choirs and their Social Potential in the Weimar Republic', *Proceedings: Society of Dance History Scholars, Twenty-Sixth Annual Conference, Stoughton, Wisconsin: Society of Dance History Scholars*, 45–50

Harrison, John F. C., ed. (1968) *Utopianism and Education: Robert Owen and the Owenites*, New York: Teachers College Press, Columbia University

Harrison, Rachel (2002) *Dorothy Elmhirst and the Visual Arts at Dartington Hall, 1925–45*, unpublished PhD thesis, Plymouth University

Hazareesingh, Kissoonsingh, ed. (1992) *A Rich Harvest: the complete Tagore/Elmhirst Correspondence and Other Writings*, Stanley, Rose Hill, Mauritius: Editions de l'Océan Indien

Hewison, Robert (1986) *Too Much: Art and Society in the Sixties 1960–75*, London: Methuen

Hodgson, John and Valerie Preston-Dunlop (1990) *Rudolf Laban: An Introduction to His Work and Influence*, Plymouth: Northcote House

Horosko, Marian ed. (2002) *Martha Graham: The Evolution of Her Dance Theory and Training*, Gainesville, Fla.: University Press of Florida, revised edition

Hulton, Peter, ed. (1985) *Theatre and Communities: A Council of Europe Workshop*, Dartington College of Arts Theatre Papers, Fifth Series, no. 16

Jeffs, Susan(2003) 'A Revolutionary Art Form: Ballet in China 1930–1960', *Dance Gazette*, no. 2, 17–19

Jeschke, Claudia (2003) 'Jooss' Wise Covenant with Death', in Jooss, Kurt and Anna Markard, *The Green Table: a Dance of Death in Eight Scenes*, Part 2, New York and London: Routledge, 19–25

Jordan, Diana (1938) *The Dance as Education*, London: Oxford University Press

Jordan, Stephanie (1987) 'Mary Fulkerson', *Dance Theatre Journal*, v.5, no. 3b, 4–6

Jordan, Stephanie (1992) *Striding Out: Aspects of Contemporary and New Dance in Britain*, London: Dance Books

Karina, Lilian and Marion Kant (2003) *Hitler's Dancers: German Modern Dance and the Third Reich*, trans. Jonathan Steinberg, New York: Berghahn Books, first German edition, 1996

Kew, Carole (1999) 'The Rise and Fall of Rudolf Laban's *Festkultur*', *Dance Research*, 17, no. 2, Winter, 73–96

Kuhns, David (1997) *German Expressionist Theatre: the Actor and the Stage*, Cambridge: Cambridge University Press

Kumar, Krishan (1991) *Utopianism*, Milton Keynes: Open University Press

Laban, Rudolf (1966) *Choreutics*, annotated and edited by Lisa Ullmann, London: Macdonald and Evans

Laban, Rudolf (1969) 'Notes on Choral Dancing', *Laban Art of Movement Guild Magazine*, no. 43, November, 5–7

Laban, Rudolf (1974) 'Extract from an address held by Mr. Laban on a meeting for community-dance in 1936', *Laban Art of Movement Guild Magazine*, no. 52, May, 6–11

Laban, Rudolf (1975) *A Life for Dance*, translated and annotated by Lisa Ullmann, London: Macdonald and Evans; published 1935 as *Ein Leben für den Tanz*

Langton, Basil (1996) 'Alan Rawsthorne', *The Creel* [Journal of the Alan Rawsthorne Society and Alan Rawsthorne Trust], v.3, no. 3, issue 10, Spring, 30–9

Lester, Garry (1997) 'Margaret Barr: Epic Individual and Fringe Dweller', *Proceedings: Society of Dance History Scholars*, Riverside, California: Society of Dance History Scholars, 9–19

Lester, Garry (2006) 'Galvanising community: Margaret Barr at Dartington Hall 1930-1934', *Brolga*, no. 25, 39-49

Lippard, Lucy (1983) *Overlay: Contemporary Art and the Art of Prehistory*, New York: The New Press

Littlewood, Joan (1994) *Joan's Book*, London: Methuen

Loewenthal, Lillian (1993) *The Search for Isadora: The Legend and Legacy of Isadora Duncan*, Pennington, NJ: Princeton Book Company

Mackrell, Judith (1992) *Out of Line: The Story of British New Dance*, London: Dance Books

Maletic, Vera (1987) *Body – Space – Expression*, Berlin, New York, Amsterdam: Mouton de Gruyter

Manning, Susan (1993) *Ecstasy and the Demon: Feminism and Nationalism in the Dances of Mary Wigman*, Berkeley and Los Angeles: University of California Press

Markard, Anna (1993) 'Jooss the Teacher: His Pedagogical Aims and the Development of the Choreographic Principles of Harmony', *Choreography and Dance*, vol. 3, Part 2, 45–51

Markard, Anna and Hermann Markard, eds. (1985) *Jooss*, Cologne: Ballett-Bühnen Verlag

Martin, John (1932)'The Dance: In England: The Dance Mime Project at Dartington Hall is a Model of United Effort', *New York Times*, 14 August, p.X5

Massie, Annette (1988) 'Elizabeth West and Western Theatre Ballet', *Dance Research*, VI, no. 1, Spring, 45–58

Mellor, David, ed. (1987) *A Paradise Lost: The Neo-Romantic Imagination in Britain 1935–1955*, London: Lund Humphries

Ministry of Education and the Central Office of Information (1952) *Moving and Growing: Physical Education in the Primary School, Part1*, London: HMSO

Ministry of Education and the Central Office of Information (1953) *Part2, Planning the Programme*, London: HMSO

Morris, Margaret (1926) *Margaret Morris Dancing*, London: Kegan Paul, Trench, Trubner and Co.

Morris, Margaret (1969) *My Life in Movement*, London: Peter Owen

Morris, Margaret (1972) *Creation in Dance and Life*, London: Peter Owen

Müller, Grete (2001) *Sigurd Leeder, Tänzer, Pädagoge und Choreograf, Leben und Werk*, Herisau: Appenzellerverlag

Munslow, Alan (1997) *Deconstructing History*, London and New York: Routledge

Nagrin, Daniel (1994) *Dance and the Specific Image: Improvisation*, Pittsburgh and London: University of Pittsburgh Press

Näslund, Erik (1978) *Birgit Cullberg*, Stockholm: P A Norstedt & Söners Förlag

Nicholas, Larraine (2004) 'Dancing in the Margins? British Modern Dance in the 1940s and 50s', in Alexandra Carter, ed. (2004) *Rethinking Dance History*, London: Routledge, 119–31

Novack, Cynthia (1990) *Sharing the Dance: Contact Improvisation and American Culture*, Madison, Wisconsin: University of Wisconsin Press

Odom, Selma Landen (1986) 'Wigman at Hellerau', *Ballet Review*, 14, no. 2, Summer, 41–53

Odom, Selma Landen (1991) *Dalcroze Eurhythmics in England: History of an Innovation in Music and Movement Education*, unpublished PhD thesis, Guildford: University of Surrey

Odom, Selma Landen (1992) 'What is Dalcrozian', *Dance Research*, x, no. 2, Autumn, 121–31

Paxton Steve (1977) 'In the midst of standing still something else is occurring and the name for that is the small dance', *Theatre Papers*, First Series, no. 4, Theatre Department, Dartington College of Arts (interview by Peter Hulton, summer 1975)

Paxton, Steve (1982) 'Contact Improvisation', *Theatre Papers*, Fourth Series, no. 5, Theatre Department, Dartington College of Arts

Paxton, Steve and Anne Kilcoyne (1993) 'On the Braille in the Body: An Account of the Touchdown Dance Integrated Workshops with the Visually Impaired and Sighted', *Dance Research*, XI, no. 1, Spring, 3–51

Paxton, Steve (2003) 'Drafting Interior Techniques', in Ann Cooper Albright and David Gere, eds. *Taken by Surprise: A Dance Improvisation Reader*, Middletown, CT: Wesleyan University Press, 175–83

Preston, Valerie (1963) *A Handbook for Modern Educational Dance*, London: Macdonald and Evans

Preston-Dunlop, Valerie (1998) *Rudolf Laban: An Extraordinary Life*, London: Dance Books

Preston-Dunlop, Valerie and Susanne Lahusen, eds. (1990) *Schrifttanz: A View of German Dance in the Weimar Republic*, London: Dance Books

Rauchway, Eric (1999) 'A Gentlemen's Club in a Woman's Sphere: How Dorothy Whitney Straight Created the New Republic', *Journal of Women's History*, 11.2, 60–85

Read, Alan (1993) *Theatre and Everyday Life: An Ethics of Performance*, London: Routledge

Rowell, Bonnie (2000) *Dance Umbrella: The First Twenty-Five years*, London: Dance Books

Rutherston, Jeannette (1934) 'The Central European Dance in England', *The Dancing Times*, December, 313–16

Rutherston, Jeannette (1935) 'The German Influence', *The Dancing Times*, October, 42–4

Ruyter, Nancy Lee Chalfa (1979) *Reformers and Visionaries: The Americanization of the Art of Dance*, New York: Dance Horizons

Samuel, Raphael, Ewan MacColl and Stuart Cosgrove (1985) *Theatres of the Left 1880–1935: Workers' Theatre Movements in Britain and America*, London: Routledge and Keegan Paul

Sayler, Oliver M. (1922) 'The Neighborhood Playhouse', *Theatre Arts Monthly*, 6, no. 1, January, 15–10

Schechter, Daniel (1996) *Searching for Memory*, New York: Basic Books

Schlicher, Suzanne (1993) 'The West German dance theatre: Paths from the twenties to the present', *Choreography and Dance*, 3, Part 2, 25–43

Shankar, Ravi (1997) *Raga Mala*, Guildford: Genesis Publications

Siegel, Marcia (1987) *Days on Earth: The Dance of Doris Humphrey*, New Haven and London: Yale University Press

Sinclair, Andrew (1995) *Arts and Cultures: The History of the 50 Years of the Arts Council of Great Britain*, London: Sinclair-Stevenson

Skinner, Joy (1999) *Over the Hill with a Magic Carpet*, Haddenham, Cambridgeshire: Fern House

Soares, Janet (1992) *Louis Horst: Musician in a Dancer's World*, Durham, N. Carolina and London: Duke University Press

Sorley Walker, Kathrine (2002) 'Westward, Ho', *Dance Now*, 11, no. 2, Summer, 55–71 and 11, no 3, Autumn, 75–88

Sorrell, Walter (1973) *The Mary Wigman Book*, Middletown, Connecticut: Wesleyan University Press

Spector, Irwin (1990) *Rhythm and Life: The Work of Emile Jaques-Dalcroze*, Stuyvesant, NY: Pendragon Press

Staff of the Elementary Division of the Lincoln School (1927) *Curriculum Making in an Elementary School*, Boston: Ginn and Company

Stöckemann, Patricia (2001) *Etwas ganz Neues muss nun entstehen: Kurt Jooss und das Tanztheater*, München: Kieser

Storey, Alan (1940) 'The Art of Kurt Jooss', *The Dancing Times*, no. 358, June, 596

Straight, Michael (1983) *After Long Silence*, London: Collins

Sturmer, Caryll von (1993) *Margaret Barr: Epic Individual*, Sydney, NSW: L. von Sturmer

Swanberg, W. A. (1980) *Whitney Father, Whitney Heiress*, New York: Charles Scribner's Sons

Szeemann, Harald (2003) 'Monte Verità', in *Être ensemble: Figures de la communauté en danse depuis le xxᵉ siècle*, Paris: Centre national de la danse, 17–40

Tagore, Rabindranath and Leonard Elmhirst (1961) *Rabindranath Tagore: Pioneer in Education*, London: John Murray

Thomas, F.G. (1932) *The New learning: An Experiment with Educational Films in the County of Devon*, London: WEA

Thomas, F.G. (1939) *The Changing Village: An Essay in Rural Reconstruction*, London: Thomas Nelson and Sons

Thomkins, Alysoun (1995) *Moving in Community*, London: Laban Centre

Toepfer, Karl (1997) *Empire of Ecstasy: Nudity and Movement in German Body Culture, 1910–1935*, Berkeley and Los Angeles: University of California Press

Tomko, Linda (1999) *Dancing Class: Gender, Ethnicity, and Social Divides in American Dance, 1890–1920*, Bloomington and Indianapolis: Indiana University Press

Tosh, John (2000) *The Pursuit of History*: Aims, *Methods and New Directions in the Study of Modern History*, 3rd edition, Harlow: Longman.

Tracy, Robert, ed. (1997) *Goddess: Martha Graham's Dancers Remember*, New York: Limelight Editions

Tufnell, Miranda and Chris Crickmay (1993) *Body, Space, Image*, 2nd edition, London: Dance Books

Ullmann, Lisa (1956) 'Recreative Dancing in the Movement Choir', *Laban Art of Movement Guild Magazine*, March, 20–7

Vaughan, David (1997) *Merce Cunningham: Fifty Years*, New York: Aperture

Venner, Katie (1990) *Regional Dance Agencies: A Feasibility Study*, London: Arts Council of Great Britain

Walker, Joanna (1989) *Katie Duck in the 1980s: Defining and Collaborating Performance Forms*, unpublished BA dissertation, Leicester Polytechnic

Wallis, Mick (1994) 'Pageantry and the Popular Front: Ideological Production in the Thirties', *New Theatre Quarterly*, 10 (38), May, 132–56

Wallis, Mick (1995) 'The Popular Front Pageant: Its Emergence and Decline', *New Theatre Quarterly*, 11 (41), February, 17–32.

Walther, Suzanne K. (1994) *The Dance of Death: Kurt Jooss and the Weimar Years*, Churr, Switzerland: Harwood Academic Publishers

White, Eric Walter (1975) *The Arts Council of Great Britain*, London: Davis-Poynter

Williamson, Audrey (1946) *Contemporary Ballet*, London, Rockcliff

Willson, F.M.G. (1997) *In Just Order Move: the progress of the Laban Centre for Movement and Dance, 1946–1996*, London: Athlone Press

Winearls, Jane (1958) *Modern Dance: The Jooss–Leeder Method*, London: A & C. Black

Winearls, Jane (1990) *Choreography: The Art of the Body*, London: Dance Books

Wit, Mara de (2000) *New Dance Development at Dartington College of Arts UK, 1971–1987*, unpublished PhD thesis, Middlesex University

Young, Michael (1996) *The Elmhirsts of Dartington*, Totnes, Devon: The Dartington Hall Trust, first published 1982

Zoete, Beryl de (1939) 'The Jooss–Leeder School of Dance at Dartington Hall', *The Dancing Times*, no. 348, September, 626–8

Audio-visual and digital sources

Towards Tomorrow: Pageant of Co-operation, produced by Frank H.W. Cox for the CWS National Film Service, 1938, available from the National Co-operative Archive

Dartington Christmas Festival, directed by John Irving, BBC TV West Region Production 1960, available from the South West Film and Television Archive

Mary O'Donnell Fulkerson, *Release*, ebook available from www.releasedance.com

Mary and James Fulkerson: Put Your Foot Down Charlie, Television South West

(TSW) production, 1983 [chor. Mary Fulkerson, mus. James Fulkerson, dancers: Mary Fulkerson, Jane Hansford, Beverley Sandwith], available from the South West Film and Television Archive

Really Artistic Theatrical Stuff, dir. Tim Watson, Television South West (TSW) production, 1983 [*Rats' Tale*, chor. Mary Fulkerson, mus. James Fulkerson, dancers: Laurie Booth, Martin Coles, Andy Cowton, Mary Fulkerson, Jane Hansford, Beverley Sandwith], available from the South West Film and Television Archive

January, dir. Kevin Crooks, production by Viola Farber Dance Company and TSW, 1984 [chor. Viola Farber, mus. Gordon Jones], available from the South West Film and Television Archive

Just Dancing Around? Richard Alston, dir. Mark Kidel, Euphoria Films for Channel 4, 1996

Speaking of Dance: Steve Paxton, directed and produced by Douglas Rosenberg, Oregon, Wis.: American Dance Festival, 1996

Touchdown Dance, Steve Paxton and Ann Kilcoyne, Exeter Arts Archives no. 3, 1993, DVD-ROM available from Arts Documentation Unit, Exeter

Improvisation, Katie Duck, Exeter Arts Archive, 2002, DVD-ROM available from Arts Documentation Unit, Exeter

The American Invasion 1962–72, director of research, Valerie Preston-Dunlop, producer Luis España, DVD, 2005

Index